Third Edition

CORNERSTONES
FOR CAREER
COLLEGE SUCCESS

Robert M. Sherfield
Professor, College of Southern Nevada

Patricia G. Moody
Dean Emerita, University of South Carolina

PEARSON

Boston • Columbus • Indianapolis • New York • San Francisco • Upper Saddle River
Amsterdam • Cape Town • Dubai • London • Madrid • Milan • Munich • Paris • Montreal • Toronto
Delhi • Mexico City • São Paulo • Sydney • Hong Kong • Seoul • Singapore • Taipei • Tokyo

Editor-in-Chief: Jodi McPherson
Acquisition Editor: Katie Mahan
Managing Editor: Shannon Steed
Development Editor: Claire Hunter
Editorial Assistant: Clara Ciminelli
Marketing Manager: Amy Judd
Production Editor: Janet Domingo
Editorial Production Service: Electronic Publishing Services Inc.
Manufacturing Buyer: Megan Cochran
Electronic Composition: Jouve
Interior Design: Electronic Publishing Services Inc.
Photo Researcher: Annie Fuller
Cover Designer: Diane Lorenzo

Credits and acknowledgments borrowed from other sources and reproduced, with permission, in this textbook appear on the appropriate page within text.

Copyright © 2013, 2010, 2006 by Pearson Education, Inc. All rights reserved. Manufactured in the United States of America. This publication is protected by Copyright, and permission should be obtained from the publisher prior to any prohibited reproduction, storage in a retrieval system, or transmission in any form or by any means, electronic, mechanical, photocopying, recording, or likewise. To obtain permission(s) to use material from this work, please submit a written request to Pearson Education, Inc., Permissions Department, One Lake Street, Upper Saddle River, NJ, 07458, or you may fax your request to 201-236-3290.

Many of the designations by manufacturers and sellers to distinguish their products are claimed as trademarks. Where those designations appear in this book, and the publisher was aware of a trademark claim, the designations have been printed in initial caps or all caps.

Library of Congress Cataloging-in-Publication Data

Sherfield, Robert M.
    Cornerstones for career college success / Robert M. Sherfield,
Patricia G. Moody. — 3rd ed.
        p.   cm.
    Includes bibliographical references and index.
    ISBN-13: 978-0-13-278935-6 (pbk.)
    ISBN-10: 0-13-278935-3 (pbk.)
  1. College student orientation—United States.   2. Vocational school
students—United States.   3. Study skills.   I. Moody, Patricia G.
II. Title.

    LB2343.32.S3 2013
    378.1'98—dc23

                                    2011041870

www.pearsonhighered.com

ISBN 10: 0-13-278935-3
ISBN 13: 978-0-13-278935-6

ROBERT M. SHERFIELD, PH.D.

Robert Sherfield has been teaching public speaking, theater, technical writing, and student success as well as working with first-year success programs for over 25 years. Currently, he is a professor at the College of Southern Nevada, teaching student success, professional communication, and drama.

An award-winning educator, Sherfield was named Educator of the Year at the College of Southern Nevada. He twice received the Distinguished Teacher of the Year Award from the University of South Carolina at Union and has received numerous other awards and nominations for outstanding classroom instruction and advisement.

He has extensive experience with the design and implementation of student success programs, including one that was presented at the International Conference on the First-Year Experience in Newcastle upon Tyne, England. He has conducted faculty development keynotes and workshops at over 400 institutions of higher education across the United States. He has spoken in 46 states and several foreign countries.

In addition to his coauthorship of *Cornerstones for Community College Success* (Pearson, 2012), he has authored or coauthored *Cornerstones for Professionalism* (Pearson, 2013), *Cornerstone: Discovering Your Potential, Learning Actively, and Living Well* (Prentice Hall, 2008), *Roadways to Success* (Prentice Hall, 2001), the trade book *365 Things I Learned in College* (Allyn & Bacon, 1996), *Capstone: Succeeding Beyond College* (Prentice Hall, 2001), *Case Studies for the First Year: An Odyssey into Critical Thinking and Problem Solving* (Prentice Hall, 2004), and *The Everything Self-Esteem Book* (Adams Media, 2004),

Sherfield's interest in student success began with his own first year in college. Low SAT scores and a dismal high school ranking denied him entrance into college. With the help of a success program, Sherfield was granted entrance into college and went on to earn five college degrees, including a doctorate. He has always been interested in the social, academic, and cultural development of students and sees this book as his way to help students enter the world of work and establish lasting, rewarding careers. Visit www.robertsherfield.com.

PATRICIA G. MOODY, PH.D.

Patricia G. Moody is Dean Emerita of the College of Hospitality, Retail, and Sport Management at the University of South Carolina, where she has served on the faculty and in administration for over 30 years. An award-winning educator, Moody was honored as Distinguished Educator of the Year at her college and as Collegiate Teacher of the Year by the National Business Education Association. She was also a top-five finalist for the Amoco Teaching Award at the University of South Carolina. She received the prestigious John Robert Gregg Award, the highest honor in her field of over 100,000 educators.

Moody has coauthored many texts and simulations, including *Cornerstones for Professionalism* (Pearson, 2013), *Cornerstones for Community College Success* (Pearson, 2012), *Cornerstone: Discovering Your Potential, Learning Actively, and Living Well* (Prentice Hall, 2008), *365 Things I Learned in College* (Allyn & Bacon, 1996), *Capstone: Succeeding Beyond College* (Prentice Hall, 2001), and *Case Studies for the First Year: An Odyssey into Critical Thinking and Problem Solving* (Prentice Hall, 2004).

A nationally known motivational speaker, consultant, and author, Moody has spoken in most states, has been invited to speak in several foreign countries, and frequently keynotes national and regional conventions. She has presented her signature motivational keynote address, "Fly Like an Eagle," to tens of thousands of people, from Olympic athletes to corporate executives to high school students.

As the dean of her college, Moody led international trips to build relationships and establish joint research projects in hospitality. Under her direction, faculty members in her college began a landmark study of Chinese tourists. She now travels the country delivering workshops, keynotes, and presentations on topics such as Managing Change, Working in the New Global Community, the Future of the Future, Student Motivation, and Emotional Intelligence. Moody also serves as a personal coach for business executives.

The third edition of *Cornerstones for Career College Success* is written specifically for career college students, focusing on their unique needs with financial aid, study tips, motivation, learning strategies, and technology. Every student story entitled How College Changed My Life is written by a student who graduated from a career college somewhere in the United States.

New to this edition is the incorporation of Bloom's Taxonomy throughout the chapters. Each chapter ends with a critical thinking activity based on Bloom's Taxonomy of Learning. Bloom triangles are located throughout the text to help students recognize the level at which they are learning.

Also new to this edition is the total incorporation of SQ3R into every chapter. Each chapter opens with an activity called Scan and Question. This feature requires students to scan the chapter and formulate mastery questions based on the chapter's information. At the end of each chapter, the SQ3R Mastery Study Sheet asks students to answer these questions for a thorough review.

Cornerstones also has a brand new chapter, Connect, which focuses on using technology in the educational setting. From learning how to master information literacy through the new D.A.R.T.S. system, to using Boolean logic for online searches, to incorporating social media into the educational plan, Chapter 5 is a thorough and realistic view of today's technology.

Chapter 2, Prosper, has been totally revised and updated to include new information about student loans, scholarships, and managing debt.

Chapter 13, Plan, has also been totally revised to include many sample cover letters and resumes, including scannable and electronic resume preparation.

Cornerstones for Career College Success will help career college students adjust to life in higher education, become self-motivated, master technology, use study strategies successfully, communicate more effectively, and create a dynamic job-search plan.

NEW TO THIS EDITION

New   **Bloom's Taxonomy**   This taxonomy helps students understand the different levels of learning and application for every course they take. See the Bloom triangles throughout the text and the end-of-chapter **Knowledge in Bloom** critical thinking applications.

New   **Chapter on technology**   Chapter 5, Connect, helps students master the ever-changing skills of information literacy, understand today's technology "language," conduct online searches more effectively using the new D.A.R.T.S. information literacy system, and monitor their online behaviors. This chapter introduces them to the basics of the most popular computer programs used in education.

Revised   **Scan and Question and SQ3R Mastery Study Sheet**   *Cornerstones* takes the most widely used study technique in higher education and incorporates it throughout the text, from opening Scan and Question activities to creating a Mastery Study Sheet at the end of each chapter. This technique helps students learn to scan a chapter, formulate questions based on chapter headings, and then answer those questions for subject mastery. New coverage teaches students how to apply SQ3R to every course. For examples, see the beginning and end of every chapter.

New   **How College Changed My Life feature**   Written by career college graduates, this feature profiles the challenges and strengths of 13 students who obtained a career college degree and entered the workforce in his/her chosen field. See this feature in every chapter.

New **Gainful Employment section**   This new material in Chapter 1 helps students understand how to make themselves valuable to employers and keep updated throughout their careers.

Revised **Chapter on finances and debt management**   This chapter helps students understand the benefits of managing money, controlling credit card debt, protecting themselves from identity theft, and managing the daily ins and outs of life in a changing economy. Information is also given on balancing checkbooks and understanding the real cost of "small things." See this updated coverage in Chapter 2.

Updated **Chapter on critical thinking**   This chapter has been updated to include new information on **effective decision making,** helping students learn to make decisions based on facts, evidence, and logic. See this updated coverage in Chapter 11.

New **Higher education and the adult learner**   This new coverage, found in Chapter 4, helps students who are returning to school. Tips and advice are given to make the most of college services and relationships.

New **Conquering the "First-Generation Gap" section**   This new material helps students who are first-generation college students understand more about college life and how to adjust to their changed world. See this new coverage in Chapter 3.

New **Bring the Change: Tips for Personal Success feature**   This recurring box suggests three to five helpful ideas for success and inspires students to implement the content by applying this to a career situation. This feature provides creative and practical ideas for student's success.

New **Do I Practice Personal Responsibility?**   This figure, found in Chapter 4, helps students understand their role in their own education.

New **How Can I Avoid the "Drive By" College Experience?**   This section helps students understand the MANY benefits of getting involved while at their institutions. See this new coverage in Chapter 4.

New **Section on conflict management**   This material helps students understand the basic causes of conflict in life and work and ways to manage such interpersonal conflict. See this new coverage in Chapter 12.

New **Sections on stress and wellness**   New information on managing stress and keeping yourself well during stressful times can be found in Chapter 7.

New **Appreciating Diversity**   This section will help students understand the value of diversity in their education and the workforce. See this new coverage in Chapter 12.

ACKNOWLEDGMENTS

We would like to thank the following individuals at the **College of Southern Nevada** for their support:

Dr. Michael Richards, *President*

Dr. Darren Divine, *Vice President for Academic Affairs*

Dr. Hyla Winters, *Associate Vice President for Academic Affairs*

Dr. Wendy Weiner, *Dean, School of Arts and Letters*

Dr. John Ziebell, *Department Chair—English*

Professor Levia Hayes, *Assistant Chair—English*

Professor Linda Gannon, *Lead Faculty—Academic and Life Strategies*

We would also like to thank individuals at **the University of South Carolina** and faculty members in the Department of Hospitality, Retail, and Sport Management.

Our fondest gratitude to the following colleagues and friends who recommended individuals for the features, **How College Changed My Life** and **From Ordinary to Extraordinary:**

Amy Baldwin, *Pulaski Technical College*

Everett Vann Eberhardt, *Northern Virginia Community College*

Cathy Dees, *DeVry University*

Rita Mikhail, *DeVry University*

Sara Reese, *Bryant and Stratton College*

Steve Makosy, *Bryant and Stratton College*

Sam Gentile, *Pima Medical Institute*

Karen McGrath, *Pima Medical Institute*

Doug Paddock, *Louisville Technical Institute*

Emily Battaglia, *IEC College*

Virginia Villanuevav, *IEC College*

Jen McCoy, *Lincoln College of Technology*

Lya Redmond, *The Art Institute of Philadelphia*

Dr. Jeff Ameen, *InterCoast College*

Geeta Brown, *InterCoast College*

To the **amazing individuals** who shared their life stories with us for the feature **From Ordinary to Extraordinary:**

Bill Clayton

Lydia Hausler Lebovic

Dino J. Gonzalez, *M.D.*

Catherine Schleigh

Vivian Wong

Matt Karres

Dr. Wayne A. Jones

Maureen Riopelle

Odette Smith-Ransome

Sylvia Eberhardt

Luke Bryan

H.P. Rama

Leo G. Borges

Mark Jones.

To the **marvelous students (current and former)** who shared their advice and experiences for **How College Changed My Life:**

Derwin A. Wallace, *DeVry University*

Kerrie Dees, *Bryant and Stratton College*

Mary Harris, *Pima Medical Institute*

William Paddock, *Louisville Technical Institute*

Christian Garcia, *UEI College*

Erica Harrison, *Lincoln College of Technology*

Sakinah Pendergrass, *The Art Institute of Philadelphia*

Eric Despinis, *ITT Technical Institute*

Zzavvalynn Orleanski, *Pulaski Technical College*

Jennifer Rosa, *InterCoast College*

Lawrence Cain, *Lincoln College of Technology*

Zack Karper, *The Art Institute of Philadelphia*

We offer our sincere thanks to the members of our **Cornerstones Advisory Council** who have provided valuable ideas and guidance throughout the development and revision of this new edition:

Emily Battaglia, *UEI Colleges*

Glenn F. Corillo, *Ph.D., ECPI University*

Patricia Davis, *Houston Community College/Southwest*

Lori Ebert, *Brown Mackie College*

Steve Forshier, *M.Ed.,R.T.(R), Pima Medical Institute*

Michelle Kloss, *South University*

Zachary Lesak, *Miller-Motte Technical College, North Charleston, SC*

Ashley Hailston McMillion, *Daymar Colleges Group*

Adam Oldach, *Western Governors University*

Anthony Siciliano, *Western Governors University*

Zachary Stahmer, *Anthem Education Group*

LaToya L. Trowers, *MBA, CMAA, CPM, COM, Mildred Elley College–NYC Metro Campus*

Reviewers for previous editions of *Cornerstones* whom we recognize with deep appreciation and gratitude:

Elvira Johnson, Central Piedmont Community College; Ryan Messatzzia, Wor-Wic Community College; Sarah K. Shutt, J. Sergeant Reynolds Community College; Kristina Leonard, Daytona Beach College; Kim Long, Valencia Community College; Taunya Paul, York Technical College; Charlie L. Dy, Northern Virginia Community College; Gary H. Wanamamker, Houston Community College; Jo Ann Jenkins, Moraine Valley Community College; Judith Lynch, Kansas State University; Timothy J. Quezada, El Paso Community College; Cathy Hall, Indiana University NW; Beverly J. Slaughter, Brevard Community College; Peg Adams, Northern Kentucky University; Sheryl Duquette, Erie Community College; Melanie Deffendall, Delgado Community College; Arthur Webb, Oklahoma State University; Stephanie Young, Butler Community College; Tara Wertz, MTI College; Diana Clennan, College of Southern Nevada; Jennifer Huss-Basquiat, College of Southern Nevada; Wayne A. Jones, Virginia State University; Barbara Auris, Montgomery County Community College, Betty Fortune, Houston Community College; Joel V. McGee, Texas A & M University; Jan Norton, University of Wisconsin–Osh Kosh; Todd Phillips, East Central College; Christian M. Blum, Bryan and Stratton College; James Briski, Katherine Gibbs School; Pela Selene Terry, Art Institute of NYC; Christina Donnelly, York Technical College; Connie Egelman, Nassau Community College; Amy Hickman, Collins College; Beth Humes, Pennsylvania Culinary Institute; Kim Joyce, Art Institute of Philadelphia; Lawrence Ludwig, Sanford-Brown College; Bethany Marcus, ECPI College of Technology; Kate Sawyer, Pittsburgh Technical Institute; Patricia Sell, National College of Business and Technology; Janis Stiewing, PIMA Medical Institute; June Sullivan, Florida Metropolitan University; Fred Amador, Phoenix College; Kathy Bryan, Daytona Beach Community College; Dorothy Chase, Community College of Southern Nevada; JoAnn Credle, Northern Virginia Community College; Betty Fortune, Houston Community College; Doroteo Franco Jr., El Paso Community College; Cynthia Garrard, Massasoit Community College; Joel Jessen, Eastfield College; Peter Johnston, Massasoit Community College; Steve Konowalow, Community College of Southern Nevada; Janet Lindner, Midlands Technical College; Carmen McNeil, Solano College; Joan O'Connor, New York Institute of Technology; Mary Pepe, Valencia Community College; Bennie Perdue, Miami-Dade Community College; Ginny Peterson-Tennant, Miami-Dade Community College; Anna E. Ward, Miami-Dade Community College; Wistar M. Withers, Northern Virginia Community College; Marie Zander, New York Institute of Technology; Joanne Bassett, Shelby State Community College; Sandra M. Bovain-Lowe, Cumberland Community College; Carol Brooks, GMI Engineering and Management Institute; Elaine H. Byrd, Utah Valley State College; Janet Cutshall, Sussex County Community College; Deborah Daiek, Wayne State University;

David DeFrain, Central Missouri State University; Leslie L. Duckworth, Florida Community College at Jacksonville; Marnell Hayes, Lake City Community College; Elzora Holland, University of Michigan, Ann Arbor; Earlyn G. Jordan, Fayetteville State University; John Lowry-King, Eastern New Mexico University; Charlene Latimer; Michael Laven, University of Southwestern Louisiana; Judith Lynch, Kansas State University; Susan Magun-Jackson, The University of Memphis; Charles William Martin, California State University, San Bernardino; Jeffrey A. Miller; Ronald W. Johnsrud, Lake City Community College; Joseph R. Krzyzanowski, Albuquerque TVI; Ellen Oppenberg, Glendale Community College; Lee Pelton, Charles S. Mott Community College; Robert Rozzelle, Wichita State University; Penny Schempp, Western Iowa Community College; Betty Smith, University of Nebraska at Kearney; James Stepp, University of Maine at Presque Isle; Charles Washington, Indiana University–Purdue University; Katherine A. Wenen-Nesbit, Chippewa Valley Technical College; *Kristina Leonard,* Daytona Beach College; *Kim Long,* Valencia Community College; *Taunya Paul,* York Technical College; *Charlie L. Dy,* Northern Virginia Community College; *Gary H. Wanamamker,* Ph. D., Houston Community College; *Jo Ann Jenkins,* Moraine Valley Community College; *Judith Lynch,* Kansas State University; *Timothy J. Quezada,* El Paso Community College; *Cathy Hall,* Indiana University NW; *Beverly J. Slaughter,* Brevard Community College; *Peg Adams,* Northern Kentucky University; *Sheryl Duquette,* Erie Community College; *Melanie Deffendall,* Delgado Community College; *Arthur Webb,* Oklahoma State University; *Stephanie Young,* Butler Community College; *Tara Wertz,* MTI College; *Diana Clennan,* College of Southern Nevada; *Jennifer Huss-Basquiat,* College of Southern Nevada; and Wayne A. Jones, Virginia State University.

Without the support and encouragement of **our supportive team at Pearson,** this book would not be possible. Our sincere thanks to Jodi McPherson, Margaret Waples, Amy Judd, Shannon Steed, Claire Hunter, Janet Domingo, Clara Ciminelli, Antionette Payne, Walt Kirby, Debbie Ogilvie, Alan Hensley, Pam Jeffries, Barbara Donlon, Cathy Bennett, Matt Mesaros, Wendy DiLeonardo, Deborah Wilson, Eric Weiss, Julie Morel, Julie Hilderbrand, and Richard Rowe. Your constant belief in us has been a most cherished gift. We are lucky to know you and are better people because of you. Thank you!

Supplemental Resources

INSTRUCTOR SUPPORT –
Resources to simplify your life and support your students.

<u>Book Specific</u>

Online Instructor's Manual – This manual is intended to give professors a framework or blueprint of ideas and suggestions that may assist them in providing their students with activities, journal writing, thought-provoking situations, and group activities. This supplement is available for download from the Instructor's Resource Center at www.pearsonhighered.com/irc

Online PowerPoint Presentation – A comprehensive set of PowerPoint slides that can be used by instructors for class presentations or by students for lecture preview or review. These slides highlight the important points of each chapter to help students understand the concepts within each chapter. Instructors may download these PowerPoint presentations from the Instructor's Resource Center at www.pearsonhighered.com/irc

MyTest Test Bank – Pearson MyTest offers instructors a secure online environment and quality assessments to easily create print exams, study guide questions, and quizzes from any computer with an Internet connection.

<u>Premium Assessment Content</u>

- Draw from a rich library of question testbanks that complement the textbook and course learning objectives.
- Edit questions or tests to fit specific teaching needs.

<u>Instructor Friendly Features</u>

- Easily create and store questions, including images, diagrams, and charts using simple drag-and-drop and Word-like controls.
- Use additional information provided by Pearson, such as the question's difficulty level or learning objective, to help quickly build a test.

<u>Time-Saving Enhancements</u>

- Add headers or footers and easily scramble questions and answer choices all from one simple toolbar.
- Quickly create multiple versions of a test or answer key, and when ready, simply save to Word or PDF format and print!
- Export exams for import to Blackboard 6.0, CE (WebCT), or Vista (WebCT)! Additional information available at www.pearsonmytest.com

MyStudentSuccessLab – Are you teaching online, in a hybrid setting, or looking to infuse technology into your classroom for the first time? It is an online solution designed to help students build the skills they need to succeed for ongoing personal and professional development at www.mystudentsuccesslab.com

Other Resources

"Easy access to online, book-specific teaching support is now just a click away!"

Instructor Resource Center – Register. Redeem. Login. Three easy steps that open the door to a variety of print and media resources in downloadable, digital format, available to instructors exclusively through the Pearson 'IRC'. www.pearsonhighered.com/irc

"Provide information highlights on the most critical topics for student success!"

Success Tips is a 6-panel laminate with topics that include MyStudentSuccessLab, Time Management, Resources All Around You, Now You're Thinking, Maintaining Your Financial Sanity, and Building Your Professional Image. Other choices are available upon request. This essential supplement can be packaged with any student success text to add value with 'just in time' information for students.

Supplemental Resources

Other Resources

"Infuse student success into any program with our 'IDentity' Series booklets!" - Written by national subject matter experts, the material contains strategies and activities for immediate application. Choices include:
- Financial Literacy (Farnoosh Torabi)
- Financial Responsibility (Clearpoint Financial)
- Now You're Thinking about College Success (Judy Chartrand et.al.)
- Now You're Thinking about Career Success (Judy Chartrand et.al.)
- Ownership (Megan Stone)
- Identity (Stedman Graham).

"Through partnership opportunities, we offer a variety of assessment options!"

LASSI – The LASSI is a 10-scale, 80-item assessment of students' awareness about and use of learning and study strategies. Addressing skill, will and self-regulation, the focus is on both covert and overt thoughts, behaviors, attitudes and beliefs that relate to successful learning and that can be altered through educational interventions. Available in two formats: Paper ISBN: 0131723154 or Online ISBN: 0131723162 (access card).

Robbins Self Assessment Library – This compilation teaches students to create a portfolio of skills. S.A.L. is a self-contained, interactive, library of 49 behavioral questionnaires that help students discover new ideas about themselves, their attitudes, and their personal strengths and weaknesses. Available in Paper, CD-Rom, and Online (Access Card) formats.

"For a truly tailored solution that fosters campus connections and increases retention, talk with us about custom publishing."

Pearson Custom Publishing – We are the largest custom provider for print and media shaped to your course's needs. Please visit us at www.pearsoncustom.com to learn more.

STUDENT SUPPORT –
Tools to help make the grade now, and excel in school later.

"Now there's a Smart way for students to save money."

CourseSmart is an exciting new choice for students looking to save money. As an alternative to purchasing the printed textbook, students can purchase an electronic version of the same content. With a CourseSmart eTextbook, students can search the text, make notes online, print out reading assignments that incorporate lecture notes, and bookmark important passages for later review. For more information, or to purchase access to the CourseSmart eTextbook, visit www.coursesmart.com

"Today's students are more inclined than ever to use technology to enhance their learning."

MyStudentSuccessLab will engage students through relevant YouTube videos with 'how to' videos selected 'by students, for students' and help build the skills they need to succeed for ongoing personal and professional development. www.mystudentsuccesslab.com

"Time management is the #1 challenge students face."

Premier Annual Planner - This specially designed, annual 4-color collegiate planner includes an academic planning/resources section, monthly planning section (2 pages/month), weekly planning section (48 weeks; July start date), which facilitate short-term as well as long term planning. Spiral bound, 6x9.

"Journaling activities promote self-discovery and self-awareness."

Student Reflection Journal - Through this vehicle, students are encouraged to track their progress and share their insights, thoughts, and concerns. 8 1/2 x 11. 90 pages.

MyStudentSuccessLab

Start Strong. Finish Stronger.
www.MyStudentSuccessLab.com

MyStudentSuccessLab is an online solution designed to help students acquire the skills they need to succeed for ongoing personal and professional development. They will have access to peer-led video interviews and develop core skills through interactive practice exercises and activities that provide academic, life, and professionalism skills that will transfer to ANY course.

It can accompany any Student Success text or used as a stand-alone course offering.

How will MyStudentSuccessLab make a difference?

Is motivation a challenge, and if so, how do you deal with it?

Video Interviews – Experience peer led video 'by students, for students' of all ages and stages.

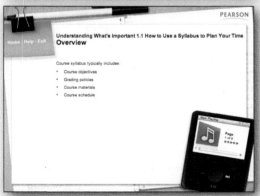

How would better class preparation improve the learning experience?

Practice Exercises – Practice skills for each topic - leveled by Bloom's taxonomy.

What could you gain by building critical thinking and problem-solving skills?

Activities – Apply what is being learned to create 'personally relevant' resources through enhanced communication and self-reflection.

MyStudentSuccessLab

Start Strong. Finish Stronger.
www.MyStudentSuccessLab.com

As an instructor, how much easier would it be to assign and assess on MyStudentSuccessLab if you had a Learning Path Diagnostic that reported to the grade book?

Learning Path Diagnostic

- For the **course**, 65 Pre-Course questions (Levels I & II Bloom's) and 65 Post-Course questions (Levels III & IV Bloom's) that link to key learning objectives in each topic.

- For each **topic**, 20 Pre-Test questions (Levels I & II Bloom's) and 20 Post-Test questions (Levels III & IV Bloom's) that link to all learning objectives in the topic.

As a student, how much more engaged would you be if you had access to relevant YouTube videos within MyStudentSuccessLab?

Student Resources

A wealth of resources like our FinishStrong247 YouTube channel with 'just in time' videos selected 'by students, for students'.

MyStudentSuccessLab Topic List -

1. A First Step: Goal Setting
2. Communication
3. Critical Thinking
4. Financial Literacy
5. Information Literacy
6. Learning Preferences
7. Listening and Taking Notes in Class
8. Majors and Careers
9. Memory and Studying
10. Problem Solving
11. Professionalism
12. Reading and Annotating
13. Stress Management
14. Test Taking Skills
15. Time Management

MyStudentSuccessLab Feature set:

Learning Path Diagnostic: 65 Pre-Course (Levels I & II Bloom's) and 65 Post-Course (Levels III & IV Bloom's) / Pre-Test (Levels I & II Bloom's) and Post-Test (Levels III & IV Bloom's).

Topic Overview: Module objectives.

Video Interviews: Real video interviews 'by students, for students' on key issues.

Practice Exercises: Skill-building exercises per topic provide interactive experience and practice.

Activities: Apply what is being learned to create 'personally relevant' resources through enhanced communication and self-reflection.

Student Resources: Pearson Students Facebook page, FinishStrong247 YouTube channel, MySearchLab, Online Dictionary, Plagiarism Guide, Student Planner, and Student Reflection Journal.

Implementation Guide: Grading rubric to support instruction with Overview, Time on Task, Suggested grading, etc.

ALWAYS LEARNING

PEARSON

Pearson Success Tips, 1/e

ISBN-10: 0132788071 • ISBN-13: 9780132788076

Success Tips is a 6-panel laminate that provides students with information highlights on the most critical topics for student success. These topics include MyStudentSuccessLab, Time Management, Resources All Around You, Now You're Thinking, Maintaining Your Financial Sanity, and Building Your Professional Image. Other choices are available upon request via our www.pearsoncustomlibrary.com program, as well as traditional custom publishing. This essential supplement can packaged with any student success text to add value with 'just in time' information for students.

Features

- **MyStudentSuccessLab** — Helps students 'Start strong, Finish stronger' by getting the most out of this technology with their book.
- **Time Management** — Everyone begins with the same 24 hours in the day, but how well students use their time varies.
- **Resources All Around You** — Builds awareness for the types of resources available on campus for students to take advantage of.
- **Now You're Thinking** — Learning to think critically is imperative to student success.
- **Maintaining Your Financial Sanity** — Paying attention to savings, spending, and borrowing choices is more important than ever.
- **Building Your Professional Image** — Students are motivated by preparing for their future careers through online and in person professionalism tips, self-branding, and image tips.
- **Additional Topics** — Topics above are 'default.' These topics include MyStudentSuccessLab, Time Management, Resources All Around You, Now You're Thinking, Maintaining Your Financial Sanity, and Building Your Professional Image. Other choices are available upon request via our www.pearsoncustomlibrary.com program, as well as traditional custom publishing. This essential supplement can be packaged with any student success text to add value with 'just in time' information for students.

Topic List

- MyStudentSuccessLab*
- Time Management*
- Resources All Around You*
- Now You're Thinking*
- Maintaining Your Financial Sanity*
- Building Your Professional Image*
- Get Ready for Workplace Success
- Civility Paves the Way Toward Success

- Succeeding in Your Diverse World
- Information Literacy is Essential to Success
- Protect Your Personal Data
- Create Your Personal Brand
- Service Learning
- Stay Well and Manage Stress
- Get Things Done with Virtual Teams
- Welcome to Blackboard!

- Welcome to Moodle!
- Welcome to eCollege!
- Set and Achieve Your Goals
- Prepare for Test Success
- Good Notes Are Your Best Study Tool
- Veterans/Military Returning Students

NOTE: those with asterisks are 'default' options; topic selection can be made through Pearson Custom Library at www.pearsoncustomlibrary.com, as well as traditional custom publishing.

PERSONALIZE THE EXPERIENCE WITH

PEARSON LEARNING SOLUTIONS

FOR STUDENT SUCCESS AND CAREER DEVELOPMENT

The Pearson Custom Library Catalog

With Pearson Custom Library, you can create a custom book by selecting content from our course-specific collections. The collections consist of chapters from Pearson titles like this one, and carefully selected, copyright cleared, third-party content, and pedagogy. The finished product is a print-on-demand custom book that students can purchase in the same way they purchase other course materials.

Custom Media

Pearson Learning Solutions works with you to create a customized technology solution specific to your course requirements and needs. We specialize in a number of best practices including custom websites and portals, animation and simulations, and content conversions and customizations.

Custom Publications

We can develop your original material and create a textbook that meets your course goals. Pearson Learning Solutions works with you on your original manuscript to help refine and strengthen it, ensuring that it meets and exceeds market standards. Pearson Learning Solutions will work with you to select already published content and sequence it to follow your course goals.

Online Education

Pearson Learning Solutions offers customizable online course content for your distance learning classes, hybrid courses, or to enhance the learning experience of your traditional in-classroom students. Courses include a fully developed syllabus, media-rich lecture presentations, audio lectures, a wide variety of assessments, discussion board questions, and a strong instructor resource package.

In the end, the finished product reflects your insight into what your students need to succeed, and puts it into practice.
Visit us on the web to learn more at www.pearsoncustom.com/studentsuccess or call 800-777-6872

ALWAYS LEARNING

PEARSON

Introducing CourseSmart, the world's largest online marketplace for digital texts and course materials.

A Smarter Way for Instructors

▶ **CourseSmart saves time.** Instructors can review and compare textbooks and course materials from multiple publishers at one easy-to-navigate, secure website.

▶ **CourseSmart is environmentally sound.** When instructors use CourseSmart, they help reduce the time, cost, and environmental impact of mailing print exam copies.

▶ **CourseSmart reduces student costs.** Instructors can offer students a lower-cost alternative to traditional print textbooks.

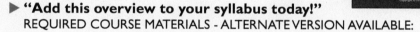

▶ **"Add this overview to your syllabus today!"**
REQUIRED COURSE MATERIALS - ALTERNATE VERSION AVAILABLE:

CourseSmart is an exciting new choice for students looking to save money. As an alternative to purchasing the printed textbook, students can purchase an electronic version of the same content. With a CourseSmart eTextbook, students can search the text, make notes online, print out reading assignments that incorporate lecture notes, and bookmark important passages for later review.

A Smarter Way for Students

▶ **CourseSmart is convenient.** Students have instant access to exactly the materials their instructor assigns.

▶ **CourseSmart offers choice.** With CourseSmart, students have a high-quality alternative to the print textbook.

▶ **CourseSmart saves money.** CourseSmart digital solutions can be purchased for up to 50% less than traditional print textbooks.

▶ **CourseSmart offers education value.** Students receive the same content offered in the print textbook enhanced by the search, note-taking, and printing tools of a web application.

CourseSmart is the Smarter Way
To learn for yourself, visit www.coursesmart.com

This is an access-protected site and you will need a password provided to you by a representative from a publishing partner.

ALWAYS LEARNING   PEARSON

BRIEF CONTENTS

CONTENTS

BEGIN

Talent alone won't make you a success. Neither will being in the right place at the right time, unless you are ready. The most important question is: "Are you ready?"—Johnny Carson

If you look at the figure printed here you will see the Chinese symbol meaning *to change*. It is made up of two symbols—the first means *to transform* or to be flexible. The second means *to do* or *to deliver*. In its purest form, the symbol means *to deliver transformation*. That is what *Cornerstones* is all about: helping you deliver or bring about transformation, positive change if you will, to your life. It is about helping you discover ways to change your thoughts, change your performance, and change your life.

Our goals in writing *Cornerstones* are to help you discover your academic, social, and personal strengths so that you can build on them, and to provide concrete and useful tools that will help you make the changes necessary for your success. We believe that in helping you identify and transform areas that have challenged you in the past, you can *discover your true potential, learn more actively, and have the career you want and deserve.*

We know that your time is valuable and that you are pulled in countless directions with work, family, school, previous obligations, and many other tasks. For this reason, we have tried to provide only the most concrete, useful strategies and ideas to help you succeed in this class and beyond.

We have spent over 60 years collectively gathering the information, advice, suggestions, and activities on the following pages. This advice and these activities have come from trial and error, colleagues, former students, instructors across the United States, and solid research. We hope that you will enjoy them, learn from them, and most of all, use them to change your life and move closer to your dreams.

Let the journey to positive change begin!

IMPORTANT FEATURES OF *CORNERSTONES* FOR *CAREER COLLEGE SUCCESS*

Throughout the text, you will find several common features to help you master the material. We hope you will use these features to become more engaged with the book, test your mastery, and practice what you have learned. The common features include:

- How College Changed My Life
- From Ordinary to Extraordinary
- Scan and Question
- Bloom's Taxonomy triangles
- Bring the Change: Tips for Personal Success
- Successful Decisions: An Activity for Critical Reflection
- Knowledge in Bloom

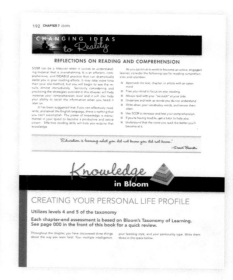

SQ3R AND SCAN AND QUESTION

What Is It and Why Do I Need to Know It?

You may be asking, "What does SQ3R mean and what could it possibly have to do with me, my text, this course, and my success?" The answer: SQ3R (S: Scan, Q: Question, 3R: Read, Recite, Review) is one of the most successful and widely used learning and study tools ever introduced.

This simple, yet highly effective mnemonic (memory trick) asks that before you actually read the chapter, you look over the contents, check out the figures and photos, look at sec-

tion headings, and review any graphs or charts. This is called *scanning.* Step 2, *question,* asks that you jot down questions that you think you will need to answer about the chapter's content in order to master the material. These questions might come from charts or figures, but most commonly, they come from the chapter's section headings. Examine this example from a section

> reported data. Crimes that result from an anomalous event, but which are excluded from reported data, highlight the arbitrary nature of the data-collection process itself.

> ### Special Categories of Crime

> **crime typology**

> A classification of crimes along a particular dimension, such as legal categories, offender motivation, victim behavior, or the characteristics of individual offenders.

> A **crime typology** is a classification scheme that is useful in the study and description of criminal behavior. All crime typologies have an underlying logic, and the system of classification that derives from any particular typology may be based on legal criteria, offender motivation, victim behavior, the characteristics of individual offenders, or the like. Criminologists Terance D. Miethe and Richard C. McCorkle note that crime typologies "are designed primarily to simplify social reality by identifying homogeneous groups of crime behaviors that are different from other clusters of crime behaviors."[65] Hence one common but simple typology contains only two categories of crime: violent and property. In fact, many crime typologies contain overlapping or nonexclusive categories—just as violent crimes may involve property offenses, and property offenses may lead to violent crimes. Thus no one typology is likely to capture all of the nuances of criminal offending.

heading from *Criminal Justice: A Brief Introduction* (6th ed.) by Frank Schmalleger (Prentice Hall, 2006). The following questions might be asked about the highlighted heading above.

1. What are the categories of crime?
2. Why do they matter?
3. What is crime typology?
4. When are categories of crime most often used?

After writing these questions from the section heading, you will read this section and then answer those questions. This technique gives you more focus and purpose for your reading. Each chapter in *Cornerstones* begins with this technique through a feature called **Scan and Question.**

We included this feature in *Cornerstones* to help you become a more active reader with greater comprehension skills in all of your other classes. SQ3R is fully discussed in Chapter 6 of this text.

BLOOM'S TAXONOMY

What Are All of Those Little Triangles Throughout My Book?

Another feature that you will notice throughout your text is small triangles followed by questions pertaining to the content. These triangles help you recognize which of the six levels of learning is being used from Bloom's Taxonomy. See the quick reference chart of Bloom's Taxonomy (Revised).

Bloom's Taxonomy (Revised)

Examining the Levels of Thinking and Learning

Levels of Thinking and Learning	What Skills You Should Have at This Level	Examples of Questions or Activities You Might Anticipate or Products You May Have to Generate
1—REMEMBERING This level is based on simple recall of information. This type of knowledge usually comes from being told or from basic reading. It is the "lowest" or most simple type of learning.	write, list, label, name, state, define, describe, identify, recognize, recall, draw, select, locate, recite, quote, order, state, reproduce, match, tell, and the five standards: who, what, when, where, and how	What is . . . , When did . . . , Why did . . . , Who were . . . , Describe the . . . , Which of the following . . . , Define the . . . , Name the . . . , Identify who . . . , Describe what happened after . . . **Sample:** What are the six levels of learning in Bloom's Taxonomy?
2—UNDERSTANDING This level determines your grasp or comprehension level of the information presented. It asks, "Do you understand the meaning?" and "Can you explain the ideas or concepts?"	summarize, describe, interpret, contrast, predict, associate, distinguish, estimate, differentiate, discuss, extend, convert, explain, generalize, give examples, rewrite, restate, classify, translate, paraphrase, illustrate, visualize, retell	How would you contrast . . . , Explain why the . . . , Summarize the main . . . , What facts show . . . , Predict the outcome of . . . , Restate the story in your own words . . . , Prepare a flow chart to illustrate . . . **Sample:** Explain why Bloom's Taxonomy is being used in *Cornerstones* and describe its importance.
3—APPLYING This level asks you to use the information you have by solving, showing, or applying that information in real-world or workplace situations. Can you use the information in a new way?	apply, demonstrate, discover, modify, operate, predict, solve, draw, dramatize, model, sketch, paint, produce, prepare, make, calculate, record, compute, manipulate, modify, use, employ	How could you use . . . , How could you solve . . . , What approach would you take . . . , Write an essay to explain why . . . , Prepare a timeline of . . . , Predict what would happen if . . . **Sample:** Prepare a plan to show how you could use Bloom's Taxonomy to get a better grade in your anatomy class.

4—ANALYZING

This level asks you to "take apart" the information for clarification, classification, and prioritizing. It also asks you to recognize what is not said (i.e., hidden meanings and unstated assumptions). This level requires that you distinguish between facts and inferences.

break down, distinguish, infer, arrange, prioritize, order, divide, categorize, appraise, test, examine, separate, deduce, choose, compare/contrast, detect, group, sequence, scrutinize, connect, outline, research, point out

How is ___ related to ___?, What conclusions can be drawn . . . , What is the relationship between . . . , Categorize the main . . . , Based on X, why is Y . . . , What were the motives behind . . . , What was the turning point in . . . , Write a survey to find out if . . .

Sample: What assumptions can be made about the rest of the term if your anatomy teacher's first two exams included 20 questions, all from level six?

5—EVALUATING

This level of thinking and learning asks you to make personal judgments about the value of issues, ideas, policies, and evidence based on your complete understanding of the information *and* based on stated judging criteria. Basically, it asks that you justify a decision, idea, or belief that you have formulated.

decide, rank, test, measure, recommend, defend, conclude, appraise, assess, judge, predict, rate, select, critique, justify, estimate, validate, measure, discriminate, probe, award, reject, grade, convince, weigh, support

Defend your position about . . . , How would you have handled "X"? Why?, Debate the issue of . . . , Prepare a paper or speech to present your ideas of . . . , What is your opinion of . . . , How would you rate . . . , What judgment could you make . . . , Justify your opinion of . . . , Based on your research, convince the reader of your paper or speech that . . . , What criteria would you use to assess the . . .

Sample: Assess how effective Bloom's Taxonomy was when used to study for your anatomy exam. Recommend two ways to improve the use of Bloom's Taxonomy for the next test.

6—CREATING

This level asks you to integrate your previous knowledge with your new knowledge and come up with new ideas, plans, and solutions. It also asks you to be able to predict outcomes based on what you have learned. This level asks you to be innovative and creative.

compose, combine, compile, create, design, generate, construct, revise, write, rewrite, tell, role play, formulate, invent, develop, modify, arrange, rearrange, prepare, assemble, set up, forecast, imagine, act, improvise, propose, substitute, integrate, incorporate

Design a plan to . . . , Write a speech or paper that . . . , Create a marketing plan that . . . , Devise a way to . . . , Compose a mnemonic that . . . , Generate a list of questions that . . . , Propose a solution to . . . , Revise the story of . . .

Sample: Write two possible test questions from each level of Bloom's Taxonomy from Chapter 1 of *Cornerstones*.

Bloom's Taxonomy (also called Levels of Thinking and Learning) is simply a way of explaining the stages at which we all acquire information. These levels, progress from simple learning and thinking (levels 1, 2, 3) to more complex learning and thinking (levels 4, 5, 6).

In addition to having correlations to Bloom's Taxonomy throughout your text, each chapter will end with an exercise called Knowledge in Bloom. This chapter-end activity is included to help you process and apply the information from the chapter.

So, Why Use Bloom in the *Cornerstones* Text?

Bloom's Taxonomy is important because it helps us determine the level at which we understand important information. For example, it is important to be able to answer questions at Level 1, such as:

Abraham Lincoln was the _____ President of the United States.

Abraham Lincoln's wife's name was _____ _____ Lincoln.

However, it is also important to be able to answer questions at levels 5 and 6, such as:

Based on your knowledge of the Civil War era, predict what would have happened to the United States without the Emancipation Proclamation. Justify your answer.

Summarize the main events that led to President Lincoln's assassination.

As you can clearly see, there is a great difference between these levels of learning. The higher the level, the more information and knowledge you need to be able to understand and respond to the question or problem.

The chapter-end activity Knowledge in Bloom will help you process and demonstrate your knowledge at different levels. This is important because you will have professors who teach and test at levels 1, 2, and 3 and those who teach and test at levels 5, 6, and 7. Learning to process and demonstrate your knowledge at every level can assist you in:

- Doing well in other classes by providing a foundation for effective studying and learning
- Learning to solve problems more thoroughly
- Predicting exam questions
- Learning how to critically evaluate and assess ideas and issues
- Learning to thoroughly and objectively research topics for papers and presentations
- Testing your own reading comprehension

A WORD ABOUT READING AND USING CORNERSTONES

We encourage you to read this text (and every text) with great care so that you can learn from the ideas presented within its pages. We also encourage you to *use* this book!

- Write in the margins
- Circle important terms
- Highlight key phrases
- Jot down word definitions in the margins
- Dog-ear the pages
- Write questions that you have in the spaces provided

Review the following page from this text to see how one student used the book to its fullest.

By treating this book like your "foundation to success," you will begin to see remarkable progress in your study practices, reading comprehension, and learning skills.

BRING the *Change*

TIPS FOR PERSONAL SUCCESS

Assume you are 90 years old and on your deathbed. You are thinking back over your life. Most likely you would think about certain people and events that have transpired. Perhaps you might want people to say or write the following about you:

- She was kind to people.
- He spent quality time with his children.
- She was a wonderful friend.
- He was always a giving person.

Now, it is your turn. Create a list of at least three things that you hope to have people say or write about you upon your death.

1. _____

_____

2. _____

_____

3. _____

_____

How can damage to your name and reputation negatively affect your overall success?

Bananastock

associated with this project and your name and grade is posted with every other group. Your group is the only group to receive an F. It doesn't feel good.

Basically, it comes down to this: Every time you make a choice, every time you complete a project, every time you encounter another person, your actions define your character and your name. People admire and respect you when you make an honorable and moral choice, especially if it is a difficult decision. Both your character and your name are exclusively yours, and you are responsible for their well-being. When you care this passionately about your reputation and character, your life is governed by protecting your name. Your actions, beliefs, and decisions are all tied to this one belief: "My name and my reputation matter and I will do nothing to bring shame or embarrassment to my name."

Point 8: Develop a Strong, Personal Guiding Statement

What is a guiding statement? How will it help me? How can I write a guiding statement?

You're wearing a t-shirt to class. It is not your normal, run-of-the-mill t-shirt, however. You designed this t-shirt for everyone to see and read. It is white with bright red letters. On the front of the t-shirt is written your ***personal guiding statement***—the words by which you live. The words govern your life. What would your t-shirt say? Perhaps you will use the golden rule, "Do unto

the words I live by

chapter one
THRIVE

CREATING SUCCESS, GUIDING CHANGE, AND SETTING GOALS

"The greatest reward of an education is to be able to face the world with an open mind, a caring heart, and a willing soul."—Robert M. Sherfield

Why read this chapter?

Because you'll learn:

- The basic truths about career colleges
- The differences between high school, college, and career
- The nuts and bolts of goal setting

Because you'll be able to:

- Apply the Essential Cornerstones for Success to your life and studies
- Create positive change in your own life
- Set realistic, attainable goals

Scan and QUESTION

Take a few moments, **scan this chapter**, and on page 28, write **five of your own questions** that you think will be important to your mastery of this material. You will also find five questions listed from your authors.

Example:

☑ **Discuss two traits employers are seeking from today's employees.** (from page 5)

☑ **What are the basic truths about the culture of career colleges?** (from page 14)

MyStudentSuccessLab

MyStudentSuccessLab (www.mystudentsuccesslab.com) is an online solution designed to help you "Start strong, Finish stronger" by building skills for ongoing personal and professional development.

Name: Robert M. Sherfield

Institution: Graduate! Spartanburg Methodist College, Lander College, University of South Carolina

Age: 52

Major: Theatre and Speech

Career: College Professor, Author, Professional Speaker

I am the son of textile workers. Both of my parents worked in a cotton mill for over 30 years. My mom graduated high school but my father only went to the third grade. My hometown is in the rural South about 35 miles from the nearest metropolitan area. I attended a small high school and had never been a good student. Because of my poor performance through the years, working full-time, and family commitments, I decided to attend a community college and then transfer to a four-year college. I never imagined how my high school performance would affect my application to college, and indeed the rest of my life. It took me years to overcome the effects of self-defeating behaviors, a horrible academic background, a negative attitude, and terrible study skills. I quickly learned that my success depended on becoming an open-minded person who knew how to set goals, work to achieve them, develop self-motivation, and study effectively. These were not easy steps for me after 12 years of failure and disappointment.

I barely finished high school with a D– average, and my SAT scores and class rank were so bad, I was denied entrance to the community college. The college granted me provisional acceptance only if I enrolled in, and successfully completed, a summer preparatory program. I graduated high school on a Friday night and began my college studies in the prep program the very next Monday morning. I never realized what lay ahead. I never realized how my life was about to change forever.

My first class that semester was English. Professor Brannon walked in, handed out the syllabus, called the roll, and began to lecture. Lord Byron was the topic for the day. My second class was Professor Wilkerson. She entered with a dust storm behind her, went over the syllabus, and before we had a chance to blink, she was involved in the first lecture. "The cradle of civilization," she began, "was Mesopotamia." We all scurried to find notebooks and pens to begin taking notes. I could not believe I was already behind on the first day. "Who teaches on the first day?" I thought.

One minute before class ended, she closed her book, looked directly at us and said, "You are in history now. You elected to take this class and you will follow my rules. You are not to be late, you are to come to this class prepared, and you are to do your homework assignments. If you do what I ask you to do, read what I've assigned to you, and do your homework activities, you will learn more about Western civilization than you ever thought possible. If you don't keep up with me, you won't know if you are in Egypt, Mesopotamia, or pure hell! Now get out!"

On the 30-mile trip home, my mind was filled with new thoughts: Lord Byron, Mesopotamia, professors who talked too fast, professors who did not talk at all, tuition, parking, and the size of the library. I knew that something was different, something had changed in me. In one day at my community college, I had tasted something intoxicating, something that was addictive. I had tasted a new world. My college experience changed my life in so many ways, but the number one thing that happened to me was that I learned how to be more comfortable in more places. Because of my experiences in college, I began to be as comfortable in New York City at a Broadway play as I was at my job in the cotton mill. I learned to be as comfortable sailing the River Thames past Big Ben and Parliament as I was working at the Buffalo Sewer District. My college experience taught me to appreciate the joys and wonders of travel, learning, and meeting new people. I had never known this before. My college experience changed my life, and I will be forever grateful to those instructors who opened the door to the world for me.

Over 30 years later, as I coauthor your *Cornerstone* text, I am still addicted to that new world I first experienced in college. Higher education changed my life, and I am still changing—with every day I live, every new book I read, every new class I teach, every new person I meet, and every new place to which I travel, I am changing. I wish the same for you.

THINK about it

1. What adversities in your past will you have to work to overcome to persist in your current studies?

2. What changes and adjustments do you think you are going to have to make in your personal and academic life to reach your goals, graduate, and enter the career you want?

THE TIMES, THEY ARE A-CHANGIN'

What Is the Relationship Between Your Education and the New Global Economy?

Why do you need to consider today's global economy when thinking about your future?

©iStockPhoto

Composer, singer, and activist Bob Dylan once wrote, "The times, they are a-changin'." Truer words have never been spoken—especially for anyone living at this moment. This is not your daddy's economy. It is not your mama's workplace, and it certainly is not your grandfather's job market. To glide over this simple truth *could be the most costly decision of your life.*

"New global economy," you might say, "Who cares about a global economy?"

"China? Who cares about the fluctuating economy in China, Russia, Dubai, or India? I live in Kansas and I'm worried about America's future."

"An iPhone? A Blackberry? An iPad? I can't even afford my bus ticket this month," you may be thinking.

While you may not be alone in thinking "This does not matter to me," you would be very wrong and exceptionally foolish to think that today's world affairs do not concern **you,** your **education,** and your **future.** Yes, it may be true that you are simply trying to get a degree in medical assisting to work in a small doctor's office in Spokane, Washington; or to obtain a degree in criminal justice to work at the local police department in Union, South Carolina; or to earn a degree in business so that you can work in banking in Stockton, California. However, no certificate, no degree, no job, and certainly no person will be exempt from the changes and challenges of "the new global economy."

"So, where does this leave *me*?" you might be asking. It leaves you in an exciting, vulnerable, challenging, scary, and wonderful place. We did not include this information to scare you or to turn you off, but rather to give you a jolt, to open your eyes to the world in which you live and workforce for which you are preparing. We included it to encourage you to use *every tool* available, *every resource* possible, *every connection* imaginable, and *every ethical, moral, and legal means* possible to prepare yourself for this ever-changing world in which we live today.

The present and the future may not be as rosy as you had hoped for, but it is here, it is real, and it is yours. However, you must know this: If you make the strategic changes in your life now, you can have a much brighter future. No workplace will be immune from the changes facing our world today, and your very survival depends on being prepared and knowing how to quickly adapt to a variety of situations.

"When it comes to the future, there are three kinds of people: those who let it happen, those who make it happen, and those who wonder what happened."

—John Richardson, Jr.

In his book *The 2010 Meltdown,* Edward Gordon (2005) writes, "Simply stated, today in America, there are just too many people trained for the wrong jobs. Many jobs have become unnecessary, technically obsolete . . . or worse yet, the job/career aspirations of too many current and future workers are at serious odds with the changing needs of the U.S. labor market" (p. 17).

However, all is not lost to you or your future. People who are skilled, possess superb oral and written communication skills, know how to solve problems, have the capacity to change, and can work well with others will be in high demand for many years to come.

What Are Employers Saying?

According to the report *College Learning for the New Global Century* (2008), "Employers want college graduates to acquire versatile knowledge and skills. Fully sixty-three percent of employers believe that too many recent college graduates do not have the skills they need to succeed in the global economy and a majority of employers believe that only half or fewer recent graduates have the skills or knowledge needed to advance or to be promoted in their companies." Other skills listed as vitally important to employers include:

Computer literacy
The ability to learn new skills quickly
Accuracy
Attention to detail
Self-confidence
Tact
Humor
Character

Whether we like it or not, a massive transformation is going on all around us in this country, as well as all over the world. Thriving in the coming years is going to be more difficult than in the past and will require certain new and different abilities and attitudes. You will need to learn the skills that will make you competitive, give you an edge, and help you master a life filled with changes and challenges. Many of these skills are outlined in Figure 1.1, Essential

Figure 1.1 Essential Cornerstones for Success in a Changing World

Seek Excellence as a Communicator
Writing, speaking, and listening skills are constantly listed by employers as mandatory for success in any profession. Few people actually possess these qualities, especially all three. If you want to put yourself ahead of the competition, then attend every class, every seminar, every meeting, and every function where you can learn more about effective writing, speaking, and listening skills.

Become a Desirable Employee
A strong work ethic will be another valuable quality that sets you apart from the other job seekers. A work ethic can include a variety of characteristics, including your pride, passion, professionalism, ability to work on a team, and ability to adapt, grow, and change. Your work ethic is how you perform at work without a job description, constant supervision, or someone threatening you. Your work ethic is not tied to what you do to get a raise or a promotion, but rather what you do because it is the right thing to do. In today's work environment, employers want to make sure that you are dedicated to your job, your company, and your colleagues. Our suggestion is to develop a strong work ethic that is healthy for you and your employer.

Practice Loyalty and Trustworthiness
Loyalty to your employer is a highly valued trait. However, one's loyalty cannot be measured by a resumé or determined by a simple interview. Proving that you have the characteristics of loyalty and trustworthiness comes over time. It may take years to establish loyalty and trustworthiness with your company and within your industry, but with hard work, dedication, and honesty, it can and will be achieved. Be forewarned, however: it may take years to build trust, but it only takes seconds to destroy it.

Walk with Confidence and Make Bold Decisions
Appropriate confidence and boldness are important to employers. There is a difference between having confidence in yourself, your work, and your decision-making ability and being cocky. Confidence comes from experience, calculated risk taking, and previous successes. Employers are looking for confident people who are not afraid to make hard decisions. They are also seeking individuals who have confidence through experience. There is a difference between bragging about doing something and actually doing it. There is a difference between being hard and making hard decisions. When you meet with the person(s) interviewing you, confidently steer the conversation toward your general and specific abilities and characteristics.

Use Critical-Thinking Skills
The ability to think your way through problems and challenges is highly valued by employers. Employers are looking for people who can distinguish fact from opinion; identify fallacies; analyze, synthesize, and determine the value of a piece of information; think beyond the obvious; see things from varying angles; and arrive at sound solutions. They also want people who possess the emotional intelligence to critically and creatively work to resolve challenges.

Manage Your Priorities Well
Setting priorities and managing time are essential to success in today's stressful workplace. Today, maybe more than any other time in human history, we are faced with more and more to do and what seems like less and less time in which to do it. Your success depends on how well you manage your priorities both personally and professionally. Priority management not only involves getting today's work accomplished, it also involves the ability to plan for your personal and professional future. Use your time wisely at work, at home, and in leisure.

Multiply by Multitasking
The ability to multitask, or accomplish several things at once, will serve you well in the workplace and at home. A recent newspaper cartoon suggested that you are too busy if you are multitasking in the shower. This may be true, but in keeping pace with today's workforce, this is another essential task—the ability to do several things at a time, and the ability to do them all very well. If you have not had much experience in multitasking, we suggest that you begin slowly. Don't take on too many things at one time. As you understand more about working on and completing several tasks at a time, you can expand your abilities in this arena. An example of multitasking at home is to have a casserole baking while clothes are washing at the same time you are researching a project on the Internet. To be successful in the fast-paced world we live in today, you must be able to manage several tasks at once—without burning dinner.

Stay Current and Build Transferable Skills
Keeping your skills and knowledge current is essential to your success. Building skills that can be transferred from one position to another is essential in today's workplace. Fine-tuning your computer skills can set you apart from many of today's applicants. Your skills need to include the ability to work with word-processing programs, spreadsheets, databases, and

PowerPoint. Some careers will require knowledge and expertise of industry software, and you will need to be an expert if this is true in your field. Learn to develop webpages, and create your own website that reflects a professional, career-oriented person. Learn to use social media for more than socializing.

Continue to Get Experience and Education

Never stop learning! You may not want to hear it, but your education will never end. You will eventually complete your formal schooling, but as long as you are working in today's global economy, you will need to keep abreast of the changes in your field. Seek out opportunities to expand your knowledge base. Get certified in areas that will make you more market-able. Take a continuing education course to brush up on changing workplace skills. Make yourself the best, most knowledgeable, most well-rounded applicant in the field.

Avoid Internet and Social Media Blunders

Don't let social media mistakes come back to haunt you and cause you to miss out on your dream job! You may think that posting that photo of yourself half-naked with a bottle of Jim Beam in one hand and a stuffed poodle in the other is cute and that your friends will love it. They may. Your current or future employer may not. What you post online today may very well come back to haunt you in the future—even if you remove it, it can still be accessed. You may not lose your current position over a crazy, spur of the moment posting, but it may cost you a future position. You may tell yourself that your Facebook, LinkedIn, or webpage is private and no one's business, but remember, nothing is private online and everything is someone's business in the world of business.

Watch Your Credit Rating

Building a good credit rating is one of the most important jobs you have. Really? My credit rating? What in the world does my credit score have to do with my employment? The answer: A great deal. More and more, employers are accessing your credit history and score as a part of the hiring procedure. Why? Because some employers believe that your credit history paints a clear picture of your working future. Bad credit history means a bad employee. Missed payments mean missed work. Low score means low morale. Careless errors mean careless job performance. This is just one of the many ways that your credit history and score can follow you for years.

Remain Open-Minded

The ability to accept and appreciate a highly diverse workplace and the inherent differences and cultures that will be commonplace is important. You will need to develop the ability to listen to others with whom you disagree or with whom you may have little in common and learn from them and their experiences. The ability to learn a new language (even if your mastery is only at a primitive, broken, conversational level) and conduct yourself in a respectable and professional style will set you apart from other employees.

Practice Accountability

The ability to accept responsibility and be accountable for all aspects of your future—including your psychological and spiritual well-being, your relationships, your health, your finances, and your overall survival skills—is vitally important. Basically, you must develop a plan for the future that states, "If this fails, I'll do this," or "If this job is phased out, I'll do this," or "If this resource is gone, I'll use this," or "If this person won't help me, this one will."

Polish Your Human Relation Skills

Polish your people skills and learn to get along with people from all walks of life. We saved this one for last, certainly not because it is least important, but because this quality is an overriding characteristic of everything listed previously. Employers are looking for individuals who have "people skills." This concept goes so much further than being a team player; it goes to the heart of many workplaces. It touches on your most basic nature, and it draws from your most inner self. The ability to get along with grouchy, cranky, mean, disagreeable, burned-out coworkers is, indeed, a rare quality. But don't be mistaken; there are those who do this, and do it well. Peak performers, or those at the "top of their game," have learned that this world is made up of many types of people and there is never going to be a time when one of those cranky, grumpy people is not in our midst. Smile. Be nice. Remain positive.

"You want to be the most educated, the most brilliant, the most exciting, the most versatile, the most creative individual in the world because then, you can give it away. The only reason you have anything is to give it away."

—Leo Buscaglia, Ph.D.

Cornerstones for Success in a Changing World. These skills will be needed for your success, personal independence, and growth in the new economy. Study them carefully as each one will help you create a positive transition to the world of work.

GAINFUL EMPLOYMENT

What Strategies Can I Use to Keep from Being Outsourced?

Go where the puck is going! Sound crazy? The great hockey champ Wayne Gretzky made the comment that ***this one step*** had been his key to success. What does it mean? He said that when he was playing hockey, he did not skate to where the puck was at the moment; he skated to where the puck was *going*. He anticipated the direction of where the puck was going to be hit, and when it came his way, he was already there—ready to play.

Think of your career in this light. Go to where it will be bright in the future, not necessarily where it is bright at this moment. Look ahead and try to determine what is going to be "hot" in the coming years, not what is hot right now. Plan ahead. Look at trends. Read. Ask questions. Stay prepared. Think in the future, not the moment.

People holding degrees and certificates are a dime a dozen. This does not mean, however, that *you* are a dime a dozen. Herein lies the challenge. How do you distinguish yourself from the countless job seekers out there? What are you going to do that sets you apart from your competition? What do you have to offer that no one else can possibly offer to an employer? Later, we will discuss some of the talents and qualities that are becoming increasingly rare, yet constantly sought after, in today's "workquake." By understanding more about these qualities, you can put yourself miles ahead of the competition.

Take some time now and work through the exercise in Figure 1.2. You will find several skills and traits for which employers are looking in the left-hand column. In the right-hand column, create two tips that outline ways ***you*** can impress a potential employer.

CREATING YOUR SUCCESS

Can You Really Create Your Future?

Is it really possible to draft a blueprint of your own future? Is it possible to "create success?" The answer is yes. The process of creating success begins with an internal idea that you have the power, the passion, and the capacity to be successful—to reach your chosen goals. It has been said that those people who are not out there creating their own future deserve the future that will be handed to them. You can be a person who creates the future for yourself and your family. Your education is one of the most important steps in this process because your education will give you options and alternatives. It will also help you create opportunities, and, according to Leo Buscaglia, writer and speaker, the healthiest people in the world are the people with the most alternatives.

"So, how do I create a successful future with more options?" you may be asking. The formula is simple, but the action required is not—and have no doubt, ***action is required.*** The formula consists of four steps:

What is the most surprising thing you have learned about your institution's curriculum thus far?

IndexOpen

1. The willingness to set clear, realistic goals and the ability to visualize the results of those goals

2. The ability to recognize your strengths and build on them

Figure 1.2   **Skills for Gainful Employment**

SKILL / TRAIT EMPLOYERS SEEK	TWO TIPS TO IMPRESS
Priority/Time Management	1. 2.
Attitude	1. 2.
Written Communication	1. 2.
Interpersonal Communication/Relationships	1. 2.
Ethics	1. 2.
Dress/Personal Grooming	1. 2.
Computer/Technology Skills	1. 2.
Decision-Making/Problem-Solving Skills	1. 2.
Confidence	1. 2.
Advanced Training/Certifications	1. 2.

3. The ability to recognize your weaknesses or challenges and work to improve them

4. The passion and desire to work at your zenith every single day to make your goals and dreams a reality

Simple? The first three are rather simple. Number four is the kicker. Truthfully, most people have little trouble with the first three; it is the work involved with number four that causes most people to give up and never reach their fullest potential—and to be handed a future over which they had little say in creating. You can create your own future, your own success, and your own alternatives.

Coming to the realization that there is no "easy street" and no "roads paved with good intentions" is also important to creating your success. In his landmark book, *Good to Great,* Jim Collins suggests that once you decide to be great, your life will never be easy again. Rid yourself of the notion that there is some easy way out, that school will be easy, or that your education will make your professional life easier. Success requires

> "Though no one can go back and make a brand new start, anyone can start from now and make a brand new ending."
> —Carl Bard

hard, passionate work on a daily basis. This passionate work may require you to change some of your thoughts, actions, and beliefs. That is what this chapter and indeed this entire course is about: Creating success through positive change.

YOUR EDUCATION AND YOU

Why Is It the Partnership of a Lifetime?

What can a career college education do for you? The list will certainly vary depending on whom you ask, but basically, career colleges can help you develop in the areas listed below. As you read through the list, place a checkmark beside the statements that most accurately reflects which skills you hope to gain from attending classes at your institution. If there are other skills that you desire to achieve from your education, write them at the end of the list.

_____ Grow more self-sufficient and self-confident
_____ Establish and strengthen your personal identity
_____ Understand more about the global world in which you live
_____ Become a more involved citizen in social and political issues
_____ Become more open-minded
_____ Learn to manage your emotions and reactions more effectively
_____ Understand the value of thinking, analyzing, and problem solving
_____ Expand and use your ethical and moral thinking and reasoning skills
_____ Develop commanding computer and information literacy skills
_____ Manage your personal resources such as time and money
_____ Become more proficient at written, oral, and nonverbal communication
_____ Grow more understanding and accepting of different cultures
_____ Become a lifelong learner
_____ Become more financially independent
_____ Enter a career field that you enjoy

Which skill is the most important to you?

_____

_____

_____

Why?

_____

_____

_____

What plans will you put into action to hone and master this skill?

_____

_____

_____

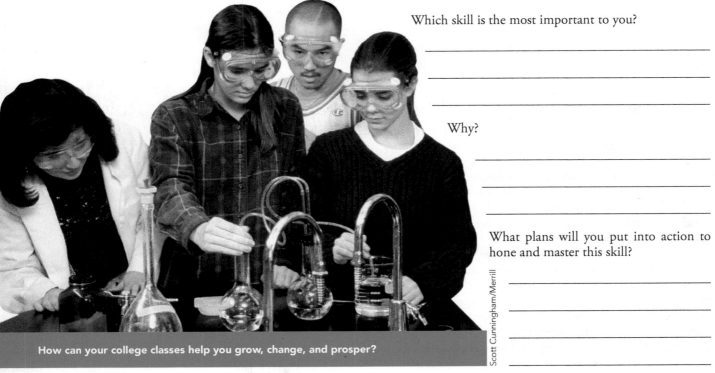

How can your college classes help you grow, change, and prosper?

Scott Cunningham/Merrill

CREATING SUCCESS THROUGH POSITIVE CHANGE

How Can You Bring Positive, Lasting Change to Your Daily Life?

Change is quite often met with resistance, not only by the person directly involved in the change, but by those around that person. As you begin to change, grow, and take control of your future, you will notice that your relationships with others may change, too. Change is not easy, and the person who initiates it (hopefully you) may not be the most popular person around. People like stability and they like things "the way they have always been." We're creatures of habit, and change creates unfamiliar ground. There will be people along the way who may try to derail your hopes. Some of your friends who have always been close may feel threatened by the differences they see in you. If you are going places, people don't like the idea of being left behind. But remember, there are going to be people pulling for you, too. There are going to be people in your life who support your dreams and goals and want nothing but the very best for you. Your courage and desire and reliance on these people will see you through hard times.

So, why is change so important to you and your future? Quite simply, change that you direct creates opportunities for you to grow and prosper in ways you may have never imagined. It allows you to become and remain competitive. It allows you to actively live in a world that is fluid and unpredictable. There are several things you need to know about creating success in your life through positive change. Consider the following ideas:

> *"Your time is limited, so don't waste it living someone else's life."*
> —Steve Jobs

1. *Change is a skill.* Change is a ***learned skill*** that any willing person can do. Period. Public speaking and learning how to drive a car are skills, and just like those activities, learning to change is a skill, too. You'll need to familiarize yourself with the tools to learn this skill.

2. *Change takes time.* Change does not happen immediately at the snap of your fingers. If you've ever taken piano, guitar, or drum lessons, you'll know it took time to learn how to play them because it is a skill—just like change. You did not learn to play overnight, just as you won't learn everything about math or nursing in one semester. Often, change is a slow, systematic series of events that eventually leads you to your desired end.

3. *Change requires an "attitude adjustment."* A contestant on the TV show *America's Got Talent* was being interviewed about her chances of success on the show. Queen Emily was an African American single mother working full time. She had given up her dream of being a professional singer years earlier to raise her children. She stated that before her audition, she stood and looked in the mirror crying. Her only thought was "My time has passed; this is never going to happen for me. Never!" Then, she looked herself in the eyes and said, "Why NOT me? I'm talented. I'm good at performing, and I KNOW I can sing. **WHY NOT ME?**" Her attitude adjustment was the key to her being able to change her life. She auditioned, surpassed thousands of contestants, and was invited to Los Angeles as one of five finalists. After *America's Got Talent*, she performed in a major show in Las Vegas, Nevada.

Corbis RF

How can surrounding yourself with positive, upbeat, optimistic people help you with personal change?

DID YOU *Know?*

ABRAHAM LINCOLN was born on February 12, 1809, in Hardin, Kentucky, to two uneducated farmers. They lived in a one-room log cabin. His mother died when he was 10 years old, just a few years after his father moved the family to Illinois.

He was raised in great poverty and only had 18 months of formal schooling. He studied very hard on his own and learned to read, write, and do mathematical problems. He went on to become a lawyer. One of his law partners once said of him, "His ambition was a great engine that knew no rest."

He lost the love of his life when he was 26, suffered a nervous breakdown at age 27, failed in business twice, lost eight elections, and suffered the death of three children all *before* he became our president and changed the course of our nation. On Good Friday, April 14, 1865, Lincoln was assassinated at Ford's Theatre in Washington, D.C., by John Wilkes Booth. (White House, n.d.).

PHOTO: Courtesy of the Library of Congress

4. *Change demands action.* While circumstances and desire may drive the need for change in your life, don't lose sight of the fact that ultimately, change is an action. It is something you must do—mentally, physically, spiritually, and intellectually. Just as Queen Emily knew, without action, her life was not going to change.

5. *Change is about working toward something, not running away from something.* If you want true, lasting, meaningful change in your life, you have to think about it as working toward good, positive, useful things, not as running away from bad, negative, unpleasant things. "Working toward" is *positive and internal.* "Running away from" is *negative and external.* Try to work *toward a goal* and not *run from a problem.*

6. *Change is about letting go and holding on.* As with any new endeavor, you will have to decide what is working in your life and what is not. By doing so, you can decide what you need to hold onto and what you finally need to let go of. You will want to hold onto the positive strengths and talents you have while letting go of the negative, destructive attitudes that you may have held in the past.

7. *Change is accomplished by having a clear, focused, directed goal.* To change something in your life, you will need to develop a clear, realistic, simple path to make that change. You may need to divide the change into smaller bits so that it does not seem so overwhelming. In their book *Switch* (2010), Chip and Dan Heath suggest "shrinking the change—that big change comes from a succession of small changes." They state, "Big problems are rarely solved with big solutions. Instead, they are most often solved by a sequence of small solutions, sometimes over weeks, sometimes over decades." If you want to change your life and lose 50 pounds, you should decide to lose five pounds first. *Just five pounds*—not 50. After the first five, your goal will be to lose five more. Before you know it, you've lost 30, 40, 50 pounds. A smaller, clearer focus helps you bring about the change and not get bogged down in the massive struggle to lose 50 pounds.

THE M & M THEORY

What Have Your Money and Your Mama Got to Do with It?

What is the M & M theory? It is quite simple really. We all pay attention to and try to protect the things that matter most to us. "Your money and your mama" are symbolic of what you care about. Most people care deeply what happens to their families, their income, their friends, their careers, and the environment, and most people do care and are concerned about our ever-changing world.

However, in the hustle and bustle of finding daycare, studying for classes, working a full-time job, cleaning the house, helping the kids with homework, and trying to prepare a meal from time to time, we may lose sight of some of the most important things in our lives. Try to keep this thought in mind: *your education*

"Forget mistakes. Forget failures. Forget everything except what you're going to do now . . . and do it."

—*Will Durant*

is important, too. In fact, it is of paramount importance to your future on many levels—culturally, socially, intellectually, and in preparing you for the future. Your education is a part of the M & M theory because it involves your money—the future financial health for you and your family.

According to one of the leading research sources in higher education, *The Chronicle of Higher Education* (2010, p. 32), first-year students had a variety of thoughts regarding a college education and money. Of the 222,000 students who responded to their survey, 78 percent responded that "being very well-off financially" was an essential or very important objective. Seventy-two percent responded that "the chief benefit of a college education is that it increases one's earning power" (Sieben, 2011).

According to the United States Bureau of Labor Statistics in its annual report, *Education and Training Pay* (2010), people with college degrees can earn considerably more than those who do not have a degree. For instance, those with a bachelor's degree average approximately $29,000 *more per year* in earnings than those with only a high school education. People with an associate's degree average approximately $10,000 more per year in earnings than those with only a high school education. For a complete look at earning power of U.S. citizens age 25 and older, see Figure 1.3.

By focusing on money in this section, we do not mean to suggest that the only reason for attending college is to make more money. As a matter of fact, we feel that it is a secondary reason. Many people *without college degrees* earn huge salaries each year. However, as the data suggest, traditionally, those with college degrees *earn more money* and *experience less unemployment.* Basically, college should make the road to financial security easier, but it should also be a place where you learn to make decisions about your values, your character, and your future. College can also be a place where you make decisions about the changes that need to occur in your life so that you can effectively manage and prosper in an ever-changing world. It can also be a place where you learn the skills to change and continue to grow long after you graduate.

Figure 1.3 **Education, Pay, and Unemployment Statistics of Full-Time Workers, 25 and Over**

UNEMPLOYMENT RATE	DEGREE	MEAN EARNINGS
2.40%	Professional degree	$146,659
1.90%	Doctorate degree	$116,305
4.00%	Master's degree	$87,913
5.40%	Bachelor's degree	$68,812
7.00%	Associate's degree	$49,835
9.20%	Some college, no degree	$47,484
10.30%	High school graduate	$39,937 not in El Paso
14.90%	Less than high school graduate	$30,958

Source: Department of the Census, Department of Labor, 2009.

THE CULTURE OF COLLEGE

What Are the Basic Truths about Career College Success?

In your lifetime, you will experience many things that influence and alter your views, goals, and livelihood. These may include things such as travel, relationships, and personal victories or setbacks. However, few experiences will have a greater influence than your career college experience. A career college education can mean hopes realized, dreams fulfilled, and the breaking down of social and economic walls. To get the most from your career college experience and to lay a path to success, it will be important to look at your expectations and the vast differences between high school, jobs you may have held, and the culture of your institution. This section will introduce you to some of the changes you can expect.

Basic Truth 1: Success Is about Making Choices, Sacrifices, and Intelligent Transitions

Life is a series of choices. Hard choices. Easy choices. Right choices. Wrong choices. Nevertheless, the quality of your life is determined by the choices you make and your willingness to evaluate your life and determine if transitions are in order. You will have many important and hard choices in the near future, such as deciding whether to devote your time to studying or partying; whether to ask for help in classes that challenge you or give up and drop out; or whether to make the sacrifices needed for your future success or take the easy road. Those choices will determine the quality of your future. Some of the choices that you make will force you to step beyond your comfort zone—to move to places that may frighten you or make you uncomfortable. That's OK. That's good. In fact, that's very good.

So what is a **comfort zone**? It sounds cozy, doesn't it? Warm and fuzzy. However, do not let the term fool you. A comfort zone is not necessarily a happy and comfortable place. It is simply a place where you are familiar with your surroundings and don't have to work too hard. It is where you feel confident of your abilities, but it is also a place where your growth stops. *It can be a prison and staying there can be a cop-out.* Successful people who have won personal and professional victories know that moving beyond one's comfort zone helps in nurturing change, reaching your potential, and creating opportunities for positive growth.

Basic Truth 2: Your Education Is a Two-Way Street

Perhaps the first thing that you will notice about higher education is that you have to **give** in order to **receive**. Not only do you have expectations of your institution and instructors, but your institution and instructors have great expectations of you. To be successful, you will need to accept substantially more responsibility for your education than you may have in the past. By attending this institution, you have agreed to become a part of its community, values, and policies. You now have the responsibility to stand by its code of academic and moral conduct, and you have the responsibility of giving your very best to every class and organization in which you are involved. And, you have a responsibility to *yourself* of approaching this new world with an open mind and curious enthusiasm. In return, your institution will be responsible for helping you reach your fullest potential and live the life you desire.

So, what are your thoughts at the moment? Respond to the following questions honestly and personally.

What sacrifices do you think you'll need to make in your personal life to be academically successful?

Stockbyte/Getty RF

B R I N G the Change

TIPS FOR PERSONAL SUCCESS

Consider the following tips to help you move beyond your comfort zone:

- Take one positive risk per week.
- Ask others for help when you need it.
- Volunteer for activities and to help others.
- Forget the past and embrace the future.

List two other tips that will help people move beyond their comfort zone.

1. _____

2. _____

1. Thus far, I think the most rewarding class and instructor this term are going to be _____
_____

2. I believe this because _____
_____

3. To date, I've learned that he or she expects me to _____
_____

> "You gain strength, experience, and confidence by every experience where you stop to look fear in the face. You must do the thing that you think you cannot."
> —Eleanor Roosevelt

Basic Truth 3: You're in Charge Here—It's All about Self-Motivation and Self-Responsibility

One person and *only* one person has the power to determine your thoughts and the direction of your future. **It is you!** You will decide the direction of your future. You are not a victim, and you will not be treated as a victim at this institution. You will not be allowed to use "victim excuses" or employ the "victim mentality." This is all about you and your desire to change your life. Higher education is not about others doing the work, but rather about you finding internal motivation and accepting responsibility for your actions, your decisions, your choices, and yourself. It is not about making excuses and blaming others. *You are in charge here.* This is your education, and no one else will be responsible for acquiring the knowledge and skills you will need to survive and thrive. No one will be able to give you personal motivation.

Regardless of your circumstances, that late paper for English is not your husband's fault. That missed lab report is not your child's problem. Your tardiness is not your mother's mistake. That unread chapter is not your partner's liability. Likewise, that 98 you scored on your drug calculation test is yours. That A you got on your paper about the criminal justice system is yours. That B+ you got on your first math test is yours. This is about *you*! Your life. Your future. Your attitude is going to greatly affect your possibility of success.

Figure 1.4 Victim and Winner Profiles

THE VICTIM	THE WINNER
The victim blames others for his/her problems.	The winner accepts responsibility for what happens in his/her life.
The victim procrastinates and makes excuses for not doing a good job.	The winner thinks ahead and plans for success.
The victim sees adversity as a permanent obstacle.	The winner sees adversity as a way to get stronger.
The victim constantly complains and has a negative mentality about most things.	The winner has an optimistic attitude and is pleasant to be with most of the time.
The victim does just enough to get by and is happy with poor grades and mediocre accomplishments.	The winner works hard to raise his/her level of achievement and constantly seeks to improve.
The victim lets life happen without trying to make things happen.	The winner has a plan, sets goals, and works everyday to make positive things happen.
The victim is always late, often absent, and always has an excuse.	The winner is on time, prepared, and rarely negligent regarding his/her responsibilities.
The victim hangs out with people who are negative, troublemakers, or party animals with low ambition and a poor work ethic.	The winner surrounds himself/herself with people who are working hard to make something of themselves and who are encouraging and motivating.

BLOOM LEVEL 1

Consider Figure 1.4 describing the differences between a "victim" and a "winner."

1. Name one person available to you (personally or professionally) who can offer you support and encouragement, and to whom you can turn when things get tough.

   _____

2. Why do you respect and/or admire this person enough to ask for help?

   _____

   _____

   _____

   _____

3. Generate a list of three questions you would like to ask this person about his or her life, how he or she "made it," and how he or she overcame adversity.

   1. _____

   2. _____

   3. _____

Basic Truth 4: Self-Management Will Be Your Key to Success

A major transition coming your way involves the workload for your courses and the choices you will need to make regarding your schedule and time. You may be assigned a significant amount of reading as homework; in fact, the amount of reading that your classes demand is usually a shock to many students. Although you may have only two or three classes in one day, the basic guideline is that for every hour spent in class, a minimum of two to three hours should be spent in review and preparation for the next class.

Quick math: If you are taking five classes and are in class for 15 hours per week, you need to spend 30 hours studying. This makes a 45-hour week—five hours more than a normal work week for most people! "Not I," you may say, and you may be right. It all depends on how wisely you use your time, how difficult the work is, and the strength of your academic background.

Basic Truth 5: This Is Not High School

It sounds so simple, but this is perhaps the most universal and important truth discussed here: College is very different from both high school and the world of work and perhaps one of the most different places you'll ever encounter. The expectations for four different areas are outlined in Figure 1.5. Review each area carefully and consider your past experiences as you study the differences.

Basic Truth 6: Eliminating the "This Isn't Harvard Syndrome" Will Be Essential to Your Success

Some students enter school with little or no perception of how much work is involved or how much effort it is going to take to be successful. They do not think that the local or online career college could possibly be "that difficult." Many even perceive an institution to be less rigorous than it actually is. Some might reason, "It's only Grace Medical Institute" or "It's just Trion Technical College." They do not think that the career college they are attending has the academic standards of a Harvard, a Yale, or a Stanford University. The truth is that your career college education is what *you make of it.* When you graduate and you are interviewing for a job, the name of your institution may hold some weight, but your skills, passion, experiences, knowledge, and thinking abilities will be the paramount "tipping point."

True, you may not be at Harvard or Yale, but the rigor of your programs, the amount of reading required, the level of math skills needed, and the degree to which critical-thinking, communication, and information literacy skills will be required may surprise you. We think that it is important to dispel the *"This Isn't Harvard" Syndrome* as quickly as possible so that you can prepare yourself for the coursework and requirements ahead and make the most of your college experience.

You've probably already attended a few of your classes and received syllabi from those classes as you read this. Examine two of your current classes. What has surprised you the most about what is going to be required of you this semester?

CLASS	SURPRISING REQUIREMENT	YOUR PLAN FOR SUCCESS
#1		
#2		

By embracing these truths about your school, learning, self-motivation, and education in general, you will have taken some very important steps toward your success.

Figure 1.5 A Guide to Understanding Expectations

	HIGH SCHOOL	CAREER COLLEGE	WORK
Punctuality and Attendance	**Expectations:** • State law requires a certain number of days you must attend • The hours in the day are managed for you • There may be some leeway in project dates **Penalties:** • You may get detention • You may not graduate • You may be considered a truant • Your grades may suffer	**Expectations:** • Attendance and participation in class are strictly enforced by many professors • Most professors will not give you extensions on due dates • You decide your own schedule and plan your own day **Penalties:** • You may not be admitted to class if you are late • You may fail the assignment if it is late • Repeated tardiness is sometimes counted as an absence • Most professors do not take late assignments	**Expectations:** • You are expected to be at work and on time on a daily basis **Penalties:** • Your salary and promotions may depend on your daily attendance and punctuality • You will most likely be fired for abusing either
Teamwork and Participation	**Expectations:** • Most teamwork is assigned and carried out in class • You may be able to choose teams with your friends • Your grade may reflect your participation **Penalties:** • If you don't participate, you may get a poor grade • You may jeopardize the grade of the entire team	**Expectations:** • Many professors require teamwork and cooperative learning teams or learning communities • Your grade will depend on your participation • Your grade may depend on your entire team's performance • You will probably have to work on the project outside of class **Penalties:** • Lack of participation and cooperation will probably cost you a good grade • Your team members will likely report you to the professor if you do not participate and their grades suffer as a result	**Expectations:** • You will be expected to participate fully in any assigned task • You will be expected to rely on coworkers to help solve problems and increase profits • You will be required to attend and participate in meetings and sharing sessions • You will be required to participate in formal teams and possess the ability to work with a diverse workforce **Penalties:** • You will be "tagged" as a non–team player • Your lack of participation and teamwork will cost you raises and promotions • You will most likely be terminated
Personal Responsibility and Attitude	**Expectations:** • Teachers may coach you and try to motivate you	**Expectations:** • You are responsible for your own learning	**Expectations:** • You are hired to do certain tasks and the company or institution fully expects this of you

	HIGH SCHOOL	CAREER COLLEGE	WORK
	• You are required by law to be in high school regardless of your attitude or responsibility level **Penalties:** • You may be reprimanded for certain attitudes • If your attitude prevents you from participating, you may fail the class	• Professors will assist you, but there is little "hand holding" or personal coaching for motivation • College did not choose you; you chose it and you will be expected to hold this attitude toward your work **Penalties:** • You may fail the class if your attitude and motivation prevent you from participating	• You are expected to be positive and self-motivated • You are expected to model good behavior and uphold the company's work standards **Penalties:** • You will be passed over for promotions and raises • You may be reprimanded • You may be terminated
Ethics and Credibility	**Expectations:** • You are expected to turn in your own work • You are expected to write your own papers, without plagiarizing **Penalties:** • You may get detention or suspension • You will probably fail the project	**Expectations:** • You are expected to turn in your own work • You are expected to write your own papers, without plagiarizing • You are expected to conduct research and complete projects based on college and societal standards **Penalties:** • Poor ethical decisions may land you in front of a student or faculty ethics committee or result in expulsion from the college • You will fail the project as well as the class • You may face deportation if your visa is dependent on your student status	**Expectations:** • You will be required to carry out your job in accordance with company policies, laws, and moral standards • You will be expected to use adult vision and standards **Penalties:** • Poor ethical decisions may cause you to be severely reprimanded or terminated, or in some cases could even result in legal consequences

BUILDING A NEW YOU

How Can You Change Your Life Through Goal Setting?

Positive change can be brought about in several ways, but the most effective way is through goal setting and having a "change plan." Think about what you really want or what you need to change in your life. More importantly, think about why you want "this thing" and what it is going to mean to your life. By thinking about what you want, what needs to change, and where you want to be, goals become easier.

Successful Decisions

AN ACTIVITY FOR CRITICAL REFLECTION

After the first week of classes, Devon was very disheartened about the difficulty of the classes for which he was registered. He did not think that he was going to have so much reading or homework and he never thought the instructors would be so demanding. He had never been strong at math, but he was just floored at how difficult his beginning math course had become. He failed his first test. He passed his first essay in English, but only with a grade of C. He seriously considered dropping out. It was just too much. It was more than he expected.

Devon knew, however, that he had to succeed. He looked at this current financial situation, his dead-end job, and his desire to work in a health profession. Dropping out would never get him there. Dropping out would never make him a better, more prepared person. Dropping out would never afford him

the opportunity to provide a better life for his family. However, Devon felt that he was just too far behind to catch up. He was at a loss as to what to do.

In your own words, what would you suggest that Devon do at this point? Pretend that Devon is enrolled at your institution. List at least two additional things that he could do to ensure his success and not drop out. Think about what services are offered and who might be of assistance to him.

1. _____

_____

2. _____

_____

"Decide you want it more than you're afraid of it."
—Bill Cosby

Goal setting itself is relatively easy—it is the personal commitment and self-motivation that requires detailed attention, hard work, and unbridled passion. The most vital step toward reaching your goal is making a personal commitment to yourself that you are going to achieve it and then committing all of your possible resources toward the completion of that goal.

Characteristics of Attainable Goals

The following characteristics will help you in your quest to bring about change through effective goal setting. Goals should be:

- *Reasonable.* Your goal should be a challenge for you, but also within reason based on your abilities.

- *Believable.* To achieve a goal, you must really believe it is within your capacity to reach it.

- *Measurable.* Your goal needs to be concrete and measurable in some way. Avoid such terms a "earn a lot" or "lose some weight."

- *Adaptable.* Your goals may need to be adapted to changing circumstances that may be happening in your life.

- *Controllable.* Your goals should be within your own control; they should not depend on the whims and opinions of anyone else.

- *Desirable.* To attain a difficult goal, you must want it very badly. You should never work toward something just because *someone else* wants it.

How to Write Your Goals to Bring about Positive Change

"I will pass my next math test with a B or better" is an example of a short-term goal. "I will purchase my first home in seven to ten years" is probably a long-term goal. During your time at school, more of your goals may be short term than long term, but you can certainly begin setting

from ORDINARY to Extraordinary

Bill Clayton
ACE Certified Personal Trainer / Post-Rehabilitation Specialist
Owner/Operator, Clayton Personal Fitness, Las Vegas, Nevada

"**I** WAS . . .**"** Those are powerful words. For example, I was the manager of the gardening department of a major retail chain. I was an employee in a shop that prints and mails inserts and flyers. I was a rock band drummer for several bands. I was a crystal meth addict. Yes . . . I was!

It seems strange to write that now, but the term "I was . . ." is impossible to erase. My friends and clients often ask me how I managed to go from the life of a meth addict to a personal trainer. The journey was a strange one and often difficult.

I began playing the drums when I was six years old and by the time I was eight, I had my first "garage band." Writing and playing music were my only passions. They were my life. After high school, I worked many odd jobs, but my love of performing never waned.

In my 20s, I had a band that steadily played gigs and I was living the life of a rocker. We traveled. We sang. We partied. We traveled some more and we partied some more . . . and more. Before I really realized what was happening with me, I had become addicted to meth. It was my life. I hung around people who used with me and they became my family. I met Kathy, the woman I would eventually marry, while performing with my band. She and I hit it off even though she knew of my addiction. One evening after we were married, Kathy and I were talking and she mentioned that she would like to have children one day. I wanted children, too. At that moment, the strangest thing came to my mind. I thought, "If she gets pregnant, I'll stop doing meth." How could I be so messed up that I would work to abolish my addiction for a child not yet born, BUT I would

> My friends and clients often ask me how I managed to go from the life of a meth addict to a personal trainer.

not consider trying to stop just for ME? That was my wake-up call. I knew I had to change my life. I was 29 years old.

I was one of the lucky ones. I was able to stop "cold turkey" on my own. I know that others are not so lucky. I began to look at my life and tried to determine what I wanted to do. I had to seriously evaluate every aspect of who and what I was. I knew that I had to set goals to get my life back on track.

I had been in a life-threatening motorcycle accident years earlier and remembered the great care I received from my physical therapist. So, I began to look at PT programs and that is when I found the personal trainer program at our local college. Something about this was very attractive to me. Again, I was lucky. I happened to find my passion and my life's vocation without much struggle.

Today, after working through my addiction, surviving a divorce, and mourning the death of my mom, I can say without a doubt that I am one of the luckiest people on Earth. Because I was willing to change and stay committed to finding a better life, I own my own gym, hold certifications from every major fitness and rehabilitation organization in America, and count each day as a true gift.

EXTRAORDINARY REFLECTION

Read the following statement and respond in your online journal or class notebook.

Mr. Clayton mentions that he was one of the "lucky ones." What role do you think luck plays in one's success? Is there a difference between luck, readiness, and action? If so, what is it?

What exactly is it going to take to achieve your biggest, most important goals?

Shutterstock

both. Goals can be lofty and soaring, but great goals can also be as simple as "I will spend two hours at the park with my children tomorrow afternoon."

Well written, exciting, and effective goals include:

- A goal statement with a target date
- Action steps
- A narrative statement
- An "I deserve it" statement
- A personal signature

The ***goal statement*** should be specific and measurable; that is, it should entail some tangible evidence of its achievement, and it should have a ***target date,*** or timeline for accomplishment. Your goal statement must also use an action verb. An example of a goal statement with an action verb and target date is: "*I will* lose 10 pounds in six weeks" or "*I am going to* join a campus club by the fifth week of this term." This is a much more powerful statement than: "I am thinking about joining a club" or "I wanna have a new car."

After you write the goal statement, you'll need to create ***specific action steps*** that explain exactly what you are going to do to reach your goal. There is no certain number of steps; it all depends on your goal and your personal commitment. An example of action steps for weight loss might be: (1) I ***will*** walk up three flights of steps daily, (2) I ***will*** meet with a personal trainer, (3) I ***will*** set an appointment with a nutrition counselor, (4) I ***will*** . . .

The next step is to write a ***narrative statement*** about what your goal accomplishment will mean to you and how your life will change because of reaching this goal. For example, if your goal is to lose 30 pounds, paint a "verbal picture" of how your life is going to look once this goal has been reached. Your verbal picture may include statements such as: "I'll be able to wear nicer clothes." "I'll feel better." "I'll be able to ride my bicycle again." "My self-esteem will be stronger." If your goals don't offer you significant rewards, you are not likely to stick to your plan.

Next, write two reasons why you deserve this goal. This is called your ***"I deserve it" statement.*** It may seem simple, but this is a complex question. Many people do not follow through on their goals because deep down, they don't feel they deserve them. The narrative statement helps you understand how your life will look once the goal is met but your "I deserve it" statement asks you to consider *why* you deserve this goal.

Finally, ***sign your goal statement.*** This is an imperative step in that your signature shows that you are making a personal commitment to see this goal to fruition. This is your name. Use it with pride. Use the goal sheet in Figure 1.6 to build your goals.

ONE LAST, IMPORTANT WORD ABOUT YOUR GOALS

What Happens When Aspirations and Behavior Collide?

Earlier in the chapter, you read about change and how to bring about a positive change in your life. One of the ideas discussed was ***"change demands action."*** Your goals demand action, too. Many students are dismayed when they realize that goals don't just happen. Dreams and plans and aspirations are fine, but the ending can be quite painful if you don't put forth the effort to bring them to fruition. To reach your goals and meet your aspirations, you may have to work

Figure 1.6 Goal Sheet

My Personal Goal

To help you get started, use this goal-setting sheet as a template for this and future goals.

Name _____

Goal Statement (with action verb and target date) _____

_____

_____

Action Steps (concrete things you plan to do to reach your goal)

1. _____

2. _____

3. _____

4. _____

5. _____

Narrative Statement (how your life will look when you reach your goal) _____

_____

_____

_____

What **obstacles** will you need to overcome to reach this goal? _____

_____

_____

I deserve this goal because:

1. _____

_____

2. _____

_____

I hereby make this commitment to myself.

_____   _____
My Signature   Date

BLOOM LEVEL 1

BLOOM LEVEL 2

BLOOM LEVEL 3

harder than you've ever worked in the past. You may have to change the way you approach things. You may have to adjust the way you think about involvement and most importantly, you may have to change the level of action that you put toward your goals.

The point at which many students leave school is the point at which their aspirations and behaviors collide. They realize that monumental changes are going to have to occur before their aspirations are met and they are simply not ready, willing, or able to make these monumental adjustments. Begin working today to employ healthy study habits; get involved in your institution's activities; work to get to know your instructors, counselors, and advisors; and reach out to people in class and beyond who can help you. Build on your strengths and work tirelessly to overcome your challenges. These steps will help you reach your goals and make your future aspirations a reality.

CHANGING IDEAS to Reality

REFLECTIONS ON CHANGE AND GOAL SETTING

The transition from one place to another is seldom easy, even when the change is what you want. Entering career college has given you the opportunity to assume new roles, develop new friendships, meet new people, work under different circumstances, and create a bountiful future. It is an opportunity to improve on who you are at this moment or to build an entirely new person if you choose to do so. Going to a career college gives you the opportunity to reflect on your strengths and consider areas where you might need to change. These changes form the very essence of the career college experience; they create wonderful new experiences and help you discover who you really are and what you have to offer the world.

As you reflect on this chapter, keep the following pointers in mind:

- Evaluate your reason(s) for attending career college and what it means to your life.
- Understand and use the Essential Cornerstones for Success.
- Work hard to be a winner, not a victim.
- Use goal setting to help you direct changes in your life.
- Don't just let change happen; get involved in your own life and learning.

"If what you believe doesn't affect how you live, then it isn't very important."

—*Dick Nogleberg*

Knowledge
in Bloom

BRINGING POSITIVE CHANGE TO YOUR LIFE

Utilizes levels 1–6 of the taxonomy

Each chapter-end assessment is based on Bloom's Taxonomy of Learning. See pages xxvi–xxviii in the front of this book for a quick review.

Explanation: After reading and reflecting thus far, you may have identified several changes that you need to make in your academic or personal life. Also, changes may have been thrust on you by choices you or those around you have made. The following model provides a method for bringing positive changes into your life and/or reshaping the changes over which you had little control.

Process: Based on Bloom's Taxonomy, the **Change Implementation Model** asks you to consider questions and recommends actions at each level of learning. The chart moves from less difficult questions (levels 1, 2, 3) to more challenging questions (levels 4, 5, 6). To begin the change process in your life, follow the steps in this chapter-end activity.

STEP 1
Review the steps of the **Change Implementation Model** based on **Bloom's Taxonomy.**

Level 1—REMEMBER	*Describe* one behavior, belief, or action that you need to change in your life. Also, list the possible obstacles that you might encounter.
Level 2—UNDERSTAND	*Explain* why this change needs to occur in order for you to be successful. Also, give two examples of the options available to you at your institution, home, or in the community for making the desired change.
Level 3—APPLY	*Use* the information from levels 1 and 2 to show your plan (action steps) to overcome the obstacles listed above.
Level 4—ANALYZE	*Compare* your current action steps to the steps you have previously taken to overcome obstacles and enact change. What conclusions can you draw from this comparison?
Level 5—EVALUATE	*Justify* what you are doing, why you need to do it, and how it is going to positively affect your life in a detailed written paragraph.
Level 6—CREATE	*Design* your plan to bring about this change in your life based on the information you have gathered from investigation and reflection. Consider using the goal-setting format illustrated in this chapter to create a plan and action steps that are truly unique to you.

STEP 2
After studying the Change Implementation Model above, read the following fictional scenario, in which you encounter difficulty in Accounting 101.

You enter your Accounting 101 class eager to take the first course in your major field. You are shocked to find that the professor begins lecturing on the first day. Not only is the material difficult to understand, so is the professor, whose first language is not English.

For homework, the professor assigns two chapters to read per class, but the lectures are not based on material found in the text. You try to study as you did in high school, but now you feel overwhelmed and isolated. The material is much harder.

After three weeks and a failed first test, you notice that the students who passed the test had formed study groups, something that you once thought only the brightest students practiced.

Using the **Change Implementation Model,** you decide to make positive changes in your study habits. As an example, plans for change are shown in Step 3.

STEP 3

Review this example and determine how you might use the **Change Implementation Model** to enact changes to save your grade in Accounting 101.

Level 1—REMEMBER	If I could, I would change my study habits in accounting and become stronger in my math skills Obstacles: fear of change, shyness, pride, and time constraints
Level 2—UNDERSTAND	Why I need change: Weak math skills causing me to fail accounting Institution: Tutoring center, math lab, professor office hours Community: Aunt works in accounting office
Level 3—APPLY	Step 1: I will join a study group. Step 2: I will make an appointment for tutoring in the math lab. Step 3: I will talk to my advisor about services available. Step 3: I will plan at least five hours per week to study for my accounting class. Step 4: I will seek help from my aunt who is an accountant.
Level 4—ANALYZE	Past: I took notes in class, looked over them before a test New: Join study group, go to tutoring center and math lab New: Talk with advisor New: Meet with my aunt for advice and assistance Conclusion: In taking personal responsibility for my education, taking calculated risks to bring about change, and asking for help, I'm more likely to pass accounting.
Level 5—EVALUATE	I am working so hard to pass accounting because I want this degree and I want the knowledge of how to run my own business. If I don't change my habits, I will not pass accounting and I will not have this degree. Without this degree, I will most likely have to work in low-paying jobs for the rest of my life. By asking for help, spending more time studying, and spending more time around people who have some of the same interests, I can develop the skills to graduate, start my own business, and help my family out financially.
Level 6—CREATE	**Goal:** I will get involved with a study group, schedule a tutor, and spend at least five hours per week studying for accounting. I will do this by the end of this week. **Action Steps:** Step 1: I will join study group/get accounting tutor. Step 2: I will talk to my advisor about services available. Step 3: I will study five hours per week for accounting class. Step 4: I will work with my boss to design a plan for more study time. Step 5: I will meet with my aunt once a week to get her help. **Narrative statement:** Basically, by getting involved and not trying to go this alone, I will begin to enjoy college more and do better in my classes. **I deserve this goal because:** I have the courage to ask for help and the intelligence to put my pride aside and seek assistance. I deserve to learn this material so that I can successfully run my own business.

STEP 4

After studying the **Change Implementation Model** example on the previous page, focus on a few things that you might want to change about your own academic life, such as study habits, motivation level, financial or time management, or attitude. Now, choose **one** of the major changes you wish to incorporate into your life from the list that you made. Using the **Change Implementation Model,** devise a strategy to effect this change.

Level 1—REMEMBER	
Level 2—UNDERSTAND	
Level 3—APPLY	
Level 4—ANALYZE	
Level 5—EVALUATE	
Level 6—CREATE	

SQ3R MASTERY STUDY SHEET

EXAMPLE QUESTION *(from page 5)*
Discuss two traits employers are seeking from today's employees.

ANSWER:

EXAMPLE QUESTION *(from page 14)*
What are the basic truths about the culture of career colleges?

ANSWER:

AUTHOR QUESTION *(from page 6)*
Identify the Essential Cornerstones for Success.

ANSWER:

AUTHOR QUESTION *(from page 7)*
Why is it important to avoid social media blunders?

ANSWER:

AUTHOR QUESTION *(from page 12)*
What is the M & M theory and how is it used?

ANSWER:

AUTHOR QUESTION *(from page 20)*
What are the characteristics of attainable goals?

ANSWER:

AUTHOR QUESTION *(from page 20)*
Why must a goal be measurable?

ANSWER:

YOUR QUESTION *(from page ___)*

ANSWER:

YOUR QUESTION *(from page ___)*

ANSWER:

YOUR QUESTION *(from page ___)*

ANSWER:

YOUR QUESTION *(from page ___)*

ANSWER:

YOUR QUESTION *(from page ___)*

ANSWER:

Finally, after answering these questions, recite in your mind the major points covered here. Consider the following general questions to help you master this material.

- What was it about?
- What does it mean?
- What was the most important thing you learned? Why?
- What were the key points to remember?

chapter two

PROSPER

MANAGING YOUR MONEY AND DEBTS WISELY

"Don't tell me where your priorities are. Show me where you spend your money, and I will tell you what they are." —James W. Frick

Why
read this chapter?

Because you'll learn:

- How to manage your money and avoid credit card trouble
- How to identify the types of financial aid available to you
- How to protect yourself against identity theft

Because you'll be able to:

- Keep your FICO score healthy
- Construct and use a budget
- Protect your credit cards and other vital information from identity theft

Scan
and QUESTION

Take a few moments, **scan this chapter,** and on page 56, write **five of your own questions** that you think will be important to your mastery of this material. You will also find five questions listed from your authors.

Example:

☑ **What are four types of financial aid?**
(from page 34)

☑ **How does a Pell Grant differ from a loan?**
(from page 35)

MyStudentSuccessLab

MyStudentSuccessLab (www.mystudentsuccesslab.com) is an online solution designed to help you "Start strong, Finish stronger" by building skills for ongoing personal and professional development.

Name: Derwin A. Wallace

Institution: Graduate! DeVry University and The Keller Graduate School of Management

Age: 44

Major: B.S. in Accounting and M.B.A., Finance Concentration

Career: Director of Corporate Investor Relations, National Association of Investor Corps

I was born in a ghetto on the West Side of Chicago. My father was a strict man from the Mississippi Delta, and his way of disciplining his children was to beat them—me included. By the sixth grade, I had a job, paid rent, and bought my own school lunches and clothes. When I was 16, I had saved enough money to buy a boom box. One night I was playing the boom box and because it was plugged into an electrical outlet, using power and increasing electrical costs, my father took the power cord and began to beat me with it. It was at this point that I knew I had to leave . . . and leave I did.

I broke into a friend's garage and wrapped myself in blankets and paper to keep from freezing to death. Later, I hid in his basement and was nearly eaten to death by rats. I began to stop by an old bakery to get their thrown-away donuts to feed the rats so they would leave me alone. That is how I survived. I went on to live in buses and abandoned buildings and cars. I was on the high school tennis team and diving team so I had a key to the school gym. I took my showers in the locker room. I lived like this for two years. After high school graduation, others went out to party and I found myself celebrating in an abandoned car.

After high school, I joined the military for a few years and was asked to leave due to acts of immaturity. After

the military, I began my college studies, but dropped out shortly thereafter because of money and many other life situations. My life was going nowhere. I lived in rented rooms for eight years. One day I decided to move to Atlanta and found myself homeless again. I began work as a telemarketer and found another room to rent. At 28, I found myself with nothing. I had a dead-end job, no education, and was dating a woman who was, unknown to me, an occasional drug user. Something had to change. My life had to change. I looked around at others and wondered why they had a nice life and I did not. Finally, I realized that I had to look at my own life and my actions before I could blame anyone else. I decided my lack of education was holding me back.

I had seen an ad for DeVry University, and I decided to investigate. I had been interested in math and accounting, and DeVry made the registration process so easy for me. They helped me with my degree plan, my financial aid, and most importantly, they encouraged and supported me. I was able to get tutoring and individual attention in the small classes. Some of my instructors worked in the accounting and investment field and shared their real-world experiences. After my first semester, I had a 4.0 and received a Georgia Lottery Scholarship. I made the Dean's List and was a President's Scholar. Because of my accounting and business classes, I began to watch the stock market. As crazy as it seems, I took the extra money from my loans and scholarships and began to invest it in stocks. After six years, I graduated with a B.S. in accounting and a M.B.A concentration in finance. My education assisted me in obtaining careers as a stock broker, financial analyst, investor relations professional, and financial controller. As director of corporate investor relations, my main responsibility is to put companies that trade in the stock market in front of investors in hopes they may purchase those companies' stock.

Education took me from living in a rat-infested basement to flying in corporate jets and working with some of the most wealthy and powerful companies in America. Just as my education gave me limitless opportunities, yours will too. Corporate America is a battlefield and you must get your armor ready. Your education is your preparation for battle—it is your boot camp for the real world.

My final piece of advice is to live below your means. Doing this gives you freedom. If you buy that BMW, the designer clothes, and the mansion on a hill and all of your money goes to pay the bills, you have lost your freedom and flexibility—you're a slave to a paycheck. The major stressor in life is to be tied to a job that you hate and can't leave because without it you will lose all your material possessions. Live below your means.

THINK about it

1. What role has your family played in shaping your experiences and future? How can you use this to your best advantage?

2. Mr. Wallace states that you should live below your means. Do you think this is good advice? Why or why not?

YOUR MONEY. YOUR FUTURE. YOUR LIFE

How Can You Take Control of Your Financial Future?

You may be wondering why a chapter on finance would be included in this text about student success. The answer is quite simple. We have known many students over the years who were academically capable, socially skilled, and managed their time and goals well. However, they were forced to leave their studies because they got into financial trouble. They did not know how to earn money, manage money, save money, or live within their means. This chapter is included to help you do all of these things so that you can get your education.

Most college students have had little to no training in managing finances. Many are ill-prepared to make sound financial decisions, find themselves in trouble, and have to leave school. It is not unusual for college graduates to accumulate significant college loan and credit card debt, as well as car loans and other financial obligations by the time they graduate. We do not want this to happen to you. Learning to manage your finances and debts wisely will certainly be one of the most important lessons you learn—and one that you will need to carry with you throughout your life and career.

One of the first steps in financial literacy is learning the difference between **standard of living** and **quality of life.** According to Sycle and Tietje (2010), your standard of living is determined by tangible things such as your ability to buy a nice car, own a fine home, wear designer clothes, eat in famous restaurants, and go out when you please. This would be considered a high standard of living. Conversely, if you live paycheck to paycheck, you have a low standard of living. However, there are many people who have a low standard of living but have an extremely high quality of life. "There are probably people living off the land in a Central American jungle who are more satisfied and content than some millionaires living in Los Angeles.

Money doesn't necessarily buy you quality of life" (Sycle and Tietje, 2010).

Quality of life is determined by the things that do not cost a great deal of money, such as love, the affection of your children, your leisure activities, and the ability to enjoy quiet times with friends and family. Money *may* improve your quality of life, but there are many rich, unhappy, sad people.

The reason you need to know the difference is because many people think that the more you make, the happier you are. This may be true if you also have the intangible things that improve your quality of life as well. But possessions alone seldom make one happy. You can live well and have a high quality of life on almost any budget if you know how to manage your finances properly. Here you will learn how to manage your money so that you can have the quality of life you want and deserve.

What would make your quality of life better?

PRACTICING DISCIPLINE AT THE RIGHT TIME

Can You Mind Your Own Business?

The time to learn to take care of your business and finances is right now so you can hit the ground running when you graduate. You might already be working in a full-time position with an opportunity to participate in a 401(k) program. Many people neglect to enroll because they don't understand and they don't want to appear ignorant by asking. You may feel that you simply can't afford to enroll and allocate that money to a retirement fund. The truth? You really can't afford not to enroll! Your future depends on it. Even if you are a typical student who is struggling to make ends meet and can't invest right now, this is the time to prepare for what comes ahead. We highly encourage you to make up your mind that you are going to be financially secure and that you are going to master the keys to saving money.

Some important tips for preparing for the future *right now* include:

- Practice ***delayed gratification.*** This is the first key to personal wealth accumulation. Even though it will probably require changing your habits, learn to develop this habit now.

- Take a ***personal finance course*** as soon as possible. You will be able to put the information into practice much sooner if you take the course early in your college career.

- If you plan to operate any kind of business, ***take accounting and tax law courses.*** Even if you plan to run a dance studio or a physical fitness center, this applies to you.

- ***Save your change every day.*** You will be surprised how quickly it adds up. You can put it in savings or invest it. You may even need it to pay the rent one month.

How many credit cards do you currently have? Do you use them wisely?

■ *Write down everything you spend.* Where can you cut costs? In what ways are you wasting money? In Figure 2.10 (p. 57), you will find a worksheet entitled Tracking Your Expenditures and Spending Habits. Use this sheet to track all of your spending for three days; then analyze your habits and develop a change plan. You'll be amazed at where your money goes.

■ *Apply for every type of financial aid* possible to assist with your education. You may not be awarded every type, but every cent helps. The following section will help you with this.

FINANCIAL AID

Is There Such a Thing as Pennies from Heaven?

Nearly two of every three students are going into debt to go to college, owing an average of more than $27,000, most often to the government (NPR Staff, 2011). Chances are good that you have already borrowed money or might need to in the future. Therefore, understanding financial aid, scholarships, loans, and grants is very important as you make decisions that will affect you for a long time. If you have to borrow money to attend school, we think you should; on the other hand, we urge you to be very frugal—even stingy—when it comes to borrowing money. A day of reckoning will come, and for many people, it's like getting hit by a freight train when they realize what this debt means to them. Because they are relatively uninformed about personal finances, many people make bad financial decisions. Many students don't have a clue as to the impact of large student loans and other debts on their future well-being.

The most well-known sources of financial assistance are from federal and state governments. Federal and state financial aid programs have been in place for many years and are a staple of assistance for many college students. Figure 2.1 indicates some sources of aid.

Each year, over $170 billion of financial aid is available. Not every school participates in every federal or state assistance program, so to determine which type of aid is available at your school, you need to contact the financial aid office. *Today!*

One of the biggest mistakes students make when thinking about financial aid is forgetting about scholarships from private industry and social or civic organizations. Each year, millions of dollars are unclaimed because students do not know about these scholarships or where to find the necessary information. Speak with someone in your financial aid office regarding all types of scholarships.

Figure 2.1 Types of Aid

TYPE	DESCRIPTION
Federal and state loans	Money that must be repaid with interest—usually beginning six months after your graduation date
Federal and state grants	Money you do not have to repay—often need-based awards given on a first-come, first-served basis
Scholarships (local, regional, and national)	Money acquired from public and private sources that does not have to be repaid—often merit based
Work study programs	Money earned while working on campus for your institution that does not have to be repaid

Figure 2.2 Eligibility for Federal Financial Aid

To receive aid from the major federal student aid programs, you must:

- Fill out a FAFSA on a yearly basis (Free Application for Federal Student Aid, www.fafsa.ed.gov)
- Have financial need, except for some loan programs
- Hold a high school diploma or GED, pass an independently administered test approved by the U.S. Department of Education, or meet the standards established by your state
- Be enrolled as a regular student working toward a degree or certificate in an eligible program; you may not receive aid for correspondence or telecommunications courses unless they are a part of an associate, bachelor, or graduate degree program
- Be a U.S. citizen
- Have a valid Social Security number
- Make satisfactory academic progress
- Sign a statement of educational purpose
- Sign a statement of updated information
- Register with the Selective Service, if required
- Not have a previous drug conviction, for some federal financial aid

Source: Adapted from *The Student Guide: Financial Aid from the U.S. Department of Education.* U.S. Dept. of Education, Washington, DC, 2010–2011.

Federal Financial Aid Types and Eligibility

PELL GRANT. This is a need-based grant awarded by the U.S. government to qualified undergraduate students who have not been awarded a previous degree. Amounts vary based on need and costs and your status as a full- or part-time student. For the 2011 school year, the full award amount was $5,550. This figure changes yearly and also may change due to congressional mandates and spending.

FEDERAL SUPPLEMENTAL EDUCATIONAL OPPORTUNITY GRANT (FSEOG). This is a need-based grant awarded to institutions to allocate to students through their financial aid offices. The amount varies between $100 and $4,000 per year, with an average award of about $750.

ACADEMIC COMPETITIVENESS GRANT (ACG). The ACG became available in 2006 for first-year college students who graduated high school after January 1, 2006, and second-year students who graduated after January 1, 2005. Students must be eligible for the Pell Grant to be considered for the ACG. Grants are awarded to first-year students who completed a rigorous high school degree (as established by state and local educational agencies) and to second-year students who maintain a 3.0 GPA.

NATIONAL SMART GRANT. The National SMART Grant (or National Science and Mathematics Access to Retain Talent Grant) is awarded to full-time students during the third and fourth years of undergraduate study. Students must also be eligible for the Pell Grant to receive a SMART Grant and must be majoring in physical, life, or computer sciences; technology; an international language deemed

Bob Daemmrich/PhotoEdit

Have you allotted enough time in your schedule to fill out your financial aid application completely and accurately?

necessary to national security; mathematics; or engineering. Students must maintain a 3.0 GPA in coursework required for the major.

STAFFORD LOAN.   Formerly known as the Guaranteed Student Loan, the Stafford Direct Loan Program is a low-interest subsidized loan. You must show need to qualify. The government pays the interest while you are in school, but you must be registered for at least half-time status. You begin repayments six months after you leave school.

UNSUBSIDIZED STAFFORD LOAN.   This Stafford Loan is a low-interest, *non-subsidized* loan. You *do not* have to show need to qualify. You are responsible for the interest on the loan while you are enrolled. Even though the government does not pay the interest, you can defer the interest and repayments until six months after you have left school.

FEDERAL PLUS LOAN.   This is a federally funded but state-administered, low-interest loan to qualified parents of students in college. The student must be enrolled at least half-time. Parents must pass a credit check and be U.S. citizens. Repayments begin 60 days after the last loan payment.

WORK STUDY.   Work study is a federally funded, need-based program that pays students an hourly wage for working on (and sometimes off) campus. Students earn at least minimum wage.

HOPE SCHOLARSHIP TAX CREDIT (HSTC).   According to FinAid.org, the HSTC provides a federal income tax credit based on the first $4,000 in postsecondary education expenses paid by the taxpayer during the tax year. The amount of the credit is 100 percent of the first $2,000 in qualified expenses and 25 percent of the second $2,000. You can apply for the HSTC for four years. The HSTC is subject to congressional changes.

PERKINS LOAN.   This is a need-based loan where the amount of money you can borrow is determined by the government and the availability of funds. The interest rate is 5 percent and repayment begins nine months after you leave school or drop below half-time status. You can take up to 10 years to repay the loan.

Tips for Applying for Financial Aid

- You *must* complete a FAFSA (Free Application for Federal Student Aid) to be eligible to receive *any* federal or state assistance. ***You AND your parents*** must apply for and obtain a PIN number to complete the FAFSA ***if you are considered a dependent***. Because much federal and state money is awarded on a first-come, first-served basis, it is advisable to complete your application as soon after January 1 as possible—even if you have to use the previous year's tax returns and update your application later. Your college's financial aid office can assist you with this process. You can also log onto www.fafsa.ed.gov to learn more.

- Do not miss a deadline. There are no exceptions for making up a missed deadline for federal financial aid!

- *Read all instructions* before beginning the process, always fill out the application completely, and have someone proofread your work.

- If documentation is required, submit it according to the instructions. Do not fail to do all that the application asks you to do.

- Never lie about your financial status.

- Begin the application process as soon as possible. Do not wait until the last moment. Some aid is given on a first-come, first-served basis. Income tax preparation time is usually financial aid application time.

- Talk to the financial aid officer at the institution you will attend. Person-to-person contact is always best. Never assume anything until you get it in writing.

- Take copies of fliers and brochures that are available from the financial aid office. Private companies and civic groups will often notify the financial aid office if they have funds available.

- Always apply for admission as well as financial aid. Many awards are given by the college to students who are already accepted.

- If you are running late with an application, find out if there are electronic means of filing.

- Always keep copies of your tax returns for each year!

- Apply for everything possible. You will get nothing if you do not apply.

Figure 2.3 Online Financial Aid Tip Guide

Consider the following online sources for learning more about and applying for different types of financial aid:

FAFSA (Free Application for Federal Student Aid)
The "must go to place" for beginning your financial aid process. You (and your parents, if you are a dependent) must complete the FAFSA to receive any federal aid.
www.fafsa.ed.gov

Federal Student Aid Portal
The U.S. government source for higher-education funding.
http://studentaid.ed.gov/PORTALSWebApp/students/english/index.jsp

FinAid! The SmartStudent Guide to Financial Aid
Great website for financial aid tools, advice, support, military aid, calculators, and various guidelines.
www.finaid.org

FastWeb
A site dedicated to helping you find scholarships. You fill out a profile and the website notifies you when a scholarship that matches your interests becomes available.
www.fastweb.com

PAY FOR COLLEGE
This site offers assistance in finding different types of aid, college costs, loans, and financing.
www.collegeboard.com/student/pay

ED.GOV (The U.S. Department of Education)
A website dedicated to helping you find various types of aid and understand payment options and guidelines.
www2.ed.gov/finaid/landing.jhtml?src=ln

FINANCIAL AID INFO
A website clearinghouse that guides you to many different financial aid websites.
www.financialaidinfo.org/useful-student-aid-websites.aspx

STUDENT LOANS

A Day of Reckoning Will Come. Will You Be Ready?

The high cost of college makes tuition out of reach for many families. For many students, the only way they can attend college is with student loans. If this is the only way you can go to college, borrow the money—but borrow no more than you absolutely must. Try not to borrow anything but tuition and perhaps enough for books and supplies. Get a job, budget, cut out extras, work in the summers, attend college via a cooperative program, enroll in online courses, live at home or find a roommate—do everything possible not to borrow more money than you must.

Many students are finding it necessary to extend their student loans over a period of 30 years just to keep their heads above water; of course, if one does that, the interest paid is also higher. For example, a student who takes 30 years to pay off a $20,000 loan at 6.8 percent will pay about $27,000 in interest plus the principal compared to $7,619 on a loan paid off in 10 years (Block, 2006). You will have to repay the money that you have borrowed. Period! *Not even bankruptcy will relieve you of this debt* because student loans are not subject to bankruptcy laws; so again, don't borrow any money you don't absolutely need. Consider the examples in Figure 2.4.

Because of the *College Cost Reduction and Access Act of 2007,* your federal student loan may be forgiven after 10 years of full-time employment in *public service,* such as the military, law enforcement, public health, public education, or social work, to name a few. However, you must have made 120 payments as a part of the Direct Loan Program. Only payments made after October 1, 2007, count toward the required 120 monthly payments. To learn more about this program, visit www.finaid.org/loans/publicservice.phtml.

Figure 2.4 Total Interest Paid

AMOUNT OF MONEY BORROWED	AVERAGE INTEREST RATE	TOTAL YEARS TO REPAY (20 YEARS IS THE AVERAGE)	MONTHLY PAYMENT	TOTAL INTEREST PAID (YOUR COST TO BORROW THE MONEY)
$ 5,000	7%	10	$ 58.05	$ 1,966.00
		20	$ 38.76	$ 4,302.40
		30	$ 33.27	$ 6,977.20
$10,000	7%	10	$116.11	$ 3,933.20
		20	$ 77.53	$ 8,607.20
		30	$ 66.53	$13,950.80
$15,000	7%	10	$174.16	$ 5,899.20
		20	$116.29	$12,909.60
		30	$ 99.80	$20,928.00
$20,000	7%	10	$232.22	$ 7,866.40
		20	$155.06	$17,214.40
		30	$133.06	$27,901.60
$30,000	7%	10	$348.33	$11,799.60
		20	$232.59	$25,821.60
		30	$199.59	$41,852.40

YOUR CREDIT HISTORY

Do You Know the Score?

Many students don't even know they have a credit score, yet this score is the single most important factor that will determine if you get approved for a mortgage, car loan, credit card, insurance, and so on. Furthermore, if you get approved, this credit score will determine what rate of interest you have to pay (Broderick, 2003). You can order one free credit score online a year by accessing the website www.annualcreditreport.com.

Range of Scores and What FICO Means for You

This information may seem trivial right now, and you might not want to be bothered with more information. But the truth is, you must pay attention to this because your credit score has long-lasting implications for almost everything you want to do. The sooner you understand the importance of this score and take steps to keep it healthy, the better off you will be.

Your credit score is referred to as a FICO score. FICO is the acronym for *Fair Issac Corporation,* the company that created the widely used credit score model. This score is calculated using information from your credit history and files. The FICO score is the reason it matters if you accumulate large debts, if you go over your credit card limits, if you are late with payments—these offenses stick with you and are not easily changed. Based on this score, you can be denied credit, pay a lower or higher interest rate, be required to provide extensive asset information in order to even get credit, or sail right through when you seek a loan.

> "Just about every financial move you make for the rest of your life will be somehow linked to your FICO score."
> —Suze Orman, Financial Planning Expert

FICO scores range from 300 to 850. A good score is considered 720 or above. The lower your FICO score, the higher interest rate you will have to pay because you will be considered a poor risk. So what's the big deal about a few points? Study Figure 2.5, and you will see how important your FICO score is when you start to finance a house or seek credit for other reasons.

Here are some tips for keeping your credit score healthy, suggested by Trudeau (2007):

- Obtain a copy of your credit report and correct any inaccuracies. Clean up any errors in your personal information: incorrect addresses, Social Security number, and employer information. Below, you will find the three major credit reporting agencies and their contact information:

  - Equifax: www.equifax.com, 1-800-685-1111
  - Experian: www.experian.com, 1-888-397-3742
  - TransUnion: www.transunion.com, 1-800-888-4213

- Review any negative credit information and correct errors. The credit reporting agencies have 30 days to investigate and respond to your inquiry. If they cannot verify a negative item within 30 days, they must remove it from your report.

- Keep all your credit card balances under 35 percent of the total credit limit available. For example, if you have a $500 limit, you should never have a balance larger than $175. To go over will lower your FICO score and might cause the credit card company to raise your rate.

- Call your creditors and ask them to lower your interest rates! This can dramatically, and immediately, lower your payments and reduce your overall debt.

- Call and ask your creditors to remove any overdraft or late fees. If you are a good customer, they will usually do this—but they won't do it unless you ask.

Figure 2.5 The Impact of FICO on Buying a Home

FICO SCORE	INTEREST RATE	PAYMENT	30 YEARS OF INTEREST
500	9.3%	$1651	$394,362
560	8.5%	$1542	$355,200
620	7.3%	$1373	$294,247
675	6.1%	$1220	$239,250
700	5.6%	$1151	$214,518
720	5.5%	$1136	$208,853

Using the table above, analyze the data. What is the difference in interest paid for someone who has a 620 FICO score and someone who has a 700 score?

What is the payment difference for someone with a 500 FICO score and a 675 score?

BLOOM LEVEL 4

- Do not open up several credit cards at once. Multiple inquiries bring your credit score down.
- Don't close credit cards if they are in good standing. The best thing for your credit score are old accounts with good credit history. Just lock them up and don't use them!
- Set up automated payments to make sure you pay your bills on time. One late payment has an extremely negative impact on your score.
- Be careful about transferring balances. If you do this too often, it will lower your FICO score.

> *"Your credit past is your credit future."*
> —Steve Konowalow

B IS FOR BUDGETING

Where Does My Money Go?

Most people have no idea where their money goes. Many just spend and spend and then borrow on credit cards to pay for additional expenses for which they have not budgeted. Knowing how much money you have and exactly how you spend it is a very important step toward financial security. Many college students pay more attention to buying than they do to budgeting, watching their credit score, or controlling their credit card debt. If you fit that mold, this is one area where change is needed.

One of the main reasons to budget is to determine the exact amount of money you need to borrow to finance your college education. Poor planning while in college can easily result in a lower standard of life after you graduate and begin paying back enormous loans. Deciding how much to borrow will affect your life long after you have completed your degree. You should also remember that you will be required to repay your student loans even if you do not graduate. As previously mentioned, even bankruptcy won't eliminate student loans.

When budgeting, you must first determine how much income you earn monthly. Complete the following chart:

Source of Income	Estimated Amount
Work	$ _____
Spouse/Partner/Parental income	$ _____
Scholarships/Loans	$ _____
Savings/Investments	$ _____
Alimony/Child support	$ _____
Other	$ _____
TOTAL INCOME	$ _____

Next, you must determine how much money you spend in a month. Complete the following chart:

Source of Expenditure	Estimated Amount
Housing	$ _____
Utilities	$ _____
Phone (home and cell)	$ _____
Internet access	$ _____
Car payment	$ _____
Car insurance	$ _____
Fuel	$ _____
Other transportation	$ _____
Clothing	$ _____
Food	$ _____
Household items	$ _____
Personal hygiene items	$ _____
Health care/insurance	$ _____
Entertainment	$ _____
Pet care	$ _____
Savings	$ _____
Other	$ _____
TOTAL EXPENDITURES	$ _____
Total Income – Total Expenditures =	$ _____

If the amount of your total expenditures is smaller than your monthly income, you are on your way to controlling your finances. If your total expenditures figure is larger than your monthly income, you are heading for a financial crisis. Furthermore, you are establishing bad habits for money management that may carry over into your life after college.

Now, consider your education and the costs associated with everything from books to supplies to child care. Using the Economic Readiness Assessment in Figure 2.6, determine how much your education (tuition, books, room, board, etc.) will cost you next semester. You will have to go to the bookstore (or online) to research the cost of your texts, and you may need to refer to your college catalog for rules regarding some of the other questions. You can also use the Internet to answer a few of the questions, but it is important that you answer them all.

Figure 2.6 Economic Readiness Assessment

Please read each question below carefully, respond with Yes or No, and then answer the question based on your financial research for **next term.** Be specific. You may have to visit the financial aid office, bookstore, or other campus resource center to answer the questions.

QUESTION	ANSWER	RESPONSE
I know exactly how much my tuition will cost next term.	YES NO	Answer: $ _____
I know the additional cost of lab fees, technology fees, and other fees associated with my courses (if any).	YES NO	Answer: $ _____
I know how much my textbooks will cost next semester.	YES NO	Answer: $ _____
I know how much my transportation will cost next semester (car payment, gas, insurance, bus passes, etc.).	YES NO	Answer: $ _____
I know how much I need to spend on supplies for next semester.	YES NO	Answer: $ _____
I know how much child care will cost next semester.	YES NO	Answer: $ _____
I know where my GPA must remain to keep my financial aid.	YES NO	Answer: _____
I know how much money I can borrow through financial aid in one academic year.	YES NO	Answer: $ _____
I know how much money I need to manage my personal budget in a single term.	YES NO	Answer: $ _____
I have estimated miscellaneous and unexpected costs that might occur during the semester.	YES NO	Answer: $ _____
I know what a FAFSA is and how and when to apply.	YES NO	Answer: _____
I know how a drug arrest could affect my financial aid.	YES NO	Answer: _____
I know the scholarships available to me and how, when, and where to apply for them.	YES NO	Answer: _____
I know how and where to apply for work study.	YES NO	Answer: _____
I know how a felony charge could affect my ability to get a job after graduation.	YES NO	Answer: _____

BLOOM LEVEL 4

BLOOM LEVEL 6

After completing your budget list, evaluating ways to cut spending, and taking a careful look at your college expenses, outline what you need to do to cut or control your expenses. Then develop a budget plan that includes your living expenses, unexpected items, college costs, and a moderate savings plan. You will probably need to also consider your spending habits chart in Figure 2.10 to make more rational and informed decisions.

Figure 2.7   Balancing Your Checkbook: A Quick Guide

Notice Check 286 and how it was recorded in the check register. You might also consider downloading your bank's check register app or use Excel to electronically balance your checkbook. Whatever method you use, work hard to keep your balances up to date to avoid overdraft charges, which are sometimes over $30 per check.

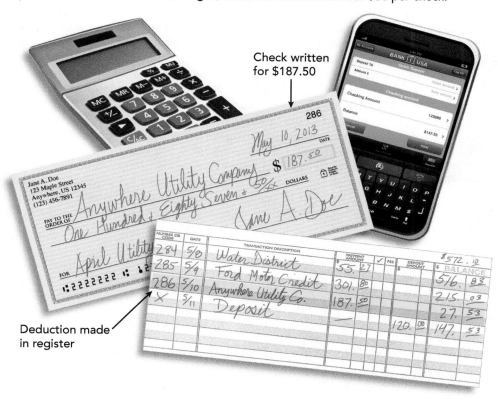

Check written for $187.50

Deduction made in register

CREDIT CARDS: LIVING ON BORROWED MONEY

Are Credit Cards Really the Worst Kind of Debt?

Credit card debt—one of the worst kinds of debt—is rising rapidly among college students as they struggle to pay tuition, buy books, and cover day-to-day living expenses. According to a Nellie Mae study (2010), 76 percent of all undergraduate college students have at least one credit card and carry an average balance of almost $2,500. As a result of over-the-top credit card marketing, terrible credit card terms and conditions, and an economy that no longer provides as many well-paying jobs with good benefits as it once did, graduates are facing overwhelming odds to achieve financial health, in large part as a result of the credit card debt from their undergraduate years (Williams, 2008).

Studies show that credit card shoppers, in general, are less price sensitive and more extravagant. When you pay with plastic, you lose track of how

> "If you can eat it, wear it, or drink it, it is not an emergency."
> —Kim Rebel, Credit Counselor

much you are spending. According to the article "Life Without Plastic" (Rosato, 2008), after McDonald's started accepting credit and debit cards in 2004, diners who paid with plastic spent $7.00 a visit on average, compared to $4.50 when they paid in cash. The article also suggests that you are less aware of what you spend if you use plastic. For example, 68 percent of students who paid cash for their books knew how much they spent. Conversely, only 35 percent of students using plastic knew what they spent. Rosato also reports that you are willing to pay more for the same stuff if you are using plastic instead of real money.

"Imagine being 30 years old and still paying off a slice of pizza you bought when you were 18 and in college. Sounds crazy, but for plenty of people, problems with credit card debt can lead to that very situation" (Collegeboard, 2008). If you borrow excessively and only pay the minimum each month, it will be very easy to find yourself over your head with credit card problems. Take the case of Joe: "Joe's average unpaid credit card bill over a year is $500, and his finance charge is 20 percent. He pays a $20 annual fee plus a $25 late fee (he was up late studying and forgot to mail in his check). Joe ends up owing $145 to his credit card company, and he still hasn't paid for any of his purchases" (Collegeboard, 2008).

Can you imagine paying for a piece of pizza for 12 years?

iStockPhoto

Most credit card companies charge a very high rate of interest—18 to 21 percent or higher. If you are late with a payment, the interest rate can go even higher. For every $1,000 you charge, you will pay from $180 to $210 each year, states Konowalow (2003). Don't be fooled by the ploy of "1.5 percent interest." This means 1.5 percent each month, which equates to 18 percent per year. The best practice is to charge no more than you can pay off each month while avoiding high interest rates. Consider the tips in Figure 2.8.

THE PITFALLS OF PAYDAY LOANS, CAR TITLE LOANS, AND RENT-TO-OWN CONTRACTS

Did You Know There's Someone Lurking on Every Corner to Take Your Money?

Many unsuspecting consumers have been duped into signing car title loans, payday loans, and rent-to-own contracts that resulted in very high monthly payments and penalties. Some were told by their title loan broker before they signed the contract that they could make a partial payment if they needed to and this would be OK. Unfortunately, the unsuspecting victims find out too late that their car is going to be repossessed due to one late or partial payment. Others realize too late that on a loan of $400, they must pay back over $500 that month. According to some reports, payday and title loan lenders have been charging as much as 250 to 350 percent interest on an annual basis. In some instances, interest rates as high as 900 percent have been charged due to poor government regulatory policies. Some states have recently enacted laws to prevent this.

Payday loans are extremely expensive compared to other cash loans. For example, a $300 cash advance on the average credit card, repaid in one month, would cost a finance charge of $13.99 and an annual interest rate of almost 57 percent, which is very high. By comparison, however, a payday loan costing $17.50 per $100 for the same $300 would cost $105 if renewed one time, or 426 percent annual interest (Payday Loan Consumer Information, 2008). As bad as credit card debt is, it pales in comparison to the pitfalls of payday loans.

Figure 2.8 **Important Facts You Need to Know about Credit Cards**

What you don't know can wreck your credit rating and ruin your life. Listed below are some of the most important things you can learn about managing credit card debt. Some of them will make you angry; others don't seem legal, but they happen all the time.

✓ Understand that credit cards are nothing more than high-interest loans—in some cases, very high! The system is designed to keep you in debt.

✓ Be aware that companies often add on new fees and change policies after customers already have signed up.

✓ If you fall behind on payments to one creditor or if your credit score drops for any reason, your rates can be raised on all your credit cards.

✓ Banks can and will abruptly switch your due date, so pay attention. Always check your bill to see if any fees or charges have been added.

✓ Avoid cards that charge an annual fee just for the privilege of carrying the card. This fee can be as high as $100 to $400 per year. If this fee is charged, it will be automatically added to your card and then you begin paying interest on the fee.

✓ Be sure your card allows for a grace period before interest is charged.

✓ Carry only one or two credit cards so you can manage your debt and not get in over your head. Do not accept or sign up for cards that you don't need.

✓ When you accept a card, sign it right away. Keep records of your credit card numbers (in a secure location) and the phone numbers to contact in case they are lost or stolen. If you lose your card, report it immediately to avoid charges.

✓ Avoid the temptation to charge. You should use credit cards only when you absolutely must and only when you can pay the full amount before interest is added. "Buy now, pay later" is a dangerous game.

✓ When you pay off a card, celebrate and don't use that as a reason to charge again. Lock that card in a safe place and leave it there.

✓ Each month, always try to pay more than the minimum payment due.

✓ Send the payment at least five days in advance. Late fees now represent the third-largest revenue stream for banks.

✓ Call the credit card company and negotiate a better rate. If they won't give you a better rate, tell them you are going to transfer the debt.

✓ If you have several credit card debts, consolidate all the amounts onto the card on which you have the lowest balance. Don't cancel your cards, because it helps your credit score if you have cards on which you have no debt. Just don't use them again!

✓ Do not leave any personal information (credit cards, Social Security numbers, checking accounts) in places where roommates or other students have access to them. Purchase a metal file box with a lock and keep it in a secure place.

✓ Consider using a debit card. Money is deducted directly from your bank account, and you cannot spend more than you actually have.

✓ If you have already gotten into credit card trouble, get **reputable** counseling. One of the best agencies is the National Foundation for Credit Counseling (NFCC).

✓ Be aware that using a credit card carelessly is similar to a drug addiction. Credit card use is habit forming and addictive!

✓ Ask yourself these questions: "If I can't pay this credit card in full this month, what is going to change next month? Will I have extra income or will I reduce my spending enough to pay for this purchase?" If the answers are "No," you don't need to make the purchase.

✓ Realize that you are building your future credit rating even though you are a student.

Once you get a credit card, immediately write "CHECK ID" across the back in RED, permananet ink.

Successful Decisions

AN ACTIVITY FOR CRITICAL REFLECTION

Jonathon enjoys school. He has made new friends, has a great relationship with his instructors, and is managing to keep his grades up. But he already has a major problem—keeping up with his expenses. He is spending a lot more money than he has coming in. He works 25 hours per week at a part-time job, but it would be difficult to work more because of his schedule at school, his family commitments, and the amount of time he needs to study for his math class.

To compound this problem, he has met a great girl, and he has tried hard to impress her by taking her to expensive clubs and dinners. Their first date cost him a bundle. He didn't have the funds so he charged everything on his new credit card. Jonathon is getting very stressed about his money situation. He's having trouble sleeping well. To top it off, his new girlfriend is talking about taking a vacation together. He knows that he will have to pay the majority of the bills on the trip. He is worried because he has already maxed out one credit card and has heavy charges on the other one. Jonathon has learned that if he charges $1,000 on his card and only makes the minimum payments, it will take 15 and a half years to pay it off. He doesn't want to disappoint his girlfriend and fears losing her if he doesn't go on the vacation. But clearly, he has to make some changes.

What are two things you would advise Jonathon to do right away?

1. _____

_____

2. _____

_____

List two other suggestions that you would make to Jonathon to help him get control of his expenses.

1. _____

_____

2. _____

_____

SMALL COSTS ADD UP!

How Much Money Will You Throw Down the Drain in Ten Years?

Many people pay more money for convenience. If you are on a tight budget, you might want to give up some conveniences so you can save more of your money. Although we want you to really live and enjoy life, we also want you to take a hard look at where your money goes. Those dimes, quarters, and dollars add up quickly. In fact, spending small amounts of money can add up to $175,000 over a ten-year period for the typical person. What if you could save some of that money and invest it? What would that money be worth to you when you are 65 and want to retire? Is having sausage biscuits and orange juice from a fast-food restaurant really worth $3.50 a day—or $1274 if you have one *every day for one year?* Did you ever stop to think if you spend $3.50 every day on fast food or coffee for ten years that you would be spending $12,740?

The Ten-Year Plan

According to the website The Digerati Life (2008), some other prime causes of money drain are:

- **Gum:** A pack a day will cost you $5,488 in ten years.

- **Bottled water:** One bottle a day will cost you almost $5,500 in ten years (most bottled water comes from no special source and is no better than tap water).

- **Eating lunch out daily:** If you only spend $9, this will cost you over $35,000 in ten years.

- **Junk food/Vending machine snacks:** This will cost you at least $4,000 in ten years if you are a light snacker, and they are empty calories.

- **Unused memberships:** Those gym memberships that look so enticing and, for many people, go unused will total over $7,500 in ten years.

- **Expensive salon visits:** Fake nails alone along with the salon visit can cost over $30,000 in ten years.

- **Cigarettes:** Not only will this terrible habit kill you and make people want to avoid you, but it will cost you over $25,000 in ten years if you smoke a pack a day.

These are just a few of the drains that take our money and keep us from being wealthy when we are older. Maybe you want to splurge at times and go for the convenience, but day in and day out, you can really save a lot of money if you budget your time and do some of these things for yourself.

Examine the information about the ***Latte Factor*** in Figure 2.9 and apply it to your own spending habits.

PROTECT YOURSELF FROM IDENTITY THEFT

Why Might Your Institution Be Ground Zero?

"Amid all the back-to-school activities and tasks that students face, one of the most important is to protect their identities. You have such busy schedules that you may unknowingly expose yourself to identity theft and fraud, particularly when you're making online purchases or engaging in social-networking web sites. We're all living in an extremely open environment where free flow of information is the norm, as opposed to the exception," said Adam Levin, co-founder of Identity Theft 911 (Yip, 2008). Because students tend to move often, their mail service may be interrupted if they don't follow through with change-of-address cards. By the time their information catches up to them, they may have already suffered from identity theft. "All these things make this group vulnerable," said Thomas Harkins, chief strategy officer of Secure Identity Systems (Yip, 2008).

People who may steal your identity are roommates, relatives, friends, estranged spouses, restaurant servers, and others who have ready access to information about you. They may steal your wallet, go through your trash, or take your mail. They can even legally photocopy your vital information at the courthouse if, for example, you have been divorced. The Internet provides thieves many other opportunities to use official-looking e-mail messages designed to obtain your personal information. Do not provide personal information over the Internet no matter how official the website might look. Reputable businesses will not inquire about your personal information in this manner.

It is very difficult, if not impossible, to catch identity thieves. While you may not be liable, you still have to spend your time filing expensive legal affidavits, writing letters, and making telephone calls to clear your good name.

DID YOU *Know?*

Can you imagine being worth over *$62 billion* and still living in the same home that you bought in 1958 for $31,500? Well, **WARREN BUFFETT,** one of the world's wealthiest people, does just that in Omaha.

Born in 1930, Mr. Buffett, a native Nebraskan, is not only one of the world's wealthiest people, most savvy investors, successful businessmen, and financial intellectuals, but also one of the most philanthropic. He recently announced that he was leaving 83 percent of his wealth to the Bill and Melinda Gates Foundation.

Having always been "financially smart," he filed his first income tax return at the age of 13 so that he could deduct the cost of his bicycle as a business expense. At age 15, he and his friend spent $25 to purchase a pinball machine, which they placed in a barber shop. A few months later, they owned three machines in different locations.

He applied to Harvard in 1950 but was denied entrance. He attended and graduated from Columbia University and began working as a stock broker. His first real business venture, the purchase of a Texaco gas station, did not work out very well. He decided to enroll in a public speaking course and began teaching an investment class at the University of Nebraska.

He later became a major shareholder in the firm Berkshire Hathaway, which purchased major shares in The Washington Post Company, ABC, Geico, Dairy Queen, and Coca-Cola. The most he has ever taken as an actual salary from all of his ventures and investments is $100,000 per year. It was reported in 2006 that Mr. Buffett does not carry a cell phone, does not have a computer at his desk, and drives his own car.

Upon his death, his children will not inherit much of his wealth. He has been quoted as saying, "I want to give my kids just enough so that they would feel that they could do anything, but not so much that they would feel like doing nothing." (Forbes, 2009; Kennon, n.d.; Wikipedia, n.d.).

PHOTO: Ron Sachs/CNP Photolink/Newscom

Figure 2.9 **The Latte Factor**

In his book *The Finish Rich Notebook* (2003), Bach states, "How much you earn has no bearing on whether or not you will build wealth." As a rule, the more we make, the more we spend. Many people spend far more than they make and subject themselves to stress, exorbitant debt, fear, and an ultimate future of poverty.

Bach uses the Latte Factor to call people's attention to how much money we carelessly throw away when we should be saving and investing for the future. He uses the story of a young woman who said she could not invest because she had no money. Yet, almost every day she bought a large latte for $3.50 and a muffin for $1.50. If you add a candy bar here, a drink there, a shake at the gym, you could easily be spending $10 a day that could be invested.

If you take that $10 per day and invest it faithfully until retirement, you would have enough money to pay cash for a home, a new car, and have money left over. This is the power of compound interest! If you are a relatively young person, you will probably work that many years and more, so you could retire with an extra $1 million in addition to any other savings you might have accumulated.

The point is that most of us have the ability to become rich, but we either lack the knowledge or the discipline to do so. Remember the Latte Factor as you begin your college career and practice it, along with other sound financial strategies, if you want to become a millionaire.

Calculate your own Latte Factor. For example, if you buy one diet soda each morning at $1.81, then your Latte Factor is $658.84 per year ($1.81 × 7 days/week × 52 weeks/year).

My daily "have to have it" is _____.

It costs $ _____ per day.

My Latte Factor is $ _____.

How to Minimize Identity Theft Risk

Criminals are very clever, and many are adept at using electronic means to steal your information. According to a variety of financial sources, there are a number of ways to avoid having your identity stolen:

- Carry only the ID and cards you need at any given time.
- Do not make Internet purchases from sites that are unsecured (check for a padlock icon to ensure safety).
- Do not write your PIN, Social Security number, or password on any information that can be stolen or that you are discarding. Do not keep this information in your wallet or exposed in your living space.
- Try to memorize your passwords instead of recording them on paper or in the computer.
- Buy a shredder and use it.
- Avoid providing your Social Security number to any organization until you have verified its legitimacy.
  - Check your credit file periodically by requesting a copy of your report.
  - Do not complete credit card applications at displays set up on campus. This exposes your personal information to people you don't know.

How careful are you when it comes to protecting your financial and medical records?

iStockPhoto

BRING the *Change*

TIPS FOR PERSONAL SUCCESS

Consider the following suggestions for improving your financial status during the semester:

- Practice delayed gratification.
- Reduce your Latte Factor.
- Talk to an advisor about taking a personal finance course next semester as an elective.

Now it is your turn. What three things could you implement to change your financial management practices?

1. _____

2. _____

3. _____

- Use your home address as your permanent mailing address rather than a temporary address while in school.

- Do not provide personal information on a social network that can be used by an identity thief. You don't know these people!

- Carry your wallet in your front pocket instead of your back pocket.

- Place a security freeze on your credit score. This prevents anyone from looking at your credit report except for companies that already have a financial relationship with you. Lenders who can't pull your credit report are unlikely to grant new credit to someone else in your name.

- Opt out of pre-approved credit offers, which are easy for identity thieves to steal. This stops credit bureaus from selling your name to lenders. Go to the opt-out website at www.optoutprescreen.com or call 888-567-8688.

- Don't use obvious passwords like your birthday, your mother's maiden name, or the last four digits of your Social Security number (Consumer Response Center, 2003; *Consumer Reports,* 2008; *The State,* 2008).

BATTLING THE BIG "IFs"

Do You Know What to Do When You Need Something?

The following list provides helpful tips for managing some important financial decisions in your life and protecting yourself when things get tough.

IF YOU NEED TO PURCHASE A CAR

- Do not purchase a new car. We know it is tempting, but the value will plummet 20 to 40 percent the moment you drive off the lot. It is just not worth it! Purchase a two- to three-year-old car from a reputable dealer.

- Don't fall in love with a car before you know everything about it. Love is blind when it comes to people . . . and cars, too!

from ORDINARY to *Extraordinary*

Leo G. Borges
Founder and Former CEO, Borges and Mahoney,
San Francisco, California

TULARE, CALIFORNIA, is still a farming community today, but in 1928 when I was born, it was totally agricultural and an exceptionally rural, detached part of the world. My parents had immigrated to California from the Azore Islands years earlier in search of a better life—the American dream. My father died when I was three years old and when I was 11, my mother passed away. Even though I was raised by my sisters, aloneness and isolation were the two primary feelings I had growing up. We were orphans. We were poor. We were farm kids. We were Portuguese—not Americans. Every day, someone reminded us of these realities. One positive thing remained, however. My mother always told us that we could be anything or have anything if we believed in it and worked hard for it.

I left home at 17 to attend a program in advertising in San Francisco. Later that year, I moved to Los Angeles and began working for a major advertising firm. From there I enlisted in the Coast Guard, and when my duty was over, I worked for an oil company and then a major leasing firm. In each position, I worked my way up the ladder, strove to do my very best, and proved that I was capable of doing anything regardless of my background.

When I was in my early forties, my best friend, Cliff, and I decided to start our own business. We were tired of working in "middle management" and knew that we could be successful if we worked hard. After much research and consulting with companies across the country, we determined that we would start a company in the water treatment business.

You may be asking yourself, "What experience did an advertising agency, an oil company, and a leasing firm give me to start a business in water treatment?" The answer is "None." However, Cliff was an excellent accountant and I

> *We were orphans. We were poor.*
> *We were farm kids. We were*
> *Portuguese—not Americans.*

was an excellent salesman. We found a third partner who was one of the leading water treatment experts in the world and we were off. It was not easy and we had to eat beans for many meals, but Borges and Mahoney, Inc., was born.

Our first office was a small storefront in San Francisco. Through the development of superior products, expert advice to clients, and outstanding customer service, we grew and grew, finally moving to our largest location in San Rafael, California. By the time we sold our business some 20 years later, we had 15 full-time employees and annual revenues in the millions of dollars.

To this day, I attribute my success to the fact that I was determined to show everyone—my sisters, cousins, aunts and uncles, former coworkers, friends and foes—that I would never let my past, my heritage, my economic background, or my history hold me back. I knew that I could be a success. Through hard work, determination, and surrounding myself with supportive, brilliant people, I proved that the American dream my parents sought years earlier is truly possible for anyone who works hard, believes in him- or herself, and doesn't give up. It is possible for you, too.

EXTRAORDINARY REFLECTION

Read the following statement and respond in your online journal or class notebook.

Mr. Borges states that through hard work, determination, and surrounding himself with supportive, brilliant people, he and his partner, Cliff, were able to become very successful in business and beyond. Whom can you call on in your life to offer support and advice and provide you with solid, smart advice? What questions do you need to ask them?

- Purchase an extended warranty, but read the terms carefully.

- Always ask for a "Carfax" and a title search, and make the dealer pay for them.

- Check to see if your state has a "Lemon Law" and if so, read it carefully.

- Don't be pressured into a sale by lines such as "This is our last one like this" and "I've got several people interested in this car." Let them have it!

- Make sure the car has passed the smog test if one is required in your state.

IF YOU NEED TO SAVE ON FUEL

- Consider carpooling.

- Make sure your car is in good running condition and that your tires are inflated properly. Get your car tuned up often.

- Drive slower and at a constant speed when possible. Driving 74 mph instead of 55 mph increases fuel consumption by as much as 20 percent.

- Check your car's air filter and fuel filter, and replace them if they are dirty.

- Do not use "jackrabbit" starts. Accelerate easily after red lights and stop signs. "Flooring it" costs money.

- When stuck in traffic, try to drive at a steady pace and not stop and start. Watch how the large trucks do this—they seldom come to a complete stop.

- Plan your trip so that you can make the most number of right turns, thus saving time at lights. Also, combine your errands so that you can make fewer trips.

- Clean out your car. Carrying around just a few extra pounds in the trunk or back-seat costs fuel.

- Stick with the wheels and tires that came with your car. If you are using larger wheels and tires than recommended, this creates more drag and weight on your car and costs you more fuel.

- Use the telephone. Often, many things can be accomplished without personal visits.

IF YOU FEEL THE URGE TO MAKE AN IMPULSE PURCHASE

- Use the 72-hour rule. Wait 72 hours to make any purchase over $50.

- If you still feel the need to purchase the item after 72 hours, consider your budget and how you are going to pay for it.

- Consider waiting until you can pay cash for the item or consider putting the item on layaway. Do not charge it!

- Purchase the item later as a reward to yourself for getting all A's in your classes.

- Think about how purchasing this item will affect your family's budget.

- Make as few trips out shopping as possible to lower your temptation to purchase things you can't afford.

iStockPhoto

Do you work hard to control everyday and impulse spending?

IF YOUR GROCERY BILL IS OUT OF CONTROL

■ Shop with a calculator, and enter each item as you place it into your cart. This will give you a great idea of what you're spending.

■ Create a menu for each day of the week, and shop only for the items on your list. Do not shop when you are in a hurry, tired, or after working all day.

■ Consider purchasing generic brands—often they are the same product with a different label.

■ Clip coupons. They actually work. Go online to your favorite product's website, and print off their online coupons. Try to shop where stores double or triple the coupon's value.

■ Consider cooking in bulk and then freezing leftovers for later in the week.

■ Look for placement of the product in the store. Items at chest level are the most expensive. Look up and down on the shelves to find less expensive items.

■ Do not shop for convenience items, such as pre-made meals, bakery items, or boneless chicken breasts. Purchase an entire chicken and cut it up. You'll save a lot of money this way.

■ Buy in bulk at one of the major warehouse stores. Often this can save a lot of money if you are buying for a large family.

IF YOUR CHILD WANTS SOMETHING THAT OTHER CHILDREN HAVE

■ Use Freecycle (www.freecycle.org). This is an non-profit organization made up of over 4600 groups with nearly 6 million members who give things away in many towns.

■ Consider giving your child a small allowance and having him or her save for this item.

■ Make the purchase a reward when your child passes a test or does something productive.

■ Try to shop "out of season" when things are cheaper—for example, buy coats in the summer.

■ Keep an eye out for bargains all year long, such as school supplies—don't wait until school is about to start and things are more expensive.

■ Consider shopping at thrift stores or yard sales. Often, items can be purchased at a fraction of the original price and are in great condition.

■ Trade with other parents. Perhaps they have an item that their child has outgrown and is still in great shape.

■ Ask others to purchase certain items for your child's birthday or other holidays. Directed gift giving is a great way to save money.

IF YOUR CREDIT CARDS ARE LOST OR STOLEN

■ Contact your local police immediately.

■ Notify your creditors immediately and request that your accounts be closed.

■ Ask the card company to furnish copies of documents that show any fraudulent transactions.

■ Refuse to pay any bill or portion of any bill that is a result of identity theft.

■ Report the theft or fraud to credit reporting agencies.

CHANGING IDEAS *to Reality*

REFLECTIONS ON FINANCIAL RESPONSIBILITY

Although many young people fail in the management of their personal finances, there is no reason that you cannot manage your financial business well. You should think about personal finance and the management of money and investments as basic survival skills that are very important to you now, as well as for the rest of your life.

Since only 10 percent of high school students graduate from high school with any kind of instruction in personal finance, learning to budget your money, make wise investments, and avoid credit card debt are priority needs of all students. As you move toward establishing yourself in a career, it is important to remember that to get what you want out of life, a significant part of your success will depend on your ability to make sound money decisions. We hope you will learn to make money work for you instead of your having to work hard for money because of poor decisions made early in life. En route to becoming a good money manager, the following tips will assist you:

- Don't get caught in the credit card trap.
- Know exactly how you are spending your money.
- Protect your credit rating by using wise money management strategies.

- Learn all you can about scholarships and grants.
- Understand the regulations about repaying student loans.
- Don't borrow any more money than you absolutely have to.
- Ask for your credit score at least once a year, and be sure you have a good one.
- Use only one or two credit cards.
- Try to pay off your credit card each month before any interest is charged.
- Write down your credit card numbers, and keep them in a safe place in case your cards are lost or stolen.
- If you get into credit card trouble, get counseling.
- Learn everything you can about investments and retirement plans.

Learning to manage your money and protect your credit rating will be as important to you as getting your degree. It is never too early to learn about money management. If you can do it when you have just a little money, it will be easier when you have more.

"Never work just for money or for power. They won't save your soul or help you sleep at night."

—*Marian Wright Edelman*

Knowledge
in Bloom

ANALYZING AND IMPROVING YOUR MONEY MANAGEMENT SKILLS

Utilizes levels 1–6 of the taxonomy

Each chapter-end assessment is based on Bloom's Taxonomy of Learning. See pages xxvi–xxviii in the front of this book for a quick review.

Process: As a beginning college student, it is not too early to map out your financial future. In this exercise, you will be asked to list some of your pressing financial concerns and discuss how you might spend more wisely. You will be asked to apply principles of financial management as you analyze your overall current financial management profile, design a plan for improvement, and critique your plan after practicing it for a week.

LEVEL 1

List three of your most pressing financial concerns:

_____

_____

_____

LEVEL 2

Give examples of how you might improve your money management techniques relative to these three concerns and spend more wisely.

_____

_____

_____

_____

_____

_____

_____

_____

LEVEL 3

Prepare a plan for improving how you spend your money in these three areas.

_____

_____

_____

_____

LEVEL 4

Analyze your current financial management practices using the information you have studied in this chapter. Discuss your income, expenses, student loans, credit card debt, impulse buying habits, and overall financial situation at the moment. Be sure to list financial concerns.

_____

_____

_____

_____

LEVEL 5

Now that you have been honest with yourself and have identified current financial practices and concerns, **design** a plan for improvement by listing steps that you will employ to practice better financial management.

_____

_____

_____

_____

_____

LEVEL 6

Follow your plan for a week. Write down everything you spend, the things you resist that you might have typically bought, and strategies you have employed to improve. After a week, **evaluate your plan** and your discipline to stick with this plan at this point.

_____

_____

_____

_____

SQ3R MASTERY STUDY SHEET

EXAMPLE QUESTION *(from page 34)* What are four types of financial aid?	**ANSWER:**
EXAMPLE QUESTION *(from page 35)* How does a grant differ from a loan?	**ANSWER:**
AUTHOR QUESTION *(from page 38)* What have you learned about student loans that might help you make better decisions?	**ANSWER:**
AUTHOR QUESTION *(from page 40)* Why is budgeting so important?	**ANSWER:**
AUTHOR QUESTION *(from page 43)* What are some of the dangers of credit card debt?	**ANSWER:**
AUTHOR QUESTION *(from page 47)* What practices will you employ to avoid identity theft?	**ANSWER:**
AUTHOR QUESTION *(from page 52)* Discuss several tips to keep your grocery bill within your budget.	**ANSWER:**
YOUR QUESTION *(from page _____)*	**ANSWER:**
YOUR QUESTION *(from page _____)*	**ANSWER:**
YOUR QUESTION *(from page _____)*	**ANSWER:**
YOUR QUESTION *(from page _____)*	**ANSWER:**
YOUR QUESTION *(from page _____)*	**ANSWER:**

Finally, after answering these questions, recite in your mind the major points covered here. Consider the following general questions to help you master this material.

- What was it about?
- What does it mean?
- What was the most important thing you learned? Why?
- What were the key points to remember?

Figure 2.10   Tracking Your Expenditures and Spending Habits

Over the course of the next three days, write down **every cent** you spend, including items such as fuel, food, bottled water, child care, newspapers, and so on. After three days, analyze your spending habits and determine at least five ways that you can cut expenses. You can use the memo feature on your smart phone to help with this exercise.

DAY 1	DAY 2	DAY 3
TOTAL FOR DAY 1 $ _____	TOTAL FOR DAY 2 $ _____	TOTAL FOR DAY 3 $ _____

What is the biggest lesson you have learned from tracking your money? What was the most shocking? Why?

_____

_____

_____

List five ways that you can cut your expenses.

1. _____

2. _____

3. _____

4. _____

5. _____

chapter three

ENGAGE

DEVELOPING YOUR PERSONAL AND ACADEMIC MOTIVATION

"To be successful you need to find something to hold on to, something to motivate you, something to inspire you." —Tony Dorsett

Why read this chapter?

Because you'll learn:

■ The difference between internal and external motivation

■ How to put adversity and failure into perspective

■ The impact of self-esteem on your values, motivation, and attitude

Because you'll be able to:

■ Define, discuss, and use the Cornerstones of Personal and Professional Success

■ Identify your values and use them to develop a strong guiding life statement

■ Evaluate your self-image to build healthier self-esteem and understand the impact of self-esteem on your values, motivation, and attitude

Scan and QUESTION

Take a few moments, **scan this chapter,** and on page 82, write **five of your own questions** that you think will be important to your mastery of this material. You will also find five questions listed from your authors.

Example:

☑ **What is the difference between internal and external motivation?** (from page 62)

☑ **How can overcoming self-defeating behaviors help you become a better student?** (from page 66)

MyStudentSuccessLab

MyStudentSuccessLab (www.mystudentsuccesslab.com) is an online solution designed to help you "Start strong, Finish stronger" by building skills for ongoing personal and professional development.

Name:	Kerrie Dees
Institution:	Graduate! Bryant and Stratton College
Age:	37
Major:	Medical Assisting
Career:	Medical Assistant

I never saw myself as a college student and certainly never thought that I'd have a college degree. I had studied and practiced hair styling for years, but due to a repetitive injury, I was forced to change careers. I woke up one day in my mid-thirties with a child and no career. With no other employable skills besides hair styling, I knew that I was going to have to make some major changes in my life—and quickly!

I saw an ad on TV for Bryant and Stratton and remembered that several of my family members had attended. I remembered them talking about the small classes and individual attention, and I decided to investigate and see if they had anything for me. I had always been curious about medical assisting and thought that I might enjoy working in a health care environment. There was one problem—I had never been a good student. I had never applied myself and learned how to study. I was worried that I would not be able to make it. My greatest challenge was finding the self-discipline and self-initiative to study and work hard. I had never done either before. The first step that I had to take was to get organized and arrange my schedule to make time for both my family and school.

After a few weeks in class, I began to see myself differently. Looking back, the greatest lesson that I learned was self-development—learning how to see the bigger picture of the world and how I fit into that picture. I began to learn what role I could play in the world of work by helping others. I soon found that I was capable of doing the work. Sure, there was hard work involved; there were doubts and fears, but finally, I was heading toward something. My self-esteem began to rise as I developed goal after goal and reached those goals through hard work and determination. If I could go back to school with a job and a child, anyone can, if they have the passion and vision.

What my education did for me was to make me marketable and employable. I now have skills that I could carry anywhere. My advice to you would be to work hard and don't take anything for granted. Get a support team at home and at school and get it quickly. I would also advise you to major in something that you love—follow your heart and your passion. You must be hungry for the degree, and it is hard to be hungry for something that you don't love.

THINK about it

1. What role do you think self-discipline will play in your success at your institution and in the world of work?

2. Examine your major right now. Is this your passion? Are you following your heart? Is this a career in which you can easily spend the next 30 years?

THE POWER AND PASSION OF MOTIVATION

What Is the Difference Between Internal and External Motivation?

Motivation can change your life! Read that statement again. *Motivation can change your life!* Ask any successful businessperson. Ask your favorite athlete or actor. Ask your classmates who ace every exam, project, or paper. It is their burning desire—their aspiration to succeed, to live an exceptional life, and reach their goals that changed their lives and got them to where they are today. Motivation is a force that can transform your attitude, alter the course of your performance, intensify your actions, and illuminate your future. Motivation can help you live a life that reflects your true potential. Motivation can help you live a life beyond your grandest dreams.

> "The moment you begin to do what you really want to do, your life becomes a totally different kind of life."
> —B. Fuller

If you have a need or desire to change your motivation level or attitude toward personal and academic success, there are steps you can take to help you with this goal. Some of the steps we describe will be easy to implement and others will greatly challenge you, but taken seriously, each step can assist you in discovering who you really are and what you want in life and help you find the motivation you need to change. No one can do this for you.

There are two types of motivation: **external and internal**. *External motivation* is the weaker of the two because, as the title suggests, there are *external forces or people* causing you to do something. You do not own it. External motivators may be things or people such as your parents, spouse, or partner pushing you to complete your degree; your supervisor telling you to do "x, y, or z" or you will be fired; or even your instructors giving you an exam to make sure you have done the reading. You may do the things asked of you, but the reason for doing them is external. You do not necessarily choose to do them on your own.

Internal motivation is uniquely yours. It is *energy* inside of you—pushing you to go after what you want. Internal motivation is a strong and driving force because you own it. There are no external forces or people telling you that you must do it—it comes from your desire *to be something, to have something, to attain a goal that you truly desire, or to solve a problem.* Successful people live in the world of internal motivation or find ways to convert external motivation into internal motivation.

A simple example of this conversion may be that your current degree requires you to take classes whose value or purpose you cannot understand. You may ask yourself, "Why would an interior design major have to take an algebra class?" The class is hard, math is not your thing, the chapters are frustrating and difficult to read, and math has little to do with your interests, career goals, or overall life plan. The challenge for you is to find an internal reason to move forward—a rationale for how math is going to help you, now and in the future. This is called *internalizing.* Perhaps you want to own your own interior design business—a business that will require the use of math. Internalizing the content of this math class and it requirements can motivate you to do well.

How can doing something you love and enjoy increase your motivation level?

Bananastock

By converting this external motivation (a requirement for your degree) into internal motivation (something that can help you run your business), the math class will become easier and more relevant, because you have found a way to link it to your success, your goals, your money, your health, your family, or your overall life plan.

By internalizing, you see that good math skills can help you land a work-study job in design shop. You find that good math skills can help you create an effective personal budget plan and help you save money. You find that the more you learn about the logic and process of math, the easier it is to solve problems and think more critically, thus helping you perform better in other classes. By silencing your negative self-talk about math (*"I hate math," "Math is so stupid," "I'm going to fail this class"*), you are able to internalize the rewards of the class and own the outcome. You have made a conversion.

THE NEED TO BE MORE

What Is the Relationship Between Motivation and Maslow?

One important way to think about motivation is to consider the work of Abraham Maslow, a renowned psychologist who in 1943 introduced the **Hierarchy of Basic Needs** in his landmark paper, "A Theory of Human Motivation." His basic premise is that every human being is motivated by a set of basic needs and we will do whatever it takes to have these things in our lives. The bottom four levels are what he calls *deficiency needs,* and they include things such as the need for food, air, water, security, family, health, sexual intimacy, self-esteem, achievement, and respect from others. The top level is called a *psychological need,* and it involves self-actualization, personal growth, and fulfillment. See Figure 3.1.

Self-actualization, the top level, is perhaps the most obscure and abstract to understand, but it is the most important when it comes to motivation. Maslow suggests that we all have a basic, driving desire to matter—to have a life where we are doing what we were meant to do. Self-actualization can also be described as living at our "peak" and to be fully ourselves. The renowned psychologist, author, and speaker Dr. Wayne Dyer describes self-actualization as meaning "You *must* be what you *can* be." By this he suggests that if you know you are living a life that is "less" than what you know you are capable of living, true happiness will never be yours.

CONQUERING THE "FIRST-GENERATION GAP"

How Do You Make It and Stay Motivated When You're the First in the Family?

Many college students are first-generation students, meaning that their parents' highest level of education is a high school diploma or less. This may not seem like such a big deal, but it can be on many levels. If you are a first-generation student, you may not have the support and understanding of family members who know firsthand the pressures of what you're going through. It may seem as if they are not supportive. This could be true, but more than likely, they are unaware how to offer support because college is new for them, too. Therefore, it is so very important that you find support beyond what your family may be able to offer. You will encounter many people at your college who are first-generation students and they can help guide you. Many non-first-generation students, faculty, staff, and personal friends will be able to offer you support, too.

Figure 3.1   Maslow's Hierarchy of Basic Needs

SELF-ACTUALIZATION
Personal growth, fulfillment,
reaching your potential
socially, compassion

ESTEEM NEEDS
Self-esteem, achievement, recognition, earning
the respect of others, independence

LOVING/BELONGINGNESS NEEDS
Friendship, family, affection, relationships, belonging in work
groups, sexual intimacy

SAFETY NEEDS
Security of body, security of employment, having resources, protection
from the elements, law, order, stability

PHYSIOLOGICAL NEEDS
Basic life needs such as air, food, water, sleep, shelter, warmth, sex, excretion

In a personal survey, first-generation students responded that their reasons for attending college were to be well off financially and provide their children with better opportunities than they had.

Statistics from years of research with first-generation students also show that many are more likely to have families of their own (spouses and children), are more likely to be older (over 30), come from families with lower incomes, work more full-time hours off campus, enroll part time, be less academically prepared, and attend community colleges. It was also found that first-generation students drop out more frequently than non-first-generation students (U.S. Department of Education, 1998).

Don't despair, however. These statistics do not have to predict your future, who you are, or where you are going. You are not tied to what others have or have not done. This is your life, your future, your beginning. Being a first-generation student can have many rewards, such as an esteemed sense of accomplishment, the ability to serve as a mentor for family and friends, and the ability to increase your socioeconomic status.

As you begin your studies, however, you may find that you face some resistance from some friends and family members. You may even find that some relationships suffer or end because of your pursuit of self-improvement. Don't let this discourage you. Again, this is one of the many changes that may occur in your personal life as you embark on your college journey.

Before ending a relationship, try talking to the other person and letting him or her know that you still care, while holding fast to the notion that your own life and your own future is of great importance, too. You may find that some people leave you. You may also find that you have to leave some people. Some friends may not be able to rejoice in the fact that you are going to college because they feel that you are leaving them behind; others will simply be jealous of the fact that you are bettering yourself and they are not. If those around you do not support you and your dreams and they cannot be reasoned with, you may have to part company for the sake of growth and future security.

As you begin your studies, let yourself undergo the whole spectrum of the college experience. Get involved with your classmates. Use college resources to your best

Shutterstock

What support groups exist on your campus to help first-generation students?

advantage. Establish meaningful relationships, and enjoy the ride. Yes, you may face challenges on a day-to-day basis, but growth and change include challenges. It only means you are moving. Expanding! Growing!

If you are a first-generation student, you can do many things to help ensure your success and graduation. They include the following:

- Deal with family conflicts and misunderstandings early and quickly. Talk with them about your plans, daily schedules, and college culture. Keep family members involved so they don't feel left out or that you are abandoning them.

- Don't let feelings of guilt or "selling out" derail your goals and plans. Yes, you may be the first in your family to attend college, but with your guidance and mentoring, you will not be the last.

- Work hard to find a support group, advisor, counselor, peer, or professor who understands your situation and ask them for advice. Talk to people. Make friends. Associate.

- Try to meet people who have been at your institution for at least one term so that you can learn "survival tips" from them.

- Immerse yourself socially and academically at your institution. Make use of every source of academic, financial, career, and cultural assistance possible.

- Find a healthy balance among your work, family, and college studies. Remember, this is your future. One way to look at this is to ask yourself, "Is my current job my future? Is it my destiny? Can I do what I am doing right now for the next 25 years?"

- Involve your family and friends in your education as much as possible. Ask them to attend events with you. Encourage them to begin their studies, too.

- Don't be ashamed of what you are doing and for trying to improve your station in life. Dimming your own light does nothing to help others see more clearly. This is a major step forward, and you should be proud of yourself for taking it.

- Have an open mind and enjoy the process. This is the time to learn, grow, explore, and prosper.

ACHIEVING YOUR POTENTIAL AND INCREASING YOUR MOTIVATION

What Are the Cornerstones of Personal and Professional Success?

"I am a winner."
"I fail at everything I do."

"I am a dedicated person."
"I don't really care about anything."

"I hate getting up in the morning."
"I can't wait for my day to start."

*"Watch your thoughts, they become words.
Watch your words, they become actions.
Watch your actions, they become habits.
Watch your habits, they become character.
Watch your character, it becomes your destiny."*

—Frank Outlaw

As you can see by the two different perspectives above, your attitude about how you approach life, relationships, problems, and goals can mean the difference between being a motivated, inspired, and successful person or a weary, frightened, and unsuccessful person.

The reason that we have included the following *Strategies for Lifetime Success* is to help you see that by focusing on you—becoming a person who knows where you're going, what you want, and what you have to offer—your motivation and passion for learning and growing will flourish. By knowing more about yourself, you can then establish a clearer vision of your true potential. Take your time and read each point carefully. Consider the questions asked and complete the chapter activities to assist you with your motivation plan.

Do you think that surrounding yourself with optimistic, motivated people will help you succeed? Why or why not?

Patrick White/Merrill

Point 1: Develop a New Attitude

Your attitude—new or old, good or bad—belongs to you. If your attitude needs changing, no one can do it for you. Now is the perfect time to begin changing your attitude if it needs an adjustment, because small changes in the way you approach life can mean major changes to your success throughout your college career.

Just as some people embrace the attitude of *learned helplessness* (letting your past or other people's failures dictate your future), you can just as easily embrace the attitude of learned optimism. A *pessimist* finds bad news in most situations; he or she lives in a world that has a cloud over it all the time. *Optimists,* on the other hand, can handle bad news and difficult challenges because they have a positive way of viewing the world. Optimists learn how to determine why things went wrong and can adjust and fix the underlying problem.

People actually create their own success, reach their goals, and become successful by embracing a positive outlook on life. Conversely, a great deal of personal misery and failure is caused by adopting a bad attitude and by embracing negative feelings and *self-defeating behaviors*. Take the assessment in Figure 3.2 to determine your current attitudes.

Figure 3.2 Is My Behavior Self-Defeating?

Review the checklist below of typical self-defeating habits that can be changed by adopting the right attitude. Place a check by the ones that relate to you and your behavior:

- ☐ I am frequently depressed, lonely, sad, frustrated, worried, or frightened.
- ☐ I spend a lot of time with people who aren't very motivated to excel in college.
- ☐ I waste a lot of time watching TV, playing video games, texting, scanning Facebook, and so on.
- ☐ I get very uptight and negative when I have to take a test.
- ☐ I am more worried about associating with friends than I am about my grades.
- ☑ I spend money that I shouldn't spend and charge things on my credit card that I can't afford.
- ☑ I eat too much junk food when I get stressed.
- ☐ I don't exercise properly when I feel depressed.
- ☐ I procrastinate a lot and I lose my temper quickly when I am under pressure.
- ☐ I tend to give up easily when things get hard.
- ☑ I am having trouble with my living arrangement.
- ☐ I have trouble making it through the day without some form of stimulant such as coffee, cigarettes, drugs, or alcohol.
- ☐ I daydream in some of my classes.
- ☑ I turn in my assignments late and make up excuses as to why.
- ☐ I daydream a lot about how things used to be.
- ☐ I cut class when I feel depressed or unprepared.
- ☐ I don't feel comfortable talking to my advisor and instructors.
- ☐ I don't feel like I am making many friends here, and I often feel lonely and discouraged.
- ☐ I do not participate in any co- or extracurricular activities.
- ☐ I spend a lot of my time doing nothing.
- ☐ I hate my job.
- ☐ Some of my classes are awful, and I cut them often.

If you checked off five or more statements on this chart, you may be experiencing self-defeating behavior. You will need to consider carefully how to eliminate these behaviors from your life as you work on a personal attitude adjustment.

Select one of the self-defeating habits that you checked from the list and state exactly what your behavior is and why you think you are experiencing this problem.

_____

_____

_____

_____

BLOOM LEVEL 1

Develop five action steps to help you change your attitude and overcome this self-defeating behavior.

1. _____

2. _____

BLOOM LEVEL 2

3. _____

4. _____

5. _____

Point 2: Make Excellence a Habit

As you work to change some of your habits and become a highly motivated person, one practice you need to embrace is excellence in everything you do. The average person is happy doing just enough to get by. Those who excel and succeed demand excellence from themselves in everything they do. If you don't think excellence matters, consider these points: Would you want a doctor who cheated his or her way through medical school to operate on you or your child? Would you want a pilot who didn't perform very well on the simulated crash test to fly your plane? Would you want to cross a bridge every day that was designed by an engineer who cheated his way through design class? Excellence matters! Figure 3.3 illustrates the importance of excellence in several real-life situations.

> *"NEVER leave well enough alone. If it ain't broke, fix it; take fast and make it faster; take smart and make it smarter; take good and make it great."*
> —Cigna Advertisement

Point 3: Overcome Your Doubts and Fears

Success is a great motivator, but so is fear. Actually, fear probably motivates more people than anything else. Unfortunately, fear motivates most people to hold back, to doubt themselves, to stay in their comfort zones, and to accomplish much less than they could have without the fear.

Your own personal fears may be one of the biggest obstacles to reaching your potential. If you are afraid, you are not alone; everyone has fears. Isn't it interesting that *our fears are learned?* As an infant, you were born with only **two fears:** a fear of falling and a fear of loud noises. As you got older, you added to your list of fears. And if you are like most people, you may have let your fears dominate parts of your life, saying things to yourself like:

> *"People become who they are. Even Beethoven became Beethoven."*
> —Randy Newman

Figure 3.3 What If 99.9% Were Good Enough?

If 99.9% were good enough, then:

- 12 newborns would be given to the wrong parents in the United States every day.
- 7 people would be buried in the wrong graves or cremated incorrectly daily in the United States.
- 292 book titles published in the United States would be shipped with the wrong covers on them this year.
- 400 entries in *Webster's Dictionary* would be misspelled.
- 1,200,000 credit cards held in the United States would have incorrect cardholder information on the black magnetic strip on the back of the card.
- 79,000 drug prescriptions would be written incorrectly this year in the United States
- 32,000 of the Library of Congress's books would be filed on the shelves incorrectly.

EXCELLENCE MATTERS!

"What if I try and fail?" "What if people laugh at me for thinking I can do this?" or "What if someone finds out that this is my dream?" You have two choices where fear is concerned. You can let fear dominate your life, or you can focus on those things you really want to accomplish, put your fears behind you, and *go for it.*

Dr. Robert Schuller, minister, motivational speaker, and author, once asked, ***"What would you attempt to do if you could not fail?"*** This is an important question for anyone, especially someone trying to increase his or her motivation level. In the spaces below, work through this idea by answering the questions truthfully. We have adapted and expanded this question for the purpose of this exercise.

1. What would you attempt to do if you could not fail?

   _____

   _____

   _____

   _____

2. Beyond the answers "I'm afraid" or "Fear," *why* are you not doing this thing?

   _____

   _____

   _____

   _____

BLOOM LEVEL 6

3. If you did this thing and were successful at it, how would your life change? Be specific.

   _____

   _____

   _____

   _____

   _____

Point 4: Put Adversity and Failure into Perspective

> *"If you fall down or if you're knocked down, try to land on your back because if you can look up, you can get up."*
> —Les Brown

Thomas Edison was once asked how it felt to fail over 1,000 times at making the light bulb work. He reportedly responded, "I have never failed at making the light bulb work. I successfully identified over 1,000 ways that it would not work." Edison looked on his unsuccessful attempts to build the electric light bulb positively. He saw it as eliminating ways that it would not work, not as failure. Failure is just a temporary byproduct of the success that lies ahead if you persevere. A part of being motivated means learning to deal with failure and setbacks. Most people compile a string of failures before they have great success.

Have you ever given up on something too quickly, or gotten discouraged and quit? That feeling is quite different from completing a goal and getting an adrenaline rush from success. Can you think of a time when you were unfair to yourself because you didn't stay with something long enough? Completing a goal feels much different than giving up. Have you ever stopped doing something you really loved because somebody laughed at you or teased you

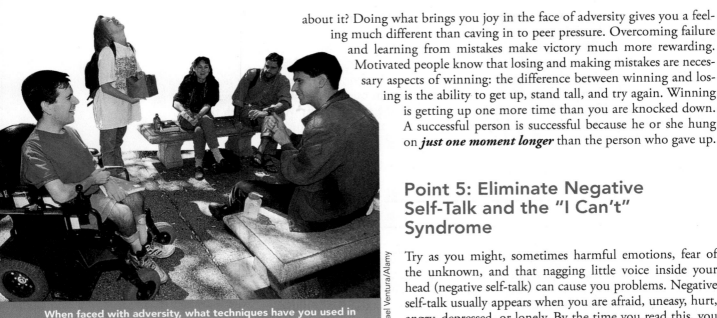

When faced with adversity, what techniques have you used in the past to survive and move on?

about it? Doing what brings you joy in the face of adversity gives you a feeling much different than caving in to peer pressure. Overcoming failure and learning from mistakes make victory much more rewarding. Motivated people know that losing and making mistakes are necessary aspects of winning: the difference between winning and losing is the ability to get up, stand tall, and try again. Winning is getting up one more time than you are knocked down. A successful person is successful because he or she hung on *just one moment longer* than the person who gave up.

Point 5: Eliminate Negative Self-Talk and the "I Can't" Syndrome

Try as you might, sometimes harmful emotions, fear of the unknown, and that nagging little voice inside your head (negative self-talk) can cause you problems. Negative self-talk usually appears when you are afraid, uneasy, hurt, angry, depressed, or lonely. By the time you read this, you may have experienced these feelings. When you experience change, your body, mind, and soul typically go through a process of physical and emotional change as well. Learning to recognize these symptoms in order to control them can help you control the stress that can accompany change. You may have to develop a new attitude.

Your attitude is yours. It belongs to you. You own it. Good or bad, happy or sad, optimistic or pessimistic, it is yours and you are responsible for it. However, your attitude is greatly influenced by situations in your life and by the people with whom you associate. Developing a winning, optimistic attitude can be hard yet extremely rewarding work and beneficial to the change process. Motivated and successful people have learned that one's attitude is the mirror to one's soul.

Listen to yourself for a few days. Are you more of an optimist or a pessimist? Do you hear yourself whining, complaining, griping, and finding fault with everything and everybody around you? Do you blame others for things that are wrong in your life? Do you blame your bad grades on your professors? Is someone else responsible for your unhappiness? If these thoughts or comments are in your head, you are suffering from the *"I CAN'T" Syndrome* (**I**rritated, **C**ontaminated, **A**ngry, **N**egative **T**houghts). This pessimistic condition can negatively influence every aspect of your life, from your self-esteem, to your motivation level, to your academic performance, to your relationships, to your career success.

If you want to eliminate *I CAN'T* from your life, consider the following tips:

■ Think about the many positive aspects of your life and show gratitude for them.

■ Work every day to find the good in people, places, and things.

■ Eliminate negative thoughts that enter your mind before you begin your day.

■ Discover what is holding you back and what you need to push you forward.

■ Visualize your success—visualize yourself actually being who and what you want to be.

■ Locate and observe positive, optimistic people and things in your life.

■ Make a list of who helps you, supports you, and helps you feel positive; then make a point to be around them more.

■ Take responsibility for your own actions and their consequences.

■ Force yourself to find five positive things a day for which to be thankful.

> "It's not the load that breaks you down, it's the way you carry it."
> —Lena Horne

You've seen the difference between an optimist and a pessimist. They are both everywhere—at work, at school, and maybe in your own family. Think of the optimist for a moment. You've probably sat next to him or her in one of your classes or seen him or her at work—the person who always seems to be happy, motivated, bubbling with personality, organized, and ready for whatever comes his or her way. Optimists greet people as they enter the room, they respond in class, they volunteer for projects, and they have a presence about them that is positive and lively. You may even look at these people out of the corner of your eye and ask, "What are they on?"

Positive, upbeat, and motivated people are easy to spot. You can basically see their attitude in the way they walk, the way they carry themselves, the way they approach people, and the way they treat others.

Be wary, however, of "the others." The ones you need to avoid. Whiners. Degraders. Attackers. Manipulators. Pessimists. Backstabbers. Abusers. Cowards. Two-faced racists, sexists, ageists, homophobes, ethnocentrists. These people carry around an aura so negative that it can almost be seen as a dark cloud above them. They degrade others because they do not like themselves. They find fault with everything because their own lives are a mess. They do nothing and then attack you for being motivated and trying to improve your life. We call them ***contaminated people.*** Contaminated people are unhappy with who they are. To make themselves feel better, they try to tear down people who are the opposite of what they are. They belittle your positive actions and try to make your life as miserable as their lives are.

Sure, everyone has bad days and bad stretches in his or her life. ***This is not the person*** we are talking about here. With contaminated people, being negative and trying to bring you down is epidemic in their lives. It is the way they operate all the time. It is constant. Having a bad day and complaining is normal for some people at various times, but contaminated people see life (and you) as negative and bad on an hourly and daily basis.

Point 6: Identify and Clarify What You Value in Life

If you have been highly motivated to accomplish a goal in the past, this achievement was probably tied to something you valued a great deal. Since most of what you do in life centers on what is truly important to you, you need to identify and then clarify what you value in your life—what really matters to you.

Values, self-esteem, motivation, and goal setting are all mixed up together, making it difficult to separate one from the other. The things you work to accomplish are directly connected to the things you value. Therefore, your *attitude* and *actions* are tied to your *values*. If you value an attitude or belief, your actions will be centered on these ideals. If you love to spend time with your friends and this is valuable to you, you will make the time for this on a regular basis. Why? Because having friends is a fundamental part of your value system. You like it and get pleasure from it, so you are motivated by it and you do it. It is that simple. Our values influence our actions. It is, once again, tied to Maslow's Hierarchy of Basic Needs.

> "Our souls are not hungry for fame, comfort, wealth, or power. These rewards create almost as many problems as they solve. Our souls are hungry for meaning, for the sense that we have figured out a way to live so that our lives matter."
> —H. Kushner

Below, you will find a wide and varied list of personal qualities. Read over them carefully and circle the ones you truly value. Be careful and selective. Do *not* just randomly circle words. As criteria for each word you circle, ask yourself, "Can I defend why I value this in my life?" and "Is this truly something I value, or something I was told to value and never questioned why?" If you value something and it is not on the list, add it to one of the spaces at the end.

Honesty	Affection	Punctuality	Respect
Frankness	Open-mindedness	Reliability	Trustworthiness
Sincerity	Wit/Humor	Spontaneity	Devotion
Frugality	Justice	Creativity	Caring

Spirituality	Friendliness	Energy	Intellect
Attentiveness	Conversation	Money	Security
Beauty	Enthusiasm	Positivism	Commitments
Foresightednes	Organization	Learning	Listening
Control	Comfort	Knowledge	Success
Athletic ability	Thoughtfulness	Independence	Courage
Safety	Fun	Excitement	Partying
Love	Friendship	Writing	Speaking
Reading	Family	Dependability	Teamwork
Time alone	Time w/friends	Phone calls	Walks
Exercise	Problem solving	Empowerment	Integrity
Service to others	Modesty	Strength	Tolerance
Imagination	Self-esteem	Food	Power
Winning	Goals	Risk taking	Change
Self-improvement	Forgiveness	Fairness	Optimism
Motivation	Trust	Direction in life	Giving
Working	Hobbies	Stability	Mentoring

_____ _____ _____ _____

_____ _____ _____ _____

_____ _____ _____ _____

_____ _____ _____ _____

Now that you have circled or written what you value, choose the five that you value the most. In other words, if you were *only* allowed to value five things in life, what five would you list below? In the space to the right of each value, rank them from 1 to 5 (1 being the most important to you, your life, your relationships, your actions, your education, and your career).

Take your time and give serious consideration to this activity, as you will need to refer back to this exercise later in this chapter.

LIST   **RANK**

✓ _____   _____

✓ _____   _____

✓ _____   _____

✓ _____   _____

✓ _____   _____

Now, look at your #1. Where did this value originate?

_____

_____

_____

_____

Defend why this is the one thing you value more than anything else in life.

_____

_____

Successful Decisions
AN ACTIVITY FOR CRITICAL REFLECTION

Your friend, Jamal, is struggling with staying motivated during his first term at school. He didn't have to study much in high school and still pulled good grades, but he has been overwhelmed with the amount of work his instructors are assigning. He knows he is not doing his best work, but he can't seem to get motivated to excel. You know he is capable because he participated in your study group several times before he stopped coming.

Lately, Jamal has begun to wake up during the night very stressed out and afraid that he is going to flunk out. His parents will be devastated if this happens because he is a first-generation student, and they have sacrificed so much for him to further his education. His fears gnaw at him all the time.

Sometimes he can see himself going home to tell his parents that he is failing. He visualizes how embarrassed he will be to tell them and his friends that he has failed. One of his instructors has told him that he has a bad attitude. He spent a long time this afternoon talking to you about his lack of motivation and how he is thinking of dropping out.

What advice and motivational tips would you offer Jamal to help him get on the right track?

1. _____

_____

2. _____

_____

_____

_____

How does this one value motivate you?

_____

_____

_____

Point 7: Take Pride in Your Name and Personal Character

"My name?" you may ask. "What does my name have to do with anything?" The answer: At the end of the day, the end of the month, the end of your career, and the end of your life, your name and your character are all that you have. Taking pride in developing your character and protecting your good name can be a powerful motivational force.

> "Your character is determined by how you treat people who can do you no good and how you treat people who can't fight back."
> —Abigail Van Buren

Imagine for a moment that you are working with a group of students on a project for your English class. The project is to receive a major grade and you and your group will present your findings to a group of 300 students at a campus forum. Your group works hard and when you present the project, your group receives a standing ovation and earns an A. The name of each individual group member is read aloud as you stand to be recognized. Your name and project are also posted in a showcase. You are proud. Your hard work paid off. Your name now carries weight with your peers and among the faculty. It feels good.

Conversely, imagine that your group slacks off; the project is poorly prepared and received by the audience and your instructors. Your group earns an F on the project. Your name is

B R I N G the *Change*

TIPS FOR PERSONAL SUCCESS

Assume you are 90 years old and on your deathbed. You are thinking back over your life. Most likely you would think about certain people and events that have transpired. Perhaps you might want people to say or write the following about you:

■ She was kind to people.

■ He spent quality time with his children.

■ She was a wonderful friend.

■ He was always a giving person.

Now, it is your turn. Create a list of at least three things that you hope to have people say or write about you upon your death.

1. _____

_____

2. _____

_____

3. _____

_____

associated with this project and your name and grade is posted with every other group. Your group is the only group to receive an F. It doesn't feel good.

Basically, it comes down to this: Every time you make a choice, every time you complete a project, every time you encounter another person, your actions define your character and your name. People admire and respect you when you make an honorable and moral choice, especially if it is a difficult decision. Both your character and your name are exclusively yours, and you are responsible for their well-being. When you care this passionately about your reputation and character, your life is governed by protecting your name. Your actions, beliefs, and decisions are all tied to this one belief: "My name and my reputation matter and I will do nothing to bring shame or embarrassment to my name."

Point 8: Develop a Strong, Personal Guiding Statement

You're wearing a t-shirt to class. It is not your normal, run-of-the-mill t-shirt, however. You designed this t-shirt for everyone to see and read. It is white with bright red letters. On the front of the t-shirt is written your ***personal guiding statement***—the words by which you live. The words govern your life. What would your t-shirt say? Perhaps you will use the golden rule, "Do unto

How can damage to your name and reputation negatively affect your overall success?

Bananastock

others . . ." It might be an adaptation of the Nike slogan, "Just Do It," or it might be something more profound such as, "I live my life to serve others and to try to make others' lives better," or "Be a blessing," or "Live, love, laugh."

Whatever your guiding statement, it must be yours. It can't be your parents', your professor's, or your best friend's statement. It must be based on something you value, and it must be strong enough to motivate you in hard, tough times. Your guiding statement must be so powerful that it will literally "guide you" when you are ethically challenged, broke, alone, angry, hurt, sad, or feeing vindictive. It is a statement that will guide you in relationships with family, friends, spouses, partners, or would-be love interests. It is a statement that gives direction to your daily actions. Think about how different your life would be if you woke up each morning and lived your guiding statement to the fullest.

One of the best ways to start working on your guiding statement is to look back at those values you earlier circled as important to you. If you value something, it may appear in your guiding statement. For example, if you circled the words *respect, giving,* and *optimism* among those you value, this is a basis for your statement. A guiding statement based on these words might read:

"I will live my life as a positive, optimistic, upbeat, motivated person who respects others and enjoys giving to others on a daily basis."

If your circled words included *integrity, honesty,* and *fairness,* your statement may read:

"My integrity is the most important thing in my life, and I will never act in any way that compromises my integrity. I will be truthful, fair, and honest in all my endeavors."

More simply, your guiding statement may read something like:

"Be reliable," "Live optimistically," or **"Never give up."**

In the space below, transfer the most important words from the value list on pages 71–72 and then work to develop your guiding statement.

The most important values were:

_____   _____

_____   _____

_____   _____

_____   _____

Using these words, draft your guiding statement. (Take your time and be sincere. You will need this statement later in the chapter.)

_____

_____

_____

_____

Point 9: Make a Commitment to Strengthen Your Self-Esteem

If you were asked to name all the areas of your life that are affected by self-esteem, what would you say? The correct answer is, "Everything." Every area of your life is affected by your self-esteem.

Self-esteem and self-understanding are two of the most important components of your personal makeup! To be truly motivated, you have got

DID YOU *Know?*

TIM MCGRAW, recording artist and country music sensation, was born in Louisiana in 1967. When he was 11 years old, he discovered that the man he believed to be his father was not and that his father was actually the famous New York Mets baseball player Tug McGraw. Tug denied that Tim was his son for seven years. When Tim was 18, Tug finally admitted that he was Tim's father.

During Tim's early recording years, his first series of singles failed so badly that he was told to give up his dream of becoming a country recording artist. One producer even told him, "You'll never make it, son. Go on home and find yourself a job."

As of today, he has sold over 40 million CDs and has 31 number one hits. His last 11 CDs debuted at number one on the Billboard charts. He has won three Grammy awards, 14 Academy of Country Music Awards, 11 Country Music Association Awards, and three People's Choice Awards. He is also married to another famous country music singer, Faith Hill (TimMcGraw.com, n.d.; Wikipedia, n.d.).

PHOTO: AllStar Picture Library/Alamy

from ORDINARY to Extraordinary

Lydia Hausler Lebovic
Jewish Holocaust Survivor
Auschwitz Concentration/Extermination Camp,
Auschwitz, Poland, 1944

"SWEET SIXTEEN." Isn't that the moment of joy for so many female teens today? It is a milestone date when childhood passes and young adulthood arrives. One can legally drive, and in many states, "Sweet Sixteen" signifies the age of consent.

My "Sweet Sixteen" was very different. Yes, I was dating, had a somewhat rebellious relationship with my mother, and socialized with friends, but in the countryside around me, World War II raged. In 1944, when I was 16, my family and I were ordered to pack 20 pounds of personal belongings and taken to "the Ghetto," a holding area for Jews in my hometown of Uzhorod, Czechoslovakia, now a part of Ukraine. I understood that the situation was not good and that things were changing, but I had no real idea of how my life would forever be altered in the coming weeks, months, and years.

After two weeks in "the Ghetto," my family, friends, neighbors, and I were ordered onto cattle cars—60 to 80 per car—and told that we were being taken to Hungary to work

in the corn and wheat fields. So there, in the darkness of night, our journey began—young, old, weak, strong, nursing mothers, and babies—all in the same cattle car with no water and only two buckets to use for a bathroom.

After two days of travel, the train stopped and the doors of the cattle car opened. My mother recognized that we were not in southern Hungary, but rather on the Hungary/Poland border in the north. She took us aside in the car and told us of her suspicion—that we were being taken to Auschwitz concentration camp. After another two days on the train, we arrived at Auschwitz in the early dawn hours.

The doors of the cattle cars opened, and the men were quickly separated from the women and the children from the adults. We were put into lines of five and marched forward. In front of every line was an SS officer. Quickly, I was pushed to the right and my mother and sister were pushed to the left. Little did I know at that point that those shoved to the right would be put to work and those shoved to the left would be dead by

to know yourself and love yourself. Many people who are in therapy are there simply because they cannot accept the fact that they are OK. Self-esteem is a powerful force in your life and is the source of your joy, your productivity, and your ability to have good relationships with others.

You might think of self-esteem as a photograph of yourself that you keep locked in your mind. It is a collective product—the culmination of everyone with whom you have associated, everywhere you've traveled, and all of the experiences you have had. William James, the first major psychologist to study self-esteem, defined it as "the sum total of all a person can call their own: the Material Me (all that you have), the Social Me (recognition and acceptance from others), and the Spiritual Me (your innermost thoughts and desires)."

Stanley Coopersmith, noted psychologist and developer of the most widely used self-esteem inventory in the United States, defined self-esteem as "a personal judgment of worthiness." Psychologist and author Nathaniel Branden defined self-esteem as "confidence in our ability to cope with the basic challenges of life." And finally, psychologist Charles Cooley called the evening. I never saw my mother or sister again after that moment. I never said goodbye. I was "Sweet Sixteen."

After the separation, my group was taken to a very large building and told to undress. We were completely shaven, sponged from head to toe with a bleach-like substance, showered, and given a uniform. We were then marched to the barracks where we would sleep 12 to 14 to a bed with 600 to 800 people per barracks. The black and white photo was taken as we marched toward the barracks from the shower facility and now hangs in the National Holocaust Museum in Washington, DC.

Some of the Jewish girls who had been in the camp for a while were considered "foremen." I remember approaching one such female. I asked her, "When do I get to see my mother and my sister?"

She took me by the arm and pointed toward the billowing chimney of the crematory. "You see that smoke? You see that ash? You smell that flesh burning? That's your mother. That's your sister." She walked away. I did not believe her at the time, but she was absolutely right. This realization remains the most distressing of all events in my life—past and present—that my mother and sister died in such a horrific manner. Gassed and cremated.

I remained in Auschwitz until I was shipped to the labor camp, Bergen-Belsen, in Germany. We were liberated on April 15, 1945. Upon liberation, I began working for the British Red Cross. Later that year, I was reunited with a friend of my brother, and we were married in November of 1945. We moved to Chile in 1947 and then to Los Angeles, California, in 1963.

I now travel the nation speaking about the events of my life and delivering the message, "NEVER AGAIN." I write this to essay to you for many reasons, but specifically to let you know this: The Holocaust did not ruin me. They did not destroy me. They did not destroy my belief in love. They did not destroy my faith in people. They did not destroy my religion or values. The events made me a stronger, more compassionate person. I went on to become a loving wife and mother, a successful businesswoman, and eventually a devoted grandmother. I refused to be ruined. I encourage you to use the adversity in your life to make you stronger, more compassionate, more caring, and more helpful to mankind.

> *Little did I know at that point that those shoved to the right would be put to work and those shoved to the left would be dead by the evening.*

EXTRAORDINARY REFLECTION

Read the following statement and respond in your online journal or class notebook.

Mrs. Lebovic suffered the death of family members during the Holocaust but she makes the statement, "The Holocaust did not ruin me. They did not destroy me. They did not destroy my belief in love. I refused to be ruined." How can adversity in your life, like that in Mrs. Lebovic's, make you a stronger and more motivated person?

it "the looking glass." Perhaps in everyday terms, we can define healthy self-esteem as "I know who I am, I accept who I am, I am OK, and I'm going to make it."

Self-esteem has five basic characteristics based on Maslow's Hierarchy of Basic Needs. They are:

- A sense of **security** (I am safe and have the basics of life—food, water, etc.)
- A sense of **identity** (I know who I am and where I'm going)
- A sense of **belonging** (I know how to love and I am loved)
- A sense of **purpose** (I know why I'm here and what I am going to do with my life)
- A sense of **personal competence** (I have the ability to achieve my goals and grow)

These characteristics are considered key to a person's ability to approach life with motivation, confidence, self-direction, and the desire to achieve outstanding accomplishments.

How can actively participating in class help build your self-esteem?

Image 100

Tips to Enhance Your Self-Esteem

TAKE CONTROL OF YOUR OWN LIFE. If you let other people rule your life, you will always have unhealthy self-esteem. Get involved in the decisions that shape your life. Seize control—don't let life just happen to you!

ADOPT THE IDEA THAT YOU ARE RESPONSIBLE FOR YOU. The day you take responsibility for yourself and what happens to you is the day you start to develop healthier self-esteem. When you can admit your mistakes and celebrate your successes knowing you did it your way, loving and respecting yourself become much easier.

REFUSE TO ALLOW FRIENDS AND FAMILY TO TEAR YOU DOWN. Combat negativity by admitting your mistakes and shortcomings to yourself (without dwelling on them) and by making up your mind that you are going to overcome them. By doing this, you are taking negative power away from anyone who would use your mistakes to hurt you.

CONTROL WHAT YOU SAY TO YOURSELF. "Self-talk" is important to your self-esteem and to your ability to motivate yourself positively. If you allow negative self-talk into your life, it will rule your self-esteem. Think positive thoughts and surround yourself with positive, upbeat, motivated, happy people.

TAKE CALCULATED RISKS. If you are going to grow to your fullest potential, you will have to learn to take some calculated risks and step out of your comfort zone. While you should never take foolhardy risks that might endanger your life or everything you have, you must constantly be willing to push yourself.

STOP COMPARING YOURSELF TO OTHER PEOPLE. You may never be able to beat some people at certain things. Does it really matter? You only have to "beat yourself" to get better. If you constantly tell yourself that you are not "as handsome as Bill" or "as smart as Mary" or "as athletic as Jack," your inner voice will begin to believe these statements, and your motivation and self-esteem will suffer. Everyone has certain strengths and talents to offer to the world.

KEEP YOUR PROMISES AND BE LOYAL TO FRIENDS, FAMILY, AND YOURSELF. If you have ever had someone break a promise to you, you know how it feels to have your loyalty betrayed. The most outstanding feature of your character is your ability to be loyal, keep your promises, and do what you have agreed to do. Few things can make you feel better about yourself than being loyal and keeping your word.

> *"To every person there comes that special moment when he is tapped on the shoulder to do a very special thing unique to him. What a tragedy if that moment finds him unprepared for the work that would be his finest hour."*
>
> —*Winston Churchill*

WIN WITH GRACE, LOSE WITH CLASS. Everyone loves a winner, but everyone also loves a person who can lose with class and dignity. On the other hand, no one loves a bragging winner or a moaning loser. If you are engaged in sports, debate, acting, art shows, or academic competitions, you will encounter winning and losing. Remember, whether you win or lose, ***if you're involved and active,*** you're already in the top 10 percent of the population. You're already more of a winner than most because you showed up and participated.

BE A GIVER. Author, speaker, and teacher Leo Buscaglia states: "You want to make yourself the most brilliant, the most talented, the most fabulous person that you can possibly be so that you can give it all away. The only reason we have anything is to be able to give it away." By giving to other people and sharing your talents and strengths, you begin to live on a level where kindness, selflessness, and others' needs gently collide. Whatever you want in this life, give it away and it will come back to you.

REFLECTIONS ON MOTIVATION AND SELF-ESTEEM

Motivation can change your life. Healthy self-esteem can change your life. You can change your life. We have discussed self-discovery and defining what you value, what role your attitude plays in your motivation, and how to surround yourself with positive, optimistic people. By focusing on *you* and determining what is important to your college studies, your career, your relationships, and your personal life, you can develop a vision of your future. If you can see your future, really see it, then you are more likely to be motivated to achieve it. Remember, we are motivated by what we value. As you continue on in the semester and work toward personal and professional motivation, consider the following ideas:

■ Convert external motivation into internal motivation.
■ Use the power of positive thinking and surround yourself with positive people.

■ Step outside your comfort zone.
■ Use your values to drive your life statement.
■ Clear up your past by forgiving those who may have hurt you.
■ Do one thing every day to strengthen your self-esteem.
■ Turn negative thoughts into positive energy.
■ Don't give in to defeat.
■ View adversity as a stepping stone to strength.
■ Picture yourself as optimistic and motivated.

Good luck to you as you begin developing the motivation and positive attitude you need to be successful in your studies and beyond.

"The thing always happens that you believe in; and the belief in a thing makes it happen."

—Frank Lloyd Wright

USING AND EVALUATING YOUR GUIDING STATEMENT

Utilizes levels 3 and 6 of the taxonomy

Each chapter-end assessment is based on Bloom's Taxonomy of Learning. See pages xxvi–xxviii in the front of this book for a quick review.

Process: Now that you have developed your guiding statement, consider how it can be used to guide you in the following situations.

Guiding Statement (as written on page 75 of this chapter):

_____
_____
_____
_____
_____
_____

HOW WILL YOUR GUIDING STATEMENT HELP:
If you have a disagreement with your supervisor at work?

_____
_____
_____
_____
_____
_____

If your class paper or project receives a failing grade from your professor?

_____
_____
_____
_____
_____
_____

If you are having a disagreement with someone for whom you care deeply (friend, spouse, partner, parent, work associate, etc.)?

_____
_____
_____
_____
_____
_____

If you see that someone is struggling and having a hard time "making it"?

_____

_____

_____

_____

_____

Now that you have had a chance to apply your guiding statement to several simulations, how would you rate its effectiveness to you and to those involved on a scale of 1 to 10 (1 being not effective at all and 10 being very effective)? Why? Discuss.

_____

_____

_____

_____

_____

_____

SQ3R MASTERY STUDY SHEET

EXAMPLE QUESTION *(from page 62)* What is the difference between internal and external motivation?	ANSWER:
EXAMPLE QUESTION *(from page 66)* How can overcoming self-defeating behaviors help you become a better student?	ANSWER:
AUTHOR QUESTION *(from page 70)* How can the "I CAN'T" Syndrome affect your classroom performance?	ANSWER:
AUTHOR QUESTION *(from page 71)* How can identifying your values help you stay motivated?	ANSWER:
AUTHOR QUESTION *(from page 73)* Define the word *character* and discuss how it plays a role in your motivation level.	ANSWER:
AUTHOR QUESTION *(from page 77)* Explain how self-esteem plays a role in one's motivation.	ANSWER:
AUTHOR QUESTION *(from page 78)* Why is loyalty important to your self-esteem?	ANSWER:
YOUR QUESTION *(from page _____)*	ANSWER:
YOUR QUESTION *(from page _____)*	ANSWER:
YOUR QUESTION *(from page _____)*	ANSWER:
YOUR QUESTION *(from page _____)*	ANSWER:
YOUR QUESTION *(from page _____)*	ANSWER:

Finally, after answering these questions, recite in your mind the major points covered here. Consider the following general questions to help you master this material.

- What was it about?
- What does it mean?
- What was the most important thing you learned? Why?
- What were the key points to remember?

chapter four
PERSIST

UNDERSTANDING THE CULTURE OF YOUR INSTITUTION

"I know the price of success: dedication, hard work, and constant devotion to the things you want to see happen." —Frank Lloyd Wright

Why read this chapter?

Because you'll learn:

■ The rules of your institution
■ How to decode your instructors
■ The value of planning for your second term

Because you'll be able to:

■ Use civility, personal decorum, self-management, and ethics to guide future plans
■ Avoid plagiarism
■ Find and use academic, campus, and personal success offices at your institution

Scan and QUESTION

Take a few moments, **scan this chapter,** and on page 105, **write five of your own questions** that you think will be important to your mastery of this material. You will also find five questions listed from your authors.

Example:

☑ **Why is it important to understand your institution's policies?** (from page 86)

☑ **How can you avoid the "drive by" college experience?** (from page 93)

MyStudentSuccessLab

MyStudentSuccessLab (www.mystudentsuccesslab.com) is an online solution designed to help you "Start strong, Finish stronger" by building skills for ongoing personal and professional development.

Name: Mary Harris
Institution: Graduate! Pima Medical Institute
Age: 45
Major: Occupational Therapy
Career: Respiratory Therapy

One day I woke up and found myself divorced, raising three children, and working in a job that did nothing for me. Sometimes I worked seven days a week, different schedules, and for very little money. I was working as a staffing coordinator, and I saw how people in the health professions were respected but, more importantly, how quickly they were hired. I also saw what they were making. At 45, I decided to go back to school to become a respiratory therapist. I knew that it was not going to be easy, but I also knew that I had to do it. I was lucky enough to be able to move myself and my children into my 83-year-old mother's home. This was not easy, but sometimes, you have to take a few steps back to leap forward.

I visited Pima Medical Institute one day to check out their program and something just felt different. I took their placement test, did well, and before I knew it, I was enrolled in a program that would change my life. When I began, the biggest challenge that I faced was getting into books and all of the readings that were required. It was very intimidating and scary at times. The classes were hard, and there were certainly times when I did not think I would make it. I quickly learned that it would take discipline and hard work. I had to make some major adjustments in my life with regards to time management and studying. It was a huge shift from working full-time—all the time—to going back to class.

The greatest lesson that I learned from Pima and from going back to school was to be confident in myself. After passing a few tests and then a few classes, I began to realize that success was possible. When I first returned to Pima, I thought that my age was going to be a problem, but I was wrong. I found myself in classes with people who were much younger and much older than I was. Age did not matter. Determination did. I also learned that with my degree, I would not have to work seven days a week, 52 weeks a year, and that I could move to any part of the country and find work in my field. I now have the freedom to spend more time with my children and to do the things I love.

If I could offer you one piece of advice as you begin your degree, it would be this: Set everything aside and work through it. Don't get distracted. Don't get discouraged. Put your effort and energy into your classes, because soon they will be over, you'll have your degree, and you can then focus on the things that bring you joy. You have to be willing to give 100 percent. If you put your shoulder to the wall and push, you'll complete your degree before you know it.

THINK
a b o u t *it*

1. Mary talks about learning self-confidence. What role will self-confidence play in your success?

2. What adjustments will you have to make in your daily life to work through your degree and give school 100 percent?

TO BE SUCCESSFUL, YOU HAVE TO LAST

How Can I Make It and Persist in My Studies?

Have you ever faced adversity and heavy odds when attempting to do something? Most everyone has. If you are one of the people who refused to let adversity hold you back, faced your fears, and continued with the project at hand, then you know how it feels to survive. You know how it feels to reach a goal when the odds were not in your favor. You know the feeling of winning. You know the value of persistence.

Conversely, have you ever given up on something and regretted it later? Do you ever think back and ask yourself, "What would my life be like if only I had done this or that?" Have you ever made a decision or acted in a way that cost you dearly? If you have, then you know how difficult it can be to begin new projects or face the future with motivation. You know the feeling of defeat. Know this, however: Defeat *does not* have to be a part of your life. It may be a part of your journey, but it does not have to be a permanent part of your life.

So what is ***persistence?*** The word itself means that you are going to stay—that you have found a way to stick it out, found a way to make it work, and found a way *to not give up.* That is what you will learn here—the tools to discover how your college works and what tools you will need to be successful. Self-management is about taking initiative—not waiting for someone to tell you how things work and not waiting until something goes wrong. Self-management is about investigating and researching ways to be successful at your college from this day forward. It is about your ability to ***last during tough times.***

KNOWING THE RULES UP FRONT

Why Do I Need to Know about Institutional Policies and Procedures?

Policies and procedures vary, but regardless, it is your responsibility to know what you can expect from your institution and what your institution expects from you. These policies can be found in the institutional catalog (traditional and online), your student handbook, or your schedule of classes, depending on your institution.

A few universal policies include the following:

■   All institutions of higher education must comply with the Federal Privacy Act of 1974 (this ensures your privacy, even from your parents in most cases).

Why is it important to establish a positive relationship with your instructors?

Shutterstock

Figure 4.1 Understanding Institutional Policy

POLICY QUESTION	RESPONSE
What is the last day to drop a class without penalty?	
Does your institution have a refund policy? If so, what is it?	
What is your institution's grade appeal policy?	
What is your institution's religious holiday policy?	
What is your institution's policy for placement testing?	
What is your institution's policy on academic probation?	
Does your institution have an attendance policy? What is it?	

BLOOM LEVEL 1

- Most institutions require placement tests (these are different from admission tests). They are used to properly advise you into the correct English, math, international languages, reading, and/or vocabulary classes.

- Most institutions adhere to a strict drop/add date. Always check with your institution for this information.

- Most institutions have an attendance policy for classroom instruction.

- Most institutions have a strict payment/refund/default policy.

- Almost every institution in the United States has an Academic Dishonesty Policy.

> "The very first step toward success in any endeavor is to become interested in it."
> —William Osler

Institutions do not put these policies and procedures in place to punish you or to make things harder; rather, they are designed to ensure that all students are treated fairly and equitably. Some of the policies are also mandated by the federal government in order for the institution to be allowed to receive federal monies. By reviewing your institution's catalog, schedule of classes, or student handbook, you can familiarize yourself with your institution's specific guidelines. Use these documents to complete Figure 4.1, Understanding Institutional Policy.

I CAN'T BELIEVE YOU GAVE ME AN F

What Is Your Role in Earning Grades?

There will be times when you are disappointed with a grade that you earn from an instructor. And yes, you do *earn an A or an F*; instructors *do not give A's or F's*. What do you do? Threaten? Sue? Become argumentative? Those techniques usually cost you more than they gain for you.

Figure 4.2 Do I Practice Personal Responsibility?

Think about a grade or project on which you scored lower than you would have liked or expected. Answer these questions truthfully to determine your role in the grading process. Place a check beside the questions that truly reflect your effort. If you have not yet turned in a project or taken an exam, consider these questions a checklist to success.

☐ I attend class regularly.

☐ I participate in class discussions and group work.

☐ I ask pointed and direct questions in class.

☐ I read my assignments, do my homework, and come to class prepared.

☐ I work with a study group.

☐ I have all of the supplies I need to be successful in this class (text, workbook, calculator, highlighters, etc.).

☐ I visit my instructor during office hours to ask questions and seek clarification.

☐ I use the academic support services on my campus (tutorial services, math lab, writing centers, communication lab, language lab, science lab, etc.).

☐ I use the library as a resource for greater understanding.

☐ I practice academic integrity.

☐ I bring my best to the class every time we meet.

Being able to answer these personal responsibility questions positively can mean the difference between success and failure with a project, assessment, or class. If you are truly concerned about the grade, talk to the instructor about the assignment. Ask the instructor to describe the most apparent problem with your assignment, and ask how you might improve your studying or how best to prepare for the next assignment.

First, remember that the grade assigned by an instructor can rarely be changed. If you made a less than satisfactory grade, there are several things that you need to do. First, be truthful with yourself and examine the amount of time you spent on the project.

Review the requirements for the assignment. Ask yourself:

- Did I miss something or omit some aspect of the project?
- Did I take an improper or completely wrong focus?
- Did I turn the project in late?
- Did I document my sources correctly?
- Did I really give it my very best?

Answering these important questions, and the ones listed in Figure 4.2, can help you determine the extent of your personal responsibility and preparation for success.

CLASSROOM CHALLENGES

What Do I Need to Know Right Now?

WHEN YOUR INSTRUCTOR'S FIRST LANGUAGE IS NOT ENGLISH. Yes, you may have instructors whose first language is not English. Institutions often hire instructors from around the world because of their expertise in their subjects. You may find that it is difficult to understand an instructor's dialect or pronunciation from time to time. If you have an instructor who is difficult to understand, remember these hints:

- Sit near the front of the room.
- Watch the instructor's mouth when you can.
- Follow the instructor's nonverbal communication patterns.

- Use a tape recorder if allowed.

- Read the material beforehand so that you will have a general understanding of what is being discussed.

- Ask questions when you do not understand the material.

WHEN YOU AND YOUR INSTRUCTOR HAVE A DISAGREEMENT.
There may be times when you clash with your instructor. It may be over a grade, an assigned project, a topic of discussion, a misunderstanding, or a personality issue. Above all, don't get into a verbal argument or physical confrontation. This will only make matters worse for everyone involved. If you have a disagreement, make sure that the instructor is your first point of contact. Unless you have spoken with him or her first and exhausted all options, approaching the department chair, the dean, the vice president, or the president will more than likely result in your being sent directly back to the instructor. If you go to the instructor's superiors before talking to the instructor, this will likely result in having him or her get upset with you.

THE GOLDEN RULE— OR JUST A CROCK

Do Civility, Classroom Etiquette, and Personal Decorum Affect Success?

You may be surprised, but the way you act in (and out) of class can mean as much to your success as what you know. No one can make you do anything or act in any way that you do not want. The following tips are provided from years of research and actual conversations with thousands of instructors teaching across the United States. You have to be the one who chooses whether to use this advice.

- Make every effort not to be late to class. If you are late for class, enter quietly. Do *not* walk in front of the instructor, don't let the door slam, don't talk on your way in, and take the seat nearest the door.

- Wait for the instructor to dismiss class before you begin to pack your bags to leave. You may miss important information, or you may cause someone else to miss important information.

- Do not carry on a conversation with another student while the instructor or another student is talking.

- Don't ask your instructor to break the rules just for you. The rules in your class syllabus are provided to everyone so that all students will be treated fairly. If you have a true, legitimate reason to ask for an extension or some other exception, talk to your instructor privately ***beforehand***.

- Do not sleep in class. If you are having problems staying awake, make changes in your personal life. If you're sleeping, you're wasting your money and time.

- If for any reason you must leave during class, do so quietly and quickly. It is customary to inform the instructor that you will be leaving early before class begins.

- If you make an appointment with an instructor, keep it. If you must cancel, a courtesy call is in order.

DID YOU *Know?*

NELSON MANDELA was born on July 18, 1918, in the small village of Mvezo, South Africa. His father had four wives and he was raised in a family of 13 children. His father died when he was nine years old. When he was 20, he found that his family had arranged a marriage for him. He was displeased with this arrangement and decided to flee to Johannesburg. There he found work as a guard for a mining company. He was fired from this job because the supervisor found out that he was a runaway.

Throughout his life, he suffered abuse and discrimination. He was asked to leave college because of his beliefs and protests. He endured a five-year trial for treason and later spent 27 years in prison for his outspoken opinions. He was released in 1990. In 1994, at the age of 76, he became the first black president of South Africa, effectively ending "white-only rule."

In 1993, President Mandela accepted the Nobel Peace Prize on behalf of all South Africans who suffered to end apartheid (Nobel Foundation, 1993).

PHOTO: Oliver Polet/Zuma/Newscom

"*Respect your efforts, respect yourself. Self-respect leads to self-discipline. When you have both firmly under your belt, that's real power.*"
—Clint Eastwood

- If you don't know how to address your instructor—that is, by Mr., Mrs., Miss, Ms., or Dr.—ask what he or she prefers or simply use "Instructor _____."

- Turn off your electronic devices (iPods, phones, etc.). Even if the device is off, take your earbuds out of your ears. Leaving them in is disrespectful.

- Be respectful of other students. Profanity and obscene language may offend some people. You can have strong, conflicting views without being offensive.

- Visit instructors during office hours. The time before and after class may not be the most appropriate time for you or the instructor. Your instructor may have back-to-back classes and may be unable to assist you.

- If you act like an adult (which you are), you'll be treated as one.

Remember that respect for others on your part will afford you the opportunity to establish relationships that otherwise you might never have had. Respect begets respect.

SELF-MANAGEMENT, ETHICS, AND YOUR FUTURE

Who Are You When No One Is Looking?

Think about these questions: What if there were no rules or laws to govern your behavior? What if there were no consequences or ramifications for any of your actions? Let's pretend for a moment that you could never go to jail or face fines or be shunned for your words, actions, or behaviors. If these statements came to pass, what would your life—or the lives of those you love—look like? This is one of the best ways to offer a practical definition of ethics. Basically, ethics is the accepted moral code or standard by which we all live, and that code is communicated many ways, including through our relationships with others. Codes of ethics vary from culture to culture, country to country, college to college, and group to group, but each carries with it certain "rules" that members of the culture, country, college, or group are expected to follow.

"Have the courage to say no. Have the courage to face the truth. Do the right thing because it is right. These are the magic keys to living your life with integrity."
—Clement Stone

Making professional or personal ethical decisions usually involves three factors or levels, as shown in Figure 4.3. They include the *law, fairness,* and your *conscience* (Anderson & Bolt, 2008). You might also consider adding three other levels: *time, pride,* and *publicity.*

MAKING MATURE DECISIONS

What Is the Importance of Academic and Personal Integrity?

As a student of higher education, you will be faced with temptations that require you to make hard choices. You have probably already been forced to make decisions based on ethics. Do I cheat and make a higher grade so I can compete with top students? Will cheating help me earn higher grades so I get a better job? Do I copy this paper from the Internet? Who will know? Why shouldn't I buy one of the term papers that is floating around my fraternity? What if I just copy someone's homework and not cheat on a test? What if I lie to the instructor and say I was sick so I can get more time for a test for which I am not prepared? What if I let someone look at

Figure 4.3 Six Levels of Ethical Decision Making

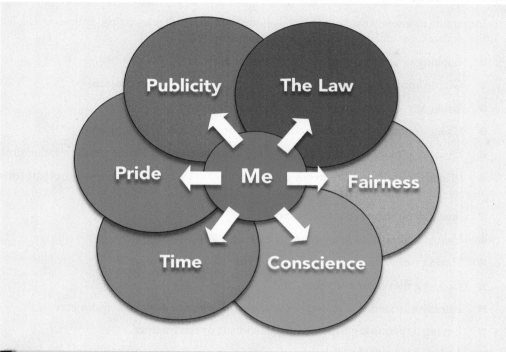

▶ Is it legal?

▶ Is it fair to me and others?

▶ Can I live with my decision?

▶ Is this decision in my long-term best interest?

▶ Could I tell my mama about it and be proud?

▶ How would I feel if this showed up on the front page of the newspaper tomorrow morning?

If you can respond positively to all six statements, this decision would most likely be in your best interest and the best interest of those around you.

my paper during a test; I'm not cheating, am I? These are all ethical questions that require you to use your personal integrity to make mature decisions.

Integrity is purely and simply making decisions about what is right and wrong according to your personal code of ethics and accepted social behavior. What will you do when nobody knows but you? It is also making decisions about what is right and wrong according to your institution's standards. As a student, you will see many people do things that you think are not right. You have to decide what is right for you and follow your values no matter what others may be doing. Just because "everyone is doing it" doesn't make it right, and certainly it doesn't make it right for you.

Even if you cheat and don't get caught, you lose. You lose respect for yourself, your self-esteem is likely to decline, and you cheat yourself of the knowledge for which you are paying. You also lose because you damage your character and the person you hope to become. Cheating can cause you to feel guilty and stressed because you are afraid that someone might find out.

"No one will question your integrity if your integrity is not questionable."

—Nathaniel Bronner, Jr.

CHEATING!

What Do You Need to Know about Academic Misconduct?

It is important to know what constitutes dishonesty in an academic setting. Following is a list of offenses that most colleges consider academic misconduct.

- Looking at another person's test paper for answers
- Giving another student answers on tests, homework, or lab projects
- Using any kind of "cheat sheets" on a test or project
- Using a computer, calculator, dictionary, or notes when not approved
- Discussing exam questions with students who are taking the same class at another time
- Plagiarism, or using the words or works of others without giving proper credit (this includes the Internet!)
- Stealing another student's class notes
- Using an annotated instructor's edition of a text
- Having tutors do your homework for you
- Copying files from a lab computer
- Bribing a student for answers or academic work such as papers or projects
- Buying or acquiring papers from individuals or the Internet
- Assisting others with dishonest acts
- Lying about reasons you missed a test or a class

THE DANGERS OF USING SOMEONE ELSE'S WORK AS YOUR OWN

How Can Plagiarizing Affect Your Future?

Plagiarism is a serious offense, and you should not take it lightly—your instructors do not! You have no doubt already heard your instructors discuss plagiarism and the ramifications of using someone else's work without proper documentation. You should strongly consider their advice and take plagiarism seriously so you do not find yourself in trouble. Some students seem to think plagiarism is merely copying someone else's work or borrowing an original idea and claiming it as their own, and of course, these acts are included in the definition. But that terminology may not adequately reflect what a serious offense this act can be. Plagiarism includes fraud, stealing, and lying. People who would never take someone's wallet or personal information may carelessly "borrow" another person's words and ideas without properly documenting them, which is just as wrong as stealing someone's money.

Plagiarism is often defined as using another's words or ideas as your own without permission. Turnitin.com (2008) provides a solution to avoiding plagiarism: "Most cases of plagiarism can be avoided by citing sources. Simply acknowledging that certain material has been borrowed, and providing your audience with the information necessary to find that source, is usually enough to prevent plagiarism." Avoiding plagiarism just takes a little more effort, but it saves you a great many problems.

> "I would prefer to fail with honor than to win by cheating."
> —Sophocles

STUDENT SERVICES AT YOUR INSTITUTION

How Do They Support Student Success?

Most institutions offer you assistance for academic, social, cultural, spiritual, and physical enrichment outside the classroom. Your tuition or student activities fee may fund many of the centers on your campus. You've paid for them; you should take full advantage of their services. Some institutional services are easier to find than others, but most are usually listed in your student handbook, college catalog, or schedule of classes. When in doubt, don't be afraid to ask your instructor, advisor, or counselor if a particular service exists. It could save you time, effort, and, in many cases, money. In Figure 4.4, conduct your own campus orientation.

CREATING A COMMUNITY AS A COMMUTER STUDENT

How Can I Avoid the "Drive By" College Experience?

Going to a career college has countless advantages. Smaller classes and more personalized attention can be life-altering as you begin your studies. However, one of the biggest complaints among students and faculty is the lack of student involvement on a commuter campus—a campus that does not offer student housing. When students do not live on campus, they tend to go to class, maybe spend some time in the library or computer center, grab a bite to eat, and then leave. You need to know that there is so much more available to you and so much more you could create to enhance your learning experience.

Check out the number of clubs, organizations, and activities available on your campus. From writing for the campus newsletter to joining the student chapter of the National Nursing Association, your career college experience is, in a large part, going to be what you make of it. Take a moment, go to your institution's website, and select at least three clubs, organizations, pre-professional associations, and/or activities that you might enjoy participating in. If there are none listed that interest you, list three that you would consider starting.

> *"If you're not actively involved in getting what you want, then you don't really want it."*
> —Peter McWilliams

1. _____

2. _____

3. _____

YOUR ADVISOR/COUNSELOR RELATIONSHIPS

May I Give You a Piece of Advice?

Your academic advisor can be enormously helpful to you throughout your college career. An advisor is usually assigned to you, although a few colleges will allow you to select your own advisor. Your advisor will help you select courses for the completion of your degree. However, you are the person most responsible for registering for classes that will count toward graduation.

Figure 4.4   Campus/Community Success Centers

CAMPUS/ COMMUNITY SERVICE	HOW IT CAN HELP YOU	PHONE NUMBER AND LOCATION
Academic advisement centers	Assists in choosing classes for each semester and offers career assessments and advice on careers.	
Computer labs	Offers students the use of e-mail, Internet services, and other online applications, usually free of charge.	
Writing centers	Offers assistance with your writing skills. Staff will not rewrite your paper for you, but they can give you advice on how to strengthen your project.	
Math centers	Offers help with math problems, one-on-one or group tutoring, and study sessions.	
Tutoring or mastery learning centers	Offers assistance in almost any subject matter. Many colleges offer this service free of charge (or for a very nominal fee).	
Language labs	Offers assistance with international languages or sign language.	
Libraries	Can be the hub of your learning experience, from printed materials to Internet usage to computer-assisted tutorials. Your library and librarians are vital to helping you succeed in your classes and become information literate.	
Veteran affairs	Offers assistance to veterans, especially with government paperwork and financial aid.	
Health services	Offers student services for physical and mental health, complete with a nurse or physician's assistant.	
International student services	Assists international students with admissions, housing, cultural adjustment, and language barriers.	
Minority student services	Offers services and programming for minority students on campus.	
Financial aid office	Assists students with federal, state, and local paperwork to apply for financial aid and scholarships. They are especially helpful in assisting with your FAFSA form each year.	
Student activities	Offers a wide variety of programming in social and cultural activities.	
Disabled student services	Offers services for students with disabilities on campus. If you have a documented disability, colleges and universities across the United States are required by law to offer you "reasonable accommodations" to ensure your success (Americans with Disabilities Act, Sec. 504). Some of these accommodations include handicapped parking, special testing centers, extended time on tests and timed projects, textbook translations and conversions, interpreters, note-taking services, and TTY/TDD services.	

BLOOM LEVEL 1

You should know as much as your advisor about your degree. Even though your advisor knows a great deal of information, everyone can make a mistake, so you should check to be sure you have been advised properly and that you are progressing toward graduation.

If you do not know why you have to take certain courses or in what sequence courses should be taken, don't leave your advisor's office until you find out. Lack of understanding of

BRING the *Change*

TIPS FOR PERSONAL SUCCESS

Consider the following tips for making the most of your relationships with professors, advisors, and counselors:

- Make an effort to get to get to know your instructor, advisor, or counselor on a personal basis. Don't avoid him or her.
- When you visit your instructor, advisor, or counselor, have a prepared list of questions ready to ask him or her.
- Volunteer for projects that allow you to work closely with your instructor, advisor, or counselor.

Now, it is your turn. Create a list of at least three more tips that you would offer a fellow classmate to assist him or her in building a positive relationship with professors, advisors, and counselors.

1. _____
   _____
   _____

2. _____
   _____

3. _____
   _____

your course sequence, your college catalog, or the requirements for graduation could mean the difference between a four-year degree, a five-year degree, or no college degree at all.

Academic advisors are not usually psychological counselors. They are assigned to assist students in completing their academic programs of study. They may offer advice on personal or career matters, but they may not be trained to assist with psychological and emotional matters. However, if you are having problems not related to your academic studies, your academic advisor may be able to direct you to the professional on campus who can best help you address certain issues and problems. Your academic advisor may be the first person to contact in times of crisis.

DEVELOPMENTAL/ REMEDIAL CLASSES

Why Is It Important to Get the Basics First?

Yes, you may need to take a developmental or remedial class. "What is that?" you may ask. A class in developmental/ remedial education offers basic skills in areas such as math, English, vocabulary, and spelling. Most students who take these classes are directed into them by the institution's placement test. It is true that most of these classes do not

Patrick White/Merrill

Do you think establishing a positive relationship with your advisor or counselor is really all that important? Why or why not?

> *"It is better to take many small steps in the right direction than to make a great leap forward only to stumble backward."*
> —Chinese Proverb

carry academic credit, do not count toward graduation, and still cost the same amount as "credit" classes. Because of this, many students try very hard to avoid these classes. This can be a huge mistake on your part. If you really need developmental classes, they will provide a foundation for you that will make the rest of your college career much easier and more successful.

If you tested and placed in a developmental English or math class, *take it!* The assessments were put into place for your well-being, not to punish you. College-level English and math classes are difficult, and if you do not know the basics, you will not do well in these and many other classes. For example, many college texts are written on the thirteenth- and fourteenth-grade levels. If you are reading and spelling on the seventh- or even tenth-grade level, you're going to be in trouble. Therefore, do yourself a favor and take the class into which you placed. You'll save yourself money, time, and a great deal of heartache! Trust us on this one.

HOW TO CALCULATE YOUR GRADE POINT AVERAGE

Does 1 + 1 Really = 2?

The grade point average (GPA) is the numerical grading system used by almost every institution in the nation. GPA determines if a student is eligible for continued enrollment, financial aid, or honors. Most colleges operate under a 4.0 system. This means that:

Each A earned is worth 4 quality points
Each B is worth 3 points
Each C is worth 2 points
Each D is worth 1 point
Each F is worth 0 points

For each course, the number of quality points earned is multiplied by the number of credit hours carried by the course. For example, suppose you are taking:

English 101 for 3 semester hours of credit earning an A ($3 \times 4 = 12$)
Speech 101 for 3 semester hours of credit earning a C ($3 \times 2 = 6$)
History 201 for 3 semester hours of credit earning a B ($3 \times 3 = 9$)
Psychology 101 for 3 semester hours of credit earning a D ($3 \times 1 = 3$)
Spanish 112 for 4 semester hours of credit earning a B ($4 \times 3 = 12$)

Then you are enrolled for 16 hours of academic credit and earned 42 quality points. Examine Figure 4.5 to see an example of this GPA calculation. In Figure 4.6, you will calculate a GPA.

GOING BACK TO COLLEGE AS AN ADULT STUDENT

Is Learning Now Really So Different Than When I Was Younger?

Surprisingly, yes. But that is not a bad thing. Learning as an adult can certainly have its challenges, such as finding child care, tending to an elderly parent, working full-time, managing a household, juggling self-esteem issues and time management constraints, and trying to maintain healthy relationships. Take heart, however, because you are not alone. The ERIC

Figure 4.5   Calculating a GPA

	GRADE	SEMESTER CREDIT		QUALITY POINTS		TOTAL POINTS
ENG 101	A	3 hours	×	4	=	12 points
SPC 101	C	3 hours	×	2	=	6 points
HIT 201	B	3 hours	×	3	=	9 points
PSY 101	D	3 hours	×	1	=	3 points
SPN 112	B	4 hours	×	3	=	12 points
		16 hours				42 total points

42 total points divided by 16 semester hours equals a GPA of 2.62 (or C+ average).

Figure 4.6   Give It a Try—Calculating Bennie's GPA

Using the information provided below, calculate Bennie's GPA.

BLOOM LEVEL 3

English 101	3 credits	Grade = A	Quality Points _____	Total _____
Chemistry 210	3 credits	Grade = C	Quality Points _____	Total _____
Chem Lab 100	1 credit	Grade = A	Quality Points _____	Total _____
Math 110	4 credits	Grade = B	Quality Points _____	Total _____
Med. Term 101	3 credits	Grade = D	Quality Points _____	Total _____
Speech 101	3 credits	Grade = B	Quality Points _____	Total _____
Total	_____ credits		Quality Points _____	Total _____

Bennie's Grade Point Average = _____

Digest (2010) suggests that almost 50 percent of today's college students are classified as adult or nontraditional. Learning as an adult can also have many advantages, such as:

■ More focus, drive, and motivation

■ Increased career focus

■ Enhanced world and life experiences

■ Workplace skills and experiences

As someone who may be returning to school after a break of a few years or 30 years, keep the following tips in mind as you begin your incredible journey:

■ Use your whole institution: Tutorial services, career counseling, library, computer centers, student activities, math and language labs. You paid for these services; don't let them to go waste.

■ Quickly discover your learning style, dominant intelligence, and personality type so that you can work to adapt your learning style to various teaching styles. Basically, you will need to learn how to process information in a timely, accurate, and compelling way.

from ORDINARY to Extraordinary

Dino J. Gonzalez, M.D.
Board-Certified Internal Medicine and
AAHIVM Certified HIV Specialist
University Medical Center Wellness Center, Las Vegas, Nevada

CAN ONE person make a difference in your life? Can one person change the course of your destiny? The answer is yes! Most definitely, yes! The person who altered the course of my future was my third-grade teacher, Mrs. Allison. She was a strong African American lady who pushed us to do our best and would not let us fail. She was hard and demanded the best from us, but she was fair and an awesome teacher. She made us bring a toothbrush from home so that we could brush our teeth after lunch. She corrected our grammar and let us know that "street English" would not fly in her class-room. She even made us do Jazzercise after lunch to teach us how to take care of our bodies. I was lucky to be under her tutelage again in the fifth grade.

Why was she so dynamic? Why did she mean so much to my life? Well, I had always been a good student in school, earning mostly A's. However, my home life was another story. I was born in 1970 in a HUD housing project in Las Vegas, Nevada, in the gang-infested 28th Street area. My mother, two brothers, and I lived in poverty. By the time I was three, my mother was bedridden and on disability due to chronic obstructive pulmonary disease, caused by a three-pack-a-day smoking habit. We were on welfare, food stamps, and the free lunch program.

As it turned out, my father never married my mother or helped support us because he was already married to another woman with children of their own. My mother did not know this until after my birth. So basically, we were on our own. Often, I felt alone in my community because I looked different. My father was Hispanic, but my mother was a blond, light-skinned Norwegian. I was not brown. I was not

- Don't be afraid of technology. You won't "blow up" the computer or the lab, and there are people on campus to help you with your technological needs. Technology is now going to be a major part of your life.

- *Never* be afraid to ask for help from your instructors, staff members, and fellow students.

- Don't let your feelings and emotions ruin your future. Yes, you may be challenged, befuddled, afraid, and even intimidated. Everyone is, regardless of age. Don't let one instructor or one experience strip you of your dreams.

- **Learn to delegate.** It is of utmost importance that students with jobs, families, re-sponsibilities, and relationships learn to let others do some of the work that you may have been doing for years. Delegate. Delegate. Delegate.

- Don't let the "process" ruin your dreams. Yes, there may be times when you simply don't understand why you have to take certain classes or complete certain projects. The process is a means to an end and if you use the process well, you'll learn a great deal. Yes, you have real-world experiences, but you can still learn many valuable things from your instructors, peers, and surroundings.

white. I felt like I did not have a real place in my community or in school. Mrs. Allison helped change all of that.

Because of her and a few close friends, I began to see the positive aspect of school and getting an education. I managed to stay away from the heavy gang influence that had engulfed my brothers. By the time I began high school, one of my brothers was already in prison because of drugs and gang activity. Because of Mrs. Allison's influence, I began to surround myself with people who were positive and worked hard. I wanted to be around people who wanted something—who had a more visionary view of the world than I had.

I was born . . . in a HUD housing project in Las Vegas, Nevada, in the gang-infested 28th Street area.

The harder I worked and studied, the better I did. I excelled in junior high and high school, and by the time I graduated, I did so with honors. I became the first person in my family to attend college. I was offered four scholarships, and they paid for everything, even giving me some spare money to live on. I had been working anywhere from 20 to 30 hours per week since I was 14 years old, but I continued to work full-time while attending college.

I had always loved science and the study of the human body, so I decided to major in chemistry and education. I began to develop a keen interest in infectious diseases and viruses. By the time I was a junior in college, I had decided to become a doctor, so I dropped my education major and focused on biology. After graduation, I applied to medical school and was accepted into the University of Nevada School of Medicine. I completed my studies, did a three-year residency, and decided to open my own practice. I became board certified in internal medicine as an HIV specialist. Six years later, my practice is hugely successful and I enjoy days filled with helping people maintain or regain their health. My dream of doing something real and helping others is now an everyday occurrence in my life.

My advice to you as a first-year college student is this: You have the power to make your dreams come true. YOU can CHANGE your life if you truly know what you want and do the work that comes with making dreams come true. Surround yourself with upbeat, positive, smart, giving, open-minded people from whom you can learn and grow. Mrs. Allison was my inspiration. Yours is out there, too.

EXTRAORDINARY REFLECTION

Read the following statement and respond in your online journal or class notebook.

Dr. Gonzalez talks about his teacher, Mrs. Allison, and how she challenged him and changed his life. What teacher(s) can you think of that have dramatically altered the course of your life?

PLANNING FOR THE NEXT STEP

What Do I Need to Do Now to Prepare for a Successful Second Term and Beyond?

You might say—and rightfully so—"I'm still trying to get through my first term. I don't have time to think beyond this." But it is never too early to plan for the future, for your next step. It is advisable to set aside some time to think about what comes next and begin preparing to take the steps to make your second term a success.

"You are the way you are because that's the way you want to be. If you really want to be any different, you will be in the process of changing right now."
—Fred Smith

Who Do You Think You Are?

This may sound strange, but the first step in successfully transitioning to anything, including your second term, is to get your head straight. Just who do you think you are, anyway? What

Successful Decisions

AN ACTIVITY FOR CRITICAL REFLECTION

JoAnne was a very shy lady who had been out of school for 27 years. When she entered her first class, she was stunned to see so many younger people and to learn that everyone seemed to have more in-depth computer skills than she did.

Horrified that her first assignment was to include a chart created in Microsoft Excel, she thought about dropping the class. "How am I going to ever learn how to turn data into a chart and insert it into a document by next week?" she thought. She even heard a classmate grumbling about dropping the class, too. Determined that she was not going to be beaten, JoAnne decided to go to the computer lab and ask

for help. Within an hour, she had learned how to make a simple chart and paste it into a document.

In your own words, what advice would you give to someone who is nervous about being in school (or back in school)? List at least two things that your classmate could do to ensure his or her success.

1. _____

_____

2. _____

_____

makes you think you can make it through your degree program? Why do you deserve to take this step, and then the next one, and so on? Any time you start to do something new, you are most likely plagued with childhood fears. You might start doubting yourself and second guessing your decisions. You might say to yourself, "I'm not smart enough to get a degree or certificate." The antidote to these kinds of deep-seated fears is to think of positive outcomes that are the opposite of the fears you are having. When doubts and fears creep into your mind, you should immediately combat this two-headed monster with a positive thought. Who do you think you are? You are a unique person who has special gifts and talents, and your time has come. Now, grab this opportunity, get ready to be successful, and plunge in without looking back. And remember, for every transition you face from now on, challenges may occur, but you have the capacity to succeed.

What qualities do nontraditional students bring to the college setting?

iStockPhoto

Can I Make It to My Second Term?

The following is a list of steps that will help you transition successfully to your second term and beyond. Put them into practice and feel the power of knowing you are ready and prepared.

BEGIN WITH THE END IN MIND. Think about how happy you will be when you finish your term and you are about to go on to your next term or pursue a job that you really want. All the way through this venture—and any venture—work hard today, but focus on the end result and enjoy the great opportunity that you have to learn and grow.

FORMULATE A CLEAR VISION ABOUT WHAT YOU WANT YOUR LIFE TO BE. This may not happen overnight, or even in a few weeks or months, but you should begin embracing certain thoughts, ideas, and pictures of what you want your life to be. Having a visual picture of what you want actually helps you move toward it. Each transition can be looked at as another step toward getting to this beautiful vision you have created in your head.

GET IN TOUCH WITH YOUR INNER FEELINGS ABOUT SCHOOL, WORK, FAMILY, AND COMMUNITY.   You will most likely never have another time when you will be as free to focus on yourself as you do right now. Even if you have a family and children, you are free to focus on you while you are in class and perhaps in between some classes. Because you are a commuting student, you will have time to think about the next step in your life as you go back and forth to school and work.

BEWARE OF THE "SECOND TERM SLUMP."   Although it is hard to pinpoint exactly what the "second term slump" really is, continuing students often find themselves confused about what they want to do, stressed because of hard decisions that need to be made, depressed because they are getting less attention in college than they did in high school, or simply tired from working, trying to spend time with a family, and keeping good grades all at the same time. This condition might invade your space as early, so be prepared to combat it. Don't wait until it is too late! Some ways to deal with the "second term slump" include the following:

- Interact with faculty and advisors and try to make a strong connection with at least one of them.

- Try to make connections with at least one or two fellow students with whom you have something in common.

- Realize that you may become less motivated and that refocusing on your purpose can help you get back on track.

- Get help as quickly as you can if you are not doing well in a particular subject.

- Talk to the instructor, hire a tutor, start a study group, or connect with a study partner.

PERSISTING FOR YOUR FUTURE

Won't You Stay for a While?

It is estimated 30 percent of college students leave during the first year and that nearly 50 percent of the people who begin college never complete their degrees (Department of Education, 2008). The age-old "scare tactic" for first-year students—"Look to your left; look to your right. One of those people will not graduate with you"—is not far from the truth. But the good news (actually, the great news) is that you do not have to become a statistic. You do not have to drop out of classes or college. You don't have to be the one who leaves. You have the power to earn your degree. Sure, you may have some catching up to do or face a few challenges, but the beauty of college is that if you want help, you can get help.

> "Striving for success without hard work is like trying to harvest where you have not planted."
>
> —David Bly

Below, you will find some powerful, helpful tips for persisting at your institution. Using even a few of them can increase your chances of obtaining your degree or certificate. Using all of them virtually assures it!

- Visit your advisor or counselor frequently and establish a relationship with him or her. Take his or her advice. Ask him or her questions. Use him or her as a mentor.

- Register for the classes in which you place when you were tested. It is unwise to register for Math 110 if you placed in Math 090 or English 101 if you placed in English 095. It will only cost you money, heartache, time, and possibly a low GPA.

- Make use of every academic service that you need, from tutoring sessions to writing centers; these are essential tools to your success.

- Work hard to learn and understand your learning style. This can help you in every class in which you enroll.

- Take steps to develop a sense of community. Get to know a few people on campus such as special faculty members and other students—people to whom you can turn for help.

- Join a club or organization. Research proves that students who are connected to the campus through activities drop out less.

- Concentrate on setting realistic, achievable goals. Visualize your goals. Write them down. Find a picture that represents your goal and post it so that you can see your goal every day.

- Work hard to develop and maintain a sense of self-esteem and self-respect. The better you feel about yourself, the more likely you will reach your goals.

- Learn to budget your time as wisely as you budget your money. You've made a commitment to college and it will take a commitment of time to bring your degree to fruition.

- If you have trouble with an instructor, don't let it fester. Make an appointment to speak with the instructor and work through the problem.

- If you feel your instructor doesn't care, it may be true. Some don't. This is where you have to apply the art of self-management.

- Find some type of strong, internal motivation to sustain you through the tough times—and there will be tough times.

- Focus on the future. Yes, you're taking many classes at one time while your friends are off partying, but in a few years, you'll have something that no party could ever offer, and something that no one can ever take away—your very own degree.

- Move beyond mediocrity. Everyone can be average. If getting a degree were easy, everybody would have one. You will need to learn to bring the best of yourself to each class.

- Focus on your career choice. Can you do what you want to do without a degree or certificate? That is perhaps the most important question when it comes to persistence. Can you have what you want, do what you want, or be who you want to be without this degree?

We wish you every success imaginable. Use us as resources, contact us, ask us questions, trust us, visit us, and allow us to help you help yourself.

"There is no secret to success. It is the result of preparation, hard work, and learning from failure."

—General Colin Powell

REFLECTIONS ON PERSISTENCE AND SELF-RESPONSIBILITY

Higher education is an exciting and wonderful place. You're meeting new people, being exposed to innovative ideas, and learning new ideas. There has never been a time when the old saying "knowledge is power" is more true. By participating in your own learning, engaging in the art of self-management, and taking initiative to learn about your institution, you are avoiding mistakes that could potentially cost you your education. Good for you!

Simply taking the time to familiarize yourself with the workings of your institution can eliminate many of the hassles that first-year students face. By doing this, you can enjoy your experience with more energy, excitement, and optimism. As you continue on in the semester and work toward self-management, consider the following ideas:

- Determine what it is going to take for you to persist and succeed at your institution.
- Practice self-responsibility.
- Guard your ethics and integrity and use civility and personal decorum.
- Know the policies and rules of your institution.
- Establish a relationship with your instructors, advisors, and counselors.
- Join a club or organization and get involved.
- Determine if you have the time to take an online class.
- Make use of student services.

Practicing self-management can help you not only in your classes but also as you enter the work of work. Strive to become a person who is accountable and responsible for his or her own life and learning.

DISCOVERING YOUR CAMPUS RESOURCES

Utilizes level 1 of the taxonomy

Each chapter-end assessment is based on Bloom's Taxonomy of Learning. See pages xxvi–xxviii in the front of this book for a quick review.

Process: Now that you have discovered more about your campus, professors, and services available, complete the following Identification and Scavenger Hunt.

QUESTION	ANSWER	LOCATION	PHONE NUMBER
If you happen to fail a test, where could you go at your institution to find assistance?			
If you are having trouble writing a paper or completing a written project, where could you go at your institution to get assistance before you turn the paper in?			
Where can you go to find out the names and meeting times of clubs and organizations at your institution?			
If you need to speak to someone about a personal health issue, stress, or overwhelming anxiety, where could you go at your institution or in the community to get help?			
What should you do if you discovered that someone broke into your car while you were in class?			
What office at your institution can help you if you're having doubts about your major or what you want to do for a career?			
Who is your advisor or counselor?			
Where is the first place you could go to at your institution to speak with someone about the technical requirements for an online class?			
Where could you look to read more about the penalties for academic dishonesty (cheating) at your institution?			

SQ3R MASTERY STUDY SHEET

EXAMPLE QUESTION *(from page 86)*
Why is it important to understand your institution's policies?

ANSWER:

EXAMPLE QUESTION *(from page 93)*
How can you avoid the "drive by" college experience?

ANSWER:

AUTHOR QUESTION *(from page 88)*
List three tips for succeeding in a class where the instructor and you do not have the same first language.

ANSWER:

AUTHOR QUESTION *(from page 89)*
Why are civility and personal decorum important in a college classroom?

ANSWER:

AUTHOR QUESTION *(from page 93)*
How can you get to know your advisor or counselor better?

ANSWER:

AUTHOR QUESTION *(from page 100)*
Why is it important to begin with the end in mind?

ANSWER:

AUTHOR QUESTION *(from page 101)*
Discuss three tips for persisting in college.

ANSWER:

YOUR QUESTION *(from page _____)*

ANSWER:

YOUR QUESTION *(from page _____)*

ANSWER:

YOUR QUESTION *(from page _____)*

ANSWER:

YOUR QUESTION *(from page _____)*

ANSWER:

YOUR QUESTION *(from page _____)*

ANSWER:

Finally, after answering these questions, recite in your mind the major points in covered here. Consider the following general questions to help you master this material.

- What was it about?
- What does it mean?
- What was the most important thing you learned? Why?
- What were the key points to remember?

chapter five

CONNECT

CONNECTING WITH TECHNOLOGY, RESEARCH, AND INFORMATION LITERACY

"It is so much easier to look for more and more information than to sit back and think about how it fits together."—Joanne Cantor

Why read this chapter?

Because you'll learn:

- How technology can assist you in all classes
- How to search a topic more easily and effectively
- The rules of the Internet (netiquette)

Because you'll be able to:

- Use the steps in the information literacy process to become a better student
- Identify a variety of search engines and various types of educational technology
- Protect your privacy online

Scan and QUESTION

Take a few moments, **scan this chapter,** and on page 134, write **five of your own questions** that you think will be important to your mastery of this material. You will also find five questions listed from your authors.

Example:

- ☑ **Why is it important to know the different types of technology used in education?**
  (from page 112)

- ☑ **What is information literacy?**
  (from page 122)

MyStudentSuccessLab

MyStudentSuccessLab (www.mystudentsuccesslab.com) is an online solution designed to help you "Start strong, Finish stronger" by building skills for ongoing personal and professional development.

How
COLLEGE CHANGED MY LIFE

Name:	William Paddock
Institution:	Graduate! Louisville Technical Institute, Louisville, Kentucky
Age:	24
Major:	Network Administration and Information Security
Career:	IT Security Specialist

I decided to go to college immediately after high school. I had three choices: go to college, get a job, or join the military. I knew that I wanted to work with computers and networks and quickly learned that to be taken seriously, I would have to have a degree. I also learned that every little detail in class or from my readings was important. Often, I've found what may seem to be an obscure or unimportant detail has come back to haunt me later on certification exams, which is why it's important to be able to soak in as much information as possible.

My greatest challenge—and success—at LTI was getting my degree and certifications. These achievements show employers that I am serious about my work and that I achieved top standing in my field. You can't really study for Microsoft Certification; you just have to know it. You have to have the knowledge under your belt from years of practice, trial and error, and use. I passed the Microsoft Certification and also received my A+ and Security Plus Certifications and became a Security Certified Network Architect (SCNA). All of this was possible because I took every class, every opportunity, every assignment, and every reading seriously.

The biggest and most important lesson that I have learned from college is that completing your degree does not complete your learning—especially in a field such as information technology. In this field, and many others, learning never stops. If you stop learning, you stop growing, and then no one will hire you. You have to continually upgrade your knowledge base. I also learned how to deal with the massive amounts of change in my field. If I had not done this, I would not have survived.

The most important thing that my education did for me was to allow me to work in the field that I love. I studied on my own, but I also took my instructors seriously and embraced what they had to offer. I would offer you this advice: take every opportunity to learn from people who are in your field of study. Always be humble and honest. There is no need to have a degree or a national certification if you cheated to get it. You will get hurt and others will too. Don't cheat yourself out of the knowledge that can come from being open, honest, and willing to take what others have to offer. Work hard, study hard, do your best, and in the end, you'll be better off for it.

THINK a b o u t it

1. William suggests that honesty is important. How will honesty benefit you in your chosen field?

2. William received several national certifications in addition to his degree. What additional training do you think you will need to be successful in your field? Why?

How much technology is too much?

iStockPhoto

THE FAST, EVER-CHANGING FACE OF TECHNOLOGY

Can Anyone Keep Up?

You've probably heard the old expression "It's like a train wreck . . . you can't look but you can't look away." Some people view today's technological changes and advances as something you can't look at, but if you look away for even a moment, you're lost. Between Twitter, Jing, Bing, VoiceThread, Facebook, Blackboard, Hulu, YouTube, and countless other programs and services, it is vital that you know the basics of these tools, as your instructors may use them in class or require you to use them beyond the class-room. At the very least, it is important to know they exist and how to find help in using these new, ever-changing learning approaches.

> "In less than three years, social media has become the most popular activity on the web."
>
> —Erik Qualman

In today's technology-driven education environment, colleges have classes, entire degrees, schedules, course listings, and other pertinent information and programs online. Office hours with faculty members may be held via a learning management program, Skype, or a social networking tool. Cooperative learning activities are held by programs such as WebEx, GoTo-Meeting, or Elluminate. Often, students are required to research or network with people outside their own institution—many times internationally. We have truly become a global society through technology. This is one reason why we all need to learn as much about new and emerging technologies as possible. Another monumental reason to learn as much about technology as possible is the fact that almost any career you pursue will be affected by the global economy, and the competition is brutal.

You may be saying, "I'm online all the time—I Facebook my friends, use Skype, e-mail my instructors, and research topics for papers and speeches." All of this is great and we encourage you to use the technology that will help you build relationships, connect with others, and continue learning. However, if you are honest with yourself, you may have to admit that much of your time online is spent on activities that do not use these tools to your educational advantage. You may also have to admit that sometimes, you are overwhelmed by the amount of information available on one topic. This chapter will help you learn the many technological tools to available to assist you in becoming a better student, researcher, writer, and employee in the twenty-first century.

SPENDING TIME ONLINE

Are You Searching, Perching, or Lurking?

You get online with a purpose, and before you know it, hours have passed and you find that you've piddled and diddled and nothing has been accomplished. This is not an uncommon occurrence. You may have had the best of intentions to go online and work or research a project, but before you know it, you've checked e-mail, watched a YouTube video, IMed three friends, Facebooked five friends, and checked your tweets. This may not be the best use of your time.

How can you spend quality time online? Consider the following tips when going online to work or complete a school assignment:

- Use your favorite e-tools (Twitter, Facebook, etc.) as a reward for getting your work done. This is a strong time management tool. Work first, then socialize and play.

- Have a plan and a timeline before you go online. If you have a topic to research, allow yourself enough time to do your work, check your messages, and network with friends later.

- When going online, do not sign into Facebook or Twitter until you have completed your work. Don't tempt yourself.

- Treat your time online as you would treat your time at work. Divide your time into work time and break time, putting your break time at the end.

- Allow yourself enough time during the day to do all of the things online that you love to do, such as network, search iTunes or Rhapsody, Google, or play games. There is nothing wrong with enjoying technology if your other work has been completed.

- Let your e-friends know when you'll be online for work and when you'll be online for socializing. Don't cross or blur the lines.

EVALUATING YOUR TECHNOLOGY SKILLS

Do I Really Need to Know Them All?

One of the most wonderful things about the world of technology is that if you have never heard of a program or don't know how to use a certain application, there is immediate, useful help online with sites such as www.butterscotch.com and www.youtube.com. If you don't know how to create a movie using Camtasia, all you have to do is go to YouTube and you can find a tutorial to assist you. If you don't know what Blackboard Course Management System is or how to use it for class, you can simply go to Google and type in "Blackboard Learning" to read about the program and take a brief demo tutorial. This is the beauty of technology. The curse? It seems to change every day. Learning to keep up with the latest trends and how to apply these to your educational process is imperative. Learning the programs, applications, and terminology is also important.

> *"Technology makes it possible for people to gain control over everything, except over technology."*
> —John Tutor

Figure 5.1 will detail some of the major programs and applications used in today's higher education setting. You may not be required to use them all, but it will be helpful to familiarize yourself with some different applications and their websites in case the need arises.

BLOOM LEVEL 3

LEARNING THE LANGUAGE OF TECHNOLOGY

What Is a Worm and Why Is It in My Computer?

As you begin to familiarize yourself with the many aspects of computer literacy, there may be terms that pop up that you have not heard before. The list of terms defined in Figure 5.2 will help you as you discover more about the world of technology and computer literacy.

BLOOM LEVEL 5

Figure 5.1 Types of Technology in Education

DESCRIPTION	PROGRAM	WEBSITE	HOW COULD YOU USE THIS PROGRAM TO HELP WITH A CLASS OR ASSIGNMENT?
Software Programs Used for word processing and creating presentations, charts, and graphs on PCs and Macs	Microsoft Office (Word, Excel, PowerPoint) Prezi Pages for Mac Google Docs	www.office.microsoft.com www.prezi.com www.apple.com/iwork/pages www.docs.google.com	
Learning Management Systems Used to offer classes and training throughout higher education and business	Blackboard Moodlerooms Elluminate Desire2Learn Instructure	www.blackboard.com www.moodlerooms.com www.pearsonmylabandmastering.com www.desire2learn.com www.instructure.com	
Group Communication Tools Used to communicate in groups and share information on your computer screen with others around the world	Twitter VoiceThread GoToMeeting WebEx	www.twitter.com www.voicethread.com www.gotomeeting.com www.webex.com	
Social Networking/Sharing Sites Used to network with business professionals who may help you find employment, chat with and make friends, keep in touch, and post the latest news and photos	Facebook Twitter LinkedIn	www.facebook.com www.twitter.com www.linkedin.com	
Photo/Video Building and Viewing Used to create and/or view videos and share them with friends or colleagues	Jing YouTube Hulu Flickr Camtasia	www.jingproject.com www.youtube.com www.hulu.com www.flickr.com www.techsmith.com	
Search/Research Engines Used to research topics of interest or that have been assigned by your professor; it is wise to use a variety of these sites instead of relying on just one	Google Dogpile Yahoo Ask Lycos Wikipedia Bing AltaVista	www.google.com www.dogpile.com www.yahoo.com www.ask.com www.lycos.com www.wikipedia.com www.bing.com www.altavista.com	
Tools to Help You Learn to Use New Technology Offer easy-to-use video tutorials to help you use some of the technologies that may be required of you in the classroom	YouTube eHow Butterscotch	www.youtube.com www.ehow.com www.butterscotch.com	

DESCRIPTION	PROGRAM	WEBSITE	HOW COULD YOU USE THIS PROGRAM TO HELP WITH A CLASS OR ASSIGNMENT?
Document-Sharing Tools Used to share your word processing documents with others for additions, comments, and editing	PBWorks Google Docs WorkZone WorkShare	www.pbworks.com www.docs.google.com www.workzone.com www.workshare.com	
Digital Note-Taking Systems Used to take notes online	MyNoteIt Yahoo! Notes Notefish Ubernote Springnote	www.mynoteit.com www.widgets.yahoo.com /widgets/notes www.notefish.com www.ubernote.com www.springnote.com	

Figure 5.2   **The Techno-pedia**

Bookmarks	These allow you to tag popular sites so that you can easily access them again—usually with one click.
Cookie	This term refers to data that is sent to your computer by a company's computer to monitor your actions while on its site. Cookies remember your log-in and password information and track what you viewed or purchased the last time you visited that site.
Dot com	.com is the most common ending for Internet addresses. However, there are many others. The following will help you direct your Internet searches:

- ■ .com: Used to search commercial, for-profit businesses
- ■ .edu: Used to search educational institutions, colleges, universities
- ■ .net: Used by Internet service providers
- ■ .gov: Used to search documents within the United States government
- ■ .org: Used to search non-profit organizations
- ■ .mil: Used to search information from the United States military
- ■ .us: Used to search any organization in specific countries such as United States (.us), United Kingdom (.uk), France (.fr), Sweden (.se), and Germany (.de)

Hacker	A modern-day bank robber. This is a person who electronically breaks into your computer and steals your private and sensitive information—often to use for illegal purposes.
HDTV/HDV	High-definition television or high-definition video. They are high-quality, crisp, visually appealing TV or video recordings.
Phishing	A scheme by hackers to acquire your private information such as passwords, log-in codes, and credit card information by using "real" companies' logos in their correspondence. They trick you into updating your information for a company or site your trust, when in actuality, you are directly providing the hacker your information. To avoid phishing schemes, do not click on suspicious links within e-mails, do not provide personal information in any format, and call the company to answer questions asked in the correspondence.

(continued)

Figure 5.2 **The Techno-pedia (continued)**

PDF	The portable document format was created by Adobe as a document-sharing format that is independent of software programs and applications such as Word and PowerPoint.
Podcast	Combines the terms *iPod* and *broadcast* into a single word. It is a video or audio file you can access on your iPhone.
Malware	Malicious software. Malware are programs that are unknowingly placed on your computer to cause technological harm. Common types of malware (viruses) are trojan horses, worms, and spyware that delete files or directory information and cause your computer to function improperly. To avoid them, do not open files from unknown sites and keep your spyware and virus programs up to date.
Right click	Refers to clicking the right button of your mouse to reveal additional menus and pop-ups. A mouse is automatically set to the left click for common tasks.
RTF	Rich text format. RTF was developed by Microsoft as a document file format to make files easier to open in most formats and programs on most computers.
URL	Universal retrieval language. The URL is the Internet address that you type into your search bar, such as www.yahoo.com, www.youtube.com, or www.pearsonhighered.com.
Web 2.0	Web 2.0 is the new age of the Internet. Web 1.0 was created as a one-sided, "you search it; we define it" tool, whereas Web 2.0 is more interactive and includes social media (Facebook, Twitter, etc.), blogs, document sharing, videos, and interactive searches.

USEFUL INTERNET SITES AND SEARCHES

How Can I Find Specific Information?

Often, you may need to find specific information. Perhaps you need to find a map of a specific country, or if a book is in print, or the population of Iowa. Figure 5.3 can help you save a great deal of time. Remember, it is always best to view a number of resources (online and in print) to ensure accuracy and validity of your information.

OR! AND! NOT! QUOTATION!

Why Will These Simple Words Save You Hours of Research Time?

If you are trying to broaden or narrow your search on a specific topic, these simple words or actions, when typed into your search engine, can save you untold time online. Boolean Logic developed the OR, AND, or NOT approach to help direct your search more effectively (Ritchie, 2010). For example, if you are writing a paper or speech on Rosa Parks and the civil rights movement and type *Rosa Parks* into Google, you will get 3,520,000 hits. If you type *civil rights movement* into Google, you will get 4,300,000 hits, for a total of 7,820,000 hits. However, if you type in *Rosa Parks AND the civil rights movement,* you will narrow your search to a total of 478,000 hits. This is still many more articles than any human can digest, but it does cut your search and combines the topics together for you.

Figure 5.3   Information Made Easy

IF YOU NEED TO KNOW:	SEARCH THESE ADDRESSES
How to locate a place or view a map	www.googleearth.com www.mapquest.com
Whether a book is in print	www.amazon.com www.barnesandnoble.com
U.S. and state population, economic, and workforce data	www.census.gov
Information about famous people	www.loc.gov www.who2.com www.biography.com/search
Unbiased information and comparisons of world religions	www.patheos.com
Federal or state legislation	www.thomas.loc.gov www.house.gov www.whpgs.org/f.htm
Magazine and newspaper articles	www.newslink.org www.ehow.com
Information about a specific country	www.infoplease.com www.countryreports.org
Information about careers	www.bls.gov www.careeroverview.com www.occupationalinfo.org
Brief contents and entire scanned books	www.books.google.com www.openlibrary.org
Simple, effective instructional videos on math, history, physics, and finance.	www.khanacademy.org

If you want to search only for Rosa Parks and not the civil rights movement, you should type *Rosa Parks NOT the civil rights movement* into your search engine. This will limit your research to topics only on Rosa Parks and not the civil rights movement. To search for as many articles on both topics as possible, you should type *Rosa Parks OR the civil rights movement* into your search engine. If you want to get the results for an exact topic, put quotation marks around the words, such as "civil rights movement." The search engine will now search those exact words only. This can be helpful when you are looking for ideas rather than exact titles, such as "death of Rosa Parks." This search will only show articles on her death and obituary.

SOCIAL MEDIA FOR EDUCATIONAL PURPOSES

Does It Really Have More Use Than Planning Lunch?

Most educational institutions and businesses are using social networking sites in numerous ways to interact with students and customers. They use these sites to send messages, offer advice, and

from ORDINARY to *Extraordinary*

Luke Bryan
Country Music Singer/Songwriter
2010 Top New Solo Vocalist, Academy of Country Music Awards

BASICALLY, I'M a country boy who grew up in the very small town of Leesburg, Georgia. During high school, I worked on my dad's farm and in his peanut and fertilizer businesses. I played sports and loved everything about outdoors. Because I loved country music, my mother often urged me to belt out George Strait songs over and over while she drove me into town to shop. When I was 14, my parents bought me an Alvarez guitar. By age 15, my father would take me down to a nearby club, Skinner's, where I shared guitar licks and lead vocals with other local country singers.

At age 16, two local songwriters who'd enjoyed some success providing tunes for Nashville artists invited me to join their twice-a-week writing sessions at a local church. By that time, I was leading my own band, playing at Skinner's and various community events.

Encouraged by everyone who heard me play, I planned to move to Nashville after high school graduation. Supported by my family, I was loading my car for the move when tragedy struck. My older brother Chris, one of my biggest supporters and one of my best friends, was killed in an auto accident the day I was to leave town. This was a devastating blow to me that still affects me today. All I wanted to

PHOTO: Kerri Edwards, Red Light Management

do was be close to my family so my plans for Nashville were put on hold.

I continued to devote myself to my music, finding escape and emotional release in my songs. I poured my feelings into my songwriting and, after enrolling at Georgia Southern University, my band and I performed nearly every weekend on campus or at nearby clubs or parties. I eventually recorded an album of 10 songs, nine of which I wrote. I played throughout my college career and was able to pay my way through Georgia Southern University playing and singing country music.

After I graduated from college, I went back home to work for my dad. I did this for a year and a half, but my heart just wasn't in it. By then, I had begun to realize that I was way too passionate about country music to turn it loose without going for it. One day my father took me for a drive. "Look, your heart is in your music," my father told me. "It's what you were meant to do. You either quit this job and move to Nashville, or I'm going to fire you." With the encouragement of my family, I headed for Nashville. My dad agreed to help support me for a year to see if I could make it in the country music business. He said, "You will always wonder if you could have made it, so you need to go try."

deliver positive advertising. We highly recommend that you familiarize yourself with as many social networking sites as possible and become an expert on at least one of them. Once you have mastered the skills needed to navigate the site, list your expertise on your resumé. Regardless of what field you enter today, most employers will be looking for social media experts to help them develop, expand, and connect with their customer base. Information regarding a few of the most popular and widely used social media is provided here.

FACEBOOK. Facebook is one of the most widely used and rapidly growing social media sites in existence. It is used to connect and communicate across social and business lines. Companies

Within two months I had signed a recording contract. I will always be grateful to my parents for their support and encouragement.

Like most new artists, I struggled in the beginning, but I tried to keep a level head and to plug myself into a positive community of singers and performers. I can tell you for sure that who you hang out with has a great impact on who you become. I advise you to surround yourself with people in your field who seem to be moving and shaking. I watched lots of my friends succeed, and this made me feel that I could make it, too. It's easy to get in with the wrong crowd in college or after you graduate, so I highly recommend that you associate with a good group of people who are trying to make something of themselves. My fellow writers and performers had a major impact on my life.

One of the biggest days in my life was signing a contract with Capitol Records. When they offered me a contract, all I could think about was "I've got to call Mama and Daddy." All my dreams and wishes came together right there in that room.

I spent many long hours preparing to tour and sing in front of big crowds. Becoming a recording artist encompasses many hours of hard work, but it has paid off. Capitol Records released my debut album in 2006. Now, I am living my dream! I have been fortunate enough to open for some of the greats in the business, like Kenny Chesney. I can't say that it's been easy breaking into a competitive field; I've worked very hard for many years, but it's all been worth it because I am beginning to see success. I've written several songs that have been well received, including "Good Direc-

> *One of the biggest days of my life was signing a contract with Capitol Records. . . . All my dreams and wishes came together right there in that room.*

tions," which was recorded by Billy Currington and climbed to number one. "Country Man," which I recorded, made the top ten. Another big hit for me was "All My Friends Say." I recently released "We Rode in Trucks" and "Do I." I wrote "Do I" with Lady Antebellum, a trio of popular, well-known country music stars. We were all thrilled when "Do I" went to the top of the charts and stayed there several weeks. Our record company, Capitol Records, gave us a Number One party in Nashville.

I now headline my own shows and my recent album, Tailgates and Tanlines, reached number one on the country music charts. I am very happy when my wife and our two little sons travel with me.

The best advice I can give you is to follow your dreams, do what you love, and trust your instincts. Don't get trapped into doing something you don't love and look forward to every day.

EXTRAORDINARY REFLECTION

Read the following statement and respond in your online journal or class notebook.

Luke mentions that he was encouraged to go after his dream by his family and friends. He also states how important it is to surround yourself with people who are on the move and believe in their dreams. Who supports you and your dreams? How have your family and friends helped you reach your goals thus far?

are using Facebook to promote their products, announce new products, interact with customers, track their customers' buying habits, and recruit and retain employees. "The fastest growing demographic of Facebook users is those twenty-five years and older" (Kabani, 2010). According to Kabani, Facebook is like a coffee shop; it is a great place to strike up a conversation. Research shows that many people use Facebook to share their personal information and identity. You can access Facebook and start your own page at www.facebook.com.

LINKEDIN.   LinkedIn is considered the professionals' site and is described by Kabani (2010) as a "buttoned-down office-networking event. If Facebook is happy hour, LinkedIn is all business,

Successful Decisions

AN ACTIVITY FOR CRITICAL REFLECTION

Anita is returning to school after a 30-year absence. When she was in high school, the biggest piece of technology was the IBM Electric Typewriter and a copy machine. She took typing in high school, but it has been years since she used the skill. She can still type but does so very slowly.

After registering for classes, Anita discovered that two of her instructors require her to access the course material from the learning management system and one instructor requires all students to work in online groups. She is terrified. She has used a computer, but only sparingly. She has a negative attitude about learning to use Facebook or Twitter and sees no point in using this technology for class. She does not have a computer at home, and she does not know if she can catch up with the skills she needs to be successful at her institution.

What suggestions would you make to Anita to help her adjust to the world of technology, social media, and online classes?

1. _____
_____

2. _____
_____

How can social media help you with your current field of study?

iStockPhoto

suit and tie." This is a site that should be treated as strictly business, and is certainly not the place to post unflattering pictures or information that might be damaging to you if a potential or current employer happened to see it. This site usually attracts well-educated people who tend to be more affluent. LinkedIn is a great place to post your resumé, because the people frequenting this site might be searching for good employees. You can post recommendations from references (with their permission, of course) or glowing letters of appreciation from customers. If someone posts a recommendation for you, you will get a message giving you an opportunity to accept or reject the recommendation's posting.

TWITTER. Twitter falls in the category of microblog. A microblog is a brief message (no more than 140 characters long) that typically uses abbreviations or Internet acronyms such as OMG (oh my god) or LOL (laugh out loud) in order to pack more information in a message. Some people are constantly sending "tweets" telling their friends every move they make. As a professional, you need to leave this behavior behind and learn how to use Twitter to deliver time-sensitive information, such as to inform your group about a special event, educational opportunity, or upcoming meeting. Twitter is an excellent way to grab online visibility, and this visibility can be positive or negative depending on your tweets.

GOOGLE +. Google+ is a new social media site competing with Facebook. It is offered by the Google search engine company. This service allows you to link and integrate your Gmail, Google maps, and other Google products into a one-stop shop.

Collaborative Communication Programs

Today many students and employees work in **virtual teams** (people who work together but are not physically located in the same place) and they find collaborative communication programs to be very helpful and effective. While there are several available, we are going to discuss three of the most popular.

WIKIS. A wiki is a webpage that can be viewed and modified by anybody with a web browser and access to the Internet—it might be called a webpage with an edit button. This means that any visitor to the wiki can change its content if they desire, enabling people to collaborate with others online easily. Wikis can be surprisingly robust and open-ended. They can be password protected if desired. Participants can add information to a wiki or edit what someone else has written.

GOOGLE DOCS.   Google Docs is a great tool for virtual teams because it is absolutely free and it enables you to create documents, spreadsheets, presentations, forms, and drawings while working from anywhere around the world simply by accessing the Internet. Some people refer to it as an online alternative to Microsoft Office, which, of course, is not free. You can share documents, presentations, forms, and spreadsheets with anyone you want from within Google Docs itself without manually finding a file and attaching it as an e-mail. It is also easy to download documents to your hard drive if you want to save a document on your computer.

SKYPE.   Skype is another great collaborative program for working, communicating, and celebrating together although users may be miles apart. This program can be used to hold a "face-to-face" video conference between two people, or an audio-only conference between more than two people. You can hold meetings, have a work session, or just visit with friends. The great thing about Skype is that the basic program is free and can be downloaded to your computer from the Internet. For a small fee, you can communicate internationally with friends and virtual team members.

MAXIMIZING THE USE OF TECHNOLOGY

How Can Tech Tools Help with Your Classes?

Regardless of your major, you are probably going to be required to use some type of technology in almost every class you take. From research to editing to communication, the use of technology in today's college classroom is almost inescapable. Consider the core classes found in many colleges, and list at least two ways that technology could help you in each of these classes (Figure 5.4). One example is given to you in each category.

PRIVACY AND SECURITY ISSUES

Did You Know You're a Published Author?

Congratulations! You're an author—that is, if you have ever sent a tweet. As of 2010, the Library of Congress has archived *every tweet* ever sent since Twitter's inception in 2006. If you have ever sent a tweet—good or bad, nice or naughty, serious or silly—you are a part of the Library of Congress. This is just one of the many examples of the lack of privacy on the web. Privacy issues can be monumental obstacles to you now and later in your life. Therefore, it is important that you guard your privacy and watch your online activities. What you post online now in a silly or romantic moment can come back later to cost you that dream job. Be careful what you post online; nothing on the Internet is private. In a world of WikiLeaks, hackers, and savvy researchers, your words and photos are public words and photos.

> "Web 2.0 presents opportunities for people to use your information for unscrupulous purposes such as identity fraud and theft."
> —Andy Pulman

To protect yourself and your online information as much as possible, consider the following tips and suggestions:

- Create a strong, uncommon password for your accounts. Try to use a combination of at least eight letters, numbers, and symbols, such as RO#99@SH.

- Do not share your passwords with anyone—not roommates, not family members, not even your best friends. Relationships change, and you may later regret providing this information.

Figure 5.4   How Can Technology Help?

CORE CLASS	DESCRIBE TWO WAYS TECHNOLOGY CAN HELP YOU BE SUCCESSFUL
English	Example: Research the proper use of a semicolon. 1. 2.
Science (biology, chemistry, physics)	Example: Watch the virtual dissection of a pig for your anatomy class. 1. 2.
International language (Arabic, Spanish, French, Russian)	Example: Initiate a Twitter "conversation" with someone from Russia and ask him or her to converse with you in his or her native language for practice. 1. 2.
Fine arts (art, music, or theater)	Example: Watch a video clip of a Broadway play or dance concert. 1. 2.
Social sciences (psychology, sociology, anthropology)	Example: Research the population trends in Africa, plot them on a map, and distinguish what those trends mean. 1. 2.
Computer science	Example: Research how to create an Excel spreadsheet. 1. 2.
Mathematics	Example: Watch a YouTube video on how to divide fractions and then practice what you have learned. 1. 2.
One class in your major field of study	1. 2.

BLOOM LEVEL 2

- Do not use common events such as your birthday, anniversary, or child's birth as your password.

- Be careful where you post your photo. Even if you post your photo on your personal Facebook page, it can be found by a simple web search.

- Use only secure websites for any type of financial transaction. Look for security seals such as Verisign, Comodo, and GeoTrust. Do *not* use your debit card on-line. If you must purchase from an online site, use credit cards or the payment site PayPal (www. paypal.com).

- Learn how to use online security features and privacy settings. These are offered for your safety and for the protection of your information.

- Don't tell your Facebook or on-line friends that you will not be home. This invites break-ins and burglary at your home.

- Install and run your security and spyware protections at least twice per week.

- Turn off or delete cookies from other sites and retailers.

- Be very wary of anyone asking for personal information to "update their records." It is probably a phishing scheme.

- Teach your children not to provide private information or to go onto unknown sites and rooms.

iStockPhoto

What is the most important thing you can do to avoid identity theft?

RIDIN' HIGH ON THE INFORMATION SUPERHIGHWAY

What Are the Rules of the Road?

Yes, there are rules for proper etiquette in an online class, when texting, IMing, tweeting, or simply conversing with friends. By knowing and applying these simple guidelines, you will be taken more seriously and so will your correspondence. Consider using the following "rules of the road" when sending e-communications.

- Never, ever send an e-mail, IM, tweet or any other type of e-communication that you would not want anyone else to read. ***E-communication is not private,*** especially when sent from a company or work computer. Information is available on the web for a long, long time.

- Avoid language that may come across as angry, mean, insult-ing, or strong. People can't see your face online and may not know you're kidding. If you use all caps, this may come across as angry.

DID YOU *Know?*

MARTIN LUTHER KING JR. was only in his early thirties and the pastor of a small Baptist church in Montgomery, Alabama, when he was thrust into the national spotlight as a leader of protests against segregation.

The movements and marches he led brought significant changes in the fabric of American life through his courage and selfless devotion. He was arrested over twenty times, traveled 6,000,000 miles, and spoke over 2,500 times wherever there was injustice or protest. His ability to prepare and deliver powerful speeches, along with his bravery and personal sacrifice, changed the world.

Martin Luther King and Coretta Scott King had four children, all of whom are involved in different aspects of civil rights. He was awarded the Nobel Peace Prize at the age of 35, the youngest man to ever receive the award.

PHOTO: Benjamin F. Forte/CNP/Newscom

- Use the 24-hour rule when responding to a heated piece of correspondence. Do not respond in anger or fear. Once the "send" button has been pressed, you can't take it back. Use restraint, reread the correspondence, and make your decision once you have cooled off.

- Read your e-mails before you send them. Check for errors in grammar, content, and fact.

- Text language (LOL, OMG, BFF, :-(BTW, FYI) is fine when texting or IMing with your friends, but not for e-mails or class projects and papers. Use it sparingly.

- If possible, let someone read your e-correspondence for accuracy and clarity. If the other person can't understand it, you need to rewrite it.

- When texting, IMing, and e-mailing, consider other people's time and how many pieces of e-correspondence they may get in one day.

- Don't forward e-correspondence that you do not have permission to forward.

- Treat people online with the same courtesy, politeness, and respect you would give them in a face-to-face situation.

- Don't use language you would not want your grandmother to read.

- Don't forward e-mail hoaxes, urban legends, or chain letters; people find them annoying and you may also be forwarding a virus. Anything promising $10 million from an overseas account is a scam, and Bill Gates is not going to give you any of his money for e-mailing your friends—even if your friend's doctor's best friend's mother's lawyer checked it out!

- If you receive an e-mail along with 15 or 20 other people, respond *only* to the person who sent the e-mail unless otherwise advised. Don't hit "reply all."

- Online e-communications, especially e-mails, should contain proper opening and closing salutations, not just content that begins and ends.

By adhering to these online "rules of the road," you will soon find that your online correspondence is more effective.

PRACTICING INFORMATION LITERACY IN THE AGE OF TECHNOLOGY

Why Is It Important to Know How to Sort Through and Evaluate Information?

Anyone—yes, *anyone*—can post information on the Internet. Most information online is not screened for accuracy, judged on truth, or critiqued for its worth. Often, much of what you find online may not even indicate an author's name. Some of it will be accurate and valuable, whereas other pieces will be full of half-truths, downright lies, and false claims. Some information will be legitimate and helpful, and some will be nothing more than a false advertisement to con you into buying something. Some will be unbiased and impartial, and some will be slanted and unbalanced by the person or company from which it was posted. Therefore, it is up to you to learn how to determine the worth, value, and accuracy of the information you find online.

Information literacy includes the skills a person needs to determine what information is needed, where to find it, how much of it is needed for a specific topic, how to analyze and organize it to create the "product," and finally, how to properly cite it. The procedure is that simple and that complex. Information literacy affects all aspects of your college career and will later play a major role in your success in the workplace. You will use information literacy when you write a paper, read an article and evaluate it, listen to presenters and determine if you believe what they are saying, or when preparing and making your own presentation. Information literacy is the cornerstone of an educated mind.

> *"More information, by overwhelming and distracting the brain, can make it harder to tap into just the core information you need."*
>
> *—Eric Kessler*

If you master the processes of information literacy in the digital age, you will gain more control over what you are learning and how you can apply it. You will become more adept at distinguishing facts from untruths while selecting points that support your topic or research problem. Regardless of your major, you cannot escape the need to locate, analyze, apply, and present information in a compelling and logical manner. You will also become a more savvy consumer because you can make informed decisions about shopping, voting, investing, purchasing a home or car, choosing your major, and a host of other important life decisions.

THE INFORMATION LITERACY PROCESS

Can You Hit the Bullseye with D.A.R.T.S.?

Becoming information literate does not just happen by opening a book or using Google. True information literacy (IL) begins by understanding the process of research. This section will help you identify and remember the steps in using IL skills. Using the **D.A.R.T.S. system for information literacy** (Figure 5.5), you can easily remember the steps, use them often, and benefit from their practicality.

Figure 5.5   The D.A.R.T.S. System for Information Literacy

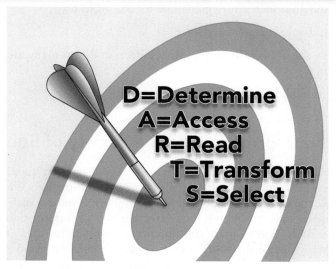

D=Determine
A=Access
R=Read
T=Transform
S=Select

© Robert Sherfield and Patricia Moody

D: Determine the Information You Need by Narrowing Your Topic

Research begins by asking a question. Suppose that you have been assigned a paper or speech and you decide to write or speak on Rosa Parks. You begin the research and type *Rosa Parks* into Google. You get 3,520,000 hits. This is just a few too many articles to read by Monday. However, if you begin with a question in mind, you can narrow your topic and determine what information you need early on.

After some thought, you decide that your research question will be "What was Rosa Parks's role in the civil rights movement?" If you Google this topic, you get 251,000 hits. Still far too many, but 3,269,000 fewer hits than before, and you have a direction to begin your paper. So, the first steps in becoming a more information literate student are to ***identify and narrow your topic*** and ***determine what information is needed on this topic***. You will also need to determine what type of information you need and want to use in your project. Do you want facts, opinions, eyewitness reports, interviews, debates, and/or arguments? Each may provide you with different types of information.

Cyber research can be an amazing tool in your educational pursuit. However, when you are faced with 3,520,000 articles on one topic, it can also become overwhelming. ***Information overload*** can have negative effects on the learning process. Angelika Dimoka, director of the Center for Neural Decision Making at Temple University, suggests that with the vast amounts of information we face in an online search, "the brain's emotion region runs as wild as toddlers on a sugar high" (Begley, 2011). We begin to make stupid mistakes and bad decisions. Our frustration and anxiety levels also soar. Too much information can lead to ***information paralysis***. This basically means that you have so much information that you don't know what to do with it—so you do nothing.

> "The booming science of decision making has shown that more information can lead to objectively poorer choices, and to choices that people come to regret."
> —A. Dimoka

The new field of decision-making research also suggests that when we are faced with too much information and too many decisions, we tend to make no decision at all. When the amount of information coming at us is coupled with the speed at which it comes, this can lead to devastating results. According to Sharon Begley in her article "I Can't Think" (2011), when faced with too much information, "we sacrifice accuracy and thoughtfulness to the false god of immediacy." We tend to make quick, bad decisions rather than slower, well-reasoned ones. It is for these reasons that step one in the D.A.R.T.S. System is imperative. When determining what information is needed on your narrowed topic, you should also make sure that you do the following:

■ Understand your instructor's guidelines for the project.

■ Understand your intended audience.

■ Determine the availability of reliable resources and how many are required by your instructor.

■ Develop a timeline to complete your project.

A: Access the Information from a Variety of Sources

After you have made your topic decision and narrowed your research question, you will want to begin the process of accessing valuable, reliable, credible information. While Wikipedia and Google are valuable tools, it is also important to use a variety of sources such as journals, scholarly books, newspapers, and maybe even interviews to gather the information needed.

You may be asking, "Is the library still important in the digital age?" Yes! The answer is an absolute yes! Many people think of libraries as quiet, tomb-like places presided over by a crabby old woman prepared to pounce on you if you ask a question or touch one of her precious books. Fortunately, that stereotype went the way of the horse and buggy. Today, libraries

BRING the Change

TIPS FOR PERSONAL SUCCESS

Consider the following strategies for polishing your information literacy skills:

- Use multiple sources to compare and contrast information.
- Use information that is current and timely.
- Always cite your sources.
- Check and verify the credibility of your sources.

Now, it is your turn. Create a list of at least three tips that you would offer fellow classmates to assist them with becoming more information literate.

1. _____

_____

2. _____

_____

3. _____

_____

are often the hub of a college campus. Your library is the key used to unlock the secrets to your education and help you become more information literate by accessing a variety of sources. Although the Internet is an amazing tool, serious research requires you to use the library and its tools, including books, maps, charts, government data, periodicals, and your librarian. It may be fun and easy to use Google, Dogpile, or Wikipedia, but you will also need to hone your library research skills and critical-thinking abilities.

> "The library is the hospital of the mind."
> —M. Tullins

Some of the things that your librarian can assist you with include helping you discover, understand, search, and use the online catalog; narrow your digital search to get to the information you need; search other libraries for information and sources not available on your campus; discover, use, and evaluate databases for almost every subject area; and make use of interlibrary loan tools. Your librarian can also help you understand your own library's online data search systems.

Becoming information literate requires you to seek and use a variety of sources; however, you must also determine how much is enough. You don't want to overwhelm yourself. When searching for your resources, keep the following tips in mind:

- Understand that information comes in a variety of media such as government documents, maps, videos, books, scholarly journals, online databases, and YouTube interviews, just to name a few.

- As you begin to put your information together to create your project, determine what information is missing and where you might locate it. You will also need to determine if you have too much information on a particular aspect of your topic.

- Manage your information carefully so that you know exactly where you found it. This will allow you to access the information later if needed and provide proper citations once your project is complete.

BLOOM LEVEL 5

Now it is your turn. Consider that you have been asked to write a paper on the value of a career college education. First, develop a brief thesis for your paper and then find at least three online resources to help you write this paper. For this exercise, **do not** use Wikipedia.

Thesis: _____

_____

_____

Source 1: _____

Citation: _____

Why is this source suitable, valid, and reliable? _____

_____

_____

Source 2: _____

Citation: _____

Why is this source suitable, valid, and reliable? _____

_____

_____

Source 3: _____

Citation: _____

Why is this source suitable, valid, and reliable? _____

_____

_____

R: Read and Evaluate the Information for Accuracy and Credibility

You have chosen your topic, narrowed it into a workable thesis, and found a variety of sources that you can use for your project. Let's say that you have found three Internet articles, one book, one YouTube video, and one journal article. It is now time to read or view your material in great detail and evaluate the information to determine if it is valid, accurate, and credible. Basically, you are working to discover if your sources present facts correctly and if the information is up-to-date, logical, fair, unbiased, and useable. By using the Credibility Checklist in Figure 5.6, you will have a better understanding of the quality of your information.

T: Transform the Information to Create Your Project

Now that you have found your information and evaluated its credibility and usefulness, it is time to actually use what you have found. It is time to transform these facts, figures, interviews, charts, graphs, and opinions into your project. You will need to determine what type of organizational pattern best suits your information. This may have been by your instructor's guidelines. Organizing the body of your paper or speech can be done using one of several proven methods:

Figure 5.6 Credibility Checklist

Are the information and author credible, valid, accurate, and reliable?	• Who is the author and what are his or her credentials, educational background, past writings, or experience? • What edition is the source? Second and third editions suggest that the source has been updated to reflect changes and new knowledge. • Who is the publisher? If the source is published by a university press, it is likely to be a scholarly publication. • Does the information appear to be valid and well researched, or does it just gloss over the material? Is it supported by evidence? • What are the author's credentials? Anyone can put anything on the web. Your task is to distinguish between the reliable and questionable, the knowledgeable and the amateur.
Is the article fact or opinion, popular or scholarly?	• What is the title of the source? This will help you determine if the source is popular, sensational, or scholarly and indicates the level of complexity. Popular journals are resources such as *Time, Newsweek, Vogue, Ebony,* and *Reader's Digest.* They seldom cite their sources. Sensational resources are often inflammatory and written on an elementary level. They usually have flashy headlines, and they cater to popular superstitions. Examples are *The Globe, The National Enquirer,* and *The Star.* • Is the source factually objective, is it opinionated, or is it propaganda? Objective sources look at all angles and report on each one honestly. • Are sources documented with footnotes or links? In scholarly works, the credibility of most writings is proven through the footnote or endnote documentation.
Is it up to date and timely?	• When was the source published? If it is a webpage, the date is usually found on the last page or the home page. Is the source current or out of date for your topic? • Look for the date that the article was last updated. Is the page dated? Is it current enough for your research or is it "stale" and outdated?
Does it have depth?	• What is the intended audience of your source? Is the information too simple, too advanced, or too technical for your audience?
Is it logical?	• Could the article be parody, humor, or satire? • Ask yourself, "Why was this page put on the web?"
Is it fair?	• Does the article present both sides of the argument? Is it balanced? • Was the article written by a neutral source on the topic?
Are the sources of the information cited? Does it include a bibliography?	• Does the writer of the book, article, or website cite his or her sources? If not, what does this mean for the credibility of the information?

Source: Adapted from Ormondroyd, Engle, and Cosgrave (2001), and UC-Berkeley (2005).

■ **Spatial organization** is when you arrange information or items according to their direction or location. If you were describing the Mall in Washington, D.C., you could begin with the Lincoln Memorial and then move on to the Reflecting Pool, the Washington Monument, and the Smithsonian.

■ **Cause–effect organization** is when you discuss the causes of a problem and then explore its effects. If you were speaking about high blood pressure, you would first examine the causes of high blood pressure, such as diet, hereditary factors, and weight, and then move on to the effects, such as heart attack and stroke.

What services are available to help you with your technology needs?

Patrick White/Merrill

- **Chronological organization** is when you present information in the order in which it happened. Speeches that deal with historical facts and how-to speeches often use chronological organization. If you were writing a paper on the history of automobiles in the United States since 1950, you would begin with the 1950s and then move to the 1960s, 1970s, 1980s, and so forth.

- **Problem-solving organization** is often used in persuasive papers to get your reader to accept your proposal. You first begin by pointing out the major problem(s) and then move on to revealing the solutions and their advantages. If you were writing about crime on college campuses, you would begin by informing the reader or listener about the problems, the crime statistics, and the personal toll on students. You would then propose solutions and tell how the solutions would help all students.

- **Topical/categorical organization** is when you group information into subdivisions or cluster information into categories. If you were writing a paper on taxes in the United States, you might categorize your information into local taxes, state taxes, federal taxes, luxury taxes, "sin" taxes, and special taxes.

- **Compare/contrast organization** is when you discuss your topic in a fashion that shows its similarities to and differences from another topic. You may be writing a paper that compares the health care system in the United States to that of England or Canada.

- **Importance/priority organization** allows you to arrange information from the most important issue to the least important or vice versa. If you were writing a paper to inform readers and listeners about buying diamonds, you might arrange your information so that you speak first about the most important aspects of diamond buying—clarity, color, and cut—and later about less important factors.

S: Select the Appropriate Documentation Style

You're not finished yet. Now, you must let your readers or listeners know where you located your information. This is called *citation* or *documentation* of your sources. You will need to document and cite all statistics, quotes, and excerpts from works that you referenced. The most common means of doing this is by quoting within the paper and then compiling a reference or bibliography sheet at the end. The following must be cited if used:

- *Any* copyrighted information (music, poems, literary works, films, photographs, videos, artwork, advertisements, plays, computer programs, audio files, etc.); most of these works require that you seek permission to use them and many require that you pay a royalty to the author or his or her heirs

- Direct quotations

- Opinions, judgments, and insights of others that you summarize or paraphrase

- Information that is not widely known

- Information that is open to dispute

- Information that is not commonly accepted

- Tables, charts, graphs, and statistics taken from a source (Kirszner and Mandell, 1995)

There are several acceptable ways to document your research. The three most widely used methods are the **MLA** (Modern Language Association), the **APA** (American Psychological Association), and the **CMS** (Chicago Manual of Style). All three styles can be explained by your librarian, through the MLA, APA, or CMS Style Guides, and/or by searching online.

Correct APA Style for the Citation of a Webpage

Sherfield, R., & Moody, P. (2011). *How to document an article found on the web.* Retrieved from www.sherfieldmoodydocuments.com

Correct MLA Style for the Citation of a Webpage

Sherfield, Robert M., and Patricia G. Moody. "How to Document an Article Found on the Web." *Name of Website,* 20 Dec. 2010. Web. 25 Mar. 2011 <www.sherfieldmoodydocuments.com>.

Correct CMS Style for the Citation of a Webpage

Sherfield, Robert M., and Patricia G. Moody. "How to Document an Article Found on the Web." Accessed March 25, 2011, www.sherfieldmoodydocuments.com.

By using the D.A.R.T.S. System of Information Literacy, you can rest assured that you are approaching the mountains of information in a more organized and reasonable fashion. These simple steps can mean the difference between information overload or information mastered.

ON THE GO AND GOING ONLINE—WHERE IT ALL COMES TOGETHER

How Do You Succeed in Distance-Education Courses?

Distance-learning classes can be great for students who may live far from campus, have transportation issues, work full time, or have families and small children. These courses have flexible hours and few, if any, class meetings. Most online classes allow you to work at your own pace, but most still have stringent deadlines for assignment submission.

Do not let anyone try to tell you that these courses are easier than regular classroom offerings; they are not. Distance-learning courses are usually more difficult for the average student because they require being highly self-disciplined. Some colleges reserve distance-learning courses for students with GPAs of 3.0 or higher. You need to be a self-starter and highly motivated to complete and do well in these courses. Take the assessment in Figure 5.7 to determine if an online class is right for you.

Figure 5.7   Distance Education Readiness Assessment

Please answer each question truthfully to determine your readiness for online learning.

1. Do you own your own computer? Yes No
2. If your computer relatively new (enough memory, CD-ROM, graphics card, wireless Internet, etc.)? Yes No
3. Can you type (not just text, but type)? Yes No
4. Are you comfortable using a computer and web technology? Yes No
5. Do you have the technical requirements for online learning (Internet access, Internet browser, Adobe, Word or compatible program, PowerPoint, Excel)? Yes No
6. Are you highly organized? Yes No

(continued)

Figure 5.7 **Distance Education Readiness Assessment (continued)**

7. Are you a good manager of time?	Yes	No
8. Are you highly motivated—a self-starter?	Yes	No
9. If you work full or part time, do you feel you have at least six to eight hours per week to spend working with each of your online classes?	Yes	No
10. If you have family issues that require a great deal of your time, do you have family support?	Yes	No
11. Do you have "down time" to spend working on your online classes?	Yes	No
12. Can you get to campus if necessary?	Yes	No
13. Do you feel comfortable chatting online with unknown persons?	Yes	No
14. Do you think you can relate to others in an online relationship?	Yes	No
15. Do you consider yourself a good reader with high-level comprehension?	Yes	No
16. Can you concentrate on your work even with online distractions (e-mail, friends, etc.)?	Yes	No
17. Do you feel comfortable calling your instructors during their office hours if you need to do so?	Yes	No
18. Do you think you will be able to take notes during an online chat or class session?	Yes	No
19. Are you comfortable with online terminology such as URL, listserv, portal, streaming video, Skype, etc.?	Yes	No
20. Are you excited about taking an online class?	Yes	No

If you answered "No" to more than three questions, you should reconsider taking an online class at this time. To prepare for future classes, you may also want to spend time researching and becoming more familiar with the questions that you marked "No." You can also speak with your advisor or professor about your possibility for success in his or her course. Your campus probably offers an online orientation from which you might benefit.

If you decide to take an online class, consider the following advice:

- If at all possible, review the course material before you register. This may help you in making the decision to enroll. Often, professors' syllabi are accessible online.
- Begin before the beginning! If at all possible, obtain the distance-learning materials (or at least the text) before the semester begins. Getting ahead give your more confidence.
- Know if your class is totally online or a hybrid course; it makes a huge difference.
- Make an appointment to meet the instructor as soon as possible. Some institutions will schedule a meeting for you. If it is not possible to meet, at least phone the professor and introduce yourself.
- Log in on a daily basis even if nothing is due. Important messages may be posted.
- Learn the required technology and software programs to be successful, and make sure you have access to these programs.
- Develop a schedule for completing each assignment and stick to it! Don't let time steal away from you. This is the biggest problem with online classes.
- Keep a copy of all work mailed, e-mailed, or delivered to the instructor.
- Always mail, e-mail, or deliver your assignment on time—early if possible.
- Take full advantage of any online orientation or training sessions.
- Participate in class, chats, and in your groups (if you are assigned a group).
- If you have computer failure, have a back-up plan.
- Alert your instructor immediately if you have family, computer, or personal problems that will prevent you from completing an assignment on time.
- Work ahead if possible.
- Find out where to go or who to call on campus should you encounter technical problems with the learning platform or getting online.
- Never be afraid to know your instructor's digital office door. Many instructors hold office hours online and welcome your comments and questions.

© Robert M. Sherfield

CHANGING IDEAS *to Reality*

REFLECTIONS ON TECHNOLOGY, RESEARCH, AND INFORMATION LITERACY

Technology is an amazing part of our lives. It is also a wicked, double-edged sword. It can bring us joy and give us heartache. It can make some tasks in life easier, and it can frustrate us to no end with others. It can help us complete tasks more quickly, but, when it fails, it can slow us down—and in some cases bring us to a complete stop. It can allow us to have continual communication, but it can also remove us from personal, face-to-face interaction. It can help us learn new information, and it can sometimes freeze our brains solid.

The most effective advice we can give you when dealing with new and ever-changing technology is this: Take one new program or application at a time and learn it well, practice it, and discover its strengths and limitations. After you have learned this program, move on to another program to continue your growth. If you are new to computers and technology in education, resist the urge to learn every step of every tool at the same time. Master what you must know to be successful, and move on to what you want to know. Build on your strengths, and let your challenges be your goals for the future.

As you work toward improving your technology, research, and information literacy skills, consider the following:

- Work hard to learn the technology tools that will help you be successful in your classes.
- Manage your time online carefully, and do your work before you play and socialize.
- Learn the terms of technology to help you grow in this field of study.
- Learn to use effective search engines, tools, and bookmarking to help save time.
- Use the D.A.R.T.S. System of Information Literacy to guide your research.
- Guard your online privacy like you would guard your personal bank account.
- Practice the tools of netiquette when online.
- Take your online classes as seriously as you take your face-to-face classes.

"Treat your password like your toothbrush. Don't let anybody else use it, and get a new one every six months."

—Clifford Stoll

Knowledge
in Bloom

BUILDING YOUR INFORMATION LITERACY SKILLS

Utilizes levels 4 and 5 of the taxonomy

Each chapter-end assessment is based on Bloom's Taxonomy of Learning. See pages xxvi–xxviii in the front of this book for a quick review.

Process: Find an in-depth website or online article about a major current event within the last month. Using the information from the article and/or website, complete the following Information Literacy Checklist and Worksheet. Justify your answers.

Event: _____

Why is this event important? _____
_____

Name of website or online article: _____

URL of website or article: _____

Publisher or affiliation: _____

Publication date: _____

Author: _____

After reading the website or article, use other sources (books, journals, or other online sites) to compare/contrast your findings and to justify your responses.

QUESTION	YOUR RESPONSE	JUSTIFY YOUR RESPONSE
Is the author's name indicated?	Yes No	Name?
Is the author of the source credible? Reliable?	Yes No	Why?
Is the source from an individual webpage, an organization, a government agency, a for-profit agency, an international source, a military site, or an educational institution?	Type:	How do you know?
Is this site easy to navigate, read, and use?	Yes No	Why?
Does the author provide contact information or can you find the contact information online?	Yes No	Contact information:
Is this source masked as an advertisement?	Yes No	Justify.
Does this source require that you have or purchase special software to view portions of the material?	Yes No	What is required? How much does it cost?

QUESTION	YOUR RESPONSE	JUSTIFY YOUR RESPONSE
Does the source provide enough information to begin a project on this topic? Does it offer an in-depth look at the topic?	Yes No	List three important facts you gained from this source.
Is the information accurate?	Yes No	Justify.
Is the article dated?	Yes No	Date of publication:
Is the information current?	Yes No	Justify.
Is the information objective and fair?	Yes No	Justify.
Is the article an opinion piece or a factual piece?	Opinion Fact	Justify.
Does the article provide both sides to the event?	Yes No	Justify.
Does the article provide live links within the piece?	Yes No	List the URL of one link.
Does the author provide footnotes and references for his or her research?	Yes No	List one of the references used to write this piece.

Based on your readings and investigations of this article or site, summarize your findings into a 250- to 300-word essay. Be certain to use the author's name, facts, dates, references, and new information learned about the event.

_____

_____

_____

_____

_____

_____

_____

_____

_____

_____

_____

_____

_____

_____

SQ3R MASTERY STUDY SHEET

EXAMPLE QUESTION *(from page 112)* *Why is it important to know the different types of technology used in education?*	**ANSWER:**
EXAMPLE QUESTION *(from page 122)* *What is information literacy?*	**ANSWER:**
AUTHOR QUESTION *(from page 111)* *How can you manage your time online more effectively?*	**ANSWER:**
AUTHOR QUESTION *(from page 118)* *What is a virtual team?*	**ANSWER:**
AUTHOR QUESTION *(from page 124)* *What is information paralysis?*	**ANSWER:**
AUTHOR QUESTION *(from page 127)* *How can you evaluate an online research source?*	**ANSWER:**
AUTHOR QUESTION *(from page 129)* *List and briefly discuss three tips for succeeding in an online class.*	**ANSWER:**
YOUR QUESTION *(from page _____)*	**ANSWER:**
YOUR QUESTION *(from page _____)*	**ANSWER:**
YOUR QUESTION *(from page _____)*	**ANSWER:**
YOUR QUESTION *(from page _____)*	**ANSWER:**
YOUR QUESTION *(from page _____)*	**ANSWER:**

Finally, after answering these questions, recite in your mind the major points covered here. Consider the following general questions to help you master this material.

- What was it about?
- What does it mean?
- What was the most important thing you learned? Why?
- What were the key points to remember?

chapter six
READ

BUILDING SUCCESSFUL READING STRATEGIES FOR PRINT AND ONLINE MATERIAL

"The difference between the right word and the almost right word is the difference between lightning and the lightning bug."—Mark Twain

Why read this chapter?

Because you'll learn:

- How to determine your reading speed and become an active reader
- How to use fixation to increase reading speed
- How to read in pieces to enhance your comprehension

Because you'll be able to:

- Calculate and use your reading speed to manage your study time more effectively
- Use the SQ3R study and reading method to best advantage
- Read passages, sections, and chapters and remember what you have read

Scan and QUESTION

Take a few moments, **scan this chapter,** and on page 158, write **five of your own questions** that you think will be important to your mastery of this material. You will also find five questions listed from your authors.

Example:

☑ **Describe the process of fixation.** (from page 142)

☑ **Why is comprehension more important than speed?** (from page 142)

MyStudentSuccessLab

MyStudentSuccessLab (www.mystudentsuccesslab.com) is an online solution designed to help you "Start strong, Finish stronger" by building skills for ongoing personal and professional development.

How
COLLEGE CHANGED

Name:	Christian Garcia
Institution:	Graduate! UEI College
Age:	33
Major:	Medical Assisting and Business Ma
Career:	Associate Director of Education, U

I come from Honduras, a country where education is a luxury and you have to be rich to obtain a degree. My native language is Spanish and during my youth, I only spoke broken, "street English." I quickly learned that without extended education, I could not advance in a career or in my private life. I knew that I had to go to college to be able to provide for myself.

After I completed high school, I enrolled in UEI College in California. I had always been interested in the medical field, so I decided to study medical assist- and work to become a medical laboratory techni- I began working in my field and decided that I d to also get a degree in business management. years later, I obtained my degree in business. er being at UEI, I realized that I not only love the field, but that I also love education and I wanted It became a dream of mine. After speaking Dean of Academic Instruction, he encouraged y dream became a reality. He gave me my first pportunity at my own alma mater. I began the program from which I graduated. ad been an instructor for a while, I had the o become a program chair. I loved this

position and realized that I had four moved on to become the associate c tion at UEI, overseeing the evening pro macy technology, medical assisting, dental as and criminal justice. Today, I work in a position that makes me happy to get out of the bed in the mornings. I followed my passion and it paid off.

The most important thing that I learned as a student was to act like the professional that you are trying to become. I was rejected for several jobs because I did not know how to dress or act in an interview. My degree and training taught me to dress properly, carry myself with pride, and speak with a purpose. I began to be the person I wanted to become.

Education has changed my life completely. It has created endless opportunities for me. It helped me get the life I dreamed of. It also taught me to live by my code: Do what you love and you'll never work a day in your life. I always tell my friends that I stopped working in 1999 because I found a career that doesn't feel like work. I also learned that in life, you have to search for your opportunities because they usually do not come to you.

ink t it

1. Christian's first language was not English. What skills will you have to upgrade to be successful your chosen field? Why? How do you plan to do this?

2. What do you think about Christian's statement "Do what you love and you'll never work a day in your life"?

READING *FUNDAMENTAL* OR JUST PURE TORTURE?

Getting Ready to Read College-Level Material

Quick question: What are the top two academic problems among students today? According to faculty members, assessments, national tests, and yes, even your peers around the nation, the two greatest problems students face today are math classes and reading comprehension—and some math problems can even be attributed to poor reading skills.

How many times have you read to the bottom of a page or completed a section in a textbook and said to yourself, "I don't remember a thing I just read"? In actuality, all of us have done this at one time or another. The strategies outlined here will help you eliminate this common occurrence from your study time. By applying these strategies, you will be able to read a page, a section, or an entire chapter so that when you reach the end, you will comprehend and remember what you just read.

As you begin to explore the methods in this chapter, you may say to yourself, "How much time do they think I have?" Although our methods do take some time, if properly used, you will never get to the bottom of a page again and not know what you've read. Think of it way: Would you rather read the material four or five times and *not* remember what you or read it one time and have it? That is the beauty knowing how to effectively read c level material. Figure 6.1 details the "six-pack" you will need to effectively read and c hend material.

DISCOVERING YOUR READING STYLE

Are You Active or Passive?

Active reading is really nothing more than a mindset (see Figure 6.2). It is as you begin the reading process. For the next few days, try approaching ments with a positive and open mind and notice the difference in your c standing, and overall comprehension. Instead of saying things like, "I stuff is worthless," reframe your self-talk into statements such as "I'm and "I think I can apply this to my life now."

Figure 6.1 **What Are the Ingre for Successful Read**

- The material you are reading
- Pens or pencils and a highlighter
- Paper for taking notes
- A dictionary (traditional or online)
- Time devoted exclusively to reading
- An open mind

Figure 6.2 Discovering Your Reading Style

Take a few moments and circle TRUE or FALSE for each of the statements below to determine if you are more of an active or passive reader.

1. I enjoy reading for pleasure.	TRUE	FALSE
2. College textbooks have little connection to my real life.	TRUE	FALSE
3. I look for the deeper meaning in words and phrases.	TRUE	FALSE
4. I seldom visualize what I am reading.	TRUE	FALSE
5. I look up words that I do not understand.	TRUE	FALSE
6. I read only what I have to read, and that is a stretch for me.	TRUE	FALSE
7. I stop reading to ponder what something means.	TRUE	FALSE
8. I never take notes when reading.	TRUE	FALSE
9. Reading brings me great joy.	TRUE	FALSE
10. My mind wanders constantly when I read.	TRUE	FALSE
11. I make time for reading even when I am not required to read.	TRUE	FALSE
12. Words are just words—they add no real meaning to my life or work.	TRUE	FALSE
13. I get excited about reading something new because I know I will learn something new and useful.	TRUE	FALSE
14. When reading, I just want to get it over with.	TRUE	FALSE
15. I usually have no trouble concentrating when reading.	TRUE	FALSE
16. I never look up words; I just read on.	TRUE	FALSE

Total of even-numbered TRUE responses _____

Total of odd-numbered TRUE responses _____

If you answered TRUE to more even numbers, you tend to be a more passive reader.
If you answered TRUE to more odd numbers, you tend to be a more active reader.

I FEEL THE NEED . . . THE NEED FOR SPEED!

Do You Know Your Personal Reading Rate?

You've heard the advertisements: "Breeze through a novel on your lunch hour," "Read an entire computer instruction book over dinner," or "Read *The New York Times* in 10 minutes." Sure, there are people who have an incredible gift for speed reading and a photographic memory, but those people are not the norm.

In Figure 6.3, you will find a passage on binge drinking. Read the section at your normal pace. Use a stopwatch or a watch with a second hand to accurately record your time, and then calculate your rate and comprehension level using the scales provided.

This section is included to give you some idea about how long it will take to read a chapter so that you can *plan your reading time* more effectively. There is an average of 450 words on a college textbook page. If you read at 150 words per minute, each page may take you an average of three minutes to read.

This is a **raw number** for just reading. It does not allow for marking, highlighting, taking notes, looking up unfamiliar words, reflecting, or comprehension. When these necessary skills are coupled with basic reading, they can sometimes triple the amount of reading time required. So, that page that you estimated would take you three minutes to read may actually take you nine to 10 minutes. This matters greatly when you have a 40-page chapter to read for homework.

iStockPhoto

Have you ever timed yourself to determine how long it takes you to read a complete chapter?

Figure 6.3 Calculating Your Reading Rate

Start Time _____ : _____ : _____
        Hour   Min.   Sec.

BINGE DRINKING

Binge drinking is classified as having more than five drinks at one time. Many people say, "I only drink once a week." However, if that one drinking spell includes drink after drink after drink, it can be extremely detrimental to your liver, your memory, your digestive system, and your overall health.

Most college students report that they do not mean to binge drink, but it is caused by the situation, such as a ballgame, a party, a campus event, or special occasion. Researchers at Michigan State University found that only 5 percent of students surveyed say they party to "get drunk" (Warner, 2002).

In their breakthrough work, *Dying to Drink*, Harvard researcher Henry Wechsler and science writer Bernice Wuethrich explore the problem of binge drinking. They suggest that "two out of every five college students regularly binge drink, resulting in approximately 1,400 student deaths, a distressing number of assaults and rapes, a shameful amount of vandalism, and countless cases of academic suicide" (Wechsler and Wuethrich, 2002).

It is a situation reminiscent of the old saying "Letting the fox guard the henhouse." After a few drinks, it is hard to "self-police," meaning that you may not be able to control your actions once the drinking starts.

Perhaps the greatest tragedy of drug and alcohol abuse is the residual damage of pregnancy, sexually transmitted diseases, traffic fatalities, verbal/physical abuse, and accidental death. You know that drugs and alcohol lower your resistance and can cause you to do things that you would not normally do, such as drive drunk or have unprotected sex. Surveys and research results suggest that students who participate in heavy episodic (HE) or binge drinking are more likely to participate in unprotected sex with multiple sex partners. One survey found that 61 percent of men who do binge drink participated in unprotected sex, as compared to 23 percent of men who do not binge drink. The survey also found that 48 percent of women who do binge drink participated in unprotected sex, as compared to only 8 percent of women who do not binge drink (Cooper, 2002).

These staggering statistics suggest one thing: alcohol consumption can cause people to act in ways in which they may never have acted without alcohol—and those actions can result in personal damage from which recovery may be impossible. (386 words)

Finishing Time _____ : _____ : _____
        Hour   Min.   Sec.

Reading time in seconds = _____

Words per minute (use the following chart) = _____

Example: If you read this passage in 2 minutes and 38 seconds, your reading time in seconds would be 158. Using the Rate Calculator Chart, your reading rate would be about 146 words per minute.

RATE CALCULATOR FOR "BINGE DRINKING" PASSAGE	
TIME IN SECONDS	WORDS PER MINUTE
40	581
50	464
60 (1 minute)	387
120 (2 minutes)	194
130	179
140	165
150	155
160	145
170	137
180 (3 minutes)	129
190	122
200	116
210	110
220	106
230	101

Test Your Comprehension Skills

Answer the following questions with T (true) or F (false) without looking back over the material.

_____ 1. Binge drinking has resulted in the deaths of students.

_____ 2. Men who binge drink have unprotected sex more often than men who do not binge drink.

_____ 3. Women who binge drink have unprotected sex no more often than women who do not binge drink.

_____ 4. "Self-policing" means that you are able to look out for yourself.

_____ 5. Binge drinking is classified as having more than three drinks at one time.

Each question is worth 20%. Comprehension = _____ %

Example: If you answered two correctly, your comprehension rate would be 40% (2 × 20%). If you answered four correctly, your comprehension rate would be 80% (4 × 20%).

Test Your Comprehension Skills Answers: 1 = T, 2 = T, 3 = F, 4 = T, 5 = F.

DEVELOPING A POWERFUL VOCABULARY

Do You Have to Be a Logodaedalian to Enjoy Words?

Thankfully, it is not every day you run across words like *logodaedalian*. (A logodaedalian is a person who has a great passion for unique, sly, and clever words and phrases.) Perhaps the best way to develop a dynamic vocabulary is through reading. By reading, you come across words that you may have never seen before. You are exposed to aspects of language that you may not have experienced in your family, neighborhood, or geographic location.

Of course, unfamiliar words in a passage, section, or chapter will not become a part of your vernacular unless you stop and look them up. This is the way to begin building a masterful vocabulary.

Let's start by looking up the noun *vernacular*. Using a dictionary (in print, online, or from a free smartphone app), take a moment and jot down the definition.

Vernacular means: _____

_____

_____

See how simple that was? Now you have a new word in your vocabulary. Actually, you have two new words in just a few paragraphs: *vernacular* and *logodaedalian*. You have taken a step toward becoming a logophile!

Here are some more tips to develop a strong vocabulary:

■ Look up words that you do not know (you can download a free dictionary on your smartphone).

■ Read often and widely—including difficult material.

■ Ask for clarifications in class and online.

■ Try to remember a word's usage, whether in a phrase, sentence, or explanation.

■ Keep a running list of words you do not know (put them in your memo section of your smartphone).

■ Make connections by rhyming the new word with familiar words.

■ Draw pictures of the word's definition on a index card.

■ Work crossword puzzles and word games such as Scrabble.

LEARNING TO READ FASTER AND SMARTER

Can You Improve Speed and Comprehension?

As you begin to practice reading for comprehension, review the following tips to help you read the material more quickly and understand it more clearly. Whenever you are faced with having to choose between *comprehension* or *speed,* choose comprehension! The following steps will help as you begin to master reading college-level material.

Learn to Concentrate

Speed and comprehension both require deep, ***mindful concentration***. Neither can be achieved without it. In order to comprehend information, your body needs to be ready to concentrate. You need sleep, rest, and proper nutrition. Most importantly, you need a quiet, peaceful place to concentrate on your reading. To increase your concentration and comprehension, consider the following:

- Reduce outside distractions such as people talking, rooms that are too hot or cold, cell phones ringing, and so on.

- Reduce internal distractions such as fatigue, self-talk, daydreaming, hunger, and emotions that cause you to think of other things.

- Set a goal for reading a certain amount of material in an allotted time. This goal can help you focus.

- Take a short break every 20 minutes. Don't get distracted and do something else; come back to your reading in three to five minutes.

- Take notes as you read. This helps reading become an active process.

- When reading online material, don't become distracted by e-mails, Facebook posts, and so on.

Overcome Fixation

Fixation is another important step in learning to read for speed and comprehension. Fixation is when your eyes stop on a single word to read it. Your eyes stop for only a fraction of a second, but those fractions add up over the course of a section or chapter. Your mind sees the words something like this:

Nutrition   is   important   to   good   health.

As you read this, you probably had six fixations because the words are spaced out. However, if they were not spaced, many people would still have six fixations. To increase your speed, try to see two words with one fixation; this will cut your reading time nearly in half. Try to see the sentence like this:

Nutrition is important   to good health.

Smith (2007) states that "research has shown that the average reader can see approximately 2.5 words per fixation." To reduce your fixation

DID YOU *Know?*

JAY LENO has always been a hard worker. Having mild dyslexia, he did not do very well in high school, getting mainly C's and D's.

Jay, however, was determined to accomplish his goals. Despite his poor grades, he was resolute about attending Emerson College in Boston.

The admissions office decided that Jay was not a good candidate for the college and refused him admission. However, he had his heart set on attending Emerson, so he sat outside the admission officer's office 12 hours a day, five days a week until he was accepted into the university.

He credits his dyslexia with helping him develop the drive and perseverance needed to succeed in comedy, and life in general.

(*Source:* Levinson Medical Center for Learning Disabilities. "Dyslexic? You're Not Alone." Retrieved from www.dyslexiaonline.com.)

PHOTO: Kathy Hutchins/Newscom

time for active reading, practice seeing two or more words with one fixation. As you practice, try to read in phrases like the example below:

Nutrition is important   **to good health. Therefore,**   **you should work hard**   **to eat proper meals**   **every day.**   **By doing this you can maintain**   **good health.**

READING ONLINE MATERIAL

Do I Need a New Set of Reading Skills?

You may be asking, "Is reading online really different from reading the printed word?" The answer is yes, especially with today's online, interactive, multimedia environment. Not too long ago, college students purchased their books or reading packets from the college bookstore and read the printed word. Today, this is not always the case. You may be required to download entire books or chapters, you will be assigned websites by your instructors, and you will sometimes decide to explore topics further through online research. Reading online requires an adjusted set of skills. You will still need to use the reading tips in this chapter, especially SQ3R, but you will also need to familiarize yourself with the strategies for successfully reading online (nontextual) material. Consider the tips offered in Figure 6.4.

Figure 6.4   Tips for Reading Online Material

- Before you even open the site, plan some undisturbed time to survey, explore, and read the site. Make it a point to avoid distractions or multitasking such as downloading songs on iTunes, reading your Facebook page, or checking e-mail. Devote this time to reading the material.
- Know why you are reading the online material.
- As you open the site, browse through (survey) it first to determine the length, view the main headings, and find out if you'll need to download plug-ins or any additional programs on your computer to access the material. Get a "feel" for the site and the matter.
- Click on any menus or tabs to determine what additional information is available.
- Work to avoid eye strain. You can do this several ways:
  - Read in periods of 20 minutes. After 20 minutes, take a short break.
  - Increase the size of your view screen to make the site larger.
  - Copy the material, paste it into a Word document, and enlarge the font so that you can read it more clearly.
- While reading, use virtual sticky notes to mark important material. You can download several free sticky notes programs by going online and searching "Free Online Sticky Notes."
- While reading, use an online highlighter to mark important material. To access an online highlighter, download one of the free online highlighting programs such as www.awesomehighlighter.com.
- While reading online, just as reading from printed material, take notes! This is one of the most important tools for memory and comprehension. As you read online material, take notes the traditional way or take virtual online notes. To do this, open a word-processing program, reduce it into the bottom menu bar, and as you read, click on it and add notes to your online page. Double space between each sentence to make it easier to read during your review period. You can also download several free online note-taking systems by searching "Free Online Note-Taking Software." You may want to consider investing in a dual monitor set-up for your computer.
- Use free text-to-speech programs to convert your online material to verbal material. If you're on the run, download any free text-to-speech program and then copy and paste the written work into the program. Next, download the file to your mp3 player or burn it to a CD. You now have "reading on the run."

Successful Decisions

AN ACTIVITY FOR CRITICAL REFLECTION

Whitney is 19 years old and just completed high school. She enrolled at Seymore Technical Institute with dreams of becoming a phlebotomist. She did well in high school, but reading has never been her strongest talent.

She became increasingly worried when she began to review her texts for the first semester. The readings were much more difficult than she expected. Further, she was stunned at the amount of reading required by each instructor.

Realizing that reading *and* comprehending were going to play a major role in her academic success, Whitney began to set aside two hours per day devoted strictly to reading, taking notes, vocabulary building, and comprehension. She was doing better but still struggling with her difficult texts and handouts.

Pretend that Whitney is a student at your institution. What services are available that you could recommend to help her improve her reading and comprehension skills?

1. _____
   _____

2. _____
   _____

What would you recommend that she do on a daily basis to improve her reading and comprehension?

1. _____
   _____

2. _____
   _____

FINDING THE MAIN IDEA

Can You Get to the Main Point?

As you should know from your English class, each paragraph or section typically has a main idea, often called a ***topic sentence.*** The topic sentence is what the paragraph or section is about. Identifying the main idea of a section can greatly aid your comprehension of the material. However, in many college texts, each paragraph will *not* have a topic sentence. Some paragraphs simply give further details of the previous paragraph. You may have to find the main idea by reading an entire section of a chapter from heading to heading.

For practice, read the following paragraph and determine the main idea—the point.

Do you remember where you were and what you were doing when you first heard about Barack Obama's election as the first African American president of the United States? Chances are good that you remember some of the details surrounding what you were doing when you heard this historic news. Experts report that most people will remember exactly where they were and what they were doing when a major event occurs. Depending on your age, you or your parents probably remember where you were when you heard about the World Trade Center. Many people who were alive when John Kennedy was assassinated remember vividly where they were, even though this event happened over fifty years ago. Events of this magnitude appear to be seared into our memories.

Circle the one option below that best describes the main idea.

1. The election of Barack Obama

2. John Kennedy's assassination

3. The fact that we tend to remember what we were doing when events of great magnitude happen

Which did you choose? Statement one, although mentioned in the first sentence of the paragraph, has very little to do with the paragraph's intended message. It is simply a prompt.

Statement two is vaguely related to the fact that we remember what we were doing during a tragic event, but doesn't actually state this. Statement three states the correct main idea for this paragraph.

Finding the topic sentence or main idea in a paragraph, section, or chapter is not hard, but it does take concentration and a degree of analytical skills. If you approach each paragraph or section as a detective searching for clues, you will soon find out how easy and effortless it is to determine main points.

Read the following paragraph and identify the topic in your own words. Justify your answer. Then, identify the main idea of the paragraph. See if you can determine what the authors really want you to know. Finally, develop (predict) one test question for this paragraph.

You *will not* have to do this for every paragraph you read in college. As you become a stronger reader, you will do this type of analysis after each heading or chapter section. But for now, as you work on building your skills as a reader, take the time to learn how to fully analyze a small portion of a chapter.

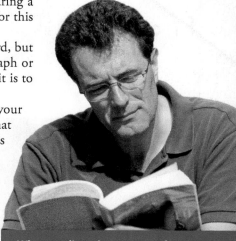

The origin of emotion is the brain. You might say that there are two minds—one that thinks (the thinking mind) and one that feels (the emotional mind). Think of thoughts and emotions as two different mechanisms for knowing and making sense of the world. The two minds are not adversarial or physically separate; rather, they operate interactively to construct your mental life. Passion (the heart) dominates reason (the mind) when feelings are intense. (Nelson & Low, 2010, p. 22)

Shutterstock

When reading, do you stop after each paragraph and think about the meaning?

Define the following terms:

mechanism _____

adversarial _____

dominate _____

The topic of this paragraph is _____

_____

_____

BLOOM LEVEL 4

Who or what is the paragraph about (the main idea)?

_____

_____

_____

_____

What does the author of the paragraph really want you to know?

_____

_____

_____

Develop one test question from this paragraph using each level of Bloom's Taxonomy as explained in the "Begin" section of this text (p. 000).

_____

_____

_____

from ORDINARY to *Extraordinary*

Sylvia Eberhardt
Fashion Model, Abercrombie and Fitch, Hollister Magazine,
and Other Top Agencies
Honors Graduate, Fairfax High School, Fairfax, Virginia
Honors Student—Howard University, Washington, D.C.

IF YOU read my resumé and looked at my professional credits, you might think I had it made—that the world had been handed to me on a silver platter and that I never wanted for anything. Nothing could be further from the truth. Although I am an honors student at Howard University and a fashion model who has worked with some of the top stores and magazines in the nation, my beginnings were anything but easy and beautiful.

I was born into a crack-infested, gang-ridden, one-bedroom house in inner-city Washington, D.C. I was raised a few doors down from a major crack house, where I saw junkies, prostitutes, and pimps on a daily basis. It was simply a way of life. Poverty surrounded me and my two siblings at every turn. Unemployment was rampant, and the streets were filled with trash and used needles. I slept in a bunk bed where nightly I could hear drug deals being made outside my window. The iron bars on the windows were the only things that separated me from the ugliness of the world outside my home.

My mother died just before I entered high school, and I was raised from that point on by my father. I was constantly teased and tormented growing up because I was so thin. My peers nicknamed me Anna (for "Anorexic"). What they did not know was that I suffered (and continue to suffer) from Crohn's disease, a life-threatening disability. Crohn's is an autoimmune disease that affects the gastrointestinal system

SQ3R TO THE RESCUE

How Can You Do It Right the First Time?

There are as many ways to approach a chapter in a textbook as there are students who read textbooks. Most would agree that there is no "right" or "wrong" way to begin the process. However, a few ways of approaching a chapter are more effective than others.

The most basic and often-used reading and studying system is the SQ3R method, developed by Francis P. Robinson in 1941. This simple, yet effective, system has proved to be a successful study tool for millions of students. SQ3R involves five steps: Scan, Question, Read, Recite, and Review. The most important thing to remember about SQ3R is that it should be used on a daily basis, not as a method for cramming. See Figure 6.5.

Scan

The first step of SQ3R is to scan, or pre-read, an assigned chapter. Every chapter in this text begins with the feature Scan and Question. This is a part of SQ3R. You begin by reading and causes rashes, severe abdominal pain, arthritis, vomiting, and weight loss.

How did I survive? How did I become an honors student at one of the top high schools in the nation? How did I become a fashion model at the age of 15? I am blessed to have an amazing, supportive father who taught me that you never have to let your past or present dictate your future. He believed and taught me that no matter how humble one's beginnings, no matter where you were born or the circumstances of your life, the test of a person's character is knowing that he or she holds his or her destiny in his or her own hands.

He taught me that I had to take responsibility for my own life. I had to be my own savior. Further, he taught my siblings and me that "you may live in the ghetto, but the ghetto does not have to live in you." He always told us that you do not have to think and act poor simply because you live in a lower-class neighborhood. He also taught us that in order to enjoy the finer things in life, you first have to experience hard times. He would say to us, "You have to ride in an old, ragged car before you can appreciate a Mercedes." His attitude helped guide and change my life.

After we moved to Virginia, I began working hard and taking college-level classes at Northern Virginia Community College while still in high school. My dream is to become a heart surgeon. I knew from the very beginning that I would have to study hard and give up many things I enjoyed doing. It paid off, however. By the end of my senior year in high school, I had over 30 college credits in math, science, anatomy, microbiology, calculus, and physiology, with a 4.0 grade point average. I won a full scholarship to Howard University and finished my first semester with a 3.92 GPA.

I write all of this to you to say, "Your life is what you make of it. You can let your past and present dictate and ruin your future, or you can get over it, work hard, believe in yourself, push yourself, and work toward your dreams." I wish you so much good luck and good fortune in your future.

> *My father taught me that "you may live in the ghetto, but the ghetto does not have to live in you."*

EXTRAORDINARY REFLECTION

Read the following statement and respond in your online journal or class notebook.

Sylvia mentions that her father would say to her that in order to enjoy the finer things in life, you first have to experience hard times: "You have to ride in an old, ragged car before you can appreciate a Mercedes." How do you plan to use your past experiences, positive or negative, to bring about positive change in your future?

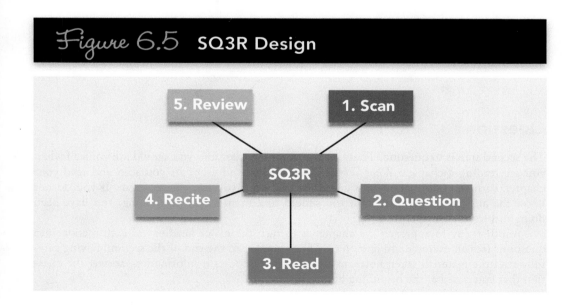

Figure 6.5 SQ3R Design

- 5. Review
- 1. Scan
- 4. Recite
- SQ3R
- 2. Question
- 3. Read

the title of the chapter, the headings, and each subheading. Look carefully at the chapter objectives, vocabulary, timelines, graphs, charts, pictures, and drawings included in each chapter. If there is a chapter summary, read it. Scanning also includes reading the first and last sentence in each paragraph. Scanning is not a substitute for reading a chapter. Reading is discussed later. Before going any further, scan the next chapter of this text using the following questions.

What is the title of the chapter? _____

What is the subheading of the chapter? _____

List the chapter major headings. _____

_____

_____

_____

Who is introduced in the "Did You Know" feature? List one thing you learned about him or her.

_____

_____

If the chapter contains quotations, which one means the most to you? Why?

_____

_____

What is the most important graph or chart in the chapter? Why?

_____

_____

Close your book and list five topics that this chapter will cover.

1. _____
2. _____
3. _____
4. _____
5. _____

Question

The second step is to question. There are five common questions you should ask yourself when you are reading a chapter: *Who? When? What? Where?* and *Why?* As you scan and read your chapter, turn the information into questions and see if you can answer them. If you do not know the answers to the questions, you should find them as you read along. You have been doing this for each chapter thus far.

Another way to approach the chapter is to turn the major headings of each section into questions (see an example in Figure 6.6). When you get to the end of the section, having carefully read the material, taken notes, and highlighted important information, answer the question that you posed at the beginning of the section.

Figure 6.6   Forming Questions from Headings

Example: If you were describing the mall in Washington, D.C., you could begin with the Lincoln Memorial and then move on to the reflecting pond, the Washington Monument, and the Smithsonian.

Cause-Effect Organization is when you arrange your information in the cause-and-effect order. You would discuss the causes of a problem and then explore its effects.

Example: If you were speaking about high blood pressure, you would first examine the causes of high blood pressure such as diet, hereditary factors, and weight and then move on to the effects such as heart attack and stroke.

> **What is cause and effect?**
> **Why is it important?**

Chronological Organization is presenting information in the order in which it happened. Speeches that deal with historical facts and how-to speeches often use chronological organization.

Example: If you were giving a speech or writing a paper on the history of automobiles in the United States since 1950, you would begin with the 50s, move to the 60s, 70s, 80s, and 90s. If you were giving a how-to speech on refinishing a table, you would begin with the first process of stripping the old paint or varnish and move forward to the last step of applying a new coat of paint or varnish.

> **What is chronological organization?**
> **When do I use chronological order?**
> **Why?**

O*rder and simplification are the first steps toward mastery.*
—THOMAS MANN

Problem Solving Organization is often used in persuasive papers and speeches. Usually, you are trying to get your reader or audience to accept your proposal. You first begin by pointing out the major problem(s) and then move on to revealing the solutions, and the advantages of the solutions.

Example: If you were writing or speaking about crime on college campuses, you would begin by informing the reader or listener about the problems, the crime statistics, and the personal toll on students. You would then propose solutions and tell how the solutions would help all students.

> **What is problem-solving organization?**
> **Which speech would require problem solving as an organizational pattern?**

Topical/Categorical Organization means grouping information into subdivisions or cluster information into categories. Some information naturally falls into specific categories, such as the different types of palm trees or the types of rollerblades available.

Example: If you were writing a speech or paper on taxes in the United States, you might categorize your information into local taxes, state taxes, federal taxes, luxury taxes, "sin" taxes, and special taxes.

> **What is topical/categorical organization?**
> **When would I use it?**

Compare/Contrast Organization means presenting your information in a fashion that shows its similarities to and differences from other information.

Example: You may be writing a paper or speech that compares the health care system in the United States to that of England or Canada.

> **When would I use compare/contrast? Why?**
> **What are the benefits?**
> **How does each type of organization differ?**

Importance/Priority Organization allows you to arrange information from the most important issue to the least or the least important to the

Read

After you scan the chapter and develop some questions to be answered from the chapter, the next step is to read the chapter. Remember, scanning is not reading. There is no substitute for reading in your success plan. Read slowly and carefully. The SQ3R method requires a substantial amount of time, but if you take each step slowly and completely, you will be amazed at how much you can learn and how much your grades will improve.

> *"There are worse crimes than burning books. One of them is not reading them."*
> —Joseph Brodsky

Read through each section. It is best not to jump around or move ahead if you do not understand the previous section. Paragraphs are usually built on each other, and so you need to understand the first before you can move on to the next. You may have to read a chapter or section more than once, especially if the information is new, technical, or difficult.

Take notes, highlight, and make marginal notes in your textbook as you read along. You own your textbook and should personalize it as you would your lecture notes. Highlight areas that you feel are important, underline words and phrases that you do not understand or that you feel are important, and jot down notes in the margins. Refer to the "Begin" section of this book in the preface to see how a text page should look after reading and using SQ3R.

As you begin to read your chapter, mark the text, and take notes, keep the following in mind:

- Read the entire paragraph before you mark anything.

- Identify the topic sentence of each paragraph and highlight it.

- Highlight key phrases.

- Don't highlight too much; the text will lose its significance. See Figure 6.7.

- Use two different color highlighters—one for "important information" and one for "very interesting information."

- Stop and look up words that you do not know or understand.

Figure 6.7 The Lowdown on Highlighting

USING YOUR DOMINANT INTELLIGENCE, PREFERRED LEARNING STYLE, AND UNIQUE PERSONALITY TYPE **177**

Introverts draw their strength from the inner world. They need to spend time alone to think and ponder. They are usually quiet and reflective. They usually make decisions by themselves. They do not like being the center of attention. They are private

S versus N (Sensing/iNtuition)

This category deals with the way we *learn and deal with information*.

Sensing types gather information through their five senses. They have a hard time believing something if it cannot be seen, touched, smelled, tasted, or heard. They like concrete facts and details. They do not rely on intuition or gut feelings. They usually have a great deal of common sense.

Intuitive types are not very detail-oriented. They can see possibilities, and they rely on their gut feelings. Usually, they are very innovative people. They tend to live in the future and often get bored once they have mastered a task.

T versus F (Thinking/Feeling)

This category deals with the way we *make decisions*.

Thinkers are very logical people. They do not make decisions based on feelings or emotions. They are analytical and sometimes do not take others' values into consideration when making decisions. They can easily identify the flaws of others. They can sometimes be seen as insensitive and lacking compassion.

Feelers make decisions based on what they feel is right and just. They like to have harmony, and they value others' opinions and feelings. They are usually very tactful people who like to please others. They are very warm people.

J versus P (Judging/Perceiving)

This category deals with the way we *live and our overall lifestyle*.

Judgers are very orderly people. They must have a great deal of structure in their lives. They are good at setting goals and sticking to them. They are the type of people who would seldom, if ever, play before their work was completed.

Perceivers are just the opposite. They are less structured and more spontaneous. They do not like timelines. Unlike the judgers, they will play before their work is done. They will take every chance to delay a decision or judgment. Sometimes, they can become involved in too many things at one time.

After you have studied the the Personality Type Chart (Figure 7.9) and other information in the chapter regarding your personality type, you can make some decisions about your study habits and even your career choices. For instance, if you scored very high in the extroversion section, it may not serve you well to pursue a career where you would be forced to work alone. It would probably also be unwise to try to spend all of your time studying alone. If you are a strong extrovert, you would want to work and study around people.

bring the CHANGE

Tips for Personal Success

Consider the following tips for making the most of your learning style, personality type, and dominant intelligence.

- Improve your weaker learning styles by incorporating at least one aspect of those learning styles into your daily study plans.

- If your personality type clashes with your professor's personality type, try to make adjustments that enable you to get through the class successfully.

- Adjust your learning style to match your professor's teaching style if possible.

- Use your primary intelligence to help you decide on your life's vocation.

Now, it is your turn. Create a list of at least three more tips that you would offer a fellow classmate to assist him or her in making the most of his or her learning style, intelligence, and personality type. Develop one strategy for each category.

1. Learning Style Tip _____

2. Multiple Intelligence Tip _____

3. Personality Type Tip _____

While reading, you will want to take notes that are more elaborate than your highlighting or marginal notes. Taking notes while reading the text will assist you in studying the material and committing it to memory. **This is a major part of learning actively.** There are several effective methods of taking notes while reading (see Figure 6.8). They include:

Charts	Outlines	Flash cards
Mind maps	Timelines	Summaries
Keywords		

Figure 6.8   Sample Note-Taking Methods

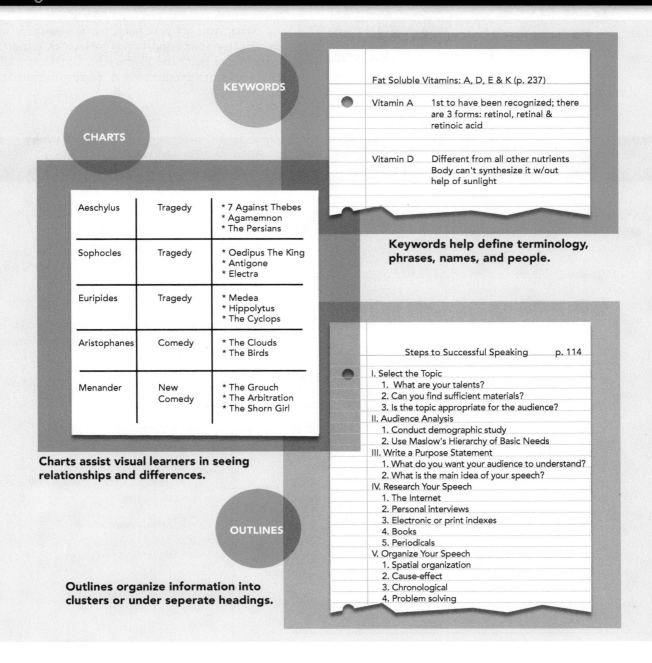

KEYWORDS

Fat Soluble Vitamins: A, D, E & K (p. 237)

Vitamin A   1st to have been recognized; there are 3 forms: retinol, retinal & retinoic acid

Vitamin D   Different from all other nutrients Body can't synthesize it w/out help of sunlight

Keywords help define terminology, phrases, names, and people.

CHARTS

Aeschylus	Tragedy	* 7 Against Thebes * Agamemnon * The Persians
Sophocles	Tragedy	* Oedipus The King * Antigone * Electra
Euripides	Tragedy	* Medea * Hippolytus * The Cyclops
Aristophanes	Comedy	* The Clouds * The Birds
Menander	New Comedy	* The Grouch * The Arbitration * The Shorn Girl

Charts assist visual learners in seeing relationships and differences.

OUTLINES

Steps to Successful Speaking   p. 114

I. Select the Topic
  1. What are your talents?
  2. Can you find sufficient materials?
  3. Is the topic appropriate for the audience?
II. Audience Analysis
  1. Conduct demographic study
  2. Use Maslow's Hierarchy of Basic Needs
III. Write a Purpose Statement
  1. What do you want your audience to understand?
  2. What is the main idea of your speech?
IV. Research Your Speech
  1. The Internet
  2. Personal interviews
  3. Electronic or print indexes
  4. Books
  5. Periodicals
V. Organize Your Speech
  1. Spatial organization
  2. Cause-effect
  3. Chronological
  4. Problem solving

Outlines organize information into clusters or under seperate headings.

As you read through a chapter in your textbook, you may find that you have to use a variety of these techniques to capture information. Try them for one week. Although taking notes while reading a chapter thoroughly is time consuming, you will be amazed at how much you remember and how much you are able to contribute in class after using these techniques. They work!

IT'S NOT OVER UNTIL IT'S OVER

What Is Reading Piece by Piece and How Can It Help?

If you are reading material that is completely new to you—difficult to understand yet important to remember—you may have to disregard paragraphs and paraphrase sections of a paragraph. This can be done with simple "tick marks" in your reading. This can be one of the most effective reading tools you will ever learn how to use.

> *"The man who does not read good books has no advantage over the man who can't read."*
>
> —Mark Twain

When you get to a point where you have "read enough," or your mind begins to wander, put a tick mark at that point (see Figure 6.9). Continue reading until you get to another section, putting tick marks in

---

Figure 6.9 Tick Mark Reading

A Brief History of Crime in America
(from F. Schmalleger, *Criminal Justice: A Brief Introduction*, 6th Edition. Prentice Hall, 2006.)

  1 What we call criminal activity has undoubtedly been with us since the dawn of history, and crime control has long been a primary concern of politicians and government leaders world-wide./ 2 Still, the American experience with crime during the last half century has been especially influential in shaping the criminal justice system of today./

  3 In this country, crime waves have come and gone, including an 1850–1880 crime epidemic, which was apparently related to social upheaval caused by large-scale immigration, and the spurt of widespread organized criminal activity associated with the Prohibition years of the early twentieth century./ 4 Following World War II, however, American crime rates remained relatively stable until the 1960s./

  5 The 1960s and 1970s saw a burgeoning concern for the rights of ethnic and racial minorities, women, the physically and mentally challenged, and many other groups. The civil rights movement of the period emphasized the equality of opportunity and respect for individuals, regardless of race, color, creed, or personal attributes./ 6 As new laws were passed and suits filed, court involvement in the movement grew. Soon, a plethora of hard-won individual rights and prerogatives, based on the U.S. Constitution, the Bill of Rights, and the new federal and state legislation, were recognized and guaranteed. By the 1980s, the civil rights movement had profoundly affected all areas of social life—from education throughout employment to the activities of the criminal justice system./

1) Criminal activity has been around since the beginning of time and has been a concern to politicians and leaders.

2) Crime in Am. has greatly shaped our criminal justice system in the past 50 years.

3) Crime in Am. has come in waves including the 1850–1880 epidemic due to immigration and a later one due to Prohibition.

4) After WWII, crime in Am. remained stable until the 60s.

5) During the 60s and 70s, Am. saw the rise of individual rights regardless of race, creed, or attributes.

6) Due to laws based on the US Constitution the C.R. Movement profoundly impacted all aspects of life in Am. including the C.J. system.

the places where you feel you have read a complete thought. You will not want to read an entire chapter at one time—simply a section, main heading to main heading. After you understand the section, move on to the next and then the next until the chapter is complete.

When you get to the end of the paragraph or section, reread the first section that you marked off. Out to the side, paraphrase that section. Then go to the next section. Look at the right-hand side of Figure 6.9 for an example.

Few techniques will assist your comprehension and retention more than this one because it requires you to be actively involved in the reading process. You are reading, paraphrasing, clarifying, and looking up words you do not know. This process is essential to you if your reading comprehension is not at the college level.

Recite

Recitation is simple, but crucial. Skipping this step may result in less than full mastery of the chapter. Once you have read a section using one or more of the previous techniques, ask yourself this simple question: "What was that all about?" Find a classmate, sit down together, and ask questions of each other. Discuss the main points of the chapter. Try to explain the information to each other without looking at your notes. If you are at home, sit back in your chair, recite the information, and determine what it means. If you have trouble explaining the information to your friend or reciting it to yourself, you probably did not understand

BRING the Change

TIPS FOR PERSONAL SUCCESS

Consider the following strategies for making the most of your reading time:

- Reduce the distractions around you. Try to find an atmosphere that is comfortable and effective for you.
- Discover what time of day is best for you to read and concentrate on your material.
- Read in sections. Don't try to read an entire chapter in one sitting. Break it down and take breaks.
- Never just skip over words or phrases that you don't understand. Look them up in a dictionary.

Now, it is your turn. Make a list of three tips you would share with a classmate that would assist him or her in becoming a better reader.

1. _____

_____

2. _____

_____

3. _____

_____

the section and you should go back and re-read it. If you can tell your classmate and yourself exactly what you just read and what it means, you are ready to move on to the next section of the chapter.

Another way to practice reciting is to use the materials you produced as you read the chapter. Hopefully, you took notes, highlighted passages, underlined phrases, and paraphrased sections. From these, you can create flash cards, outlines, mind maps, timelines, and keyword note cards. Using these materials is another way to "recite" the material.

Review

After you have read the chapter, immediately go back and read it again. "What?!! I just read it!" Yes, you did. And the best way to determine whether you have mastered the information is once again to survey the chapter; review marginal notes, highlighted areas, and vocabulary words; and determine whether you can answer the questions you posed the during the "Question" step of SQ3R. This step will help you store and retain this information in long-term memory.

REFLECTIONS ON READING AND COMPREHENSION

SQ3R can be a lifesaver when it comes to understanding material that is overwhelming. It is an efficient, comprehensive, and doable practice that can dramatically assist you in your reading efforts. It may take more time than your old method, but you will begin to see the results almost immediately. Seriously considering and practicing the strategies we have outlined will help increase your comprehension level, and it will also help your ability to recall the information when you need it later on.

It has been suggested that if you can effectively read, write, and speak the English language, there is nothing that you can't accomplish. The power of knowledge is monumental in your quest to become a productive and active citizen. Effective reading skills will help you acquire that knowledge.

As you continue to work to become an active, engaged learner, consider the following tips for reading comprehension and retention:

- Approach the text, chapter, or article with an *open mind*.
- Free your mind to focus on your reading.
- Always read with your "six-pack" at your side.
- Underline and look up words you do not understand.
- Write down your vocabulary words and review them often.
- Use SQ3R to increase and test your comprehension.
- If you're having trouble, get a tutor to help you.
- Understand that the more you read, the better you'll become at it.

"The knowledge of words is the gateway to learning."

—W. Wilson

Knowledge

in Bloom

READING FOR COMPREHENSION

Utilizes levels 1–6 of the taxonomy

Each chapter-end assessment is based on Bloom's Taxonomy of Learning. See pages xxvi–xxviii in the front of this book for a quick review.

Process: Read the following story carefully, looking up words that you do not understand, highlighting phrases that you think are important, and paraphrasing in the spaces provided. When reading the story, use the SQ3R method. We've done paragraph 1 for you as an example.

The Life and Death of Harvey Milk

READ THIS SECTION, IDENTIFY UNFAMILIAR WORDS, HIGHLIGHT IMPORTANT WORDS AND PHRASES	LOOK UP WORDS THAT NEED TO BE DEFINED	PARAPHRASE THE MAIN IDEA IN YOUR OWN WORDS
More <u>perplexing</u> things have happened, but a Twinkie caused the death of Harvey Milk. That's right. In 1978, defense lawyers using the "Twinkie Defense" explained an <u>inexplicable</u> murder away. This was the first mainstream trial to use the "I am not responsible for my actions" defense.	*Unfamiliar words and definitions* Perplexing = confusing or puzzling Inexplicable = not easily explained, unreasonable	*The main idea of this paragraph is:* In 1978, defense lawyers used a new strategy called "the Twinkie Defense" to explain why someone murdered Harvey Milk.
Harvey Milk was the first openly gay man elected to a significant office in America. In 1977, Milk was elected as a member of the San Francisco Board of Supervisors. This was quite challenging at this point in U.S. history when most people, including many psychologists and religious leaders, still classified homosexuality as deviant and a mental illness.	*Unfamiliar words and definitions*	*The main idea of this paragraph is:* _____ _____ _____ _____ _____
Harvey Milk is to the gay rights movement what Martin Luther King Jr. is to the civil rights movement. Before King, little was happening with the CRM, and before Milk, little was happening with the GRM. He changed the face of California politics and paved the way for countless other gays and lesbians to enter the world of politics.	*Unfamiliar words and definitions*	*The main idea of this paragraph is:* _____ _____ _____ _____ _____

READ THIS SECTION, IDENTIFY UNFAMILIAR WORDS, HIGHLIGHT IMPORTANT WORDS AND PHRASES	LOOK UP WORDS THAT NEED TO BE DEFINED	PARAPHRASE THE MAIN IDEA IN YOUR OWN WORDS
Dan White, a staunch anti-gay advocate, served on the board with Milk. They were constantly at odds with each other and often engaged in verbal confrontations.	*Unfamiliar words and definitions*	*The main idea of this paragraph is:* _____
White had been a policeman and a fireman in San Francisco before running for office. While running for office, he vowed to restore "family values" to the city government. He vowed to "rid San Francisco of radicals, social deviants, and incorrigibles."	*Unfamiliar words and definitions*	*The main idea of this paragraph is:* _____
Dan White was one of the most conservative members of the board, and many proposals brought to the board by Milk and the mayor of San Francisco, George Moscone, were defeated because of the heavily conservative vote led by White.	*Unfamiliar words and definitions*	*The main idea of this paragraph is:* _____
At that time, the Board of Supervisors was made up of 11 members; six of them, including Dan White, were conservative and had the power to defeat most, if not all of the liberal measures brought before the board. This did not fare well with Harvey Milk and the other liberal members of the board.	*Unfamiliar words and definitions*	*The main idea of this paragraph is:* _____
Because the job offered diminutive wages, Dan White soon realized that he could not support his family on $9,800 per year, and he submitted his resignation to Mayor Moscone. This did not sit well with the people who elected him, and they urged him to reconsider. When he tried to rescind his resignation, Mayor Moscone refused. This decision was made in part because Harvey Milk convinced Moscone to deny White's reinstatement.	*Unfamiliar words and definitions*	*The main idea of this paragraph is:* _____
In a fit of wrath over the decision, Dan White entered the San Francisco City Hall on the morning of November 27, 1978, through a basement window. He went to Mayor Moscone's office and shot him in the chest, and as he lay dying, White shot him again in the head.	*Unfamiliar words and definitions*	*The main idea of this paragraph is:* _____

READ THIS SECTION, IDENTIFY UNFAMILIAR WORDS, HIGHLIGHT IMPORTANT WORDS AND PHRASES	LOOK UP WORDS THAT NEED TO BE DEFINED	PARAPHRASE THE MAIN IDEA IN YOUR OWN WORDS
White then walked calmly down the hall and asked to see Harvey Milk. Once inside the office, he slew Milk with two bullets to the brain. He then left City Hall, called his wife, spoke with her in person at St. Mary's Cathedral, and then turned himself in.	*Unfamiliar words and definitions*	*The main idea of this paragraph is:* _____ _____ _____ _____ _____
It is reported that policemen representing the city of San Francisco shouted, cheered, and applauded when news of the murders reached the police department.	*Unfamiliar words and definitions*	*The main idea of this paragraph is:* _____ _____ _____ _____ _____
Dan White's defense lawyers used a "diminished capacity" defense, suggesting that he was led to his actions by too much sugar from junk food. The lawyers convinced a jury that he was not himself and his senses were off-kilter. This became known as the "Twinkie Defense."	*Unfamiliar words and definitions*	*The main idea of this paragraph is:* _____ _____ _____ _____ _____
Dan White was convicted of second-degree manslaughter and was sentenced to only seven years for two premeditated murders. After serving only five years, he was released. The "Twinkie Defense" had worked.	*Unfamiliar words and definitions*	*The main idea of this paragraph is:* _____ _____ _____ _____ _____
In 1985, after being released from Soledad Prison, Dan White walked into his garage, took a rubber hose, connected it to his car's exhaust, and killed himself with carbon monoxide poisoning. He was 39 years old. His tomb reads, "Daniel J. White (1946–October 21, 1985), Sgt. U.S. Army, Vietnam." Cause of death: Suicide.	*Unfamiliar words and definitions*	*The main idea of this paragraph is:* _____ _____ _____ _____ _____

Sources: "He Got Away with Murder," retrieved from www.findagrave.com; "The Pioneer Harvey Milk," retrieved from www.time.com; "Remembering Harvey Milk," retrieved from www.lambda.net.

In 100 words or less, thoroughly summarize this entire article. Be certain to include dates, names, places, and circumstances. Pretend that you have to explain this entire story to an eight-year-old. This exercise will help you become more adept at the essential cornerstone skill of knowledge.

SQ3R MASTERY STUDY SHEET

EXAMPLE QUESTION *(from page 142)*
Describe the process of fixation.

ANSWER:

EXAMPLE QUESTION *(from page 142)*
Why is comprehension more important than speed?

ANSWER:

AUTHOR QUESTION *(from page 138)*
Differentiate between passive and active reading.

ANSWER:

AUTHOR QUESTION *(from page 143)*
Discuss three strategies for reading online material.

ANSWER:

AUTHOR QUESTION *(from page 149)*
What are some effective ways of taking notes while reading?

ANSWER:

AUTHOR QUESTION *(from page 152)*
How can you use tick marks to help you improve your reading ability?

ANSWER:

AUTHOR QUESTION *(from page 153)*
Why is recitation an important part of reading comprehension?

ANSWER:

YOUR QUESTION *(from page ___)*

ANSWER:

YOUR QUESTION *(from page ___)*

ANSWER:

YOUR QUESTION *(from page ___)*

ANSWER:

YOUR QUESTION *(from page ___)*

ANSWER:

YOUR QUESTION *(from page ___)*

ANSWER:

Finally, after answering these questions, recite in your mind the major points covered here. Consider the following general questions to help you master this material.

- What was it about?
- What does it mean?
- What was the most important thing you learned? Why?
- What were the key points to remember?

chapter seven

PRIORITIZE

MANAGING YOUR TIME, STRESS, AND HEALTH WISELY

"If you want to make good use of your time, you've got to know what's most important and then give it all you've got." —Lee Iacocca

Why read this chapter?

Because you'll learn:

- The relationship between time management, your value system, and self-discipline
- How you spend your time and develop a "to do" list based on your findings
- How to deal with the major stressors in your life

Because you'll be able to:

- Simplify your life
- Avoid distractions and interruptions in your daily life
- Beat procrastination and get more done

Scan and QUESTION

Take a few moments, **scan this chapter,** and on page 191, write **five of your own questions** that you think will be important to your mastery of this material. You will also find five questions listed from your authors.

Example:

☑ **What are the components of self-discipline?** (from page 164)

☑ **How can I simplify my life and get more done?** (from page 168)

MyStudentSuccessLab

MyStudentSuccessLab (www.mystudentsuccesslab.com) is an online solution designed to help you "Start strong, Finish stronger" by building skills for ongoing personal and professional development.

How

COLLEGE CHANGED MY LIFE

Name:	Erica R. Harrison
Institution:	Graduate! Lincoln College of Technology
Age:	22
Major:	Medical Administrative Assistant
Career:	Medical Assistant

I knew that I wanted a better job and a better life for myself. I quickly realized that a high school diploma would not get me those things in today's world. I knew that I loved the medical field and that I wanted to work with patients. I enrolled at Lincoln Tech because they promised hands-on experiences and that was what I needed and wanted. After my classes, I enrolled in an externship program through the college. I worked with preparing patients' charts, taking appointments, working with x-rays, and helping patients with referrals. This clinical experience was great and gave me real-world knowledge. I knew that I had found my calling.

After graduation, I realized that I had gained the experiences through my classes and my externship to help me be successful in my first position in a pediatric office. There, I performed vitals on patients, conducted labs, assisted with tests, and prepared patients with their pre-operation procedures. I was using my education.

During college, the biggest challenge for me was staying motivated. I had to fight the outside forces that continually wanted me to do just enough to get by. I had to learn how to do as much as I needed to do and not just what I wanted to do. For me, I learned that focus was the most important aspect of motivation. You have to learn how to harness your determination into a vision of your future. You have to set goals for everything and work toward them with passion and energy. Without these hard-learned lessons, I would not have a career today—I'd just have a job. I wake up in the mornings and know that I am going to do something that I love and not just another dead-end job.

One of the most important things that college taught me was to look into the future as a source of motivation. If I looked into the future without a degree, what would my life be? If I looked into the future with a degree, what would my life be? This exercise taught me how to eliminate the obstacles that threatened my future and obtain my degree.

The biggest lesson that I learned in college beyond the required elements of my field of study was that I had to believe in myself. I know that sounds trivial, but it is vitally important. You have to believe that this degree and a better life are possible for you. You can't sit around waiting for the future to get better, for someone to wave a magical wand and give you your dream job. You have to make our own future. Your training and degree will be the first step in making your future.

THINK
about it

1. Erica mentions that her externship was very beneficial to her future employment. What do you hope to learn from your internship or externship? How will this help you?

2. What will your future look like without a college degree?

TIME—YOU HAVE ALL THERE IS

Can You Take Control of Your Life and Make the Most of Your Time?

You can definitely say four things about time: *It is fair. It does not discriminate. It treats everyone the same. Everyone has all there is.* No person has any more or less hours in a day than the next person. It may seem that Gary or Tamisha has more time that you do, but they do not. In a 24-hour span we all have 1,440 minutes. No more. No less. There is one more thing you can definitely say about time, too: **it can be cruel and unrelenting.** It is one of the few things in our lives that we cannot stop. There are no time-out periods, no breaks, and try as we might, we can't turn it back, shut it down, or stop it. The good news, however, is that by learning how to manage our time more effectively, we don't need to slow it down or stop it. We can learn how to get things done and have more time for joy and fun.

So, how do you spend your time? Some people are very productive, while others scramble to find a few moments to enjoy life and have quality relationships. According to time management and personal productivity expert Donald Wetmore (2008), "The average working person spends less than two minutes per day in meaningful communication with their spouse or significant other and less than 30 seconds per day in meaningful communication with their children." Think about that for a moment. *Thirty seconds.* If you think that is amazing, consider the following list. As strange as it may seem, these figures are taken from the Bureau of Labor Statistics of the U.S. Department of Census (2006). During your ***working years*** (age 20–65, a 45-year span), you spend an average of:

- 16 years sleeping
- 2.3 years eating
- 3.1 years doing housework
- 6 years watching TV
- 1.3 years on the telephone

This totals **28.7 years of your working life** doing things that you may not even consider in your time management plan. What happens to the remaining 16.3 years? Well, you will spend **14 of those years working,** which leaves you with 2.3 years, or only 20,000 hours during your working life, to embrace joy, spend time with your family, educate yourself, travel, and experience a host of other life-fulfilling activities. Dismal? Scary? It does not have to be. By learning how to manage your time, harness your energy and passion, and take control of your day-to-day activities, 2.3 years can be a long, exciting, productive time.

Why is it that some people seem to get so much more done than other people? They appear to always be calm and collected and have it together. Many people from this group work long hours in addition to going to school. They never appear to be stressed out, and they seem to be able to do it all with grace and charm. Uggh!

iStockPhoto

Shutterstock

Shutterstock

Do the figures regarding how we spend our time surprise you? Where do you think most of your "free" time goes?

You are probably aware of others who are always late with assignments, never finish their projects on time, rarely seem to have time to study, and appear to have no concrete goals for their lives. Sometimes, we get the idea that the first group accomplishes more because they have more time or because they don't have to work or they don't have children or they are smarter or have more help. Some of these reasons may be true, but in reality, many of these people have learned how to overcome and beat procrastination, tie their value system to their time management plan, and use their personal energy and passion to accomplish more.

"I can't do any more than I am doing right now," you may say to yourself. But is that really true? One of the keys to managing your time is to consider your values. What you value, enjoy, and love, you tend to put more passion, energy, and time toward. Do you value your family? If so, you make time for them. Do you value your friends? If so you make time for them. Now you have to ask yourself, "How much do I value my education? How important is it that I succeed in college and get my degree?" If you highly value education, you will find that you make more time for your studies, your classes, and your projects. **We spend time on what we value!**

TIME MANAGEMENT AND SELF-DISCIPLINE

Do You Have What It Takes to "Git 'er Done?"

Time management is actually about managing you! It is about taking control and assuming responsibility for the time you are given on this earth. The sooner you understand and get control of how you use your time, the quicker you will be on your way to becoming successful in college and many other activities. Learning to manage your time is a lesson that you will use throughout your studies and beyond. **You can't control time,** but you can control yourself. Time management

> "Self-discipline is teaching ourselves to do the things necessary to reach our goals without becoming sidetracked by bad habits."
> —Denis Waitley

is basically self-discipline—and self-discipline involves self-motivation. Time management is paying attention to how you are spending your most valuable resource and then devising a plan to use it more effectively. This is one of the goals of this chapter.

The word *discipline* comes from the Latin word meaning "to teach." Therefore, *self-discipline* is really about "teaching ourselves" (Waitley, 1997). Self-discipline implies that you have the ability to teach yourself how to get more done when things are going well and when they are not going so well. If you have self-discipline, you have learned how to hold it all together when things get tough, when you feel beaten, and when defeat seems just around the corner. It also means that when you have important tasks to complete, you can temporarily pull yourself away from enjoyable situations and fun times until those tasks have been completed. Consider the chart in Figure 7.1 regarding self-discipline. **Self-discipline is really about four things: making choices, making changes, using willpower, and taking responsibility.**

Once you have made the **choice** to engage in your education, stop procrastinating, and mange your time more effectively, you have to make the **changes** in your thoughts and behaviors to bring those choices to fruition. Then, you have to **accept responsibility** for your actions and take control of your life. You have to call on your **inner strength or willpower**—and you *do* have willpower. It may just be hidden or forgotten, but you do have it. You have the ability to empower yourself to get things done. No one can do this for you. You are responsible for your life and your actions. Self-discipline and willpower help you move in the direction of your dreams. Even in the face of fear, anxiety, stress, defeat, and darkness, self-discipline will help you find your way.

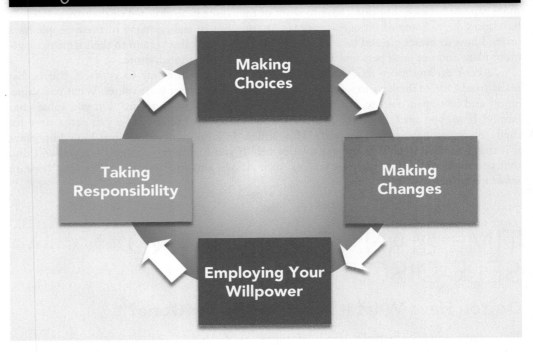

Figure 7.1 **Components of Self-Discipline**

Willpower and self-discipline are all about ***re-training your mind*** to do what *you* want it to do and not what *it* wants to do. It is about eliminating the negative self-talk that so often derails us and causes us to procrastinate and get stressed out. By re-training your mind and resisting the urge to simply "obey" your subconscious, you are basically re-training your life. Consider the following situations:

- You come home from class, tired and weary. Your subconscious mind tells you to sit down, put your feet up, and watch TV for a while. You have to tell your mind, "NO! I am going to take a short walk around the block to get my adrenaline flowing, and then I'm going to read my chapter for homework."

- You look at your desk or study space and see all of the books and papers you have gathered for your research paper. Your subconscious mind tells you to just ignore it for a while; there's still time to get it done! You have to tell your mind, "ABSO-LUTELY NOT! I'm going to get those articles organized and make an outline of my paper before I do anything else today. Period."

- You come home tired and hungry and your mind tells you to eat that candy bar or donut. You have to tell your mind, "NO WAY! I am going to have an apple instead. It is better for me and my memory to avoid sugar right now."

"Begin doing what you want to do now. We are not living in eternity. We have only this moment, sparkling like a star in our hand and melting like a snowflake."
—Marie B. Ray

By re-training your mind and paying attention to your subconscious, you can re-train yourself to develop the self-discipline and willpower to get things done and avoid the stress caused by procrastination. Willpower gives you strength to stay on track and avoid the guilt associated with putting things off or not doing them at all. Guilt turns to frustration, frustration turns to anger, and before you know it, your negative self-talk and subconscious mind have "won" and nothing gets done. You have the power to change this.

I'LL DO IT WHEN I HAVE A LITTLE FREE TIME

Is Time Really "Free"?

Shutterstock

How can becoming a more organized person help you manage your time more effectively?

What is "free time" and when does it happen? We've all used that expression at one time or another: "I'll do that when I get a little more free time," or "I'm going to wait until I find a little more time." Can time be found? Is time free? Do we ever have a moment to call our own? The answer is "maybe," but free time has to be created by you, and it can only be created by getting the things done that must be completed for your success.

Free time is *not* time that you simply create by putting off work that needs to be done. Free time is *not* time that is spent procrastinating. Free time is *not* time that you take away from your duties, chores, studies, family, and obligations. That is **borrowed time**, and if you know the rules of good behavior, you know that anything you borrow, you must repay. When are you going to find the time to "repay" these blocks of time to yourself? Usually, you don't, and that is when and where you get into trouble and your stress levels start to rise.

Free time *is* time that you reward yourself with when you have completed your studies, tasks, chores, and obligations. Free time *is* time that you have created by planning ahead and avoiding procrastination. Free time *is* time that you enjoy when your work is done and you can sit and enjoy your life, family, and friends because the pressures and guilt of poor time management are not haunting you. One of your goals in managing your time more effectively is to create more free time in your life for joy. Joy will not come to you, however, if you have projects looming over your head.

PLANNING, DOODLING, OR BEGGING

What Type of Person Are You, Anyway?

We all have different personality types, but did you know we also have different time management personalities? Consider the list in Figure 7.2 explaining the different negative time management personalities. Respond YES or NO to each management style. Then, out to the side, explain why you think this type represents you and your daily thoughts on time, if it does. Then, in the last column, list at least one strategy that you can implement to overcome this type of negative time management style.

ABSOLUTELY NO . . . WELL, MAYBE

Do You Know How to Say No?

"No, I'm sorry, I can't do that" is perhaps one of the most difficult phrases you must learn to say when it comes to effective time management. "Jeez, I should have never agreed to do this in the first place" is perhaps one of the most common phrases used when you don't know how to say "no." If you continually say "yes" to everyone and every project, then quickly, you have no time left for yourself, your family, your friends, and your projects. Many of us are taught from an early

Figure 7.2 Time Management Types

TYPE	EXPLANATION	DO YOU HAVE ANY OF THESE TENDENCIES?		WHAT ACTIONS MAKE YOU LIKE THIS TYPE OF PERSON?	WHAT CAN YOU DO TO BEGIN ELIMINATING THIS TYPE OF BEHAVIOR?
The Circler	Doing the same things over and over again and again and hoping for a different result; basically, going around in circles.	YES	NO		
The Doodler	Not paying attention to details, doing things that do not really matter to the completion of your project.	YES	NO		
The Squanderer	Wasting too much time trying to "get ready" to study or work and never really getting anything done until it is too late to do a good job.	YES	NO		
The Beggar	Expecting time to stop for you after you've wasted time doing nothing or going in circles, then becoming frustrated when you don't have enough time.	YES	NO		
The Planner	Planning out your project so carefully and meticulously that by the time you have everything you think you need, there is no time to really do the project.	YES	NO		
The Hun	Waiting too late to plan or get things done and then stomping on anyone or anything to get the project done with no regard for others' feelings, time, or relationships.	YES	NO		
The Passivist	Convincing yourself that you'll never get it all done and that there is no use to try anyway.	YES	NO		

age that *no* is a bad word and that we should always try to avoid saying it to others. However, we are not taught that never saying "no" can cause us undue stress, feelings of guilt and frustration, and throw our time management plans into disarray. Now that you have so much going on from so many different projects, the word *no* needs to become a part of your everyday vocabulary. By learning to say "no" to a few things, you can begin to say "yes" to many other things—things that you want to do, things that you need to do, and things that will actually help others in the long run. "No" is not rude; it is simply a way of managing your time so that you have more time to say "yes" to what is important and useful.

> "Time is the most valuable and most perishable of our possessions."
> —John Randolph

LEARNING TO SAY NO: IT'S AS SIMPLE AS *NOT* SAYING YES

- Think before you answer out loud with an insincere or untrue "yes."

- Make sure you understand exactly what is being asked of you and what the project involves before you give an answer.

- Review your schedule to see if you really have the time to do a quality job. (If you have to have an answer immediately, it is "no." If you can wait a few days for me to finish project X and review my schedule, the answer may be "yes.")

- Learn the difference between assertiveness (politely declining) and rudeness ("Have you lost your mind?").

- Say "no" at the right times (to the wrong things) so that you can say "yes" at the appropriate times (to the right things).

- Learn how to put yourself and your future first (for a change). By doing this, you can say "yes" more often later on.

- Inform others of your time management schedule so that they will have a better understanding of why you say "no."

- If you must say "yes" to an unwanted project (something at work, for example), try to negotiate a deadline that works for everyone—you first!

iStockPhoto

Do you think saying "no" is rude or necessary?

- Keep your "no" short. If you have to offer an explanation, be brief so that you don't talk yourself into doing something you can't do and to avoid giving false hope to the other person. If the answer is "no" right now and it will be "no" in the future, say so now.

- Offer suggestions to the other person as to who may be able to help them or when you might be available (if it is in your best interest to accept this request at any time).

- If you feel you simply have to say "yes," try to trade off with the other person and ask him or her to do something on your list.

- Put a time limit on your "yes." For example, you might agree to help someone but you could say, "I can give you 30 minutes and then I have to leave."

Your Turn

You are taking four classes, and the reading and homework are mounting day by day. Your family needs you, your friends think you've abandoned them, and you want to continue to do a good job at work. Your schedule is tight, and you have things planned down to the hour in order to be able to get it all done well. Suddenly, you are asked to help with a project for disadvantaged children that seems very worthy and timely. You know that your schedule is full, but your conscience begins to gnaw at you and you really do want to help.

Applying the tips from the list above, predict how you might be able to address this situation.

BLOOM LEVEL 3

_____

_____

_____

_____

BEGINNING YOUR DAY WITH PEACE

Can You Start Your Day as a Blank Page and Simplify Your Life?

Imagine a day with nothing to do! That may be difficult, if not impossible, for you to conceive of right now. But as an exercise in building your own day from scratch and simplifying your life, think about having a day where you build your schedule and where you do not have to be constrained by activities and projects that others have thrust on you. Think about a day where you are in charge. Crazy? Impossible? Outrageous? Maybe not as much as you think.

Yes, you will need to plot activities such as work, class, and family duties into your daily calendar, but you will also need to learn how to schedule time for fun activities, time for silence and peace, and time to be alone with your thoughts. By learning how to build your schedule each evening from scratch, you have the opportunity to plan a day where you simplify your life. There is an old quote that states, "If you want to know what you value in your life, look at your checkbook and your calendar." Basically, this suggests that we spend our money and time on things we value.

TWELVE WAYS TO SIMPLIFY YOUR LIFE

- Know what you value, and work hard to eliminate activities that are not in conjunction with your core value system. This can be whittled down to one statement: "Identify what is important to you. Eliminate everything else."

- Get away from technology for a few hours a day. Turn off your computer, cell phone, iPod, and other devices that can take time from what you value.

- Learn to delegate. You may say to yourself, "My family does not know how to use the washing machine." Guess what? When all of their underwear is dirty, they'll learn how to use it. Don't enable others to avoid activities that complicate your life.

- Make a list of everything you are doing. Prioritize this list into what you enjoy doing and what fits into your value system. If you can only feasibly do three or four of these activities per day, draw a line after number four and eliminate the rest of the list.

- Do what is essential for the well-being of you and your family and eliminate everything else.

- Don't waste time saving money. **Wisely** spend money to save time. Don't drive across town to save three cents per gallon on fuel or 10 cents for a gallon of milk. If you plan ahead, many cost- and time-saving situations will present themselves.

- Clean your home of clutter and mess. Work from cleanliness. De-clutter and organize. Make sure everything has a place.

- Donate everything you don't need or use to charity. Simplifying your life may also mean simplifying your closets, drawers, cabinets, and garage.

- Go through your home or apartment and eliminate everything that does not bring you joy or have sentimental value. If you don't love it, ditch it.

- Clean up the files on your computer. Erase everything that you don't need or want so that you can find material more easily. If you have not used the file in a month, put it on a flash drive for later use.

- Live in the moment. Yes, it is important to plan for the future, but if you ignore "the moment," your future will not be as bright.

- Spend a few moments each morning and afternoon reflecting on all of the abundance in your life. Learn to give thanks and learn to do nothing (Zen Habits, 2008; Get More Done, 2009).

BLOOM LEVEL 6

Figure 7.3 **Simplify Your Life**

Two things I can do to simplify my life at home

Two things I can do to simplify my life at work

Two things I can do to simplify my life at school

Two things I can do to simplify my life with my children

Two things I can do to simplify my life with my
spouse/partner/loved one

Two things I can do to simplify my financial matters

In Figure 7.3, compile a list that can help you simplify your life in each category. Add only those things to the list that you can actually do on a daily basis.

PROCRASTINATION: THE DREADED "P" WORD

How Can You Beat It Once and for All?

It's not just you! Almost everyone procrastinates, and then we worry and tell ourselves, "I'll never do it again if I can just get through this one project." We say things to ourselves like, "If I can just live through this paper, I will never wait until the last minute again." But someone comes along with a great idea for fun, and off we go. Or there is a great movie on TV, the kids want to play a game of ball, you go to the refrigerator for snack, and before you know it, you reward yourself with free time before you have done your work.

> "If you have to eat two frogs,
> eat the ugliest one first."
> —Brian Tracy

The truth is simple: We tend to avoid the hard jobs in favor of the easy ones. Even many of the list makers fool themselves. They mark off a long list of easy tasks while the big ones still loom in front of them. Many of us put off unpleasant tasks until our back is against the wall. So why do we procrastinate when we all know how unpleasant the results can be? Why aren't we disciplined, organized, and controlled so we can reap the rewards that come from being prepared? Why do we put ourselves through so much stress just by putting things off?

The biggest problem with procrastination, even beyond not getting the job, task, or paper completed, is *doing it poorly* and then suffering the stress caused by putting it off or turning in a subpar project. By putting the project off, you have cheated yourself out of the time needed to bring your best to the table. Most likely, you are going to hand over a project with your name on it that is not even close to your potential. And to top it off, more stress is created by this vicious cycle of "I'll do it tomorrow—or this weekend."

What has procrastination cost you? This is perhaps one of the most important questions that you can answer with regard to managing your time more effectively. Did it cost you a good grade? Did it cost you money? Did it cost you your reputation? Did it cost you your dignity? Did it cost you your ability to do your best? ***Procrastination is not free.*** Every time you do it, it costs you something. You need to determine what it is worth.

Successful Decisions
AN ACTIVITY FOR CRITICAL REFLECTION

Darius is a single father of two young daughters. He and his wife divorced several years ago and he was granted custody of Alice and Marianne. Shortly after the divorce, Darius was laid off from his job as a construction foreman. He had been making a very good living, but now, it was hard to make ends meet. He could not find another job that paid well enough to support the three of them.

Therefore, he decided to go back to school to pursue his dream of becoming a draftsman. His classes, along with his new part-time job, demanded much of his time. He found that he was spending much less time with his daughters than he had in the past—and he did not like this at all.

His daughters were cast in the school play and the performance was scheduled for Friday night—the same night as one of his drafting classes. He knew that he had a conflict on his hands. He knew that class was very important, but so was supporting his daughters. In your own words, what would you suggest that Darius do at this point? List at least three things that he could do handle this situation, manage his time to meet all of his obligations, and maintain his sanity.

1. _____
_____

2. _____
_____

3. _____
_____

In order to beat procrastination, you will also need to consider *what type* of procrastinator you are. Each type requires a different strategy and different energy to overcome, but make no doubt about it, success requires overcoming all degrees and types of procrastination. Which are you? Consider Figure 7.4.

Take a moment and complete the Time Management Assessment in Figure 7.5 (page 172). Be honest and truthful with your responses. The results of your score are provided after the assessment.

Procrastination is quite simply a bad habit formed after many years of practice. There are reasons, however, that cause us to keep doing this to ourselves. Often, we let our negative self-talk cause us to procrastinate. We allow our negative attitude to override what we know is best for us. An attitude adjustment may be just the thing you need to overcome the trap of procrastination. Consider the following negative statements. On the right-hand side, rewrite the statement to become a positive, procrastination-beating statement.

NEGATIVE STATEMENT	POSITIVE STATEMENT
I'll do it at 9:30 when this TV show is off.	_____
I'm tired.	_____
I can't concentrate.	_____
This is too hard.	_____
This is boring.	_____
I don't know why anyone would ask me to do this crazy stuff.	_____

Learning to apply this type of positive thinking can help you beat the procrastination trap and manage your time and life more effectively.

Figure 7.4 **Procrastinator Types**	

Chronic Procrastinator	You procrastinate all of the time in most aspects of your life including social situations, financial affairs, career decisions, personal responsibilities, and academic projects. Usually, you do not meet any deadlines if you complete the project at all. It is going to take a great deal of thought, planning, and energy to overcome this type of procrastination.
Moderate Procrastinator	You procrastinate much of the time. You usually get things done, but it is not your best work and you create a great deal of stress in your own life. It is going to take a fair amount of planning and energy to overcome this type of procrastination. With some planning, your projects could be much more effective and you could eliminate much stress and guilt.
Occasional Procrastinator	You occasionally put things off. You do not do this often, but when you do, you feel guilty and rush to get the project completed. Sometimes you turn in work that is not your best. You are good at planning most things, but you do need to concentrate on sticking to your plan and not letting unscheduled events obstruct your success.

GETTING THE MOST OUT OF THIS MOMENT

Do You Know the Causes of and Cures for Procrastination?

Below, you will find a list of the 10 most common causes of procrastination and some simple, doable, everyday strategies that you can employ to overcome each cause. We have provided three strategies for each cause. Add at least two of your own strategies to overcome this type of procrastination.

SUPERHUMAN EXPECTATIONS AND TRYING TO BE A PERFECTIONIST

- Allow yourself more time than you think you need to complete a project.
- Realize that no one, including you, is (or ever will be) perfect. Perfection does not exist.
- Allow enough time to do your very best and let that be that. If you plan and allow time for excellence, you can't do more.
- _____
- _____

Figure 7.5 Time Management Assessment

Answer the following questions with the following scale:

1 = Not at all   2 = Rarely   3 = Sometimes   4 = Often   5 = Very often

1. I prioritize my tasks every day and work from my priority list.		1 2 3 4 5
2. I work hard to complete tasks on time and not put them off until the last minute.		1 2 3 4 5
3. I take time to plan and schedule the next day's activities the night before.		1 2 3 4 5
4. I make time during my daily schedule to study and get my projects completed so that I can have more quality time at home.		1 2 3 4 5
5. I study and get my work done before I take fun breaks.		1 2 3 4 5
6. I analyze my assignments to determine which ones are going to take the most time and then work on them first and most often.		1 2 3 4 5
7. I have analyzed my daily activities and determined where I actually spend my time.		1 2 3 4 5
8. I know how to say "no" and do so frequently.		1 2 3 4 5
9. I know how to avoid distractions and how to work through unexpected interruptions.		1 2 3 4 5
10. I do not let "fear of the unknown" keep me from working on a project.		1 2 3 4 5
11. I know how to overcome apathy toward a project.		1 2 3 4 5
12. I know how to fight and overcome my own laziness.		1 2 3 4 5
13. I know how to reframe a project that may not interest me so that I can see the benefit in it and learn from it.		1 2 3 4 5
14. I know how to break down a major, complex, or overwhelming task to get it done in pieces and then put it all together.		1 2 3 4 5
15. I build time into my schedule on a daily or weekly basis to deal with unexpected interruptions and distractions.		1 2 3 4 5

YOUR TOTAL SCORE: _____

RESULTS: **60–75** You manage your time well and you know how to build a schedule to get things done. Your productivity is high. You don't let procrastination rule your life.

45–59 You are good at doing some things on time, but you tend to procrastinate too much. Learning how to build and work from a priority list may help you manage your time more effectively.

30–44 You need to work hard to change your time management skills and learn how to set realistic goals. Procrastination is probably a major issue for you, causing you much stress and worry. Working from a priority list can help you greatly.

29–below Your time management skills are very weak, and without change and improvement, your success plan could be in jeopardy. You could benefit from learning to set realistic goals, working from a priority list, and reframing your thought process toward tasks.

FEAR OF NOT KNOWING HOW TO DO THE TASK

- Ask for clarification from whoever asked you to do the project.
- Read as much as you can about the task at hand and ask for help.
- Break up big tasks into small ones.
- _____
- _____

LACK OF MOTIVATION

- Reframe your attitude to find the benefit in any task.
- Consider how this task will help you reach your overall goals and dreams.
- Take time to do the things you love, creating a healthy balance in your life.
- _____
- _____

FEAR OF FAILING OR FEAR OF THE TASK BEING TOO HARD

- Start the project with positive, optimistic thoughts.
- Face your fears; look them right in the face and make a decision to defeat them.
- Visualize your successful completion of the project.
- _____
- _____

Photolibrary RF

Is there a difference between laziness, procrastination, and resting?

NO REAL PLAN OR GOAL FOR GETTING THE TASK DONE

- Set reasonable, concrete goals that you can reach in about 20 to 25 minutes.
- Draw up an action plan the night before you begin the project.
- Look at completing the project in terms of your long-range goals and your overall life plan.
- _____
- _____

CONSIDERING THE TASK TOO UNPLEASANT OR UNINTERESTING

- Realize that most tasks are not as unpleasant as we've made them out to be.
- Do the hardest tasks first and save the easiest for last.
- Schedule tasks that you consider unpleasant to be done during your peak hours.
- _____
- _____

UTTER LAZINESS AND/OR APATHY

- Concentrate on the rewards of managing yourself and your time more effectively.
- Give yourself a time limit to accomplish a task.
- Set a regular, realistic time for study and stick to it.
- _____
- _____

DISTRACTIONS AND/OR LACK OF FOCUS

- Ask for help from your professors, advisor, counselor, or other professionals.
- Start on the difficult, most boring tasks first.

from ORDINARY to *Extraordinary*

Maureen Riopelle
President & Founder, Mary's Circle of Hope—The Mary
Maguire Foundation, Milford, Ohio

THINGS COULD not have been going better! I was a star basketball player recruited by hundreds of colleges and was a top pick by the University of Iowa. My dream of going to college, becoming an Olympic athlete, and later becoming a sportscaster was so close I could see it all happening. But life has a funny way of turning on a dime.

I had suffered knee problems for many years and most doctors attributed it to "growing pains." I continued to play sports in high school despite the pain. By the time I got to the University of Iowa, I finally saw a few specialists at the urging of my coaches, but the diagnosis was inconclusive. They knew my knee was in serious disrepair and that I had lost over 35 percent of the range of motion. They just couldn't figure out why.

After the surgery, my knees actually began to worsen. Doctors feared a massive infection and after more tests, another surgery was scheduled. It was then determined that the plica in my knees had hardened and formed so much scar tissue it seemed to almost form another "bone" in my leg. I was told that I would probably have to have surgery every two years to repair the damage and that I only had a 50/50 chance of ever walking again.

In a relatively brief period of time, I went from a college basketball standout and Olympic hopeful to losing my scholarship, dropping out of college, and potentially facing the rest of my life on crutches or in a wheelchair. I had five surgeries in seven months, and I spent that summer in a wheelchair and on crutches, but within a year, I was walking on my own again. Within a year and a half I walked my first 5k.

I attribute my recovery to my drive and determination. When necessary, I am the most stubborn person you'll ever meet. When I was told that I would not walk, run, or play basketball again, I took it as a personal challenge to prove everyone wrong: "I'll show you." I eventually went back to college

> *In a brief period of time, I went from a college basketball standout and Olympic hopeful to losing my scholarship, dropping out of college, and potentially facing the rest of my life on crutches or in a wheelchair.*

and graduated with a 4.0 GPA. After graduation, I began working, and life was moving along. Little did I know that within a few short years, I would again have to call on that teenager who years earlier had told herself, "I'll show you."

One morning I found a lump in my breast and immediately met with my doctor, who scheduled a mammogram. After the test, I was told that everything was fine. But there was a little voice in my head that said, "You need to ask someone else. Get a second opinion." This little voice saved my life. I did, indeed, have breast cancer, and it had even spread to my lymph nodes. My determination and strong will to live and beat the odds became my salvation once again. After surgery and treatment, there are no signs of cancer.

Both of these experiences, while trying and frightening, have led me to my real calling in life: founding Mary's Circle of Hope—The Mary Maguire Foundation, a non-profit organization dedicated to the support of women cancer survivors. We help provide financial assistance; health, fitness, and nutritional assistance; empowerment retreats and workshops; and additional services that help the woman go from surviving to thriving. Being able to help others thrive in the face of adversity has become my passion and focus in life. Visit us at www.marymaguirefoundation.org.

EXTRAORDINARY REFLECTION

Read the following statement and respond in your online journal or class notebook.

Ms. Riopelle suffered a major setback with her health, causing her to lose her scholarship and drop out of college for a time. What advice would you give to someone who is facing a life-threatening health problem with regard to persistence, internal motivation, positive thinking, and determination?

- Weed out your personal belongings and living space. Organization helps you manage your time and get to work.

- _____

- _____

CHOOSING FUN BEFORE RESPONSIBILITY

- Reward yourself when you have accomplished an important body of work.

- Don't get involved in too many organizations, accept too many commitments, or overextend yourself so that you can concentrate on what needs to be done.

- Consider the consequences of not doing what you're responsible for doing.

- _____

- _____

WAITING FOR THE "RIGHT" MOOD

- Avoid whining and complaining and realize that the right mood can be created by you at any time.

- Just do it! Force yourself to jump into the task.

- Work during your peak hours of the day.

- _____

- _____

EVALUATING HOW YOU SPEND YOUR TIME

Do You Know Where Your Time Goes?

So how do you find out where you time goes? The same way that you find out where your money goes—you track it. Every 15 minutes for one week, you will record exactly how you spent that time. This exercise may seem a little tedious at first, but if you will complete the process over a period of a week, you will have a much better concept of where your time is being used. Yes, that's right—for a week, you need to keep a written record of how much time you spend sleeping, studying, eating, working, getting to class and back, cooking, caring for children, watching television, doing yard work, going to movies, attending athletic events, hanging out, doing laundry, whatever.

Take your plan with you and keep track of your activities during the day. To make things simple, round off tasks to 15-minute intervals. For example, if you start walking to the cafeteria at 7:08, you might want to mark off the time block that begins with 7:00. If you finish eating and return to your home at 7:49, you can mark off the next two blocks. You will also want to note the activity so you can evaluate how you spent your time later. Study the example that is provided for you in Figure 7.6.

In Figure 7.7, you will find a daily time log for you to use for this exercise. Remember to take these pages with you and record how you are spending your time during the day. As you progress through the week, try to improve the use of your time. When you finish this exercise, review how you spent your time.

Figure 7.6   How Do You Really Spend Your Time?

7:00	get up	7:00			12:15
	& shower	7:15			12:30
	✕	7:30	Walked to Union	12:45
	Breakfast	7:45	1:00	Ate lunch	1:00
8:00		8:00			1:15
		8:15			1:30
	Read paper	8:30		Talked w/ Joe	1:45
	Walked to class	8:45	2:00		2:00
9:00	English 101	9:00		Went to book	2:15
		9:15		store	2:30
		9:30		Walked to	2:45
		9:45	3:00	my room	3:00
10:00		10:00		Called Ron	3:15
		10:15			3:30
		10:30			3:45
	Walked to class	10:45	4:00	Watched	4:00
11:00	History 210	11:00		TV	4:15
		11:15			4:30
		11:30		Walked to	4:45
		11:45	5:00	library	5:00
12:00		12:00			5:15

ELIMINATING DISTRACTIONS AND INTERRUPTIONS

When Is Enough Really Enough?

If you were diligent and kept an accurate account of all of your time, your evaluation will probably reveal that much of your time is spent dealing with distractions, getting side-tracked, and handling interruptions. These three things account for much of the time wasted within a 24-hour period. In Figure 7.8 (page 179), you will find a list of some of the most common distractions faced by college students. Consider how you might deal with these distractions in an effective, assertive manner.

PLANNING AND PREPARING

Is There a Secret to Time Management?

In the past, you may have said to yourself: "I don't have time to plan." "I don't like to be fenced in and tied to a rigid schedule." "I have so many duties that planning never works." Scheduling does not have to be a tedious chore or something you dread. Scheduling can be your lifeline to more free time. After all, if you build your own schedule, it is yours! As much as you are able, build your schedule the way you want and need it.

Figure 7.7 Daily Time Sheet

Monday			Tuesday			Wednesday	
6:00	6:00	6:00		6:00	6:00		6:00
	6:15			6:15			6:15
	6:30			6:30			6:30
	6:45			6:45			6:45
7:00	7:00	7:00		7:00	7:00		7:00
	7:15			7:15			7:15
	7:30			7:30			7:30
	7:45			7:45			7:45
8:00	8:00	8:00		8:00	8:00		8:00
	8:15			8:15			8:15
	8:30			8:30			8:30
	8:45			8:45			8:45
9:00	9:00	9:00		9:00	9:00		9:00
	9:15			9:15			9:15
	9:30			9:30			9:30
	9:45			9:45			9:45
10:00	10:00	10:00		10:00	10:00		10:00
	10:15			10:15			10:15
	10:30			10:30			10:30
	10:45			10:45			10:45
11:00	11:00	11:00		11:00	11:00		11:00
	11:15			11:15			11:15
	11:30			11:30			11:30
	11:45			11:45			11:45
12:00	12:00	12:00		12:00	12:00		12:00
	12:15			12:15			12:15
	12:30			12:30			12:30
	12:45			12:45			12:45
1:00	1:00	1:00		1:00	1:00		1:00
	1:15			1:15			1:15
	1:30			1:30			1:30
	1:45			1:45			1:45
2:00	2:00	2:00		2:00	2:00		2:00
	2:15			2:15			2:15
	2:30			2:30			2:30
	2:45			2:45			2:45
3:00	3:00	3:00		3:00	3:00		3:00
	3:15			3:15			3:15
	3:30			3:30			3:30
	3:45			3:45			3:45
4:00	4:00	4:00		4:00	4:00		4:00
	4:15			4:15			4:15
	4:30			4:30			4:30
	4:45			4:45			4:45
5:00	5:00	5:00		5:00	5:00		5:00
	5:15			5:15			5:15
	5:30			5:30			5:30
	5:45			5:45			5:45
6:00	6:00	6:00		6:00	6:00		6:00
	6:15			6:15			6:15
	6:30			6:30			6:30
	6:45			6:45			6:45
7:00	7:00	7:00		7:00	7:00		7:00
	7:15			7:15			7:15
	7:30			7:30			7:30
	7:45			7:45			7:45
8:00	8:00	8:00		8:00	8:00		8:00
	8:15			8:15			8:15
	8:30			8:30			8:30
	8:45			8:45			8:45
9:00	9:00	9:00		9:00	9:00		9:00
	9:15			9:15			9:15
	9:30			9:30			9:30
	9:45			9:45			9:45
10:00	10:00	10:00		10:00	10:00		10:00
	10:15			10:15			10:15
	10:30			10:30			10:30
	10:45			10:45			10:45
11:00	11:00	11:00		11:00	11:00		11:00
	11:15			11:15			11:15
	11:30			11:30			11:30
	11:45			11:45			11:45
12:00	12:00	12:00		12:00	12:00		12:00

(continued)

Figure 7.7 Daily Time Sheet (continued)

Thursday		Friday		Saturday		Sunday	
6:00	6:00	6:00	6:00	6:00	6:00	6:00	6:00
	6:15		6:15		6:15		6:15
	6:30		6:30		6:30		6:30
	6:45		6:45		6:45		6:45
7:00	7:00	7:00	7:00	7:00	7:00	7:00	7:00
	7:15		7:15		7:15		7:15
	7:30		7:30		7:30		7:30
	7:45		7:45		7:45		7:45
8:00	8:00	8:00	8:00	8:00	8:00	8:00	8:00
	8:15		8:15		8:15		8:15
	8:30		8:30		8:30		8:30
	8:45		8:45		8:45		8:45
9:00	9:00	9:00	9:00	9:00	9:00	9:00	9:00
	9:15		9:15		9:15		9:15
	9:30		9:30		9:30		9:30
	9:45		9:45		9:45		9:45
10:00	10:00	10:00	10:00	10:00	10:00	10:00	10:00
	10:15		10:15		10:15		10:15
	10:30		10:30		10:30		10:30
	10:45		10:45		10:45		10:45
11:00	11:00	11:00	11:00	11:00	11:00	11:00	11:00
	11:15		11:15		11:15		11:15
	11:30		11:30		11:30		11:30
	11:45		11:45		11:45		11:45
12:00	12:00	12:00	12:00	12:00	12:00	12:00	12:00
	12:15		12:15		12:15		12:15
	12:30		12:30		12:30		12:30
	12:45		12:45		12:45		12:45
1:00	1:00	1:00	1:00	1:00	1:00	1:00	1:00
	1:15		1:15		1:15		1:15
	1:30		1:30		1:30		1:30
	1:45		1:45		1:45		1:45
2:00	2:00	2:00	2:00	2:00	2:00	2:00	2:00
	2:15		2:15		2:15		2:15
	2:30		2:30		2:30		2:30
	2:45		2:45		2:45		2:45
3:00	3:00	3:00	3:00	3:00	3:00	3:00	3:00
	3:15		3:15		3:15		3:15
	3:30		3:30		3:30		3:30
	3:45		3:45		3:45		3:45
4:00	4:00	4:00	4:00	4:00	4:00	4:00	4:00
	4:15		4:15		4:15		4:15
	4:30		4:30		4:30		4:30
	4:45		4:45		4:45		4:45
5:00	5:00	5:00	5:00	5:00	5:00	5:00	5:00
	5:15		5:15		5:15		5:15
	5:30		5:30		5:30		5:30
	5:45		5:45		5:45		5:45
6:00	6:00	6:00	6:00	6:00	6:00	6:00	6:00
	6:15		6:15		6:15		6:15
	6:30		6:30		6:30		6:30
	6:45		6:45		6:45		6:45
7:00	7:00	7:00	7:00	7:00	7:00	7:00	7:00
	7:15		7:15		7:15		7:15
	7:30		7:30		7:30		7:30
	7:45		7:45		7:45		7:45
8:00	8:00	8:00	8:00	8:00	8:00	8:00	8:00
	8:15		8:15		8:15		8:15
	8:30		8:30		8:30		8:30
	8:45		8:45		8:45		8:45
9:00	9:00	9:00	9:00	9:00	9:00	9:00	9:00
	9:15		9:15		9:15		9:15
	9:30		9:30		9:30		9:30
	9:45		9:45		9:45		9:45
10:00	10:00	10:00	10:00	10:00	10:00	10:00	10:00
	10:15		10:15		10:15		10:15
	10:30		10:30		10:30		10:30
	10:45		10:45		10:45		10:45
11:00	11:00	11:00	11:00	11:00	11:00	11:00	11:00
	11:15		11:15		11:15		11:15
	11:30		11:30		11:30		11:30
	11:45		11:45		11:45		11:45
12:00	12:00	12:00	12:00	12:00	12:00	12:00	12:00

Figure 7.8   Common Distractions

COMMON DISTRACTIONS	MY PLAN TO OVERCOME THESE DISTRACTIONS
Friends/family dropping by unexpectedly	
Technology (playing on YouTube, Facebook, iTunes, Google, etc.)	
Constant phone calls that do not pertain to anything of importance	
Not setting aside any time during the day to deal with the unexpected	
Friends/family demanding things of you because they do not understand your schedule or commitments	
Not blocking private time in your daily schedule	
Being disorganized and spending hours piddling and calling it "work"	
Playing with your children or pets before your tasks are complete (and not scheduling time to be with them in the first place)	
Saying "yes" when you need to say "no"	
Other distractions faced by you	

To manage your time successfully, you need to spend some time planning. To plan successfully, you need a calendar that has a week-at-a-glance or month-at-a-glance section, as well as sections for daily notes and appointments. If you have not bought a calendar, you can download one from the Internet or create one using Word or another computer program.

Planning and Organizing for School

Each evening, you should take a few minutes (and literally, that is all it will take) and sit in a quiet place and make a list of all that needs to be done tomorrow. Successful time management comes from planning the night before! Let's say your list includes:

Research speech project	Exercise
Study for finance test on Friday	Buy birthday card for mom
Read Chapter 13 for chemistry	Wash the car
Meet with chemistry study group	Take shirts to dry cleaner
Attend English class at 8:00 am	Buy groceries
Attend mgt. class at 10:00 am	Call Janice about weekend
Work from 2:00–6:00 pm	

Now, you have created a list of tasks that you will face tomorrow. Next, separate this list into three categories:

MUST DO	NEED TO DO	WOULD LIKE TO DO
Read Chapter 13 for Chem.	Research speech project	Wash the car
Study for finance test on Fri.	Buy birthday card for mom	Call Janice
Exercise	Shirts to cleaner	
English class @ 8:00	Buy groceries	
Mgt. class @ 10:00		
Meet w/chem study gp.		
Work from 2:00–6:00 pm		

Don't get too excited yet. Your time management plan is *not finished.* The most important part is still ahead of you. Now, you will need to rank the items in order of their importance. You will put a 1 by the most important tasks, a 2 by the next most important tasks, and so on in each category.

MUST DO	NEED TO DO	WOULD LIKE TO DO
1 Read Chapter 13 for Chem.	1 Research speech project	2 Wash the car
2 Study for finance test on Fri.	2 Buy birthday card for mom	1 Call Janice
3 Exercise	3 Shirts to cleaner	
1 English class @ 8:00	2 Buy groceries	
1 Mgt. class @ 10:00		
2 Meet w/chem study gp.		
1 Work from 2:00–6:00 pm		

Now, you have created a plan to actually get these tasks done! Not only have you created your list, but now you have divided tasks into important categories, ranked them, and made a written commitment to complete them.

Now, take these tasks and schedule them into your daily calendar (see Figure 7.9). You would schedule category 1 (MUST DO) first, category 2 (NEED TO DO) next, and category 3 (WOULD LIKE TO DO) last. Remember, never keep more than one calendar. Always carry it with you, and always schedule your tasks immediately so that you won't forget them.

DID YOU *Know?*

TINA TURNER, born and raised Anna Mae Bullock in Nutbush, Tennessee, was abandoned by her migrant worker parents. She was raised by her grandmother and worked in the cotton fields as a child. She endured a rough and very abusive marriage. She was repeatedly beaten and raped by her husband, Ike. During their divorce hearings, she had to defend the right to even keep her name. She went on to record many number-one hits such as "Private Dancer" and "What's Love Got to Do with It?" She has won seven Grammy awards, has a star on the Hollywood Walk of Fame, is listed in the Rock and Roll Hall of Fame, and was the subject of a motion picture starring Angela Bassett.

PHOTO: Daily Mirror/MirrorPix/Newscom

STRESS? I DON'T HAVE ENOUGH TIME FOR STRESS!

Do You Feel Like You're Going to Explode?

The word *stress* is derived from the Latin word *strictus,* meaning "to draw tight." Stress is your body's response to people and events in your life; it is the mental and physical wear and tear on your body as a result of everyday life and all that you have to accomplish. Stress is inevitable, and it is not in itself bad. It is your response to stress that determines whether it is good stress (*eustress*) or bad stress (*distress*). The same event can provoke eustress or distress, depending on the person experiencing the event. Just as "one person's trash is another's treasure," so one person's eustress may be another person's distress.

The primary difference between eustress and distress is in your body's response. It is impossible to exist in a totally stress-free environment; in

Figure 7.9   Daily Calendar

DAY *Monday*

Time	Task	Priority	Complete?
6:00			Yes No
6:30			Yes No
7:00	*Study for finance*		Yes No
7:30	↓		Yes No
8:00	*English 101*		Yes No
8:30			Yes No
9:00	↓		Yes No
9:30	*Read Pg. 1–10 of Chem. Chapter*		Yes No
10:00	*Management 210*		Yes No
10:30			Yes No
11:00	↓		Yes No
11:30	*Finish Reading Chem. Chapter*		Yes No
12:00			Yes No
12:30	↓		Yes No
1:00	*Meet w/Chemistry group (take lunch)*		Yes No
1:30	↓		Yes No
2:00	*Work*		Yes No
2:30			Yes No
3:00			Yes No
3:30			Yes No
4:00			Yes No
4:30			Yes No
5:00			Yes No
5:30			Yes No
6:00	↓		Yes No
6:30	*Dinner/run by grocery store*		Yes No
7:00	↓		Yes No
7:30	*Internet Research for speech*		Yes No
8:00			Yes No
8:30	↓		Yes No
9:00	*call Janice @ w/end*		Yes No
9:30			Yes No

fact, some stress is important to your health and well-being. Good stress can help you become more motivated and even more productive. It helps your energy level, too. It is only when stress gets out of hand that your body becomes distressed. Some physical signs of distress are:

Headaches	Dry mouth	Twitching/Trembling
Muscular tension and pain	Hypertension and chest pain	Abdominal pain
Fatigue	Insomnia	Apprehension
Coughs	Impotence	Jitters
Abdominal pain and diarrhea	Heartburn and indigestion	Diminished performance
Mental disorders	Suicidal tendencies	Decreased coping ability

If you begin to experience any of these reactions for an extended period of time, your body and mind are probably suffering from undue stress, anxiety, and pressure. This can lead to a very unhealthy situation. You may even require medical attention for hypertension. Test your stress by completing the assessment in Figure 7.10.

Figure 7.10 Test Your Stress

Take the following Stress Assessment to determine the level of distress you are currently experiencing in your life. Check the items that reflect your behavior at home, work, or school, or in a social setting.

- ☐ 1. Your stomach tightens when you think about your schoolwork and all that you have to do.
- ☐ 2. You are not able to sleep at night.
- ☐ 3. You race from place to place trying to get everything done that is required of you.
- ☐ 4. Small things make you angry.
- ☐ 5. At the end of the day, you are frustrated that you did not accomplish all that you needed to do.
- ☐ 6. You get tired throughout the day.
- ☐ 7. You need some type of drug, alcohol, or tobacco to get through the day.
- ☐ 8. You often find it hard to be around people.
- ☐ 9. You don't take care of yourself physically or mentally.
- ☐ 10. You tend to keep everything inside.
- ☐ 11. You overreact.
- ☐ 12. You fail to find the humor in many situations others see as funny.
- ☐ 13. You do not eat properly.
- ☐ 14. Everything upsets you.
- ☐ 15. You are impatient and get angry when you have to wait for things.
- ☐ 16. You don't trust others.
- ☐ 17. You feel that most people move too slowly for you.
- ☐ 18. You feel guilty when you take time for yourself or your friends.
- ☐ 19. You interrupt people so that you can tell them your side of the story.
- ☐ 20. You experience memory loss.

Total Number of Check Marks

0–5 = Low, manageable stress

6–10 = Moderate stress

11+ = High stress, could cause medical or emotional problems

I DON'T THINK I FEEL SO WELL

What Is the Relationship Between Poor Time Management, Monumental Stress, and Your Health?

There are probably as many stressors in this world as there are people alive. For some people, loud music causes stress. For others, a hectic day at the office with people demanding things and equipment breaking down causes stress. For others, that loud music and a busy day at the office are just what the doctor ordered—they love it and thrive off of the energy and demands. For some people, being idle and sitting around reading a book cause stress, whereas others long for a moment of peace walking on the beach or just sitting out in the backyard with a good book. One thing is for sure: poor planning and "running out of time" are on most people's list of major stressors.

BRING the Change

TIPS FOR PERSONAL SUCCESS

Consider the following tips for dealing with and reducing stress in your life:

- Use relaxation techniques such as visualization, listening to music, and practicing yoga.
- Let minor hassles and annoyances go. Ask yourself, "Is this situation worth a heart attack, stroke, or high blood pressure?"
- Don't be afraid to take a break. Managing your time can help you take more relaxation breaks.

Now, it is your turn. Create a list of at least two more tips that you would offer a fellow classmate to assist him or her with reducing unhealthy stress in his or her life.

1. _____

2. _____

Most stress does not "just happen" to us. We allow it to happen by not planning our day or week. We allow our to do list to get out of hand (or we do not create a to do list), and before we know it, our lives are out of control because of all of the activities we are required to accomplish or because of the things we agreed to do. Because of poor planning and procrastination, we become anxious and nervous about not getting it all done. By planning, prioritizing, and developing a action strategy, we can actually lower our stress level and improve our general health and our memory.

Medical research has shown that exposure to stress over a long period of time can be damaging to your body. Many of the physical and mental symptoms of stress were mentioned earlier, but consider these effects as well. Stress can also have an effect on your *memory.* When you are stressed, your brain releases *cortisol,* which has effects on the neurons in your brain. Over time, cortisol can be toxic and damage parts of the hippocampus—the part of the brain that deals with memory and learning. Therefore, learning to control stress by managing your time more effectively can be a key to better memory. The amygdala, the part of the brain that causes "fight or flight," is also affected negatively by prolonged stress, causing you to say and do things you regret later.

Other physical symptoms include *exhaustion,* in which one part of the body weakens and shifts its responsibility to another part and causes complete failure of key organ functions. *Chronic muscle pain* and malfunction are also affected by unchecked stress. "Chronically tense muscles also result in numerous stress-related disorders including headaches, backaches, spasms of the esophagus and colon (causing diarrhea and constipation), posture problems, asthma, tightness in the throat and chest cavity, some eye problems, lockjaw, muscle tears and pulls, and perhaps rheumatoid arthritis" (Girdano, Dusek, & Everly, 2009).

As you can see from this medical research, stress is not something that you can just ignore and hope it will go away. It is not something that is overblown and insignificant. It is a real, bona fide condition that can cause many physical and mental problems from simple exhaustion to death. By learning how to recognize the signs of stress, what causes you to be stressed out, and effectively dealing with your stress, you can actually control many of the negative physical and emotional side effects caused by prolonged stress (see Figure 7.11).

Figure 7.11 Three Types of Major Stressors in Life

TYPE	CAUSE	WHAT YOU CAN DO TO REDUCE STRESS
Situational		
	Change in physical environment	• If at all possible, change your residence or physical environment to better suit your needs. If you can't change it, talk to the people involved and explain your feelings.
	Change in social environment	• Work hard to meet new friends who support you and on whom you can rely in times of need. • Get involved in some type of school activity. • Enroll in classes with friends, and find a campus support group.
	Daily hassles	• Try to keep things in perspective, and work to reduce the things that you allow to stress you out. • Allow time in your schedule for unexpected events. • Find a quiet place to relax and study.
	Poor time management	• Work out a time management plan that allows time to get your projects complete while allowing time for rest and joy, too. • Create to do lists.
	Conflicts at work, home, and school	• Read about conflict management in Chapter 12 and realize that conflict can be managed. • Avoid "hot" topics such as religion or politics if you feel this causes you to engage in conflicts. • Be assertive, not aggressive or rude.
	People	• Try to avoid people who stress you out. • Put people into perspective and realize that we're all different, with different needs, wants, and desires. • Realize that everyone is not going to be like you.
	Relationships	• Work hard to develop healthy, positive relationships. • Move away from toxic, unhealthy relationships and people who bring you down. • Understand that you can never change the way another person feels, acts, or thinks.
	Death of a loved one	• Try to focus on the good times you shared and what they meant to your life. • Remember that death is as much a part of life as living. • Talk about the person with your friends and family—share your memories. • Consider what the deceased person would have wanted you to do.
	Financial problems	• Cut back on your spending. • Seek the help of a financial planner. • Determine why your financial planning or spending patterns are causing you problems. • Apply for financial assistance.

TYPE	CAUSE	WHAT YOU CAN DO TO REDUCE STRESS
Psychological		
	Unrealistic expectations	• Surround yourself with positive people, and work hard to set realistic goals with doable timelines and results. • Expect and anticipate less.
	Homesickness	• Surround yourself with people who support you. • Call or visit home as often as you can until you get more comfortable. • Meet new friends on campus through organizations and clubs.
	Fear	• Talk to professors, counselors, family, and friends about your fears. Put them into perspective. • Visualize success and not failure. • Do one thing every day that scares you to expand your comfort zone.
	Anxiety over your future and what is going to happen	• Put things into perspective and work hard to plan and prepare, but accept that life is about constant change. • Talk to a counselor or advisor about your future plans, and develop a strategy to meet your goals. • Don't try to control the uncontrollable. • Try to see the "big picture" and how "the puzzle" is going to come together.
	Anxiety over your past	• Work hard to overcome past challenges, and remember that your past does not have to dictate your future. • Learn to forgive. • Focus on your future and what you really want to accomplish.
Biological		
	Insomnia	• Watch your caffeine intake. • Avoid naps. • Do not exercise two hours prior to your normal bedtime. • Complete all of your activities before going to bed (studying, watching TV, e-mailing, texting, etc.). Your bed is for sleeping.
	Anxiety	• Laugh more. Share a joke. • Enjoy your friends and family. • Practice breathing exercises. • Talk it out with friends. • Learn to say "no" and then do it. • Turn off the TV if the news makes you anxious or nervous.
	Weight loss/gain	• Develop an exercise and healthy eating plan. • Meet with a nutrition specialist on campus or in the community. • Join a health-related club or group.
	Reduced physical activities	• Increase your daily activity. • If possible, walk to class instead of drive. • Take the stairs instead of the elevator.
	Sexual difficulties/ dysfunction	• Seek medical help in case something is physically wrong. • Determine if your actions are in contradiction with your value system.

TIME, STRESS, DEPRESSION, AND ANXIETY

What Does One Have to Do with the Other?

Most people never make the connection, but not managing your time properly can cause more than stress—it can cause depression, anxiety, and a host of other mental, emotional, and physical problems. When you're rushing around trying to complete a project at the last moment, your stress level rises, and with higher levels of stress, depression and anxiety begin to creep in. Many of our mental and emotional issues can be addressed by allowing ourselves enough time to do a project well and not stress out over it. Yes, there are many causes of depression and anxiety, but managing your time well can help with reducing the levels of both.

SILENT PROBLEMS OF THE MIND

How Do You Control Depression and Anxiety Disorders?

Depression is a term used to describe feelings ranging from feeling blue to utter hopelessness. The use of "I'm depressed" to mean "I'm sad" or "I'm down" is a far cry from the illness of clinical depression. Depression is a sickness that can creep up on an individual and render that person helpless if it is not detected and properly treated.

There are several major types of depressions. They include the following:

- **Situational depression.** Situational depression is a feeling of sadness due to disappointments, bad news, daily frustrations, or "people problems."

- **Clinical depression.** Clinical depression is major depression and is characterized by the inability to enjoy life, loss of interest in things you once loved doing, self-hatred, feelings of utter worthlessness, and suicidal thoughts. Clinical depression is diagnosed when these feelings last at least two weeks.

- **Dysthymia.** Dysthymia is classified as mild to moderate depression and can last a long time—two years or more. There are times that you can't remember not being depressed, and it is hard to enjoy life, family, or friends.

- **Seasonal depression.** Seasonal depression is caused by the weather or by the changing seasons of the year. Some people are depressed by rain; others are depressed by a lack of sunshine.

- **Postpartum depression.** Postpartum depression, sometimes called "the baby blues," occurs after the birth of a child. It can be a very serious condition where the mother avoids the child or even wants to cause harm to the child. It can occur up to a year or more after birth.

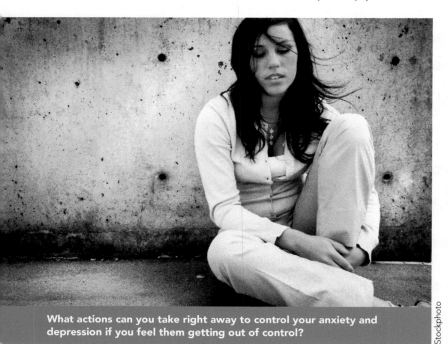

What actions can you take right away to control your anxiety and depression if you feel them getting out of control?

iStockphoto

Figure 7.12   Are You Clinically Depressed? Signs and Symptoms

Feelings of helplessness and hopelessness	You have a bleak outlook, as though nothing will ever get better and nothing can be done to improve your situation.
Loss of interest in daily activities	You have lost interest in or the ability to enjoy former hobbies, social activities, or physical affection.
Appetite or weight changes	You lose or gain significant amount of weight, changing by more than 5 percent of your body weight within a month.
Sleep changes	You experience insomnia, especially waking up in the early hours of the morning, or you oversleep.
Psychomotor agitation or retardation	You feel either overstimulated and restless or sluggish and physically slowed down.
Loss of energy	You feeling exhausted and drained—even small tasks are tiring or take longer.
Self-loathing	You feel worthless or guilty; you are overly critical of your perceived faults and mistakes.
Concentration problems	You cannot focus and you have memory trouble and difficulty making decisions.

Source: Adapted from HelpGuide.org.

Anxiety

According to the Anxiety Disorders Association of America, anxiety disorders are the most common mental illness in the United States—with more than 13 percent of adults suffering from some form of anxiety disorder. Learning to cope with anxiety allows you to focus and maintain balance in your health and academic welfare. There are several ways to proactively approach dealing with anxiety: relaxation techniques such as yoga, music or dance therapy, and meditation; cognitive behavior therapy or other forms of therapy; and medication.

If you are feeling depressed or your anxiety has reached a level where you cannot control it, but your depression seems minor or situational, try some of these helpful hints for picking yourself up out of the blues:

- Get physical exercise—it releases endorphins, which help to stimulate you and give you a personal high.

- Spend time talking with a good friend; share your thoughts and feelings.

- Control your self-talk. If you're feeding yourself negative words, change to positive thoughts.

- Do something special for yourself: Take a long walk in the park, watch a favorite movie, listen to a special CD, or visit a friend.

- Nurture yourself by doing things you love and enjoy and that bring you peace.

- Never be afraid or ashamed to seek professional assistance.

REFLECTIONS ON TIME AND STRESS MANAGEMENT

Managing your time and reducing your level of stress are two skills that you will need for the rest of your life. By learning to avoid procrastination and taking the time to enhance the quality of your life, you are actually increasing your staying power as a college student. Further, as you enter the world of work, both of these skills will be necessary for your success. Technological advances, fewer people doing more work, and pressure to perform at unprecedented levels can put your life in a tailspin, but with the ability to plan your time and reduce your own stress level, you are making a contribution to your own success.

As you continue this term in college and work toward managing your time and stress level, consider the following ideas:

- Make a to do list every evening to plan for the next day.
- Always include time for friends, joy, and adventure in your schedule.
- Avoid procrastination by practicing the "just do it" mentality.
- Work hard to lose the "superhuman" and perfectionist attitudes.
- Delegate everything that you can.
- Plan your day and week to avoid becoming too stressed.
- To reduce stress, take a few moments to relax in private.
- When stress is overwhelming, take time to decompress.

Good luck to you as you develop your plan for managing your time and stress.

> "I wanted a perfect ending. Now I've learned, the hard way, that some poems don't rhyme, and some stories don't have a clear beginning, middle and end. Life is about knowing, having to change, taking the moment and making the best of it without knowing what is going to happen next."
>
> —Gilda Radner

REDUCING STRESS IN YOUR EVERYDAY LIFE

Utilizes levels 4, 5, and 6 of the taxonomy

Each chapter-end assessment is based on Bloom's Taxonomy of Learning. See pages xxvi–xxviii in the front of this book for a quick review.

Take a moment and examine your academic and personal life right now. You probably have many things going on and may feel as if you're torn in many directions.

If you had to list the one major stressor in your life at this moment, what would it be?

_____

_____

_____

_____

_____

_____

Why is this stressor a major cause of stress in your life?

_____

_____

_____

_____

_____

_____

_____

What does this stressor do to your time management plan?

_____

_____

_____

_____

_____

_____

Are there other people or things contributing to this stressor? In other words, is someone or something making the matter worse? If so, who or what?

_____

_____

_____

_____

_____

_____

A *narrative statement* is a statement that "paints a verbal picture" of how your life is going to look once a goal is reached. Reflect for a moment, and then write a paragraph predicting how your life would change if this major source of stress were gone. Be realistic and optimistic. How would alleviating this stressor help with your time management plan?

_____

_____

_____

_____

_____

_____

_____

_____

_____

_____

_____

_____

_____

_____

_____

_____

_____

As you know, accomplishing anything requires action. Now that you have a picture of how your life would look if this stress was gone, develop a plan from beginning to end to eliminate this stressor from your life.

Step 1: _____

_____

Step 2: _____

_____

Step 3: _____

_____

Step 4: _____

_____

Step 5: _____

_____

SQ3R MASTERY STUDY SHEET

EXAMPLE QUESTION *(from page 164)* What are the components of self-discipline?	**ANSWER:**
EXAMPLE QUESTION *(from page 168)* How can I simplify my life and get more done?	**ANSWER:**
AUTHOR QUESTION *(from page 164)* How can self-discipline help you prioritize your tasks more effectively?	**ANSWER:**
AUTHOR QUESTION *(from page 164)* What are the benefits of learning how to say "no"?	**ANSWER:**
AUTHOR QUESTION *(from page 169)* What are three strategies to prevent procrastination?	**ANSWER:**
AUTHOR QUESTION *(from page 180)* How does good stress differ from bad stress?	**ANSWER:**
AUTHOR QUESTION *(from page 181)* What are some of the physical and mental symptoms of stress?	**ANSWER:**
YOUR QUESTION *(from page ____)*	**ANSWER:**
YOUR QUESTION *(from page ____)*	**ANSWER:**
YOUR QUESTION *(from page ____)*	**ANSWER:**
YOUR QUESTION *(from page ____)*	**ANSWER:**
YOUR QUESTION *(from page ____)*	**ANSWER:**

Finally, after answering these questions, recite in your mind the major points covered here. Consider the following general questions to help you master this material.

- What was it about?
- What does it mean?
- What was the most important thing you learned? Why?
- What were the key points to remember?

chapter eight

LEARN

DISCOVERING YOUR LEARNING STYLE, DOMINANT INTELLIGENCE, AND PERSONALITY TYPE

"We are led to truth by our weaknesses as well as our strengths." —Parker Palmer

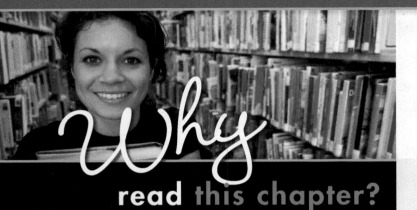

Why read this chapter?

Because you'll learn:

- Several historical theories about how we learn
- The steps in learning something new
- To use your learning style, dominant intelligence, and personality type to increase your learning power

Because you'll be able to:

- Create a study plan based on your learning style and dominant intelligence
- Use your personality type to improve studying, learning, and career development
- Develop a Personal Life Profile based on your strengths, challenges, and interests

Scan and QUESTION

Take a few moments, **scan this chapter,** and on page 216, write **five of your own questions** that you think will be important to your mastery of this material. You will also find five questions listed from your authors.

Example:

☑ **What is the difference between a learning style and a learning strategy?** (from page 203)

☑ **What is the definition of tactile learning, and how do you use it?** (from page 206)

MyStudentSuccessLab

MyStudentSuccessLab (www.mystudentsuccesslab.com) is an online solution designed to help you "Start strong, Finish stronger" by building skills for ongoing personal and professional development.

How

Name: Sakinah Pendergras
Institution: Graduate! The Art Institute of Philadelphia
Age: 28
Major: Culinary Arts
Career: Saucier and Pastry Development

My performance during my first semester at The Art Institute was so horrible that I was put on academic probation and was not going to make it to my second semester. I procrastinated and did not do the work to be successful as a student. I was called into my advisor's office for the bad news. I begged her to give me another chance and she did. My advisor, Lya Redmond, saved my academic life. She believed in me.

I thought I knew what college was all about. How hard could it be? I had already served my country in the Army and the National Guard. College was supposed to be a breeze compared to the "real world." I was wrong. After my disastrous first term, my advisor enrolled me in a student success course and I finally learned how to learn. I learned how to work hard and build my own skills and confidence.

I have always had a passion for food and knew that I wanted to work in the food service industry. I also knew that I needed a degree to be taken seriously in this demanding field. My instructors at The Art Institute shared their knowledge and experience and prepared me for a career.

One of the biggest benefits of my education is that employers take notice when you have a degree listed beside your name. It gives you credibility. It gives you experiences that you would not have had without the hands-on training from experts around the world. My education has afforded me the opportunity to meet new people, travel abroad, and have confidence in myself.

My advice to you as you begin your journey is first and foremost, to seek help when you know you need it. Don't wait around until it is too late. Finally, spend time with your instructors. Learn from them. Ask them questions. Work hard to understand! Listen to the advice and lessons they offer you because they have the knowledge to help you reach your goals. Yes, they may give you criticism, but it is only to help you grow in your field and become successful. They believe in you. You have to believe in yourself, too.

THINK about it

1. Sakinah mentioned that she waited until it was almost too late to seek help. List at least three places at your institution you can seek help in an area where you might be facing challenges.

2. Which instructor is the most approachable this term? Why? How do you plan to approach him or her with a challenge or issue?

WE HOPE YOU LEARNED YOUR LESSON!

What Is This Thing Called Learning, Anyway?

In its purest and simplest form, learning is a **cognitive mental action** in which new information is acquired or old information is used in a new way. Learning can be **conscious** or **unconscious.** Do you remember the very day you learned how to walk or talk? Probably not. This learning was more of an unconscious nature. However, you probably do remember studying the 50 states or subtraction or reading an Edgar Allan Poe poem for the first time. This learning was more conscious in nature. Learning can also be **formal** (schooling) or **informal** ("street knowledge"). Learning can happen in many ways, such as through play, trial and error, mistakes, successes, repetition, environmental conditioning, parental discipline, social interactions, media, observation, and yes, through formal study methods.

Learning is what you do **for** yourself; it is not done **to** you. Try as they might, parents may discipline you time and time again, but until you learn the lesson trying to be taught, it will not be learned. Teachers can talk until they are blue in the face about the 13 original colonies, but until you commit them to memory, they will not be learned. That is what this chapter is all about—helping you discover how and why you learn, and assisting you in finding the best way to learn so that you can do the learning for yourself on a more effective level.

Have you encountered people with learning styles different from yours? How?

Bananastock RF

"Many things in life cannot be transmitted well by words, concepts, or books. Colors that we see cannot be described to a person born blind. Only a swimmer knows how swimming feels; the non-swimmer can get only the faintest idea of it with all the words and books in the world. And so it goes. Perhaps it is better to say that all of life must first be known experientially. There is no substitute for experience, none at all."

—Abraham H. Maslow

What Do the Experts Say?

The question still begs, **how do we really learn?** By studying a textbook? By reading a newspaper? By looking at pictures? By interviewing someone about a topic? By watching a movie? By trying something to see if it works? Yes, but the process is much more complex than this. Study Figure 8.1 and consider what some of the leading experts throughout history have said about how we learn.

As you can see from these historical experts in the fields of learning, educational psychology, and philosophy, there are many theories on just how we learn best. Perhaps the most important thing to take from these examples is tied into Jean Piaget's theory of **holistic learning**—that as individuals with diverse and varied needs, backgrounds, and experiences, we require a variety of stimuli to help us learn, and that we all learn differently at different stages in our lives from a variety of things.

GIVE YOUR BRAIN A WORKOUT

Can I Really Learn All This Stuff?

Yes! Yes! Yes! You can learn! Think about all that you have already learned in your lifetime. You learned how to eat, walk, talk, play, make decisions, dress yourself, have a conversation, tie your shoes, make your bed, ride a bicycle, play a sport, drive a car, protect yourself, make associations

Figure 8.1 Learning Through the Ages

SOCRATES	Around 300 B.C., the great Greek philosopher Socrates introduced his theory of learning. He believed that we learn by asking questions. This is called the *Socratic Method*.
PLATO	Socrates' student Plato expanded on this theory and believed that we learn best by dialogue, or the *Dialectic Method*, which involved "the searcher" beginning a conversation on a topic and having a dialogue with "an expert." Plato believed that through this back-and-forth conversation, knowledge could be acquired.
LAO-TSE	In the fifth century B.C., the Chinese philosopher Lao-Tse wrote, "If you tell me, I will listen. If you show me, I will see. But if you let me experience, I will learn." He was one of the first to proclaim that active, involved learning was a viable form of acquiring information.
KUNG FU-TSE (CONFUCIUS)	Confucius first introduced the case study, which included telling stories or parables and then having people discuss the issues in the case to learn and acquire knowledge.
JOHN LOCKE	In 1690, the English philosopher John Locke introduced the theory of "the blank slate." He believed that all humans are born with empty minds and that we learn information about the world through what our senses bring to us (sensory learning). He believed that learning is like a pyramid—we learn the basics and then build on those simple principles until we can master complex ideas.
JEAN-JACQUES ROUSSEAU	In the 1760s, the French philosopher Jean-Jacques Rousseau expanded on a theory that suggests that people learn best by experiencing rather than by listening. In other words, we learn best by doing something rather than being told how someone else did it. He was the first to thoroughly introduce individual learning styles, believing that learning should be natural to us and follow our basic instincts and feelings.
J. B. WATSON	In the early 1900s, an American psychologist, J. B. Watson, developed the theory of behaviorism, believing that we learn best by conditioning or training. His theory was based on that of Pavlov (and his dog) and held the tenet that we act and learn in certain ways because we have been conditioned or trained to do so. If a dog (or a person) is fed when it rings a bell, the dog (or the person) quickly learns to ring the bell when it wants to be fed.
JEAN PIAGET	In the mid-1900s, Swiss psychologist Jean Piaget introduced the groundbreaking theory of holistic learning. This theory is widely held today as one of the most important breakthroughs in educational psychology. He believed that we learn best by experiencing a wide variety of stimuli, such as reading, listening, experimenting, exploring, and questioning.
BENJAMIN BLOOM	In 1956, Benjamin Bloom introduced his Taxonomy of Learning (modeled and discussed throughout this text). Bloom believed in a mastery approach to learning. This theory suggests that we learn simple information and then transform that information into more complex ideas, solutions, and creations. His was an idea of learning how to process and actually use information in a meaningful way.

based on observations, use a cell phone, play a video game, ask questions, and countless other simple and highly complex skills. There is proof that you *can* learn because you *have* learned in the past. The old excuse of "I can't learn this stuff" is simply hogwash! You have the capacity to know more, do more, experience more, and acquire more knowledge. Your brain is a natural learning machine, just as your heart is a natural pumping machine. It is in our nature to learn every single day. You just have to understand how this process works in order to make the most of your brain's natural learning power. And you have to devote the time necessary to learn the basics of something new

"The mind is not a vessel to be filled, but rather a fire to be kindled."
—Plutarch

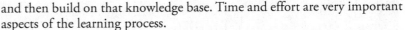

DID YOU Know?

PABLO PICASSO, the world renowned, trend-setting artist, was born in Spain. He had a hard time in school and is said to have had a very difficult time with reading. He was diagnosed with a learning disability and his formal education never really benefited him. He left his college-level courses at the Academy of Arts in Madrid after less than a year of study. However, because of his immense artistic talent, he changed the way the world looks at art through his cubist interpretation of the universe. He is listed in the *Guinness Book of World Records* as the most prolific painter in history, having completed nearly 14,000 paintings.

PHOTO: Dalmas/Sipa Press/Newscom

and then build on that knowledge base. Time and effort are very important aspects of the learning process.

You also have to give your brain a "workout" to make sure it stays in shape. Just as your body needs exercise and activities to stay in shape, your brain does, too. When you work out your brain and use it to learn new material, your brain releases a chemical called *cypin* (sigh-pin). Cypin is found throughout the body, but in the brain, it helps build new branches, like a tree sprouting new growth. In a nutshell, when you exercise your brain, your brain rewards you with new learning patterns and new learning receptors. This is sometimes referred to as *neuroplasticity* (new-ro-plas-tis-i-ty), or the brain's ability to change with new knowledge.

THE LEARNING PROCESS

What Are the Steps to Active, Authentic Learning?

"Human beings have an innate learning process, which includes a motivation to learn" (Smilkstein, 2003). You may be saying to yourself, "If I have a natural, innate ability to learn, then why is chemistry so difficult for me to master? Why is English such a crazy language with so many rules?" The answer could rest in the notion that you are going against your natural, neurological learning pattern—that you are being taught, or trying to learn by yourself, in a way that is unnatural to you, and your brain simply is having trouble adapting to this unnatural process.

BLOOM LEVEL 2

If you learn best by doing and touching, *you need to do and touch.* If you learn best by listening and questioning, you need to *listen and question.* If you learn best by reading and studying in a quiet place, you need to *find a quiet place to read and study.* Basically, you must figure out your natural inclination for learning and build on it. You will also need to understand that learning takes time and people need different amounts of time to master material. Janet may learn Concept X in a few hours, but it may take William three days of constant practice to learn the same concept. One thing is true: The more involved you are with the information you are trying to learn, the more you retain.

In the chart in Figure 8.2, we have tried to simplify thousands of years of educational study on the topic of learning. Basically, learning something new can happen in the six steps outlined there.

As a practice activity, research one of the following topics (all of which we purposefully chose because of their uniqueness or esotericism) using the six steps in the Figure 8.2 to discover something new. You can do this in your notebook or online journal. Remember, however, you will need to devote some time to this activity. Learning new information does not happen instantaneously. You will also need to use a variety of sources. Do not depend solely on Wikipedia! Yes, there are other sources out there!

POSSIBLE TOPICS

- What was Kristallnacht?
- Why and how long can a cockroach live without a head? Why?
- Who invented the electric chair and why?
- What is Sanskrit?
- How is paper made?
- Who was Vlad the Impaler? What famous character did his life inspire?

Figure 8.2 The Learning Process

1. Motivation to learn the material is the first step in the learning process. You have to possess the internal motivation and passion to want to learn what is being presented or what you are studying. You must also be motivated enough to devote the time to learning something new. Deep, purposeful learning does not happen in an instant; it takes work, patience, and yes, motivation.

2. Understand the material through ambitious curiosity, keen observations, purposeful questioning, intense studying, eager determination, robust effort, and time devoted to task. You must be able to answer such questions as: Who is involved? What happened? When did it happen? Where did it happen? How did it happen? How could it have happened? What does it all mean? Why is it important? What is the relationship between *x* and *y*? You should be able to describe it, discuss it, give examples, put the information into your own words, and tell others about it clearly.

3. Internalize the material by asking, How can this information affect my life, my career, my studies, and my future? Why does this information matter? How can I control my emotions regarding the value of this information? If I think this information is useless, how can I change this perception?

4. Apply the material by asking, How can I use this information to improve? How can I use this information to work with others, to develop new ideas, or to build meaningful conclusions? Can I demonstrate it? Can I share this information with or teach this information to others intelligently? It is possible to practice what I have learned?

5. Evaluate the material by determining the value of what you just learned. Ask yourself, Do I trust my research and sources? Have I consulted others about their findings and knowledge? What did they learn? What can I learn from them? Have I asked for feedback? Can I debate this information with others?

6. Use the material to grow and change. Ask yourself, How could I take this information (or the process of learning this information) and change my life, attitudes, or emotions? How could this information help me grow? What can I create out of this new information? How can I expand on this knowledge to learn more?

UNDERSTANDING YOUR STRENGTHS

What Are the Advantages of Discovering and Polishing Your Talents?

Here you will have the opportunity to complete three inventories: one to identify your **learning style,** one to identify your **personality type,** and one to identify your **dominant intelligence.** Later, you will have the opportunity to pull all of this information together to help you understand your learning patterns and to formulate a learning plan for the future.

These assessments are in no way intended to "label you." They are not a measure of how smart you are. They do not measure your worth or your capacities as a student or citizen. The

Figure 8.3 Take the MIS (Multiple Intelligences Survey)

Directions: Read each statement carefully and thoroughly. After reading the statement, rate your response using the scale below. There are no right or wrong answers. This is not a timed survey. The MIS is based, in part, on Howard Gardner's 1983 book, *Frames of Mind*.

3 = Often Applies   2 = Sometimes Applies   1 = Never or Almost Never Applies

_____ 1. When someone gives me directions, I have to visualize them in my mind in order to understand them.

_____ 2. I enjoy crossword puzzles and word games like Scrabble.

_____ 3. I enjoy dancing and can keep up with the beat of music.

_____ 4. I have little or no trouble conceptualizing information or facts.

_____ 5. I like to repair things that are broken, such as toasters, small engines, bicycles, and cars.

_____ 6. I enjoy leadership activities on campus and in the community.

_____ 7. I have the ability to get others to listen to me.

_____ 8. I enjoy working with nature, animals, and plants.

_____ 9. I know where everything is in my home, such as supplies, gloves, flashlights, camera, and compact discs.

_____ 10. I am a good speller.

_____ 11. I often sing or hum to myself in the shower or car or while walking or just sitting.

_____ 12. I am a very logical, orderly thinker.

_____ 13. I use a lot of gestures when I talk to people.

_____ 14. I can recognize and empathize with people's attitudes and emotions.

_____ 15. I prefer to study alone.

_____ 16. I can name many different things in the environment, such as clouds, rocks, and plant types.

_____ 17. I like to draw pictures, graphs, and charts to better understand information.

_____ 18. I have a good memory for names and dates.

_____ 19. When I hear music, I "get into it" by moving, humming, tapping, or even singing.

_____ 20. I learn better by asking a lot of questions.

_____ 21. I enjoy playing competitive sports.

_____ 22. I communicate very well with other people.

_____ 23. I know what I want and I set goals to accomplish it.

_____ 24. I have some interest in herbal remedies and natural medicine.

_____ 25. I enjoy working puzzles and mazes.

_____ 26. I am a good storyteller.

_____ 27. I can easily remember the words and melodies of songs.

_____ 28. I enjoy solving problems in math and chemistry and working with computer programming problems.

_____ 29. I usually touch people or pat them on the back when I talk to them.

_____ 30. I understand my family and friends better than most other people do.

_____ 31. I don't always talk about my accomplishments with others.

_____ 32. I would rather work outside around nature than inside around people and equipment.

_____ 33. I enjoy and learn more when seeing movies, slides, or videos in class.

_____ 34. I am a very good listener, and I enjoy listening to others' stories.

_____ 35. I need to study with music.

_____ 36. I enjoy games like Clue, Battleship, chess, and Rubik's Cube.

_____ 37. I enjoy physical activities, such as bicycling, jogging, dancing, snowboarding, skateboarding, and swimming.

_____ 38. I am good at solving people's problems and conflicts.

_____ 39. I have to have time alone to think about new information in order to remember it.

_____ 40. I enjoy sorting and organizing information, objects, and collectibles.

Refer to your score on each individual question. Place that score beside the appropriate question number below. Then, tally each line across and put the total at the side.

SCORE					TOTAL ACROSS	CODE
1 _____	9 _____	17 _____	25 _____	33 _____	_____	Visual/Spatial
2 _____	10 _____	18 _____	26 _____	34 _____	_____	Verbal/Linguistic
3 _____	11 _____	19 _____	27 _____	35 _____	_____	Musical/Rhythmic
4 _____	12 _____	20 _____	28 _____	36 _____	_____	Logical/Mathematical
5 _____	13 _____	21 _____	29 _____	37 _____	_____	Bodily/Kinesthetic
6 _____	14 _____	22 _____	30 _____	38 _____	_____	Interpersonal
7 _____	15 _____	23 _____	31 _____	39 _____	_____	Intrapersonal
8 _____	16 _____	24 _____	32 _____	40 _____	_____	Naturalistic

MIS Tally

Look at the scores on the MIS. What are your top three scores? Write them in the spaces below.

Top Score	_____	Code	_____
Second Score	_____	Code	_____
Third Score	_____	Code	_____

This tally can help you understand where some of your strengths may be. Again, this is not a measure of your worth or capacities, nor is it an indicator of your future successes. Read the following section to better understand multiple intelligences.

© Robert M. Sherfield

three assessments are included so that you might gain a better understanding of your dominant intelligence, identify your learning style, and discover your strongest personality type.

There are no right or wrong answers, and there is no one best way to learn. We hope that you will experience a "wow" or "aha!" moment as you explore and discover new and exciting components of your education. We also hope that you will learn the skills needed to more effectively use your dominant traits and improve your less dominant characteristics.

UNDERSTANDING MULTIPLE INTELLIGENCES

Why Is It Important to Discover New Ways of Looking at Yourself?

In 1983, Howard Gardner, a Harvard University professor, developed a theory called *multiple intelligences* (MI). In his book *Frames of Mind,* he outlines seven intelligences that he feels are possessed by everyone: visual/spatial, verbal/linguistic, musical/rhythmic, logical/mathematical, bodily/kinesthetic, interpersonal, and intrapersonal. In 1996, he added an eighth intelligence: naturalistic. For more information about the intelligences, see Figure 8.4.

In short, if you have ever done things that came easily for you, you were probably drawing on one of your well-developed intelligences. On the other hand, if you have tried to do things that are very difficult to master or understand, you may be dealing with material that calls on one of your less developed intelligences. If playing the piano by ear comes easily to you, your musical/rhythmic intelligence may be very strong. If you have trouble writing an English paper,

Figure 8.4 Understanding and Using the Eight Intelligences

INTELLIGENCE	HOW TO USE IT
Visual/Spatial (picture smart) Thinks in pictures, knows where things are in the house, loves to create images and work with graphs, charts, pictures, and maps.	• Use visuals in your notes, such as timelines, charts, graphs, and geometric shapes. • Work to create a mental or visual picture of the information at hand. • Use colored markers to make associations or to group items together. • Use mapping or webbing so that your main points are easily recognized. • Re-type your notes on the computer; consider using a spreadsheet. • When taking notes, draw pictures in the margins to illustrate the main points. • Visualize the information in your mind.
Verbal/Linguistic (word smart) Communicates well through language, likes to write, is good at spelling, is great at telling stories, loves to read books.	• Establish study groups so that you will have the opportunity to talk about the information. • Using the information you studied, create a story or a skit. • Read as much information about related areas as possible. • As you read chapters, outline them in your own words. • Summarize and recite your notes aloud.
Musical/Rhythmic (music smart) Loves to sing, hum, and whistle; comprehends music; responds to music immediately; performs music.	• Listen to music while studying (if it does not distract you). • Write a song, jingle, or rap about the chapter or information. • Take short breaks from studying to listen to music, especially classical music. • Commit the information being studied to the music from your favorite song.
Logical/Mathematical (number smart) Can easily conceptualize and reason, uses logic, has good problem-solving skills, enjoys math and science.	• Strive to make logical connections between subjects. • Don't just memorize the facts; apply them to real-life situations. • As you study the information, think of problems in society and how this information could solve those problems. • Organize the material in a logical sequence. • Create analyzing charts. Draw a line down the center of the page, put the information at hand in the left column, and analyze, discuss, relate, and synthesize it in the right column. • Allow yourself some time to reflect after studying.
Bodily/Kinesthetic (body smart) Learns through body sensation, moves around a lot, enjoys work involving the hands, is graced with some athletic ability.	• Don't confine your study area to a desk or chair—move around, explore, go outside. • Act out the information. • Study with a group of people, and change groups often. • Use charts, posters, flash cards, and chalkboards to study. • When appropriate or possible, build models using the information studied. • Verbalize the information to others. • Use games such as chess, Monopoly, Twister, or Clue when studying. • Trace words as you study them. • Use repetition to learn facts; write them many times. • Make study sheets.
Interpersonal (people smart) Loves to communicate with other people, possesses great leadership skills, has lots of friends, is involved in extracurricular activities.	• Study in groups. • Share the information with other people. • Teach the information to others. • Interview outside sources to learn more about the material at hand. • Have a debate with others about the information.

INTELLIGENCE	HOW TO USE IT
Intrapersonal (self smart) Has a deep awareness of own feelings, is very reflective, requires time to be alone, does not get involved with group activities.	• Study in a quiet area. • Study by yourself. • Allow time for reflection and meditation about the subject matter. • Study in short time blocks, and then spend some time absorbing the information. • Work at your own pace.
Naturalistic (environment smart) Has interest in the environment and in nature; can easily recognize plants, animals, rocks, and cloud formations; may like hiking, camping, and fishing.	• Study outside whenever possible. • Categorize information. • Relate the information to the effect on the environment whenever possible. • When given the opportunity to choose your own topic or research project, choose something related to nature. • Collect your own study data and resources. • Organize and label your information. • Keep separate notebooks on individual topics so that you can add new information to each topic as it becomes available to you.

your verbal/linguistic intelligence may not be as well developed. This does not mean that you will never be able to write a paper; it simply means that this is not your dominant intelligence, and you may need to spend more time on this activity.

In Figure 8.4, you will find each intelligence described and some helpful tips to assist you in creating a study environment and study habits using the eight intelligences. Read each category, because you may need to improve your less dominant intelligence in some of the classes you take. This list can help you build on your strengths and develop your less dominant areas.

UNDERSTANDING LEARNING STYLES THEORY

Why Is It Important to Know How I Learn?

A learning style (LS) is "the way in which each learner begins to concentrate on, process, and retain new and difficult information" (Dunn and Griggs, 2000). There is a difference between a *learning style* and a *learning strategy.* A learning style is innate and involves your five senses. It is how you best process information that comes to you. A learning strategy is how you might choose to learn or study, such as by using note cards, flip charts, or color slides. Learning strategies also involve where you study (such as at a desk, in bed, in the library, in a quiet place, with music, etc.), how long you study, and what techniques you use to help you study (such as mnemonics, cooperative learning teams, or SQ3R).

If you learn best by *seeing* information, you have a more dominant *visual learning style.* If you learn best by *hearing* information, you have a more dominant *auditory learning style.* If you learn best by *touching or doing,* you have a more dominant *tactile learning style.* You may also hear the tactile learning style referred to as *kinesthetic* or *hands-on.*

Some of the most successful students master information and techniques by using all three styles. If you were learning how to skateboard, you might learn best by *hearing someone* talk about the different styles or techniques. Others might learn best by *watching a video* where someone demonstrates the techniques. Still others would learn best by actually getting on the board and *trying it.* Those who engage all of their senses gain the most.

After taking the LEAD in Figure 8.5 and reading more about learning styles, list at least three concrete strategies that you can employ to enhance your learning strategies for each of the three areas.

Figure 8.5 Take the LEAD (Learning Evaluation and Assessment Directory)

Directions: Read each statement carefully and thoroughly. After reading the statement, rate your response using the scale below. There are no right or wrong answers. This is not a timed survey. The LEAD is based, in part, on research conducted by Rita Dunn.

3 = Often Applies   2 = Sometimes Applies   1 = Never or Almost Never Applies

_____ 1. I remember information better if I write it down or draw a picture of it.

_____ 2. I remember things better when I hear them instead of just reading or seeing them.

_____ 3. When I get something that has to be assembled, I just start doing it. I don't read the directions.

_____ 4. If I am taking a test, I can "see" the page of the text or lecture notes where the answer is located.

_____ 5. I would rather the professor explain a graph, chart, or diagram than just show it to me.

_____ 6. When learning new things, I want to "do it" rather than hear about it.

_____ 7. I would rather the instructor write the information on the board or overhead instead of just lecturing.

_____ 8. I would rather listen to a book on tape than read it.

_____ 9. I enjoy making things, putting things together, and working with my hands.

_____ 10. I am able to quickly conceptualize and visualize information.

_____ 11. I learn best by hearing words.

_____ 12. I have been called "hyperactive" by my parents, spouse, partner, or professor.

_____ 13. I have no trouble reading maps, charts, and diagrams.

_____ 14. I can usually pick up on small sounds like bells, crickets, and frogs, and distant sounds like train whistles.

_____ 15. I use my hands and gesture a lot when I speak to others.

Refer to your score on each individual question. Place that score beside the appropriate question number below. Then, tally the total for each line at the side.

SCORE					TOTAL ACROSS	CODE
1 _____	4 _____	7 _____	10 _____	13 _____	_____	Visual
2 _____	5 _____	8 _____	11 _____	14 _____	_____	Auditory
3 _____	6 _____	9 _____	12 _____	15 _____	_____	Tactile

© Robert M. Sherfield

LEAD SCORE

Look at the scores on the LEAD. What is your top score?

Top Score _____   **Code** _____

WANTED: A VISUAL LEARNER WITH TACTILE SKILLS

Do You Know the Differences Between Your Primary Learning Style and Your Dominant Intelligence?

As discussed earlier, a *learning style* and a *learning strategy* are different. A learning style and a *dominant intelligence* are also quite different. When you read over the descriptions of MI

Successful Decisions

AN ACTIVITY FOR CRITICAL REFLECTION

Kristin knew that her most powerful learning style was visual. She knew that she had always learned best when she could "see" the information in pictures, charts, graphs, PowerPoints, videos, or other powerful visuals. Kristin also knew that when she was able to get involved with the information, she seemed to retain it better. She did not know what this was called, but later learned that she was also a tactile or "hands-on" learner.

When she discovered that different people have different ways of learning and instructors have different ways of teaching, things began to make more sense to her. She wondered why she had also done poorly in classes that were all lecture—like her history class. This semester, she was becoming increasingly worried about her literature class. It, too, was all lecture about poems, plays, and sonnets. She decided to go to the Tutoring Center to find out what she could do to retain the information more effectively. Her tutor showed her how to make the terms and ideas more "visual" by drawing pictures beside each one, using colors in her notes, creating small storyboards, and creating a visual image of what was being discussed.

In your own words, what would you suggest that a classmate do if he or she was having trouble understanding, interpreting, or remembering information from a class in drawing where there was very little discussion or lecture and he or she is a very strong auditory learner? List at least three things that could be done to strengthen his or her less dominant intelligence, learning style, and/or personality type. Think about what services are offered on your campus and what people might be of assistance to him or her.

1. _____
2. _____
3. _____

theory and LS theory, you probably noticed several common elements. Both theories deal with the visual, auditory, and tactile (or kinesthetic). There are also similarities between the two theories, but the differences are great and important.

Simply stated, you can have a visual learning style and yet *not have* visual/spatial as your dominant intelligence. "How can this be possible?" you may be asking. It may be that you **learn best** by watching someone paint a picture—watching his or her brush stokes, method of mixing paints, and spatial layout. (This is your dominant *visual learning* style.) However, you may not be as engaged or as talented at actually painting as the person you watched. Your painting may lack feeling, depth, and expression. You may find it hard to paint anything that is not copied from something else. You can't visualize a landscape in your mind because your visual/spatial intelligence is not very strong. In other words, you are not an innate artist at heart. This is an example of how your visual learning style can be a strong way for you to learn, but your visual/spatial intelligence may not be your dominant intelligence.

In your own words, compare and contrast your primary learning style with your dominant intelligence. Give one example.

BLOOM LEVEL 2

Figure 8.6 Learning Styles

In the space below, use the information from the LEAD and the information on learning styles to create a study plan for each learning style.

VISUAL LEARNING STYLE
(Eye Smart)

Thinks in pictures. Enjoys visual instructions, demonstrations, and descriptions; would rather read a text than listen to a lecture; an avid note-taker; needs visual references; enjoys using charts, graphs, and pictures.

I can improve my visual learning style by...

1. _____
_____
2. _____
_____
3. _____
_____

AUDITORY LEARNING STYLE
(Ear Smart)

Prefers verbal instructions; would rather listen than read; often tapes lectures and listens to them in the car or at home; recites information out loud; enjoys talking, discussing issues, and verbal stimuli; talks out problems.

I can improve my auditory learning style by...

1. _____
_____
2. _____
_____
3. _____
_____

TACTILE LEARNING STYLE
(Action Smart)

Prefers hands-on approaches to learning; likes to take notes and uses a great deal of scratch paper; learns best by doing something, by touching it, or manipulating it; learns best while moving or while in action; often does not concentrate well when sitting and reading.

I can improve my tactile learning style by...

1. _____
_____
2. _____
_____
3. _____
_____

BLOOM LEVEL 6

UNDERSTANDING PERSONALITY TYPE

Are You ENFJ, ISTP or ENTJ, and Why Does It Matter?

In 1921, Swiss psychologist Carl Jung published his work *Psychological Types.* In this book, Jung suggested that human behavior is not random. He felt that behavior follows patterns, and these patterns are caused by differences in the way people use their minds. In 1942, Isabel Briggs-Myers and her mother, Katharine Briggs, began to put Jung's theory into practice. They developed the Myers-Briggs Type Indicator, which after more than 50 years of research and refinement has become the most widely used instrument for identifying and studying personality.

Personality typing can "help us discover what best motivates and energizes each of us as individuals" (Tieger and Barron-Tieger, 2007). The questions on the PAP in Figure 8.7 will

Figure 8.7   Take the PAP (Personality Assessment Profile)

Directions: Read each statement carefully and thoroughly. After reading the statement, rate your response using the scale below. There are no right or wrong answers. This is not a timed survey. The PAP is based, in part, on the Myers-Briggs Type Indicator (MBTI) by Katharine Briggs and Isabel Briggs-Myers.

3 = Often Applies   2 = Sometimes Applies   1 = Never or Almost Never Applies

_____ 1a. I am a very talkative person.

_____ 1b. I am a more reflective person than a verbal person.

_____ 2a. I am a very factual and literal person.

_____ 2b. I look to the future and I can see possibilities.

_____ 3a. I value truth and justice over tact and emotion.

_____ 3b. I find it easy to empathize with other people.

_____ 4a. I am very ordered and efficient.

_____ 4b. I enjoy having freedom from control.

_____ 5a. I am a very friendly and social person.

_____ 5b. I enjoy listening to others more than talking.

_____ 6a. I enjoy being around and working with people who have a great deal of common sense.

_____ 6b. I enjoy being around and working with people who are dreamers and have a great deal of imagination.

_____ 7a. One of my motivating forces is to do a job very well.

_____ 7b. I like to be recognized. I am motivated by my accomplishments and awards.

_____ 8a. I like to plan out my day before I go to bed.

_____ 8b. When I get up on a non-school or non-work day, I just like to let the day "plan itself."

_____ 9a. I like to express my feelings and thoughts.

_____ 9b. I enjoy a great deal of tranquility and quiet time to myself.

_____ 10a. I am a very pragmatic and realistic person.

_____ 10b. I like to create new ideas, methods, or ways of doing things.

_____ 11a. I make decisions with my brain.

_____ 11b. I make decisions with my heart.

_____ 12a. I am a very disciplined and orderly person.

_____ 12b. I don't make a lot of plans.

_____ 13a. I like to work with a group of people.

_____ 13b. I would rather work independently.

_____ 14a. I learn best if I can see it, touch it, smell it, taste it, or hear it.

_____ 14b. I learn best by relying on my gut feelings or intuition.

_____ 15a. I am quick to criticize others.

_____ 15b. I compliment others very easily and quickly.

_____ 16a. My life is systematic and organized.

_____ 16b. I don't really pay attention to deadlines.

_____ 17a. I can be myself when I am around others.

_____ 17b. I can be myself when I am alone.

_____ 18a. I live in the here and now, in the present.

_____ 18b. I live in the future, planning and dreaming.

_____ 19a. I think that if someone breaks the rules, the person should be punished.

_____ 19b. I think that if someone breaks the rules, we should look at the person who broke the rules, examine the rules, and look at the situation at hand before a decision is made.

(continued)

Figure 8.7 Take the PAP (Personality Assessment Profile) (continued)

_____20a. I do my work, then I play.

_____20b. I play, then do my work.

Refer to your score on each individual question. Place that score beside the appropriate question number below. Then, tally the total for each line at the side.

SCORE					TOTAL ACROSS	CODE
1a _____	5a _____	9a _____	13a _____	17a _____	_____	E Extrovert
1b _____	5b _____	9b _____	13b _____	17b _____	_____	I Introvert
2a _____	6a _____	10a _____	14a _____	18a _____	_____	S Sensing
2b _____	6b _____	10b _____	14b _____	18b _____	_____	N iNtuition
3a _____	7a _____	11a _____	15a _____	19a _____	_____	T Thinking
3b _____	7b _____	11b _____	15b _____	19b _____	_____	F Feeling
4a _____	8a _____	12a _____	16a _____	20a _____	_____	J Judging
4b _____	8b _____	12b _____	16b _____	20b _____	_____	P Perceiving

PAP Scores

Look at the scores on your PAP. Is your score higher in the E or I line? Is your score higher in the S or N line? Is your score higher in the T or F line? Is your score higher in the J or P line? Write the code to the side of each section below.

Is your higher score	**E or I**	Code _____
Is your higher score	**S or N**	Code _____
Is your higher score	**T or F**	Code _____
Is your higher score	**J or P**	Code _____

© Robert M. Sherfield

help you discover whether you are an **E or I** (**E**xtroverted or **I**ntroverted), **S or N** (**S**ensing or i**N**tuitive), **T or F** (**T**hinking or **F**eeling), and **J or P** (**J**udging or **P**erceiving). When all of the combinations of E/I, S/N, T/F, and J/P are combined, there are 16 personality types. Everyone will fit into *one* of the following categories:

ISTJ	ISFJ	INFJ	INTJ
ISTP	ISFP	INFP	INTP
ESTP	ESFP	ENFP	ENTP
ESTJ	ESFJ	ENFJ	ENTJ

Let's take a look at the four major categories of typing. Notice that the higher your score in one area, the stronger your personality type is for that area. For instance, if you scored 15 on the E (extroversion) questions, this means that you are a strong extrovert. If you scored 15 on the I (introversion) questions, this means that you are a strong introvert. However, if you scored 7 on the E questions and 8 on the I questions, your score indicates that you possess almost the same amount of extroverted and introverted qualities. The same is true for every category on the PAP.

B R I N G the *Change*

TIPS FOR PERSONAL SUCCESS

Consider the following tips for making the most of your learning style, personality type, and dominant intelligence:

- Improve your weaker learning styles by incorporating at least one aspect of those learning styles into your daily study plans.
- If your personality type clashes with your professor's personality type, try to make adjustments that enable you to get through the class successfully.
- Adjust your learning style to match your professor's teaching style, if possible.
- Use your primary intelligence to help you decide on your life's vocation.

Now, it is your turn. Create a list of at least three more tips that you would offer a fellow classmate to assist him or her with making the most of his or her learning style, intelligence, and personality type. Develop one strategy for each category.

1. Learning Style Tip

_____

_____

2. Multiple Intelligence Tip

_____

_____

3. Personality Type Tip

_____

_____

E Versus I (Extroversion/Introversion)

This category deals with the way we *interact with others and the world around us—how we draw our energy.*

Extroverts prefer to live in the outside world, drawing their strength from other people. They are outgoing and love interaction. They usually make decisions with others in mind. They enjoy being the center of attention. There are usually few secrets about extroverts.

Introverts draw their strength from the inner world. They need to spend time alone to think and ponder. They are usually quiet and reflective. They usually make decisions by themselves. They do not like being the center of attention. They are private.

S Versus N (Sensing/Intuition)

This category deals with the way we *learn and deal with information.*

Sensing types gather information through their five senses. They have a hard time believing something if it cannot be seen, touched, smelled, tasted, or heard. They like concrete facts

from ORDINARY to *Extraordinary*

Chef Odette Smith-Ransome
Hospitality Instructor
The Art Institute of Pittsburgh, Pittsburgh, Pennsylvania

AT THE age of 15, I found myself constantly in conflict with my mother, until one day I stood before her as she held a gun to my head. It was at that moment I knew I had to leave my parents' home—not just for my emotional well-being, but for my actual life and survival. My father was a good man, but he did not understand the entire situation with my mother's alcohol and diet pill addiction, and he could do little to smooth out the situation between my mother and me. To complicate matters even more, my brother had just returned home from fighting in Vietnam and everyone was trying to adjust. It was a horrible time in the house where my ancestors had lived for over 100 years. So, I packed my clothes, dropped out of the tenth grade, and ran over 1,000 miles away to Charleston, South Carolina.

My first job was as a waitress. I worked in that job for over three years, realizing more every day that I was not using my talents and that without an education, I was doomed to work for minimum wage for the rest of my life. During this time, I met a friend in Charleston who was in the Navy. When he was released, he offered to take me back to Pittsburgh. I agreed, and on my return, I went to work in the kitchen of a family-owned restaurant. They began to take an interest in me and made me feel proud of my work. I then decided to get my GED and determine what road to take that would allow me to use my culinary talents and help others at the same time.

I began my associate's degree, which required that students complete an apprenticeship. We worked 40 hours per week, Monday through Thursday, under the direction of a

and details. They do not rely on intuition or gut feelings. They usually have a great deal of common sense.

Intuitive types are not very detail-oriented. They can see possibilities, and they rely on their gut feelings. Usually, they are very innovative people. They tend to live in the future and often get bored once they have mastered a task.

T Versus F (Thinking/Feeling)

This category deals with the way we *make decisions.*

Thinkers are very logical people. They do not make decisions based on feelings or emotions. They are analytical and sometimes do not take others' values into consideration when making decisions. They can easily identify the flaws of others. They can sometimes be seen as insensitive and lacking compassion.

Feelers make decisions based on what they feel is right and just. They like to have harmony, and they value others' opinions and feelings. They are usually very tactful people who like to please others. They are very warm people.

master chef, and we were in class eight hours a day on Friday. My apprenticeship was at the Hyatt Regency in Pittsburgh. In order to obtain my degree, I had to pass the apprenticeship, all of the classes, and a bank of tests that proved my proficiency in a variety of areas. If I failed one part of the tests, I could not get my degree. Proudly, I passed every test, every class, and my apprenticeship.

My first professional job came to me on the recommendation of a friend. I interviewed for and was hired to become the private chef for the chancellor of the University of Pittsburgh. I loved the job, and it afforded me the opportunity to get my bachelor's degree. So, I juggled a full-time job, a two-year-old child, and a full load of classes. As I neared the end of my degree, I was offered a fellowship at the University of Pittsburgh that trained people to teach students with special needs. I graduated Cum Laude and began teaching and working with people who had cerebral palsy at Connelley Academy. I loved the work, and the position solidified my desire to work with adults.

From there I taught at the Good Will Training Center and later at the Pittsburgh Job Corps, where my culinary team won a major national competition. Today, I am an instructor at The Art Institute of Pittsburgh, helping others reach their

So, I packed my clothes, dropped out of the tenth grade, and ran over 1,000 miles away to Charleston, South Carolina.

dreams of working in the hospitality industry. In 2005, I was named Culinary Educator of the Year by the American Culinary Federation. I try to let my life and my struggles serve as a light for students who have faced adversity and may have felt that their past was going to determine their future. My advice to my students—and to you—is this: *Never* let anyone tell you that you can't do it, that you're not able to do it, that you don't have the means to do it, or that you'll never succeed. You set your own course in life, and you determine the direction of your future.

EXTRAORDINARY REFLECTION

Read the following statement and respond in your online journal or class notebook.

Chef Smith-Ransome had to literally leave her family to protect her life. Think about your family situation at the moment. Are your family members supportive of your efforts? Do they offer you support? Are they working with you to help you achieve your goals? If so, how does this make you stronger? Do they offer you guidance?

J Versus P (Judging/Perceiving)

This category deals with the way we *live and our overall lifestyle.*

Judgers are very orderly people. They must have a great deal of structure in their lives. They are good at setting goals and sticking to their goals. They are the type of people who would seldom, if ever, play before their work was completed.

Perceivers are just the opposite. They are less structured and more spontaneous. They do not like timelines. Unlike judgers, they will play before their work is done. They will take every chance to delay a decision or judgment. Sometimes, they can become involved in too many things at one time.

After you have studied Figure 8.8 and other information regarding your personality type, you can make some decisions about your study habits and even your career choices. For instance, if you scored very strong in the extroversion section, it may not serve you well to pursue a career where you would be forced to work alone. It would probably be unwise to try to spend all of your time studying alone. If you are a strong extrovert, you would want to work and study around people.

Figure 8.8 A Closer Look at Your Personality Type

ISTJ: THE DUTIFUL (7–10% OF AMERICANS)	ISFJ: THE NURTURER (7–10% OF AMERICANS)	INFJ: THE PROTECTOR (2–3% OF AMERICANS)	INTJ: THE SCIENTIST (2–3% OF AMERICANS)
Have great power of concentration; very serious; dependable; logical and realistic; take responsibility for their own actions; not easily distracted	Hard workers; detail-oriented; considerate of others' feelings; friendly and warm to others; very conscientious; down-to-earth and like to be around the same	Enjoy an atmosphere where all get along; do what is needed of them; have strong beliefs and principles; enjoy helping others achieve their goals	Very independent; enjoy challenges; inventors; can be skeptical; perfectionists; believe in their own work, sometimes to a fault
Possible Careers: Accountant, purchasing agent, real estate agent, IRS agent, corrections officer, investment counselor, law researcher, technical writer, judge, mechanic	**Possible Careers:** Dentist, physician, biologist, surgical technician, teacher, speech pathologist, historian, clerical worker, bookkeeper, electrician, retail owner, counselor	**Possible Careers:** Career counselor, psychologist, teacher, social worker, clergy, artist, novelist, filmmaker, health care provider, human resource manager, coach, crisis manager, mediator	**Possible Careers:** Economist, financial planner, banker, budget analyst, scientist, astronomer, network specialist, computer programmer, engineer, curriculum designer, coroner, pathologist, attorney, manager

ISTP: THE MECHANIC (4–7% OF AMERICANS)	ISFP: THE ARTIST (5–7% OF AMERICANS)	INFP: THE IDEALIST (3–4% OF AMERICANS)	INTP: THE THINKER (3–4% OF AMERICANS)
Very reserved; good at making things clear to others; interested in how and why things work; like to work with their hands; can sometimes be misunderstood as idle	Very sensitive and modest; adapt easily to change; respectful of others' feelings and values; take criticism personally; don't enjoy leadership roles	Work well alone; must know others well to interact; faithful to others and their jobs; excellent at communication; open-minded; dreamers; tend to do too much	Extremely logical; very analytical; good at planning; love to learn; excellent problem solvers; don't enjoy needless conversation; hard to understand at times
Possible Careers: Police officer, intelligence officer, firefighter, athletic coach, engineer, technical trainer, logistic manager, EMT, surgical technician, banker, office manager, carpenter, landscape architect	**Possible Careers:** Artist, chef, musician, nurse, medical assistant, surgeon, botanist, zoologist, science teacher, travel agent, game warden, coach, bookkeeper, clerical worker, insurance examiner	**Possible Careers:** Entertainer, artist, editor, musician, professor, researcher, counselor, consultant, clergy, dietitian, massage therapist, human resources manager, events manager, corporate leader	**Possible Careers:** Software designer, programmer, systems analyst, network administrator, surgeon, veterinarian, lawyer, economist, architect, physicist, mathematician, college professor, writer, agent, producer

ESTP: THE DOER (6–8% OF AMERICANS)	ESFP: THE PERFORMER (8–10% OF AMERICANS)	ENFP: THE INSPIRER (6–7% OF AMERICANS)	ENTP: THE VISIONARY (4–6% OF AMERICANS)
Usually very happy; don't let trivial things upset them; have very good memories; very good at working with things and taking them apart	Very good at sports and active exercises; good common sense; easygoing; good at communication; can be impulsive; do not enjoy working alone; have fun and enjoy living and life	Creative and industrious; can easily find success in activities and projects that interest them; good at motivating others; organized; do not like routine	Great problem solvers; love to argue either side; can do almost anything; good at speaking/motivating; love challenges; very creative; do not like routine; overconfident
Possible Careers: Police officer, firefighter, detective, military, investigator, paramedic, banker, investor, promoter, carpenter, chef, real estate broker, retail sales, insurance claims agent	**Possible Careers:** Nurse, social worker, physician assistant, nutritionist, therapist, photographer, musician, film producer, social events coordinator, news anchor, fund raiser, host, retail sales	**Possible Careers:** Journalist, writer, actor, newscaster, artist, director, public relations, teacher, clergy, psychologist, guidance counselor, trainer, project manager, human resources manager	**Possible Careers:** Entrepreneur, manager, agent, journalist, attorney, urban planner, analyst, creative director, public relations, marketing, broadcaster, network solutions, politician, detective

ESTJ: THE GUARDIAN (12–15% OF AMERICANS)	ESFJ: THE CAREGIVER (11–14% OF AMERICANS)	ENFJ: THE GIVER (3–5% OF AMERICANS)	ENTJ: THE EXECUTIVE (3–5% OF AMERICANS)
"Take charge" people; like to get things done; focus on results; very good at organizing; good at seeing what will not work; responsible; realists	Enjoy many friendly relationships; popular; love to help others; do not take criticism very well; need praise; need to work with people; organized; talkative; active	Very concerned about others' feelings; respect others; good leaders; usually popular; good at public speaking; can make decisions too quickly; trust easily	Excellent leaders; speak very well; hard working; may be workaholics; may not give enough praise; like to learn; great planners; enjoy helping others reach their goals
Possible Careers: Insurance agent, military, security, coach, credit analyst, project manager, auditor, general contractor, paralegal, stockbroker, executive, information officer, lawyer, controller, accounts manager	**Possible Careers:** Medical assistant, physician, nurse, teacher, coach, principal, social worker, counselor, clergy, court reporter, office manager, loan officer, public relations, customer service, caterer, office manager	**Possible Careers:** Journalist, entertainer, TV producer, politician, counselor, clergy, psychologist, teacher, social worker, health care provider, customer service manager	**Possible Careers:** Executive, senior manager, administrator, consultant, editor, producer, financial planner, stockbroker, program designer, attorney, psychologist, engineer, network administrator

Source: Adapted from Tieger and Barron-Tieger, 2007; and Personality Type Portraits, 2008.

CHANGING IDEAS *to Reality*

REFLECTIONS ON LEARNING HOW TO LEARN

Unlike an IQ test, learning styles, multiple intelligence, and personality type assessments do not pretend to determine if you are "smart" or not. These assessments simply allow you to look more closely at how you learn, what innate strengths you possess, and what your dominant intelligence may be.

Discovering your learning style can greatly enhance your classroom performance. For example, finally understanding that your learning style is visual and that your professor's teaching style is totally verbal (oral) can answer many questions about why you may have performed poorly in the past in a strictly "lecture class." Now that you have discovered that you are a feeling extrovert, you can better understand why you love associating with others and learn a great deal by working in groups. And now that you have discovered that your primary intelligence is logical/mathematical, you know why math and science are easier for you than history or literature.

Possessing this knowledge and developing the tools to make your learning style, dominant intelligence, and personality type work for you, not against you, will be paramount to your success. As you continue to use your learning style, dominant intelligence, and personality type to enhance learning, consider the following:

- Get involved in a variety of learning and social situations.
- Use your less dominant areas more often to strengthen them.
- Read more about personality typing and learning styles.
- Surround yourself with people who learn differently from you.
- Try different ways of learning and studying.
- Remember that inventories do not measure your worth.

By understanding how you process information, learning can become an entirely new and exciting venture for you. Good luck to you on this new journey.

"Education is learning what you did not know you did not know."

—Daniel Boorstin

Knowledge
in Bloom

CREATING YOUR PERSONAL LIFE PROFILE

Utilizes levels 4 and 5 of the taxonomy

Each chapter-end assessment is based on Bloom's Taxonomy of Learning. See pages xxvi–xxviii in the front of this book for a quick review.

Throughout the chapter, you have discovered three things about the way you learn best: your multiple intelligence, your learning style, and your personality type. Write them down in the spaces below:

My **dominant intelligence** is: _____

My **primary learning style** is: _____

My **strongest personality type** is: _____

Now that you see them all together, think of them as a puzzle that you need to assemble. In other words, what do they look like all together? What do they mean? How do they affect your studies, your relationships, your communication skills, and your career choices?

Example: If Mike's dominant intelligence is interpersonal, his learning style is verbal, and his personality type is ENFJ, connecting the dots may suggest that he is the type of person who loves to be around other people and learns best by listening to or explaining how something is done. He is a person who would probably speak out in class, be more of a leader than a follower, and start a study group, because he is outgoing, organized, and very much a goal setter. Mike is the type of person who values relationships and listens to what

others are saying. He is a person who shares and does not mind taking the time to explain things to others. He could easily become a good friend.

Some of the challenges Mike could encounter might involve taking a class where discussions are rare, having to sit and never share ideas or views, or having a professor who is not very organized and skips around. He would not deal very well with peers who are disrespectful and do not pull their own weight in the study group. He might also have a hard time with group members or classmates who are very quiet and prefer to observe rather than become involved. He would have trouble being around people who have no goals and direction in life. He might also run into some trouble because he is a very social person and loves to be around others in social settings. He may overcommit himself to groups and clubs, and on occasion, he may socialize more than study.

As you can see, Mike's Personal Life Profile tells us a great deal about his strengths and challenges. It also gives him an understanding of how to approach many different situations, capitalize on his strengths, and work to improve his weaker areas.

Now, it is your turn. Take your time and refer to the chapter for any information you may need. Examine your assessments and create your own profile in the four areas listed below. Discuss your strengths and challenges for each area.

THE PERSONAL LIFE PROFILE OF _____

Academic Strengths:

_____

_____

Academic Challenges:

_____

_____

Communication Strengths:

_____

_____

Communication Challenges:

_____

_____

Relationship Strengths:

_____

_____

Relationship Challenges:

_____

_____

Career Strengths:

_____

_____

Career Challenges:

_____

_____

Looking at all of this together, write an extensive paragraph about what this means about you. Include thoughts on your learning style, your personality, your study habits, your communication skills, and your overall success strategy.

_____

_____

_____

_____

_____

_____

_____

_____

SQ3R MASTERY STUDY SHEET

EXAMPLE QUESTION (*from page 203*) What is the difference between a learning style and a learning strategy?	**ANSWER:**
EXAMPLE QUESTION (*from page 206*) What is the definition of tactile learning, and how do you use it?	**ANSWER:**
AUTHOR QUESTION (*from page 197*) Discuss at least three theories of learning from the historical figures discussed.	**ANSWER:**
AUTHOR QUESTION (*from page 201*) Who is Howard Gardner, and why is his work important?	**ANSWER:**
AUTHOR QUESTION (*from page 204*) Explain the difference between your learning style and your dominant intelligence.	**ANSWER:**
AUTHOR QUESTION (*from page 205*) What is the difference between a visual learning style and a visual intelligence?	**ANSWER:**
AUTHOR QUESTION (*from page 206*) How can your personality type affect your career aspirations?	**ANSWER:**
YOUR QUESTION (*from page _____*)	**ANSWER:**
YOUR QUESTION (*from page _____*)	**ANSWER:**
YOUR QUESTION (*from page _____*)	**ANSWER:**
YOUR QUESTION (*from page _____*)	**ANSWER:**
YOUR QUESTION (*from page _____*)	**ANSWER:**

Finally, after answering these questions, recite in your mind the major points covered here. Consider the following general questions to help you master this material.

- What was it about?
- What does it mean?
- What was the most important thing you learned? Why?
- What were the key points to remember?

RECORD

CULTIVATING YOUR LISTENING SKILLS AND DEVELOPING A NOTE-TAKING SYSTEM THAT WORKS FOR YOU

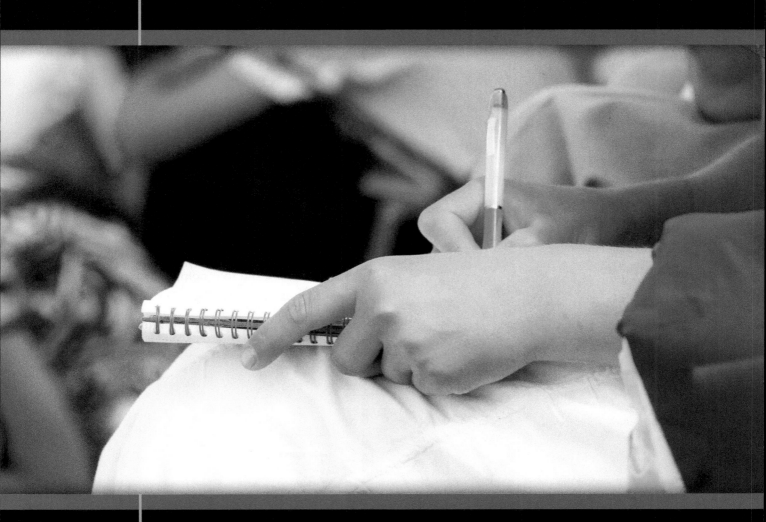

"To listen well is as powerful a means of communication as to talk well." —Chinese Proverb

Why read this chapter?

Because you'll learn:

- The difference between listening and hearing
- How to overcome the obstacles to listening
- The importance of taking notes

Because you'll be able to:

- Use the L-STAR note-taking system
- Apply the outline, Cornell, and mapping note-taking systems
- Determine which note-taking style works best for certain classes

Scan and QUESTION

Take a few moments, **scan this chapter,** and on page 242, write **five of your own questions** that you think will be important to your mastery of this material. You will also find five questions listed from your authors.

Example:

☑ **What are the four components of the Chinese verb "to listen"?** (from page 221)

☑ **Why is it important to identify keywords during a lecture?** (from page 226)

MyStudentSuccessLab

MyStudentSuccessLab (www.mystudentsuccesslab.com) is an online solution designed to help you "Start strong, Finish stronger" by building skills for ongoing personal and professional development.

Name:	Eric Despinis
Institution:	Graduate! ITT Technical Institute
Age:	33
Major:	Information Technology
Career:	IT System Administrator and Project Manager

My education helped me develop a clear vision of what I wanted, where I was going, and how to get there. When you know what you want and understand what it is going to take to achieve it, you apply the effort to make it work. I am a full-time student and a single parent. There have been times when the stress was just incredible and almost insurmountable. I know that my education is important, but so is my family. I had to learn how to make it all work together if I was going to be successful at anything. Sacrifices had to be made. Yes, there were days when it was all overwhelming—on those days, I stepped back, remembered my vision and my plan, and played with my son. He is the most important thing in my life, and our future depends on my success.

My journey has been a long and interesting one. I served in the military for almost a decade. I learned many things about information technology and electrical engineering in the Navy, but I knew that I would have to have a degree to succeed in today's world of work. With a degree, I'm one step ahead of someone who just has experience. That may not be fair, but it is the truth.

In my field of information technology, there is something new that comes along every day. *Every* day! Without my training, I would not be able to process all of the changes that are required to be successful. I would not be able to keep up. My education taught me how to expect the unexpected and know the unknown.

There were many times during my education when it all seemed like it was too much—that I was not going to make it. However, I learned to ask for help and rely on my instructors. I learned that they were there to help me, not fail me. They wanted me to succeed, and yours want you to succeed, too. They want to help you clear the many hurdles in your life. I would say to you from experience: stick with it, believe in yourself, let others help you, and you'll get there. Your degree will be worth every dollar, every day, and every sacrifice you make to earn it.

THINK about *it*

1. How important is your success to you and your family? What sacrifices are you willing to make to obtain your degree?

2. Eric mentioned that something new comes along in his profession every day. What preparations are you making to deal with the many changes that will be coming your way in your chosen profession?

THE IMPORTANCE OF LISTENING

"You cannot truly listen to anyone and do anything else at the same time."

—M. Scott Peck

Why Does Listening Really Matter in Classes and Relationships?

Listening is a survival skill. Period! It is that simple! "I know listening is important," you might say, but few ever think of the paramount significance listening has on our everyday lives. It is necessary for:

- Establishing and improving relationships
- Personal growth
- Showing respect to others
- Professional rapport
- Showing empathy and compassion
- Learning new information
- Understanding others' opinions and views
- Basic survival
- Entertainment
- Health

How much time do you think you spend listening every day? Research suggests that we spend almost 70 percent of our waking time communicating, and **53 percent of that time is spent in listening situations** (Adler, Rosenfeld, and Proctor, 2010). Effective listening skills can mean the difference between success or failure, A's or F's, relationships or loneliness, and in some cases and careers, life or death.

For students, good listening skills are critical. Over the next two to four years, you will be given a lot of information through lectures. Cultivating and improving your active listening skills will help you to understand the material, take accurate notes, participate in class discussions, communicate with your peers more effectively, and become more actively engaged in your learning process.

How can becoming a critical listener help you in and out of the classroom?

Photodisc/Getty RF

I THINK I HEARD YOU LISTENING

Is There Really a Difference Between Listening and Hearing?

No doubt you've been in a communication situation in which a misunderstanding took place. Perhaps you heard something incorrectly, or someone heard you incorrectly, or it could be that someone heard your message but misinterpreted it. These communication blunders arise because we tend to view listening (and communication in general) as an automatic response when in fact it is not.

Listening is a learned, voluntary activity. You must choose to do it. It is a skill, just like driving a car, painting a picture, or playing the piano. Becoming an active listener requires practice, time, mistakes, guidance, and active participation.

Hearing, however, is not learned; it is automatic and involuntary. If you are within range of a sound, you will probably hear it, although you may not be listening to it. Hearing a sound does not guarantee that you know what it is or from where it came. Listening actively, though, means making a conscious effort to focus on the sound and determine what it is.

Listening Defined

According to Adler, Rosenfeld, and Towne (2006), the drawing of the Chinese verb "to listen" (shown in Figure 9.1) provides a comprehensive and practical definition of listening.

To the Chinese, listening involves your *ears*, your *eyes*, your ***undivided attention,*** and your ***heart.*** Do you make it a habit to listen with more than your ears? The Chinese view listening as a whole-body experience. People from Western cultures seem to have lost the ability to involve their whole body in the listening process. We tend to use only our ears, and sometimes we don't even use them very well.

At its core, listening is "the ability to hear, understand, analyze, respect, and appropriately respond to the meaning of another person's spoken and nonverbal messages" (Daly and Engleberg, 2006). Although this definition involves the word *hear,* listening goes far beyond just the physical ability to catch sound waves.

The first step in listening *is* hearing, but true listening involves one's full attention and the ability to filter out distractions, emotional barriers, cultural differences, and religious biases. Listening means that you are making a conscious decision to understand and show reverence for the other person's communication efforts.

Listening needs to be personalized and internalized. To understand listening as a whole-body experience, we can define it on three levels:

1. Listening with a **purpose**
2. Listening **objectively**
3. Listening **constructively**

Figure 9.1   **Chinese Verb "To Listen"**

Successful Decisions

AN ACTIVITY FOR CRITICAL REFLECTION

Jennifer greatly disliked her biology instructor. She could not put her finger on *why* she disliked her, but Dr. Lipmon just rubbed her the wrong way. This had been the case since the first day of class.

Other students seemed to like her and were able to carry on conversations with her—but not Jennifer. "Why?" she thought. "Why do I dislike her so much? She's not a bad teacher," she reasoned, "But I just can't stand to listen to her."

Jennifer decided to sit back for the next week and really try to figure out what the main problem was. As she sat in class and listened, she figured it out: she and Dr. Lipmon had completely different views on many things, including evolution and woman's reproductive rights.

Every time Dr. Lipmon made a statement contrary to Jennifer's core beliefs, she cringed. She "shut down" and refused to listen any further. She transferred her dislike of Dr. Lipmon's lectures and opinions onto her as a person. She knew this was affecting her grade and her knowledge base in class, but did not know how to manage or change the situation.

In your own words, what would you suggest that Jennifer do at this point? Pretend that she is enrolled at your institution. List at least three things that she could do to ensure her success. Think about what services are offered and what people might be of assistance to her.

1. _____

_____

2. _____

_____

3. _____

_____

Listening with a purpose suggests a need to recognize different types of listening situations—for example, class, worship, entertainment, and relationships. People do not listen the same way in every situation.

Listening objectively means listening with an open mind. You will give yourself few greater gifts than the gift of knowing how to listen without bias and prejudice. This is perhaps the most difficult aspect of listening. If you have been cut off in mid-conversation or mid-sentence by someone who disagreed with you, or if someone has left the room while you were giving your opinion of a situation, you have had the experience of talking to people who do not know how to listen objectively.

Listening constructively means listening with the attitude: "How can this be helpful to my life, my education, my career, or my finances?" This type of listening involves evaluating the information you hear and determining whether it has meaning to your life. Sound easy? It is more difficult than it sounds because, again, we all tend to shut out information that we do not view as immediately helpful or useful. To listen constructively, you need to know how to listen and store information for later.

FOUR LISTENING STYLES DEFINED

What Is Your Orientation?

According to interpersonal communication expert, author, and educator Steven McCornack (2007), there are *four different listening styles.* They are action-oriented, time-oriented, people-oriented, and content-oriented. Study Figure 9.2 to determine which best describes you as a listener.

Which style best describes you? _____

_____

Figure 9.2 Four Listening Styles

Action-Oriented Listeners:
- Want to get their messages quickly and to-the-point
- Do not like fluff and grow impatient when they perceive people to be wasting their time
- Become frustrated when information is not orderly
- Are quick to dismiss people who ramble and falter when they speak.

Time-Oriented Listeners:
- Want their information in brief, concise messages
- Are consumed with how much time is taken to convey a message
- Set time limits for listening (and communicating in general)
- Will ask people to "move the message along" if they feel it is taking too long

People-Oriented Listeners:
- Are in contrast to time- and action-oriented listeners
- View listening as a chance to connect with other people
- Enjoy listening to people so that relationships can be built
- Become emotionally involved with the person communicating

Content-Oriented Listeners:
- Enjoy an intellectual challenge
- Like to listen to technical information, facts, and evidence
- Enjoy complex information that must be deciphered and filtered
- Carefully evaluate information and facts before forming an opinion
- Enjoy asking questions

What are the pros of being this type of listener _____

_____

_____

What are the cons of being this type of listener? _____

_____

_____

LISTENING CAN BE SO HARD

Can You Really Overcome the Obstacles to Listening?

Several major obstacles stand in the way of becoming an effective listener. To begin building active listening skills, you first have to remove some barriers.

Obstacle 1: Prejudging

Prejudging, one of the biggest obstacles to active listening, means that you automatically shut out what is being said. You may prejudge because you don't like or agree with the information or the person communicating. You may also have prejudging problems because of your environment, culture, social status, or attitude.

DO YOU PREJUDGE INFORMATION OR ITS SOURCE?   Answer yes or no to each of the following questions:

1. I tune out when something is boring.   Yes   No
2. I tune out when I do not agree with the information.   Yes   No
3. I argue mentally with the speaker about information.   Yes   No
4. I do not listen to people I do not like.   Yes   No
5. I make decisions about information before I understand all of its   Yes   No
   implications or consequences.

If you answered yes to two or more of these questions, you tend to prejudge in a listening situation.

TIPS FOR OVERCOMING PREJUDGING

- Listen for information that may be valuable to you as a student. Some material may not be pleasant to hear but may be useful to you later on.

- Listen to the message, not the messenger. If you do not like the speaker, try to go beyond personality and listen to what is being said, without regard to the person saying it. Conversely, you may like the speaker so much that you automatically accept the material or answers without listening objectively to what is being said.

- Try to remove cultural, racial, gender, social, and environmental barriers. Just because a person is different from you or holds a different point of view does not make that person wrong; and just because a person is like you and holds a similar point of view does not make that person right. Sometimes, you have to cross cultural and environmental barriers to learn new material and see with brighter eyes.

Obstacle 2: Talking

Not even the best listener in the world can listen while he or she is talking. The next time you are in a conversation with a friend, try speaking while your friend is speaking—then see if you know what your friend said. To become an effective listener, you need to learn the power of silence. Silence gives you the opportunity to think about what is being said before you respond. The first rule of listening is to stop talking. The second rule of listening is to stop talking. And, you guessed it—the third rule of listening is to stop talking.

ARE YOU A TALKER RATHER THAN A LISTENER?   Answer yes or no to the following questions:

1. I often interrupt the speaker so that I can say what I want.   Yes   No
2. I am thinking of my next statement while others are talking.   Yes   No
3. My mind wanders when others talk.   Yes   No
4. I answer my own questions.   Yes   No
5. I answer questions that are asked of other people.   Yes   No

If you answered yes to two or more questions, you tend to talk too much in a listening situation.

TIPS FOR OVERCOMING THE URGE TO TALK TOO MUCH

- Avoid interrupting the speaker. Force yourself to be silent at parties, family gatherings, and friendly get-togethers. You should not be unsociable, but force yourself to be silent for 10 minutes. You'll be surprised at what you hear. You may also be surprised how hard it is to do this. Test yourself.

From ORDINARY to *Extraordinary*

Catherine Schleigh
Customer Service Coordinator, Kinko's-FedEx, Inc.,
Philadelphia, Pennsylvania

I **DON'T LIKE** to speculate, but I would say that few college students in the United States had to take a bus two and a half hours each way to attend classes five days a week. I did. I would also speculate that few college students became the primary caregiver for his or her mother at the age of seven. I did. I might also speculate that few people feel as lucky, proud, and honored to simply hold his or her head high and say, "I made it." I am. My name is Catherine Schleigh, and despite my past family history and personal struggles, I am a first-generation college graduate and hold a professional position with a major corporation in one of the most wonderful cities in America.

Growing up, I had no real family so to speak of. My dad left my mom and me when I was young, and from the age of seven, I was left to care for my mother, who is a diagnosed paranoid schizophrenic. Growing up, I received no help, no support, and no encouragement from her or any member of my family. Often, she would not take her medications (or the medications had been improperly prescribed), and she would be physically, emotionally, and verbally abusive to me. It was hard to watch her talk to herself or invisible people. We lived in a very poor, drug-infested, gang-populated area of Philly, and many times, I could not see how I would ever survive.

> *I was left to care for my mother, who is a diagnosed paranoid schizophrenic.*

I managed to complete high school and began attending Job Corp, studying business. From there, I began my college studies, majoring in business administration. I had to work very hard, and the adjustment from high school to college was massive. I had to learn how to motivate myself, but the most important thing I learned was that there are people in this world who will help you if you let them.

Some of my instructors did not understand my situation at first. I cried a lot in class, did not have my projects completed from time to time, and basically lived the life of an introvert. Once everyone learned that I was caring for my mother, traveling five hours a day to class, and struggling just to eat, they became my family. They taught me that I had to put my education first. They taught me that without an education, I would most likely have to work in dead-end jobs for the rest of my life. I began to really look at all of the people in my neighborhood, and I made a committed decision that I was not going to fall prey to the temptations of alcohol, sex, unemployment, and drugs.

As I began to succeed in classes, my self-esteem became healthier. I began to understand how to support myself, take pride in my successes, and help others in any way possible. I still struggle with my mother as she seeks therapy and better medical care, but I also know that I must take care of my own life and keep working toward my own goals. My life is my first priority.

Today, I am an honors graduate. I completed my Bachelor of Arts in business administration with a GPA of 3.50. At the graduation ceremony, I was presented an award by the faculty and staff for my dedication, hard work, and for overcoming all odds to obtain my degree. I hope in some small way that my story can help you hold on and reach your dreams. Happiness and success are possible for you.

EXTRAORDINARY REFLECTION

Read the following statement and respond in your online journal or class notebook.

Ms. Schleigh had no family support. As a matter of fact, once her father was gone, she was the primary caregiver for her mother. How has your family support (or lack of support) affected your studies? Do you think it is important to have your family's support to succeed?

- Ask someone a question, and then allow that person to answer the question. Too often we ask questions and answer them ourselves. Force yourself to wait until the person has formulated a response. If you ask questions and wait for answers, you will force yourself to listen.

- Concentrate on what is being said at the moment, not what you want to say next.

Obstacle 3: Becoming Too Emotional

Emotions can form a strong barrier to active listening. Worries, problems, fears, and anger can keep you from listening to the greatest advantage. Have you ever sat in a lecture, and before you knew what was happening, your mind was a million miles away because you were angry or worried about something? If you have, you know what it's like to bring your emotions to the table.

DO YOU BRING YOUR EMOTIONS TO THE LISTENING SITUATION?   Answer yes or no to the following questions:

1. I get angry before I hear the whole story.	Yes	No
2. I look for underlying or hidden messages in information.	Yes	No
3. Sometimes, I begin listening on a negative note.	Yes	No
4. I base my opinions of information on what others are saying or doing.	Yes	No
5. I readily accept information as correct from people whom I like or respect.	Yes	No

If you answered yes to two or more of these questions, you tend to bring your emotions to a listening situation.

TIPS FOR OVERCOMING EMOTIONS

- Know how you feel before you begin the listening experience. Take stock of your emotions and feelings ahead of time.

- Focus on the message; determine how to use the information.

    - Create a positive image about the message you are hearing.

    - Avoid overreacting and jumping to conclusions.

Do you find it easy or hard to pick up the clues a professor gives in class that may indicate important test information?

iStockPhoto

LISTENING FOR KEYWORDS, PHRASES, AND HINTS

Do Professors Really Offer Test Clues in Their Lectures?

Learning how to listen for keywords, phrases, and hints can help you become an active listener and an effective note-taker. For example, if your English instructor begins a lecture by saying, "There are 10 basic elements to writing poetry," jot down the number 10 under the heading "Poetry" or number your notebook page 1 through 10, leaving space for notes. If at the end of class you listed six elements to writing poetry, you know that you missed a part of the lecture. At this point, you need to ask the instructor some questions.

Here are some key phrases and words to listen for:

in addition to	another way	above all
most important	such as	specifically
you'll see this again	therefore	finally
for example	to illustrate	as stated earlier
in contrast	in comparison	nevertheless
the characteristics of	the main issue is	moreover
on the other hand	as a result of	because

Picking up on *transition words* such as these will help you filter out less important information and thus listen more carefully to what is most important. There are other indicators of important information, too. You will want to listen carefully when the instructor:

- Writes something on the board

- Uses a PowerPoint Presentation

- Uses computer-aided graphics

- Speaks in a louder tone or changes vocal patterns

- Uses gestures more than usual

- Draws on a flip chart

LISTENING IN DIFFICULT SITUATIONS

What Do You Do When English Is Your Second Language?

For students whose first language is not English, your coursework can present some uniquely challenging situations. One of the most pressing and important challenges is the ability to listen, translate, understand, and capture the message on paper in a quick and continuous manner. According to Lynn Forkos, professor and coordinator of the Conversation Center for International Students at the College of Southern Nevada, the following tips can be beneficial:

- Don't be afraid to stop the instructor to ask for clarification. Asking questions allows you to take an active part in the listening process. If the instructor doesn't answer your questions sufficiently, make an appointment to speak with him or her during office hours.

- If you are in a situation where the instructor can't stop or you're watching a movie or video in class, listen for words that you do understand and try to figure out unfamiliar words in the context of the sentence. Jot down questions you need to ask later.

- Enhance your vocabulary by watching and listening to TV programs such as *Dateline, 20/20, Primetime Live, 60 Minutes,* and

DID YOU *Know?*

THOMAS EDISON invented the light bulb, the phonograph, the battery, the forerunner to the movie camera, and 1,089 other creations. He was also kicked out of school at age 12. His teachers thought he was too dumb to remain in class because of his constant questioning. He was deaf in one ear and 80 percent deaf in the other. He also had what would today be called ADHD. At one point during his career, he had to borrow money from a friend to avoid starvation.

Edison read constantly, had an incredible memory, and sometimes worked 20 hours a day. One of the most important scientists in history, Edison led the world into the modern era with his inventions.

PHOTO: Album/Newscom

the evening news. You might also try listening to a radio station such as National Public Radio as you walk or drive.

■ Write down the majority of what that the instructor puts on the board, overhead, or PowerPoint. You may not need every piece of information, but this technique gives you (and hopefully your study group) the ability to sift through the information outside of class. It also gives you a visual history of what the instructor said.

■ Finally, if there is a conversation group or club that meets at your institution, take the opportunity to join. By practicing language, you become more attuned to common words and phrases. If a conversation group is not available, consider starting one of your own.

TAKING EFFECTIVE NOTES

Is It Just a Big, Crazy Chore?

Go to class, listen, and write it down. Read a text, take notes. Watch a film, take notes. Is it really that important? Actually, knowing how to take useful, accurate notes can dramatically improve your life as a student. If you are an effective listener and note-taker, you have two of the most valuable skills any student could ever use. There are several reasons why it is important to take notes:

■ You become an active part of the listening process.

■ You create a history of your course content when you take notes.

■ You have written criteria to follow when studying.

■ You create a visual aid for your material.

■ Studying becomes much easier.

■ You retain information at a greater rate than non-note-takers.

■ Effective note-takers average higher grades than non-note-takers (Kiewra & Fletcher, 1984).

TIPS FOR EFFECTIVE NOTE TAKING

How Can I Write It Right?

You have already learned several skills you will need to take notes, such as cultivating your active listening skills, overcoming obstacles to effective listening, and familiarizing yourself with key phrases used by instructors. Next, prepare yourself mentally and physically to take effective notes that are going to be helpful to you. Consider the following ideas as you think about expanding your note-taking abilities.

■ **Physically and mentally "attend class."** This refers to classroom and online instruction. This may sound like stating the obvious, but it is surprising how many students feel they do not need to do anything to learn.

■ **Come to class prepared.** Scan, read, and use your textbook to establish a basic understanding of the material before coming to class. It is always easier to take notes when you have a preliminary understanding of what is being said. Coming to class prepared also means bringing the proper materials for taking notes: lab manuals, pens, a notebook, and a highlighter.

Good note-taking skills help you do more than simply record what you learn in class or read in a book so that you can recall it. These skills can also help reinforce that information so that you actually know it.

Shutterstock

- **Bring your textbook to class.** Although many students think they do not need to bring their textbooks to class if they have read the homework, you will find that many instructors repeatedly refer to the text while lecturing. The instructor may ask you to highlight, underline, or refer to the text in class, and following along in the text as the instructor lectures may also help you organize your notes.

- **Ask questions and participate in class.** Two of the most critical actions you can perform in class are to ask questions and to participate in the class discussion. If you do not understand a concept or theory, ask questions. Don't leave class without understanding what has happened and assume you'll pick it up on your own.

THE L-STAR SYSTEM

Are You Seeing Stars?

One of the most effective ways to take notes begins with the **L-STAR system** outlined in Figure 9.3.

This five-step program will enable you to compile complete, accurate, and visual notes for future reference. Along with improving your note-taking skills, using this system will enhance your ability to participate in class, help other students, study more effectively, and perform well on exams and quizzes.

L: Listening

One of the best ways to become an effective note-taker is to become an active listener. A concrete step you can take toward becoming an active listener in class is to sit near the front of the room, where you can hear the instructor and see the board and overheads. Choose a spot that allows you to see the instructor's mouth and facial expressions. If you see that the instructor's face has become animated or expressive, you can bet that you are hearing important information. Write it down. If you sit in the back of the room, you may miss out on these important clues. If you are listening to an instructor who is online, be certain to take notes, jot down questions for later, and participate as often as allowed.

Figure 9.3 The L-STAR System

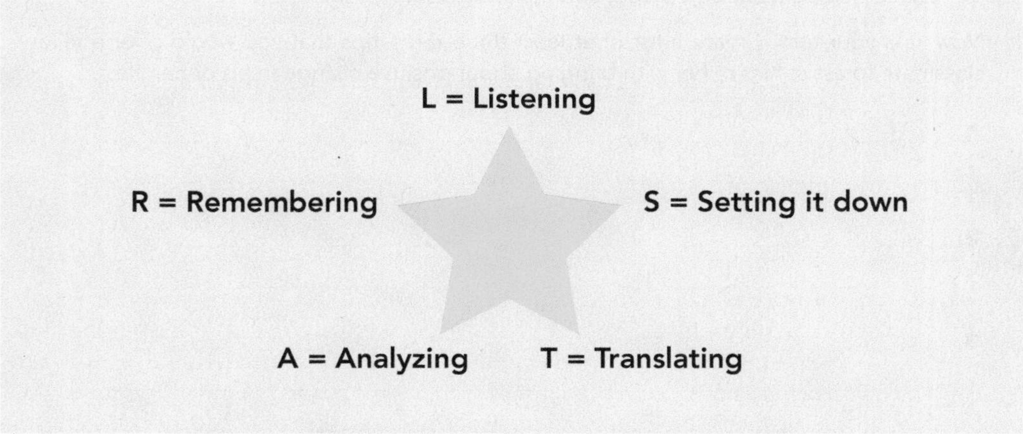

L = Listening

R = Remembering

S = Setting it down

A = Analyzing

T = Translating

S: Setting It Down

The actual writing of notes can be a difficult task. Some instructors are organized in their delivery of information; others are not. Some stick to an easy-to-follow outline and others ramble around, making it more difficult to follow them and take notes. Your listening skills, once again, are going to play an important role in determining what needs to be written down. In most cases, you will not have time to take notes verbatim. Some instructors talk very fast. You will have to be selective about the information you choose to write down. One of the best ways to keep up with the information being presented is to develop a shorthand system of your own. Many of the symbols you use will be universal, but you may use some symbols, pictures, and markings that are uniquely your own. Some of the more common symbols are:

w/	with	w/o	without
=	equals	≠	does not equal
<	less than	>	greater than
%	percentage	#	number
&	and	^	increase
+	plus or addition	–	minus
*	important	etc.	and so on
e.g.	for example	vs	against
esp.	especially	"	quote
?	question	. . .	and so on

BRING the *Change*

TIPS FOR PERSONAL SUCCESS

Consider the following tips for improving your listening skills and taking notes more effectively:

- Sit near the front of the room and establish eye contact with the instructor.
- Read the text or handouts beforehand to familiarize yourself with the upcoming information.
- Come to class with an open mind and positive attitude about learning.
- Listen purposefully, objectively, and constructively.

Now, it is your turn. Create a list of at least three more tips that you would offer a fellow classmate to assist him or her with bringing about positive change in his or her life.

1. _____
2. _____
3. _____

These symbols can save you valuable time when taking notes. Because you will use them frequently, it might be a good idea to memorize them.

T: Translating

Translating can save you hours of work as you begin to study for exams. Many students feel that this step is not important, or too time consuming, and leave it out. Don't. Often, students take notes so quickly that they make mistakes or use abbreviations that they may not be able to decipher later.

After each class, go to the library or some other quiet place and review your notes. You don't have to do this immediately after class, but before the end of the day, you will need to rewrite and translate your classroom notes. This process gives you the opportunity to put the notes in your own words and to incorporate your text notes into your classroom notes. This practice also provides a first opportunity to commit this information to memory.

Translating your notes helps you to make connections between previous material discussed, your own personal experiences, readings, and new material presented. Translating aids in recalling and applying new information. Few things are more difficult than trying to reconstruct your notes the night before a test, especially when they were made several weeks earlier.

A: Analyzing

This step takes place while you translate your notes from class. When you analyze your notes, you are asking two basic questions: (1) What does this mean? and (2) Why is it important? If you can answer these two questions about your material, you have almost mastered the information. Though some instructors will want you to spit back the exact same information you were given, others will ask you for a more detailed understanding and a synthesis of the material. When you are translating your notes, begin to answer these two questions using your notes, textbook, supplemental materials, and information gathered from outside research. Once again, this process is not simple or quick, but testing your understanding of the material is important. Remember that many lectures are built on past lectures. If you do not understand what happened in class on September 17, you may not be able to understand what happens on September 19. Analyzing your notes while translating them will give you a more complete understanding of the material.

R: Remembering

Once you have listened to the lecture, set your notes on paper, and translated and analyzed the material, it is time to study, or remember, the information. Some effective ways to remember information include creating a visual picture, reading the notes out loud, using mnemonic devices, and finding a study partner. Chapter 10 will help you with these techniques and other study aids.

THREE COMMON NOTE-TAKING SYSTEMS

Why Doesn't Everyone Listen and Take Notes the Same Way?

There are three common note-taking systems: (1) the **outline** technique; (2) the **Cornell** or split-page technique (also called the T system); and (3) the **mapping** technique.

THE OUTLINE TECHNIQUE

Easy as A, B, C—1, 2, 3?

The outline system uses a series of major headings and multiple subheadings formatted in hierarchical order (see Figure 9.4). The outline technique is one of the most commonly used note-taking systems, yet it is also one of the most misused systems. It can be difficult to outline notes in class, especially if your instructor does not follow an outline while lecturing.

When using the outline system, it is best to get all the information from the lecture and afterward to combine your lecture notes and text notes to create an outline. Most instructors would advise against using the outline system of note taking in class, although you may be able to use a modified version. The most important thing to remember is not to get bogged down in a system during class; what is critical is getting the ideas down on paper. You can always go back after class and rearrange your notes as needed.

Figure 9.4 **The Outline Technique**

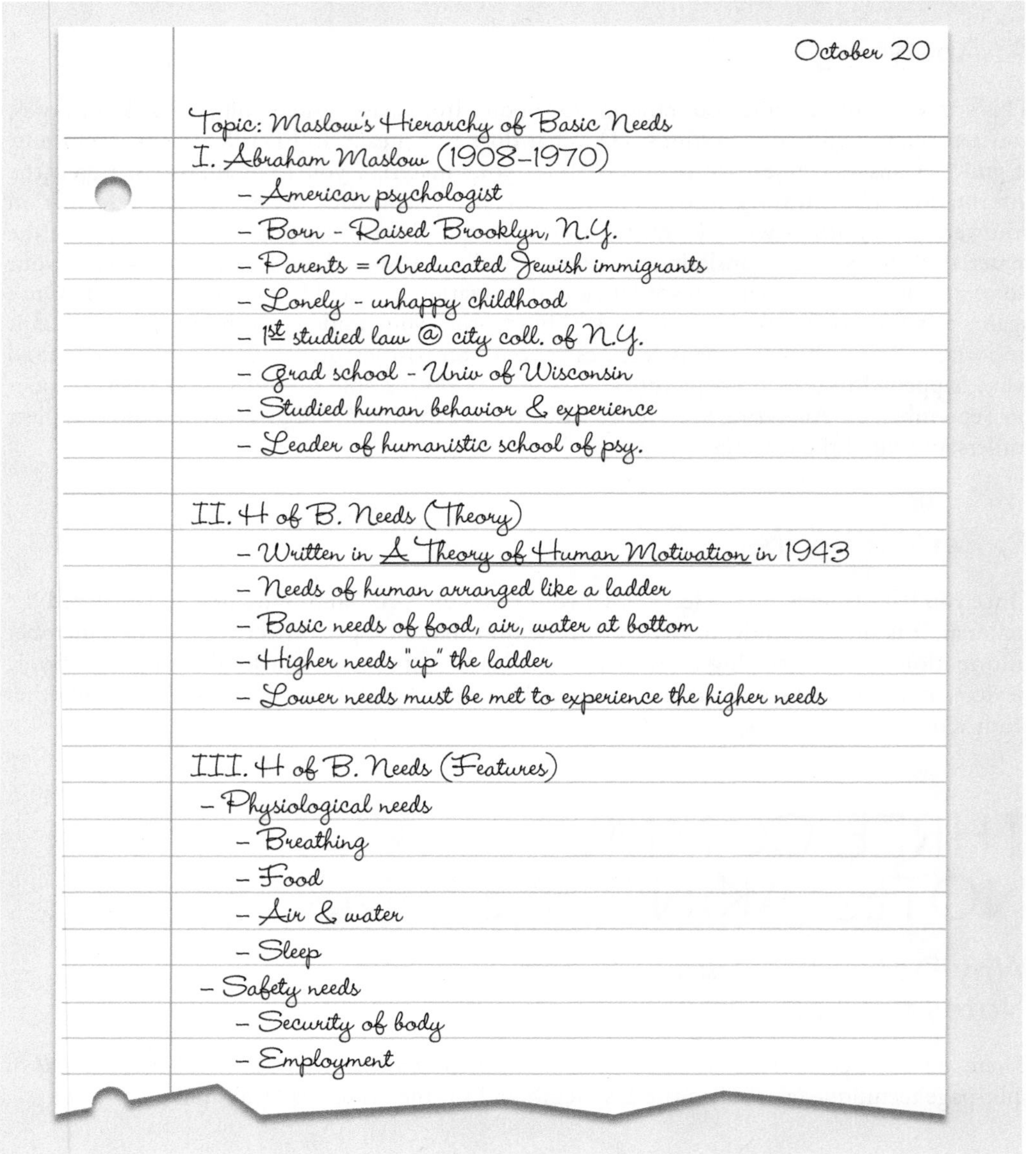

```
                                                    October 20

    Topic: Maslow's Hierarchy of Basic Needs
    I. Abraham Maslow (1908–1970)
        – American psychologist
        – Born - Raised Brooklyn, N.Y.
        – Parents = Uneducated Jewish immigrants
        – Lonely - unhappy childhood
        – 1st studied law @ city coll. of N.Y.
        – Grad school - Univ of Wisconsin
        – Studied human behavior & experience
        – Leader of humanistic school of psy.


    II. H of B. Needs (Theory)
        – Written in A Theory of Human Motivation in 1943
        – Needs of human arranged like a ladder
        – Basic needs of food, air, water at bottom
        – Higher needs "up" the ladder
        – Lower needs must be met to experience the higher needs


    III. H of B. Needs (Features)
      – Physiological needs
          – Breathing
          – Food
          – Air & water
          – Sleep
      – Safety needs
          – Security of body
          – Employment
```

If you are going to use a modified or informal outline while taking notes in class, you may want to consider grouping information together under a heading as a means of outlining. It is easier to remember information that is logically grouped than to remember information that is scattered across several pages. If your study skills lecture is on listening, you might outline your notes using the headings "The Process of Listening" and "Definitions of Listening."

After you have rewritten your notes using class lecture information and material from your textbook, your notes may look like those in Figure 9.4.

THE CORNELL (MODIFIED CORNELL, SPLIT PAGE, OR T) SYSTEM

A Split Decision?

The basic principle of the Cornell system, developed by Dr. Walter Pauk of Cornell University, is to split the page into two sections, each to be used for different information. Section A (the left column) is used for questions that summarize information found in Section B (the right column); Section B is used for the actual notes from class. The blank note-taking page should be divided, as shown in Figure 9.5.

Figure 9.5 Cornell Frame

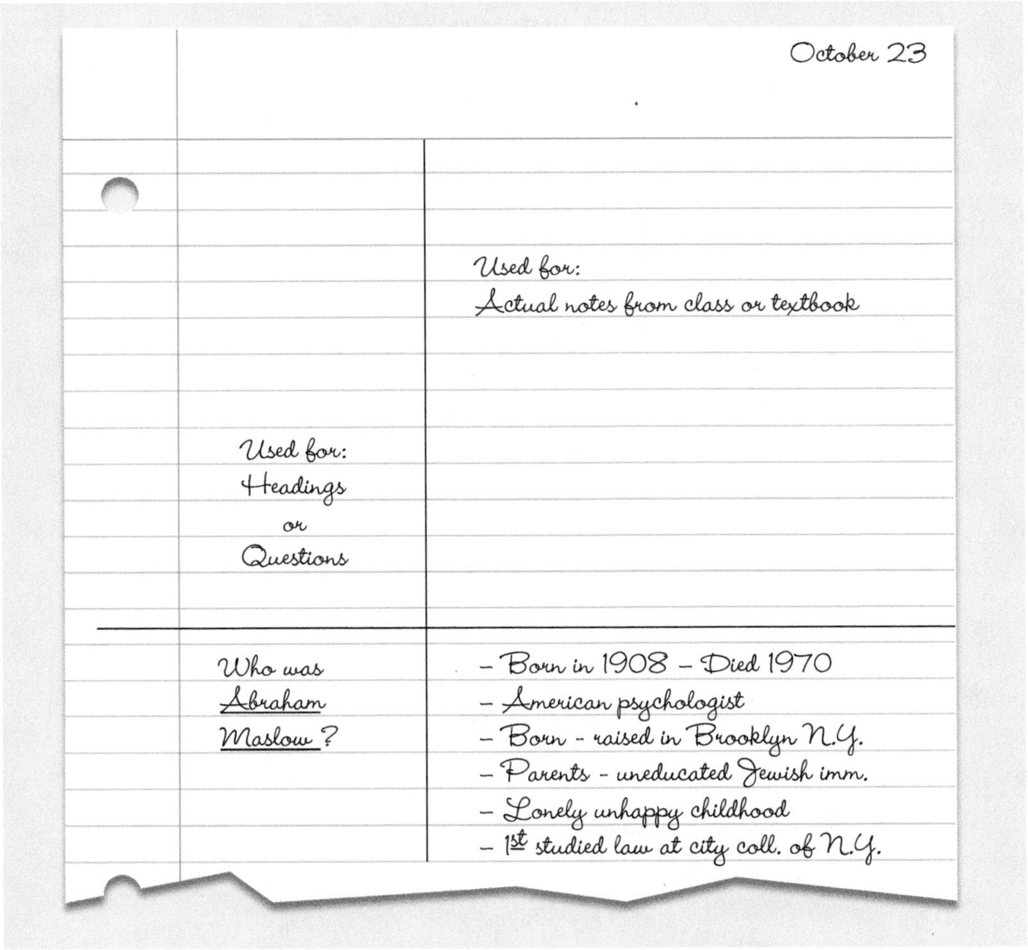

> October 23
>
> Used for:
> Actual notes from class or textbook
>
> Used for:
> Headings
> or
> Questions
>
> | Who was Abraham Maslow ? | – Born in 1908 – Died 1970 |
> | | – American psychologist |
> | | – Born - raised in Brooklyn N.Y. |
> | | – Parents - uneducated Jewish imm. |
> | | – Lonely unhappy childhood |
> | | – 1st studied law at city coll. of N.Y. |

The Cornell system is sometimes modified to include a third section at the bottom of the page for additional or summary comments. In such cases, the layout is referred to as a "T system" for its resemblance to an upside-down T. To implement the Cornell system, you will want to choose the technique that is most comfortable and beneficial for you; you might use mapping (discussed next) or outlining on a Cornell page. An example of outline notes using the Cornell system appears in Figure 9.6.

Figure 9.6 Outline Using a Cornell Frame

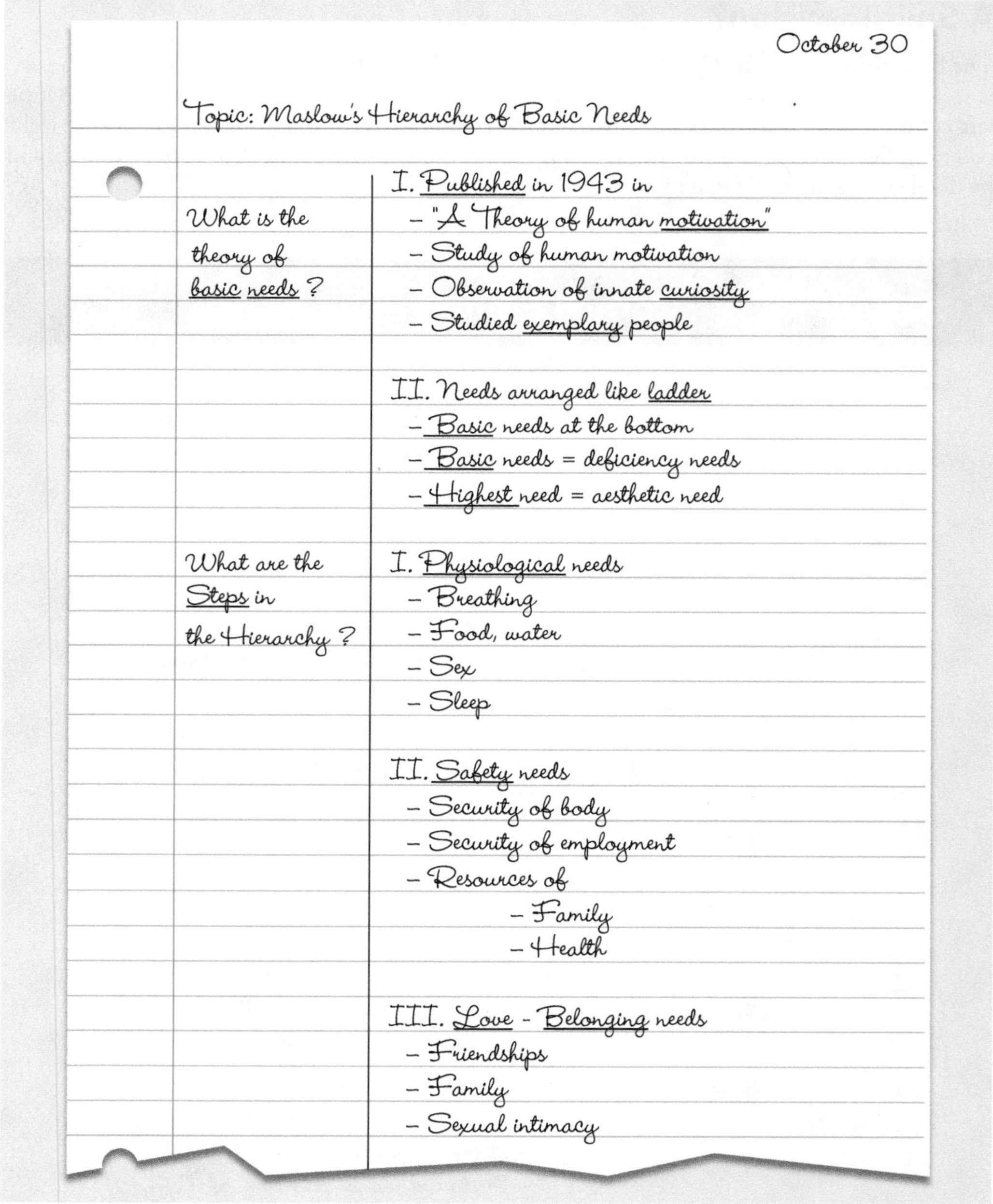

October 30

Topic: Maslow's Hierarchy of Basic Needs

What is the theory of basic needs?

I. Published in 1943 in
  – "A Theory of human motivation"
  – Study of human motivation
  – Observation of innate curiosity
  – Studied exemplary people

II. Needs arranged like ladder
  – Basic needs at the bottom
  – Basic needs = deficiency needs
  – Highest need = aesthetic need

What are the Steps in the Hierarchy?

I. Physiological needs
  – Breathing
  – Food, water
  – Sex
  – Sleep

II. Safety needs
  – Security of body
  – Security of employment
  – Resources of
      – Family
      – Health

III. Love - Belonging needs
  – Friendships
  – Family
  – Sexual intimacy

THE MAPPING SYSTEM

Are You Going Around in Circles?

If you are a visual learner, the mapping system may be especially useful for you. The mapping system of note taking generates a picture of information (see Figure 9.7). The mapping system creates a map, or web, of information that allows you to see the relationships among facts or ideas. A mapping system using a Cornell frame might look something like the notes in Figure 9.8.

The most important thing to remember about each note-taking system is that *it must work for you.* Do not use a system because your friends use it or because you feel that you should use it. Experiment with each system or combination to determine which is best for you.

Always remember to keep your notes organized, dated, and neat. Notes that cannot be read are no good to you or to anyone else.

Figure 9.7 The Mapping System

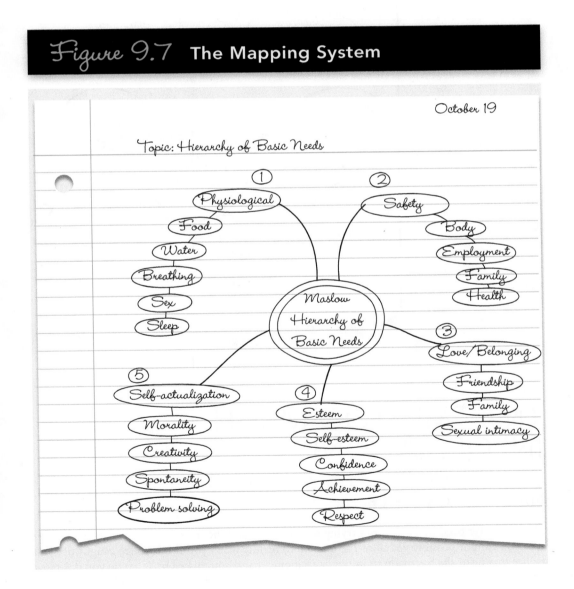

Figure 9.8 The Mapping System in a Cornell Frame

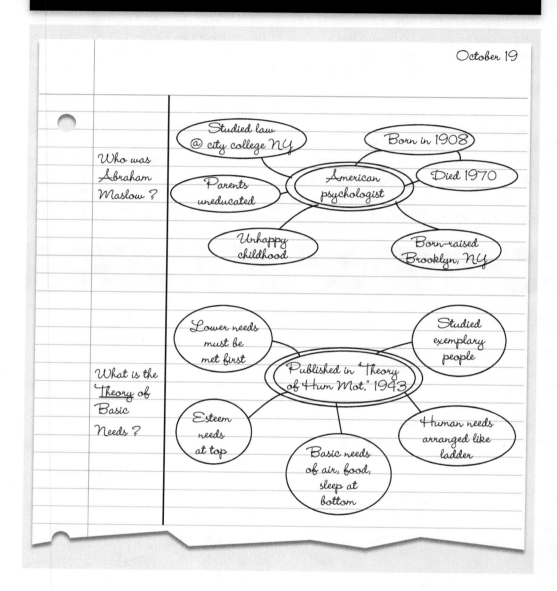

TMI! TMI! (TOO MUCH INFORMATION)

What Do I Do If I Get Lost While Taking Notes During the Lecture?

Have you ever been in a classroom trying to take notes and the instructor is speaking so rapidly that you cannot possibly get all of the information? Just when you think you're caught up, you realize that he or she has made an important statement and you missed it. What do you do? How can you handle, or avoid, this difficult note-taking situation? Here are several hints:

- Raise your hand and ask the instructor to repeat the information.

- Ask your instructor to slow down.

- If he or she will do neither, leave a blank space with a question mark at the side margin (see Figure 9.9). You can get this information after class from your instructor, a classmate, or your study buddy. This can be a difficult task to master. The key is to focus on the information at hand. Focus on what is being said at the exact moment. Don't give up!

- Meet with your instructor immediately after class or at the earliest time convenient for both of you.

- Form a note-taking group that meets after each class. This serves two purposes: (1) you can discuss and review the lecture, and (2) you will be able to get the notes from one of your note-taking buddies.

Figure 9.9 What to Do If You Get Lost

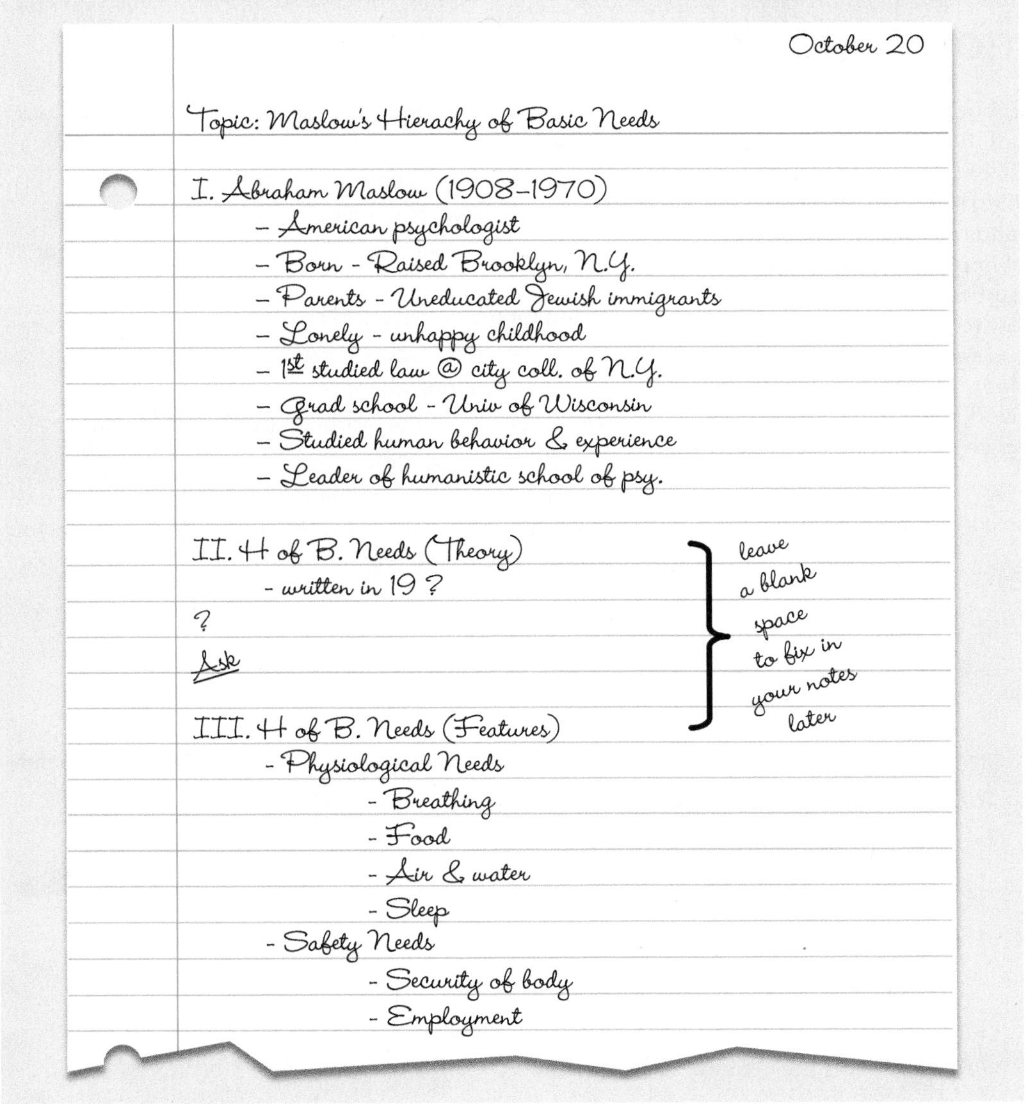

October 20

Topic: Maslow's Hierachy of Basic Needs

I. Abraham Maslow (1908–1970)
  – American psychologist
  – Born – Raised Brooklyn, N.Y.
  – Parents – Uneducated Jewish immigrants
  – Lonely – unhappy childhood
  – 1st studied law @ city coll. of N.Y.
  – Grad school – Univ of Wisconsin
  – Studied human behavior & experience
  – Leader of humanistic school of psy.

II. H of B. Needs (Theory)
  – written in 19 ?
?
Ask

} leave a blank space to fix in your notes later

III. H of B. Needs (Features)
  – Physiological Needs
    – Breathing
    – Food
    – Air & water
    – Sleep
  – Safety Needs
    – Security of body
    – Employment

- Never lean over and ask questions of another student during the lecture. This will cause that student to lose the information as well. It will probably annoy your peers and the instructor, too.

- Rehearse your note-taking skills at home by taking notes from TV news magazines or channels like the History Channel.

- Ask the instructor's permission to use a tape recorder during the lecture. Do not record a lecture without permission. We suggest that you try to use other avenues, such as the ones listed earlier, instead of taping your notes. It is a time-consuming task to listen to the lecture for a second time. However, if this system works for you, use it.

CHANGING IDEAS to Reality

REFLECTIONS ON LISTENING AND NOTE-TAKING

Yes, listening is a learned skill, but it is more than that. It is a gift that you give to yourself. It is a gift that promotes knowledge, understanding, stronger relationships, and open-mindedness. Good listening skills can help you manage conflict, avoid misunderstandings, and establish trusting relationships. Perhaps most importantly at this point in your life, listening can help you become a more successful student. Once you learn how to listen with your whole body and mind, you will begin to see how your notes, your grades, your attitude, your relationships, and your learning processes change. As you work toward improving your listening skills and developing your note-taking system, consider the following:

- When listening, evaluate the content before you judge the messenger.

- Keep your emotions and preconceived notions in check while listening.
- Sit where you can see and hear the instructor.
- Listen for "how" something is said.
- Listen to the "entire story" before making a judgment call.
- Listen for major ideas and keywords.
- Use a separate notebook for every class.
- Use abbreviations whenever possible.
- Write down what the instructor puts on the board or PowerPoint.

Becoming adept at listening and developing your own note-taking system are two essential skills that can help you become a more active learner.

"Listening is an attitude of the heart, a genuine desire to be with another person."

—J. Isham

Knowledge
in Bloom

LISTENING WITH AN OPEN MIND

Utilizes levels 4 and 5 of the taxonomy

Each chapter-end assessment is based on Bloom's Taxonomy of Learning. See pages xxvi–xxviii in the front of this book for a quick review.

Explanation: Seldom (if ever) would you pop in a CD, click your iPod, or tune your radio to a station that you strongly disliked. It just does not seem like a good use of time, and it is not something that you would probably enjoy on a daily basis. However, for this exercise, we are going to ask that you do precisely that and then apply what you've experienced and learned to several questions and the four **Essential Cornerstones for Success** from Chapter 1.

Process: Over the course of the next few days, find a song from your least favorite genre. If you are a huge fan of R&B, then move away from that genre and choose something from a genre of which you are not particularly fond. You might choose an old country song or a song from rap or bluegrass. If you enjoy listening to "easy love songs," try something different, such as metal or swing. The only stipulation is that the song must have lyrics.

You will have to listen to the song several times to answer the following questions. However, it is important to read the questions **before** you listen to the song—particularly question 2. The key to this exercise is to practice listening with an open mind, listening for content, and listening to words when barriers are in the way. (The barrier would be the music itself.)

1. What is the song's title and artist?

_____

_____

_____

_____

_____

2. What emotional and mental response did you have to the music the first time you listened to it? Why do you think you had this response?

_____

_____

_____

_____

_____

3. While listening to the song, what happened to your appreciation level? Did it increase or decrease? Why?

_____

_____

_____

_____

_____

4. In your opinion, what was the message (theme) of the song?

_____

_____

_____

_____

_____

5. What were you most surprised about with the song? The lyrics? The actual music? Your like or dislike of the song? The artist's voice?

_____

_____

_____

_____

_____

6. If you had to say that you gained or learned one positive thing from this song, what would it be?

_____

_____

_____

_____

_____

7. From memory, list at least two statements, comments, or quotes from the song.

_____

_____

_____

_____

_____

Now, consider how becoming a more effective listener can help you with each of the following.

By enhancing my listening skills, I can become more **open-minded** by:

_____

_____

_____

_____

_____

_____

By enhancing my listening skills, I can become more **creative** by:

_____

_____

_____

_____

_____

_____

By enhancing my listening skills, I can become more **knowledgeable** by:

_____

_____

_____

_____

_____

_____

By enhancing my listening skills, I can become more **resourceful** by:

_____

_____

_____

_____

_____

_____

SQ3R MASTERY STUDY SHEET

EXAMPLE QUESTION *(from page 221)*
What are the four components of the Chinese verb "to listen?"

ANSWER:

EXAMPLE QUESTION *(from page 226)*
Why is it important to identify keywords during a lecture?

ANSWER:

AUTHOR QUESTION *(from page 222)*
What is objective listening?

ANSWER:

AUTHOR QUESTION *(from page 222)*
List and define the four listening styles.

ANSWER:

AUTHOR QUESTION *(from page 229)*
Discuss the five steps in the L-STAR note-taking system.

ANSWER:

AUTHOR QUESTION *(from page 235)*
When would be the best time to use the mapping system of note taking? Justify your answer.

ANSWER:

AUTHOR QUESTION *(from page 236)*
What steps can you take to recover if you get behind when taking notes?

ANSWER:

YOUR QUESTION *(from page ____)*

ANSWER:

YOUR QUESTION *(from page ____)*

ANSWER:

YOUR QUESTION *(from page ____)*

ANSWER:

YOUR QUESTION *(from page ____)*

ANSWER:

YOUR QUESTION *(from page ____)*

ANSWER:

Finally, after answering these questions, recite in your mind the major points covered in this chapter. Consider the following general questions to help you master this material.

- What was it about?
- What does it mean?
- What was the most important thing you learned? Why?
- What were the key points to remember?

chapter ten
STUDY

DEVELOPING YOUR MEMORY, STUDY, AND TEST-TAKING SKILLS

"We can learn something new any time we believe we can." — Virginia Satir

Why
read this chapter?

Because you'll learn:

- How to study more effectively
- How to use memory tricks to retain information
- Tips for taking different types of assessments

Because you'll be able to:

- Apply memory techniques to your study efforts
- Use mnemonic devices to help with memory
- Take tests with confidence

Scan
and QUESTION

Take a few moments, **scan this chapter**, and on page 271, write **five of your own questions** that you think will be important to your mastery of this material. You will also find five questions listed from your authors.

Example:

☑ **Why are mnemonics important?**
(from page 251)

☑ **Discuss three strategies for studying math.**
(from page 259)

MyStudentSuccessLab

MyStudentSuccessLab (www.mystudentsuccesslab.com) is an online solution designed to help you "Start strong, Finish stronger" by building skills for ongoing personal and professional development.

$\mathcal{H}ow$ COLLEGE CHANGED MY LIFE

Name:	Zzavvalynn Orleanski
Institution:	Graduate! Pulaski Technical College
Age:	35
Major:	Associate of Arts Degree
Career:	Special Education

I flunked out the first time I went to college—in part because I didn't think I could do it. I felt overwhelmed by everything. However, as I looked at my life, I knew that I had to do something about my future. I am a single parent with three special-needs children, and I not only need to provide for them, but I want to be a role model for them as well. I am the only one who has the daily responsibility for raising and inspiring them. My children and our future are my motivation for going back and doing it right.

As I started at Pulaski Technical College, I had to enroll in several remedial classes and I was nervous because of my first college experience. As I began to understand more and experience success in class, I began to feel more comfortable with learning. I had a student success course and my instructor, Amy Baldwin, taught me strategies for putting together a study plan. Other instructors always encouraged and reassured me that I was doing well. My biology instructor taught me study techniques that he used when he was a first-year student. My instructors believed in me, and I realized that if they believed in me, I needed to believe in myself.

I began to work harder, study smarter, believe in myself, and before I knew it, I was on the Dean's List. I even surprised myself. I discovered that my hard work was paying off, which gave me even more self-confidence. Finally realizing that I had the capacity to succeed was one of the greatest lessons I learned in college. Pulaski Technical College became a haven for me while I dealt with the drama in my life. It was a place that made me fulfilled. Learning new and exciting things became my strength.

I would like to share two pieces of advice with you. First, don't quit. Don't give up. Don't drop out. If you do, it becomes very hard to go back and you may never get your degree. Second, develop strong relationships with your instructors and have a persistent positive attitude. Despite the many situations I faced at home and at school, I realized that a positive attitude was going to help me so much more than a negative attitude when it came to reaching my goal of becoming a special education teacher. Through what I have learned, I hope to be able to teach others not to give up when they face challenging times.

Think about it

1. Zzavvalynn states that she was overwhelmed at times. What is the most overwhelming thing that you have faced since beginning college? How are you dealing with this issue?

2. Zzavvalynn called her college "a haven . . . a place that fulfilled me." What sentence would you use to describe your college experience thus far? Why?

I FORGOT TO REMEMBER!

Do You Understand the Facts and Myths about Memory Function?

"My brain is full." MYTH
"Certain foods can help with memory development." FACT
"Proper sleep and exercise can help you retain more information." FACT
"I can't remember another thing." MYTH
"Being closed-minded can hurt your memory development." FACT
"Drugs and alcohol can help me remember more." MYTH

Several studies suggest that it is impossible to fill our brains full. One study in the 1970s concluded that if our brains were fed 10 new items of information every second for the rest of our lives, we would never fill even half of our memory's capacity (Texas A&M University, 2009).

At times, you may feel that if you study or read or learn any more, you'll forget everything. Some researchers suggest that we never forget anything—the material is simply "covered up" by other material, but it is still in our brain. The reason we can't recall that information is that it was not important enough, not stored properly, or not used enough to keep it from being covered up.

According to nineteenth-century German philosopher Friedrich Nietzsche, "The existence of forgetting has never been proved; we only know that some things don't come to mind when we want them."

So, why is it so hard to remember the dates of the Civil War or who flew with Amelia Earhart or how to calculate the liquidation value of stocks or the six factors in the communication process? The primary problem is that we never properly filed or stored this information.

What would happen if you saved a research paper on the computer and did not give it a file name? When you needed to retrieve that paper, you would not know how to find it. You would have to search through every file until you came across the information you needed. Memory works in much the same way. We have to store it properly if we are to retrieve it easily at a later time.

This section will detail how memory works and why it is important to your studying efforts. Following, you will find some basic facts about memory.

What study techniques have you used in the past to help you commit information to long-term memory?

Shutterstock

■ Everyone remembers some information and forgets other information.

■ Your senses help you take in information.

■ With very little effort, you can remember some information.

■ With rehearsal (study), you can remember a great deal of information.

■ Without rehearsal or use, information is forgotten.

■ Incoming information needs to be filed in the brain if you are to retain it.

■ Information stored, or filed, in the brain must have a retrieval method.

■ Mnemonic devices, repetition, association, and rehearsal can help you store and retrieve information.

Psychologists have determined that there are three types of memory: **sensory** memory; **short-term or working** memory; and **long-term** memory.

Sensory memory stores information gathered from the five senses: taste, touch, smell, hearing, and sight. Sensory memory is usually temporary, lasting about one to three seconds, unless you decide that the information is of ultimate importance to you and make an effort to transfer it to long-term memory.

Short-term or working memory holds information for a short amount of time. Consider the following list of letters:

jmplngtoplntstsevng

Now, cover them with your hand and try to recite them.

It is almost impossible for the average person to do so. Why? Because your working memory bank can hold a limited amount of information, usually about five to nine separate new facts or pieces of information at once (Woolfolk, 2006). However, consider this exercise. If you break the letters down into smaller pieces and add *meaning* to them, you are more likely to retain them. Example:

jum   lng   to   plnts   ts   evng

This still may not mean very much to you, but you can probably remember at least the first two sets of information—jum lng.

Now, if you were to say to yourself, this sentence means "Jump Long To Planets This Evening," you are much more likely to begin to remember this information. Just as your memory can "play tricks" on you, you can "play tricks" on your memory.

Although it is sometimes frustrating when we "misplace" information, it is also useful and necessary to our brain's survival that every piece of information that we hear and see is not in the forefront of our minds. If you tried to remember everything, you would not be able to function. As a student, you would never be able to remember all that your instructor said during a 50-minute lecture. You have to take steps to help you remember important information. Taking notes, making associations, drawing pictures, and visualizing information are all techniques that can help you move information from your short-term memory to your long-term memory bank.

Long-term memory stores a lot of information. It is almost like a hard drive on your computer. You have to make an effort to put something in your long-term memory, but with effort and memory techniques, such as rehearsal, practice, and mnemonic devices, you can store anything you want to remember there. Long-term memory consists of information that you have heard often, information that you use often, information that you might see often, and information that you have determined necessary and/or important to you. Just as you name a file on your computer, you name the files in your long-term memory. Sometimes, you have to wait a moment for the information to come to you. While you are waiting, your brain's CD-ROM is spinning. If the information you seek is in long-term memory, your brain will eventually find it, if you stored it properly. You may have to assist your brain in locating the information by using mnemonics and other memory devices.

B R I N G the *Change*

TIPS FOR PERSONAL SUCCESS

Consider the following tips for making time for studying and committing information to long-term memory:

■ Study daily to avoid having to "cram" the night before your test.
■ Form a study group with people who are motivated and keep you on track.
■ Keep up with your daily readings and homework.

Now, it is your turn. Create a list of at least three more tips that you would offer a fellow classmate to assist him or her with making time in his or her life to study.

1. _____

2. _____

3. _____

THIS ISN'T YOUR DADDY'S VCR

How Can You Use *VCR3* to Increase Memory Power?

Countless pieces of information are stored in your long-term memory. Some of it is triggered by necessity, some may be triggered by the five senses, and some may be triggered by experiences. The best way to commit information to long-term memory and retrieve it when needed can be expressed by:

V: Visualizing
C: Concentrating
R: Relating
R: Repeating
R: Reviewing

Consider the following story:

As Katherine walked to her car after her evening class, she heard someone behind her. She turned to see two students holding hands walking about 20 feet behind her. She was relieved. This was the first night that she had walked to her car alone.

Katherine pulled her book bag closer to her as she increased her pace along the dimly lit sidewalk between the Salk Biology Building and the Horn Center for the Arts. "I can't believe that Shana didn't call me," she thought to herself. "She knows I hate to walk to the parking lot alone."

As Katherine turned the corner onto Suddith Street, she heard someone else behind her. She turned but did not see anyone. As she continued to walk toward her car, she heard the sound again. Turning to see if anyone was there, she saw a shadow disappear into the grove of hedges along the sidewalk.

Startled and frightened, Katherine crossed the street to walk beneath the streetlights and sped up to get closer to a group of students about 30 feet in front of her. She turned once more to see if anyone was behind her. Thankfully, she did not see anyone.

By this time, she was very close to her car. The lighting was better and other students were around. She felt better, but vowed never again to leave class alone at night.

To **visualize** information, try to create word pictures in your mind as you hear the information. If you are being told about the Revolutionary War battle of Camden, South Carolina, try to see the soldiers and the battlefield, or try to paint a mind picture that will help you to remember the information. You may also want to create visual aids as you read or study information.

As you read Katherine's story, were you able to visualize her journey? Could you see her walking along the sidewalk? Did you see the two buildings? What did they look like? Could you see the darkness of her path? Could you see that shadow disappearing into the bushes? Could you see her increasing her pace to catch up to the other students? What was she wearing?

If you did this, then you are using your visual skills—your *mind's eye*. This is one of the most effective ways to commit information to long-term memory. See it, live it, feel it, and touch it as you read and study it, and it will become yours.

Concentrating on the information given will help you commit it to long-term memory. Don't let your mind wander. Stay focused. If you find yourself having trouble concentrating, take a small break (two to five minutes) and then go back to work.

Relating the information to something that you already know or understand will assist you in filing or storing the information for easy retrieval. Relating the appearance of the African zebra to the American horse can help you remember what the zebra looks like. You may not know what the building in Katherine's story looked like, but try to see her in front of a building at your school. Creating these types of relationships increase memory retention of the material.

Repeating the information out loud to yourself or to a study partner facilitates its transfer to long-term memory. Some people have to hear information many times before they can commit it to long-term memory. Memory experts agree that repetition is one of the strongest tools to increase the retention of material.

Reviewing the information is another means of repetition. The more you see and use the information, the easier it will be to remember it when the time comes. As you review, try to remember the main points of the information.

Walter Pauk (2007), educator and inventor of the Cornell note-taking method, concluded from a research study that people reading a textbook chapter forgot 81 percent of what they had read after 28 days. With this in mind, it may behoove you to review Katherine's story (and other material in your texts) on a regular basis. Reviewing is a method of repetition and of keeping information fresh. Using the five points just discussed, work through the questions in Figure 10.1.

Shutterstock

Do you find that studying in the library, at home, or somewhere else is most effective for you? Why?

BLOOM LEVEL 1

Figure 10.1   Remembering Katherine

Without looking back, answer the following questions about Katherine. Use the power of your visualization and concentration to recall the information.

1. What was the name of the biology building? _____

2. Did she see the shadow before or after she saw the two people behind her? _____

3. What were the two people behind her doing? _____

4. What was the name of the arts building? _____

5. Why did she cross the street? _____

6. How far ahead of her was the group of students? _____

7. When she saw the group of students in front of her, how far was she from her car? _____

8. What was Katherine's friend's name? _____

THE CAPABILITY OF YOUR MEMORY

What Is the Difference Between Memorizing and Owning?

Why don't you forget your name? Why don't you forget your address? The answer is that you know that information. **You own it.** It belongs to you. You've used the information often enough and repeated it often enough that it is highly unlikely that you will ever forget it. Conversely, why can't you remember the details of Erickson's Stages of Development or Maslow's Hierarchy of Basic Needs or Darwin's Theory of Evolution? Most likely because you memorized it and never "owned" it.

> "The illiterate of the 21st century will not be those who cannot read and write, but those who cannot learn, unlearn, and relearn."
>
> —Alvin Toffler

Knowing something means that you have made a personal commitment to make this information a part of your life. For example, if you needed to remember the name Stephen and his phone number of 925-6813, the likelihood of your remembering this depends on *attitude*. Do you need to recall this information because he is in your study group and you might need to call him, or because he is the caregiver for your infant daughter while you are in class? How badly you need that name and number will determine the commitment level that you make to either *memorizing* that information (and maybe forgetting it) or *knowing* it (and making it a part of your life).

In Figure 10.2. you will find two photos. Follow the directions above each photo. Then answer the accompanying questions.

Figure 10.2 Seeing Clearly

Consider the first picture only. Study it carefully.
Look at everything from left to right, top to bottom.

Now, notice the picture and pay close attention to the areas marked.

Notice the people on the trampoline

Notice the storage building

Notice the color of the protective padding

Notice the green foliage

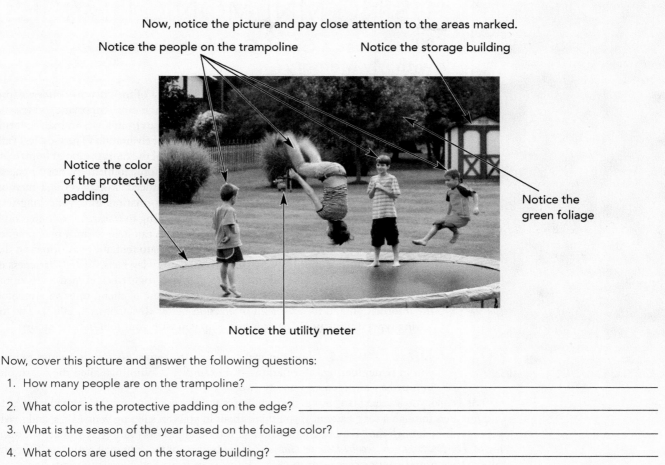

Notice the utility meter

Now, cover this picture and answer the following questions:

1. How many people are on the trampoline? _____

2. What color is the protective padding on the edge? _____

3. What is the season of the year based on the foliage color? _____

4. What colors are used on the storage building? _____

5. Is there one utility meter or two? _____

6. How many children are in the air? _____

7. Are the children all male, female, or mixed? _____

8. How many people are wearing striped shirts? _____

9. What type of fence surrounds the house? _____

10. What colors are used on the house? _____

11. Is the house made of one material or more? _____

12. What color are the flowers on the bush? _____

"NOT FAIR!" you may be saying right now. "We were not asked to look at the fence, the colors on the house, or what people are wearing." Regardless, could you answer all of the questions without looking? The purpose of this exercise is to help you understand the real difference between casually looking at something and *really* looking at something. To truly know something, you have to go beyond what is on the surface—even beyond reading and studying what was asked of you. You have to examine more than you are told or more than what is pointed out for you. To own information, you have to be totally committed to examining every detail, every inch, and every angle of it. You will need to practice and master the technique of "going beyond."

Mnemosyne, The Mother of the Muses (oil on canvas), Leighton, Frederic (1830-96)/ Private Collection/Photo © Christie's Images/The Bridgeman Art Library

The Greek goddess of memory, Mnemosyne.

USING MNEMONIC DEVICES

What Does a Greek Goddess Have to Do with My Memory?

The word *mnemonic* is derived from the Greek goddess of memory, ***Mnemosyne*** (pronounced *ne-MO-ze-knee*). She was considered one of the most important goddesses of all time because it was believed that memory separated us from lower animal life forms. It was believed that memory was the very foundation of civilization (The Goddess Path, 2009). Memory was so very important because most of the transmission of human history depended on oral stories and parables committed only to memory, not on paper.

In modern times, a ***mnemonic device*** (pronounced *ni-män-ik*) is a memory trick or technique that assists you in putting information into your long-term memory and pulling it out when you need it. According to research into mnemonics and their effectiveness, it was found that mnemonics can help create a phenomenon known as the ***bizarreness effect.*** This effect causes us to remember information that is bizarre or unusual more rapidly than normal, everyday facts. "The bizarreness effect occurs because unusual information and events trigger heightened levels of our attention and require us to work harder to make sense of them; thus we remember the information and its associated interaction better" (McCornack, 2007). The following types of mnemonic devices may help you with your long-term memory.

JINGLES/RHYMES.   You can make up rhymes, songs, poems, or sayings to assist you in remembering information—for example, "Columbus sailed the ocean blue in fourteen hundred and ninety-two."

As a child, you learned many things through jingles and rhymes. You probably learned your ABCs and numbers through a song pattern. If you think about it, you can still sing your ABCs, and maybe your numbers through the "Ten Little Indians" song. You could probably sing every word to the opening of *The Brady Bunch, Scooby-Doo,* or *Gilligan's Island* because of the continual reruns on TV. Some advertisements and commercials seem to stick with us even if we find them annoying. Jingles and rhymes have a strong and lasting impact on our memory—especially when repetition is involved.

SENTENCES.   You can make up sentences such as "Some men can read backward fast" to help you remember information. Another example is "**P**lease **e**xcuse **m**y **d**ear **A**unt **S**ally," which corresponds to the order of the mathematical operations: **p**arentheses, **e**xponents, **m**ultiplication, **d**ivision, **a**ddition, and **s**ubtraction.

Other sentences in academic areas include:

1. **M**y **V**ery **E**lderly **M**other **J**ust **S**aved **U**s **N**icely is a sentence mnemonic for the planets in order from the sun: Mercury, Venus, Earth, Mars, Jupiter, Saturn, Uranus, Neptune.

2. **E**very **G**ood **B**ird **D**oes **F**ly is a sentence mnemonic for the line notes in the treble clef in music.

3. **S**ome **M**en **H**elp **E**ach **O**ther is a sentence mnemonic for the Great Lakes from **west to east:** Superior, Michigan, Huron, Erie, Ontario.

WORDS.   You can create words. For example, **Roy G. Biv** may help you to remember the colors of the rainbow: red, orange, yellow, green, blue, indigo, and violet.

Other word mnemonics include:

1. **HOMES** is a word for the Great Lakes in no particular order: **H**uron, **O**ntario, **M**ichigan, **E**rie, **S**uperior.
2. **FACE** is a word mnemonic for the space notes in the treble clef.

STORY LINES.   If you find it easier to remember stories than raw information, you may want to process the information into a story that you can easily tell. Weave the data and facts into a creative story that can be easily retrieved from your long-term memory. This technique can be especially beneficial if your instructor gives essay exams, because the "story" that you remember can be what was actually told in class.

ACRONYMS.   An acronym is a word that is formed from the first letters of other words. You may see reruns for the famed TV show M*A*S*H. This is an acronym for Mobile Army Surgical Hospital. If you scuba dive, you know that SCUBA is an acronym for Self-Contained Underwater Breathing Apparatus. Other common acronyms include:

NASA (**N**ational **A**eronautics and **S**pace **A**dministration)

NASCAR (**N**ational **A**ssociation of **S**tock **C**ar **A**uto **R**acing)

NASDAQ (**N**ational **A**ssociation of **S**ecurities **D**ealers **A**utomated **Q**uotations)

NATO (**N**orth **A**tlantic **T**reaty **O**rganization)

BART (**B**ay **A**rea **R**apid **T**ransit)

Figure 10.3   The Pegging System

PEGGING.   The pegging system uses association, visualization, and attachment to aid in memory. With this system, you mentally "attach" what you want to remember to something that is already familiar to you—the pegs that you create. This is a visual means to remember lists, sequences, and even categories of information.

Pretend that you are looking at a coat rack mounted on the wall with 10 pegs sticking out of it, as shown in Figure 10.3. Just as you would hang hats or coats on the pegs of a rack, you can hang information there, too.

For the sake of explaining this technique more thoroughly, we have named 10 pegs for you with corresponding rhyming words. You, however, can name your pegs anything that would be easy for you to remember. Once you memorize these pegs, you can attach anything to them with visualization and imagination. The key to using the pegging mnemonic system is to name your pegs *once* and use those names each time you hook information to them. This way, they become second nature to you.

For our example, our 10 pegs are named:

1 = sun	6 = sticks
2 = shoe	7 = heaven
3 = bee	8 = gate
4 = shore	9 = line
5 = alive	10 = sin

Repeat these until you have memorized them.

To attach the information that you want to remember to the peg, you use visualization to attach a term or word to that peg. For example, if you wanted to remember a shopping list that included (1) ice cream, (2) rice, (3) Ajax, (4) milk, (5) water, and (6) cookies, this might be your visualization plan.

1 - sun	You see ice cream melting in the **sun.**
2 - shoe	You see a **shoe** being filled with rice.
3 - bee	You see Ajax being sprinkled on a **bee.**
4 - shore	You see milk instead of water rushing to the **shore** in waves.
5 - alive	You see water keeping you **alive** on a deserted island.
6 - sticks	You see cookies being offered to you on a **stick** (like a s'more).

Read over this list one more time and you'll be surprised at how easy it is to remember your shopping list. It becomes even easier when *you* name your pegs and *you* create the visualization. If you need more than 10 pegs, you can create as many as you need.

Suppose that we wanted to remember a list of ***Essential Cornerstones for Success*** (passion, motivation, knowledge, resourcefulness, creativity, adaptability, open-mindedness, communication, accountability, and vision). If your instructor suggested that you need to know this list, in order, for your midterm exam, use the pegging system to memorize it.

1 - sun	I look at the **sun** on a beautiful day with **passion.**
2 - shoe	I walk in my **shoes** with **motivation.**
3 - bee	I see a **bee** flying around that seems to be very **knowledgeable.**
4 - shore	The **shore** washes many **resources** to the beach.
5 - alive	My brain is **alive** because I use **creativity.**
6 - sticks	I see a **stick** bending into a half circle, making it very **adaptable.**
7 - heaven	Believing in **heaven** takes **open-mindedness.**
8 - gate	Many **gates** open for people who know how to **communicate.**
9 - line	If you walk a straight **line,** you are will be **accountable.**
10 - sin	It is a **sin** to lack **vision.**

Read over these one more time, then cover the list and you'll be amazed at how easy it is to repeat it. You will, of course, need to study each one to know what it means, but now, you have the list memorized, in order.

HAKUNA MATATA

How in the World Can I Study with Small Children in the House?

For many college students, finding a place or time to study is the hardest part of studying. Some students live at home with younger siblings; some students have children of their own. If you have young children in the home, you may find the following hints helpful when it comes time to study.

STUDY AT SCHOOL.   Your schedule may have you running from work to school directly to home. Try to squeeze in even as little as half an hour at school for studying, perhaps immediately before or after class. A half hour of pure study time can prove more valuable than five hours at home with constant interruptions.

CREATE CRAFTS AND HOBBIES.   Your children need to be occupied while you study. It may help if you have crafts and hobbies available that they can do while you are involved with studying. Choose projects your children can do by themselves, without your help. Depending on their ages, children could make masks from paper plates, color, do pipe cleaner art or papier-mâché, use modeling clay or dough, or build a block city. Explain to your children that you are studying and that they can use this time to be creative; when everyone is finished, you'll share what you've done with each other. Give them little awards for their work and for helping you have quiet time to study.

IndexOpen

Do you think it is a good idea to involve your children (or younger siblings) in your education? Why or why not?

From ORDINARY to *Extraordinary*

H. P. Rama
CEO, JHM Hotels, Greenville, South Carolina

I **HAVE LED** a life filled with a great variety of experiences, trials, challenges, and triumphs. Born in Africa, I was sent to India to live with my grandparents and to go to school when I was just five years old. I lived away from my parents, whom I missed greatly, in a little farming village in India where I finished school and ultimately earned an undergraduate degree. I knew I wanted to come to the United States and pursue the American dream, so at age 21 I left India and arrived in this country with only $2 in my pocket.

I had to get a job quickly, so I took the first job offered to me as a dishwasher, which I quit in just four hours. My next job was as a waiter at a Howard Johnson's restaurant in Manhattan. While I worked to support myself, I attended Xavier University to pursue my MBA. My life was primarily one of work and sacrifice as I worked hard to pay my expenses and to graduate with this degree I prized so much. While working at Howard Johnson's, I paid attention to everything that happened around me because I had no intentions of remaining a waiter all my life. I was absorbing knowledge of the hotel and restaurant business, which I would put to use later. At the time, I had no intention of becoming a hotelier. My goal was to go into banking. I always say that I became an accidental hotelier, but this field has served me well and offered me many opportunities. I was pursuing the American dream, and that was all that mattered. I considered myself fortunate to have this great opportunity to be in the United States, to be going to school, and to have a job that supported me.

After receiving my MBA from Xavier, I worked as a staff accountant for 14 months. In 1973 I had an opportunity to buy my first hotel in Pomona, California. My brother and I bought the hotel, and we had only two employees other than the two of us. We worked 24/7 and lived behind the office. There was no job that we did not do. But we were chasing the dream, and we were off and running with no idea of how many opportunities we would have.

Then I moved east, still focused on achieving the American dream, and bought a 36-room hotel in Buffalo, Tennessee.

My wife and I did everything—front desk, night duty, all the maintenance. We both worked very hard, long hours. In 1977 we moved to Greenville, South Carolina, and bought a foreclosed property from a bank. In 1983 I bought four Howard Johnson hotels—just 13 years after working for Howard Johnson's as a waiter. Over the years my brothers and I have owned and developed 78 hotels and still own 38 today.

We developed a five-star hotel in India in 1990, and today we are expanding and adding other hotels. We are most proud of the fact that we are developing a mixed-use development in India that will include a Hospitality College campus, a retailing and entertainment campus, a hospital campus, and luxury accommodations. We are using our knowledge learned in this wonderful country to continue the dream in India.

> At the age of 12, I left India and arrived in this country with $2.00 in my pocket.

In 1999, I was named Chairman of the American Motel and Hotel Lodging Association, which was a significant honor for me. Because I wanted to give back to this field that has done so much for me, I donated $1 million for scholarships for hospitality students. In 1989 I was the founding member of the Asian American Hotel Owners Association. Today I serve on several Boards of Advisors for Hospitality programs and was named an Executive Ambassador by Cornell University, in which I speak to graduate students about my experiences.

My advice to students today is this: Anything is possible if you have the vision, pay the price, work hard, and take risks. I have been very blessed, but I have also worked very hard. And I am living proof that the American dream is alive and well.

EXTRAORDINARY REFLECTION

Read the following statement and respond in your online journal or class notebook.

Mr. Rama worked his way up the ladder and became Chairman of the American Motel and Hotel Lodging Association, a major organization. What top honors do you hope to achieve in your own career? Why? How would they change your life?

STUDY WITH YOUR CHILDREN.   One of the best ways to instill the value of education in your children is to let them see you participating in your own education. Set aside one or two hours per night when you and your children study. You may be able to study in one place, or you may have separate study areas. If your children know that you are studying and you have explained to them how you value your education, you are killing two birds with one stone: you are able to study, and you are providing a positive role model as your children study with you and watch you.

RENT MOVIES OR LET YOUR CHILDREN WATCH TV.   Research has shown that viewing a limited amount of educational television, such as *Sesame Street, Reading Rainbow,* or *Barney and Friends,* can be beneficial for children. If you do not like what is on television, you might consider renting or purchasing age-appropriate educational videos for your children. This could keep them busy while you study, and it could help them learn as well.

INVITE YOUR CHILDREN'S FRIENDS OVER.   What?! That's right. A child who has a friend to play or study with may create less of a distraction for you. Chances are your children would rather be occupied with people their own ages, and you will gain valuable study time.

HIRE A SITTER OR EXCHANGE SITTING SERVICES WITH ANOTHER STUDENT.   Arrange to have a sitter come to your house a couple of times a week if you can afford it. If you have a classmate who also has children at home, you might take turns watching the children for each other. You could each take the children for one day a week, or devise any schedule that suits you both best. Or you could study together and let your children play together while you study, alternating homes.

ASK IF YOUR COLLEGE HAS AN ON-SITE DAYCARE CENTER LIKE THE BOYS AND GIRLS CLUB.   Some colleges provide daycare facilities at a reduced cost, and some provide daycare at no charge. It is certainly worth checking out.

TALK TO THE FINANCIAL AID OFFICE AT YOUR INSTITUTION.   In some instances, there will be grants or aid to assist you in finding affordable daycare for your child.

Studying at any time is hard work. It is even harder when you have to attend to a partner, children, family responsibilities, work, and a social life as well. You will have to be creative in order to complete your degree. You are going to have to do things and make sacrifices that you never thought possible. But if you explore the options, plan ahead, and ask questions of other students with children and with responsibilities outside the classroom, you can and will succeed.

DID YOU Know?

MICHAEL JORDAN was born in Brooklyn, New York, in 1963. During his sophomore year in high school, Michael tried out for his varsity basketball team. However, because he was only 5'11" he was considered too short to play and he was cut from the team. He was devastated, but this experience only increased his determination to make the team and excel.

The following summer, he grew by four inches, and with this growth spurt and intense training, he not only made the team but averaged over 25 points per game during his last two years in high school.

Jordan then attended the University of North Carolina, where he was named ACC Freshman of the Year. In 1984, he made the NBA draft for the Chicago Bulls. He led the NBA in scoring for 10 seasons, holds the top career and playoff scoring averages, and is today considered by many to be the most accomplished basketball player ever to hit the court.

PHOTO: Greg Forwerck/Ai Wire/Newscom

STUDYING IN A CRUNCH

Tomorrow? What Do You Mean the Test Is Tomorrow?

Let's be straight upfront. No study skills textbook will ever advise you to cram. It is simply a dangerous and often futile exercise in desperation. You will never read the words "Don't waste your time studying—just cram the night before so you can party harder and longer!" Cramming is just the opposite of what this whole chapter is about—knowing versus memorizing. Cramming

Figure 10.4 A Quick Reference Guide to Studying Math and Science

Before Class

- Never take a math or science course (or any course for that matter) for which you are not prepared. If you think you need or test into a basic, remedial, or transitional class, take it! Look at it as a chance to start over with new hope and knowledge.
- Understand that most math and science classes build on previous knowledge. If you begin the class with a weak background, you must work very hard to learn missed information.
- Avoid taking math or science classes during "short" terms if possible. The more time you spend with the material, the better, especially if math and/or science is not your strongest subject.
- Know your own learning style. If you're visual, use colors, charts, and photos. If you're auditory, practice your listening skills. If you're tactile, work to create situations where you can "act out" or touch the material.
- Prepare yourself before class by reading the chapter. Even if you don't understand all of it, read through the material and write down questions about material you did not understand.
- Scan all of the introductory and summation materials provided in the text or study guides.
- Join a study group. If there is not one, start one. Cooperative learning teams can be life savers.
- Seek tutorial assistance on campus from the first day. Visit the center and get familiar with how it operates. Get to know the people who work there. Don't wait until you get behind to seek assistance.

During Class

- Come to every class, study group, or lab.
- Control your own anger and frustration. The past is the past and you can't change any part of it—but you can change you future. Learn to make your negative self-talker be quiet!
- Ask questions. Ask questions. Ask questions. Ask questions . . . and be specific in your questioning. Don't just say, "I don't understand that." Ask detailed and specific questions such as, "I don't understand why $f(x + h)$ doesn't equal $f(x) + f(h)$." Or, "I don't understand the difference between 'algia' and 'dynia.' Why are two different words used for pain?"
- Slow down and read the material carefully.
- Find the formulas and write them down on note cards.
- Write down the explanatory remarks made by the instructor such as:
  - How you get from one step to the next
  - How this problem differs from other problems
  - Why you need to use formula x instead of formula y
  - Whether any steps were combined
- Try to learn from a general to specific end. That is, try to get a feeling of the overall goal of the material before you hone in on smaller problems.
- Write down any theorem, formula, or technique that the instructor puts on the board, overhead, or PowerPoint.
- Leave a space in your notes for any material you missed or did not understand. This will help you keep your notes organized when you go back after class and add the explanation.
- Bring Post-it notes, strips of paper, or bookmarks to class with you so that you can "tag" pages with important information and concepts.

After Class

- Visit your instructor's office. (Make an appointment to visit during office hours.)
- Fill in the missing information in your notes by reviewing the text, going to your study group, or getting clarification from your instructor.

- Practice the problems in your text or study guide and then practice them again, and again, and again until they become second nature. Much of math and science is learned by DOING . . . so DO . . . and then DO again.
- Apply what you learned in class or lab. Find a way to make it "speak" to your life in a practical way.
- Continually review all of the theorems, formulas, concepts, and terms from each chapter so they become second nature to you.
- When doing practice tests, pretend that you are in an actual test and adhere to the timelines, rules, and policies of your instructor. This helps replicate the actual testing situation.

Before the Test

- Ask questions that will reduce your anxiety such as:
  - What is the point value of each question?
  - How many questions will be on the test?
  - Will the questions be multiple choice, etc . . .?
  - What materials do I need to bring to class?
  - Will I be allowed to use a calculator or any other technology?
  - Is there a time limit on the test?
  - What is the overall grade value of the test?
- Make every effort to attend any study or review sessions offered by the instructor or peers

During Tests

- Read the directions carefully.
- Quickly glance over the test to determine the number of questions and the degree of difficulty as related to the time you have to complete the test.
- Work by the clock. If you have 60 minutes to take a test that has 120 questions, this means you have about 30 seconds per question.
- Begin by solving the problems that are easiest or most familiar to you.
- Read the questions on the test carefully, more than once, and don't jump to conclusions.
- Determine which formulas you will need to use.
- Decide how you want to solve the problem.
- Check your work by using multiple solving techniques. (If the problem is division, can it be checked with multiplication? This is called *opposite operations*.)
- Draw pictures if you encounter word problems. Visualization is very important.
- Show all of your work, even if it is not required. This will help the instructor (and you) see what you did correctly and/or incorrectly.
- Recheck every answer if you have time.
- Work backwards if at all possible. This may help answer the question and catch mistakes.
- After you've completed the answer, reread the question to determine if you did everything the question asked you do to.
- Never erase your margin work or mistakes. This wastes time, and you may erase something that you need (or worse, something that was correct).

After Tests

- Immediately after the test, try to determine if the majority of test questions came from classroom notes, your textbook, your study guide, or from your homework. This will help you prepare for the next test.
- Think about the way you studied for this test and how you could improve your techniques for the next time. Consider the amount of time spent studying for this test.
- Once the test is graded, determine what caused you to lose the most points: Simple errors? Applying incorrect formulas or theorems? Misunderstanding the questions asked? Intensified test anxiety? Poor study habits in general?

© Robert M. Sherfield

will not help you own the material; it can only help you memorize a few things for storage in short-term memory. You may spend several hours cramming, and shortly after the test, the information is gone, evaporated, vanished!

But, let's be straight about something else. We know that you may have obligations that take enormous hours from your week. This is simply a matter of fact in the twenty-first century. So, there may be occasions when time runs out and the only option is to cram. If you find yourself in this spot, consider the following tips and suggestions for cramming. These probably won't get you an A, but they may help you with a few questions.

DEPRESSURIZE.   Just tell yourself up front what you are doing. Don't pretend that cramming is going to save you. Let yourself realize that you are memorizing material for short-term gain and that you won't be able to keep it all. With this admission, your stress will diminish.

DITCH THE BLAME GAME.   You know you're at fault, so accept that and move on. Sitting around bemoaning your fate will not help; it will just take up more of your valuable time. Just tell yourself, "I messed up this time; I won't let it happen again."

KNOW THE SCORE.   When cramming, it is important to know what you're cramming for. If you're cramming for a multiple-choice test, you'll need different types of information than for an essay test. Know what type of test it is for which you are studying.

READ IT QUICK.   Think about **H2 FLIB.** This is a mnemonic for: read the **h**eadings, **h**ighlight the important words, read the **f**irst sentence of every paragraph, read the **l**ast sentence of every paragraph, read the **i**ndented and **b**oxed material. This can help you get through the chapter when pinched for time.

MAKE CONNECTIONS.   As you are reading, quickly determine if any of the information has a connection with something else you know. Is there a comparison or contrast? Is there a relationship of any kind? Is there a cause and effect in motion? Can you pinpoint an example to clarify the information? Is there a mnemonic that can help you with this information? These questions can help you with retention and long-term memory commitment.

USE YOUR SYLLABUS OR STUDY GUIDE.   If your instructor lists questions that you should know (mastery questions) in the syllabus, or if he or she gave you a study sheet (or you developed your own study sheet), this is the place to start. Answer those questions. If you don't have either, look to see if the text gives study questions at the end of the chapter. Try to answer the questions using the text and your lecture notes.

SEE IT.   Visualizing the information through mapping, diagrams, photos, drawings, and outlines can help you commit this information to short-term memory.

CHECK YOUR NOTES.   Did the professor indicate that certain things were important for the test?

REPEAT!   Repeat! Repeat! Repetition is the key to committing information to memory. After you read information from the text or lecture notes, repeat it time and time again. When you think you've got it, write it down, and then repeat it again.

CHOOSE WISELY.   If you're cramming, you can't do it all. Make wise choices about which material you plan to study. This can be driven by your study sheet, your lecture notes, or questions in your syllabus (if they are listed).

Information is going to leave you when you cram. Don't rely on it for the next test or the final. You will need to go back and relearn (truly understand) the information you "crammed" to commit it to long-term memory.

USING STUDY GROUPS

How Can I Use Study Groups to Help Me Learn?

There may be situations where you will need or want to study in a group. You may find a study group at your institution, or your may establish a study group online through your learning management system discussion board, Skype, WebEx, GoToMeeting, or other electronic meeting sites. Study groups can be extremely helpful because they give you the opportunity to listen to others, ask questions, share information, cover more ground, solve problems, brainstorm ideas, and develop a support system.

The following tips will help you when you establish or join a study group:

- Limit the number of participants to three to five people, and spend some time getting acquainted. Exchange contact information if you're comfortable doing so.

- Each member should make a personal commitment to bring his or her best to the group each time you meet.

- Members of the group should be able to get along with each other, take and give constructive criticism, and make valued contributions.

- Limit the group to those people who can meet at the specified times, dates, and locations.

- Set rules so that all members know the objectives and goals of the study period.

- Limit the study time to two to three hours—longer periods tend to be less productive.

- All members of the group should be prepared, share, and participate.

- The study group should have a goal for each session.

- Assignments should be made for the next study session so that everyone comes prepared and you can cover the material that needs to be learned.

- Select a leader so that you reach your goals during the meeting.

- Use the study group as a supplement to, not a replacement for, the class.

THINKING ABOUT TESTING

Can Changing My Attitude and Reducing Test Anxiety Really Help?

Yes, both are necessary to help you get you through tests. A positive or negative attitude can truly mean the difference between success and failure. With an attitude adjustment and some basic preparation, you can overcome a good deal of your anxiety about tests and do well. You can reduce anxiety when you are in control of the situation, and you can gain control by convincing yourself that you *can be* and *will be* successful. If you think positively and can honestly say that you have done everything possible to prepare for a test, then the results will most likely be positive.

Silencing your negative self-talk is one of the most powerful things you can do for yourself. Consider the following tips for reducing test anxiety during your next test. You will not be able to employ them all, but if you learn and use a few new ones each time, before you know it, you'll be a testing pro!

- Prepare yourself emotionally for the test, control your self-talk, and be positive.

- Study and learn the material—no, you can't study too much!

- Ask peers who have had a certain professor what type of tests he or she gives.

- Arrive early for the test (at least 15 minutes early).

- Come to the test with everything you need: pencils, calculator, and other supplies.

- Listen to the instructor before the test begins, know his or her rules about testing, and read the instructions.

- Keep an eye on the clock during the test so that you can finish on time. However, don't let time cause you undue stress or anxiety.

- Answer what you know first—the questions that are easiest for you.

- Check your answers, but remember, your first response is usually correct.

- Find out exactly what the test will cover ahead of time.

- Ask the instructor for a study sheet. You may not get one, but it does not hurt to ask!

- When you get the test, jot down any mnemonics you might have developed on the back or at the top of a page.

PREPARING FOR THE TEST

What Should I Find Out Before the Test Begins?

Several classes before the test is scheduled, **quiz your instructor** about the logistics and specifics of the test. This information can help you study more effectively and eliminate the anxiety that comes with uncertainty. If you don't know if the test is going to be true–false or essay or both, it is much more difficult to study. Some questions you need to ask are:

1. What types of questions will be on the test?

2. How many questions will be on the test?

3. Is there a time limit on the test?

4. Will there be any special instructions, such as use pen only or use a number 2 pencil?

5. Is there a study sheet?

6. Will there be a review session?

7. What is the grade value of the test?

8. What chapters or sections will the test cover?

Asking these simple questions will help you know what type of test will be administered, how you should prepare for it, and what supplies you will need.

TEST-TAKING STRATEGIES AND HINTS FOR SUCCESS

What Do I Do When I Can't Remember the Answer?

Almost every test question will elicit one of three types of responses from you as the test taker:

What techniques help reduce your anxiety and negative self-talk during quizzes and exams?

Patrick White/Merrill

- Quick-time response

- Lag-time response

- No response

You have a *quick-time response* when you read a question and know the answer immediately. You may need to read only one keyword in the test question to know the correct response. Even if you have a quick-time response, however, always read the entire question before answering. The question may be worded in such a way that the correct response is not what you originally expected. By reading the entire question before answering, you can avoid losing points to careless error.

You have a *lag-time response* when you read a question and the answer does not come to you immediately. You may have to read the question several times or even move on to another question before you think of the correct response. Information in another question will sometimes trigger the response you need. Don't get nervous if you have a lag-time response. Once you've begun to answer other questions, you usually begin to remember more, and the response may come to you. You do not have to answer questions in order on most tests.

No response is the least desirable situation when you are taking a test. You may read a question two or three times and still have no response. At this point, you should move on to another question to try to find some related information. When this happens, you have some options:

1. Leave this question until the very end of the test.

2. Make an intelligent guess.

3. Try to eliminate all unreasonable answers by association.

4. Watch for modifiers within the question.

Successful Decisions

AN ACTIVITY FOR CRITICAL REFLECTION

After the second week of classes, Jose was devastated over his first test score. The instructor put the range of grades on the board, and he was even more shocked to see that many people passed the test and that his score was in the bottom 10 percent.

He began asking classmates if they did well or not and found some who had made A's and others who had made D's. When he spoke with one classmate, Letty, she told him that he should just chill and take a cheat sheet to class. "The instructor never looks, man, and she left the classroom twice. She'll never know. That's how I got my A."

"Cheat," Jose thought, "I don't think I can do that." He knew that others had made better grades than he over the years, but he also knew that he had never once cheated on an exam. Ever.

Jose went to the Tutoring Center and worked with a tutor on content and on how to take a test more effectively. On the next test, Jose scored a C. "It may not be the best grade in the class," he thought, "But it is all mine. I did it."

In your own words, what two suggestions would you give Jose to improve his grades without cheating?

1. _____

_____

2. _____

_____

Remember these important tips about the three types of responses:

1. Don't be overly anxious if your response is quick; read the entire question and be careful so that you don't make a mistake.

2. Don't get nervous if you have a lag-time response; the answer may come to you later, so just relax and move on.

3. Don't put down just anything if you have no response; take the remaining time and use intelligent guessing.

What Are Some Tips for Test Taking?

Before you read about the strategies for answering these different types of questions, think about this: ***There is no substitute for studying!*** You can know all the tips, ways to reduce anxiety, mnemonics, and strategies on earth, but if you have not studied, they will be of little help to you.

STRATEGIES FOR MATCHING QUESTIONS.   Matching questions frequently involve knowledge of people, dates, places, or vocabulary. When answering matching questions, you should:

■ Read the directions carefully.

■ Read each column before you answer.

■ Determine whether there are an equal number of items in each column.

■ Match what you know first.

■ Cross off information as you use it.

■ Use the process of elimination for answers you might not know.

■ Look for logical clues.

■ Use the longer statement as a question; use the shorter statement as an answer.

Sample Test 1

DIRECTIONS: Match the information in column A with the correct information in column B. Use uppercase letters.

GOALS, MOTIVATION, AND SELF-ESTEEM

A

_____ They can be long- or short-term, social,
            academic, religious, or financial
_____ They bring out the worst in you
_____ "I CAN'T" Syndrome
_____ Your "true self"
_____ Listening with an open mind

B

A. Child within
B. Objectivity
C. Contaminated people
D. Negative thoughts
E. Goals

STRATEGIES FOR TRUE–FALSE QUESTIONS.   True–false tests ask if a statement is true or not. True–false questions can be some of the trickiest questions ever developed. Some students like them; some hate them. There is a 50/50 chance of answering correctly, but you can use the following strategies to increase your odds on true–false tests:

- Read each statement carefully.

- Watch for keywords in each statement—for example, negatives.

- Read each statement for double negatives, such as "not untruthful."

- Pay attention to words that may indicate that a statement is true, such as *some, few, many,* and *often.*

- Pay attention to words that may indicate that a statement is false, such as *never, all, every,* and *only.*

- Remember that if any part of a statement is false, the entire statement is false.

- Answer every question unless there is a penalty for guessing.

Sample Test 2

Place "T" for true or "F" for false beside each statement.

NOTE-TAKING SKILLS

1. _____ Note taking creates a history of your course content.
2. _____ "Most importantly" is not a key phrase.
3. _____ You should always write down everything the instructor says.
4. _____ You should never ask questions in class.
5. _____ The L-STAR system is a way of studying.
6. _____ W/O is not a piece of shorthand.
7. _____ You should use 4-by-6-inch paper to take classroom notes.
8. _____ The outline technique is best used with lecture notes.
9. _____ The Cornell method should never be used with textbook notes.
10. _____ The mapping system is done with a series of circles.

STRATEGIES FOR MULTIPLE-CHOICE QUESTIONS.   Many college instructors give multiple-choice tests because they are easy to grade and provide quick, precise responses. A multiple-choice question asks you to choose from among two to five answers, sometimes to complete a sentence. Some strategies for increasing your success in answering multiple-choice questions are the following:

- Read the question and try to answer it before you read the answers provided.

- Look for similar answers; one of them is usually the correct response.

- Recognize that answers containing extreme modifiers, such as *always, every,* and *never,* are usually wrong.

- Cross off answers that you know are incorrect.

- Read all the options before selecting your answer. Even if you believe that A is the correct response, read them all.

- Recognize that when the answers are all numbers, the highest and lowest numbers are usually incorrect.

- Recognize that a response written as a joke is usually wrong.

- Understand that the most inclusive answer is often correct.

- Understand that the longest answer is often correct.

- If you cannot answer a question, move on to the next one and continue through the test; another question may trigger the answer you missed.

- Make an educated guess if you must.

- Answer every question unless there is a penalty for guessing.

Sample Test 3

DIRECTIONS: Read each statement and select the best response from the answers given below.

STUDY SKILLS

1. Which statement is true according to the U.S. Bureau of Labor Statistics?
   A. Men earn more than women.
   B. Women earn more than men.
   C. People with a bachelor's degree earn the most money of any education level.
   D. Males and females earn just about the same amount of money.

2. To calculate a GPA, you would:
   A. divide quality points by the number of semester hours.
   B. multiply total points by quality points.
   C. divide total points by the number of semester hours.
   D. multiply the quality points by the total points.

3. To be an effective priority manager, you have to:
   A. be very structured and organized.
   B. be very unstructured and disorganized.
   C. be mildly structured and organized.
   D. know what type of person you are and work from that point.

4. Objective listening is:
   A. judging the speaker and not the message.
   B. listening with an open mind.
   C. mentally arguing with the speaker so you an formulate questions.
   D. listening using the elements of the Korean verb "to listen."

STRATEGIES FOR SHORT-ANSWER QUESTIONS. Short-answer questions, also called fill-in-the-blanks, ask you to supply the answer yourself, not select it from a list. Although "short answer" sounds easy, these questions are often very difficult. Short-answer questions require you to draw from your long-term memory. The following hints can help you answer this type of question successfully:

- Read each question and be sure that you know what is being asked.

- Be brief in your response.

- Give the same number of answers as there are blanks; for example, _____ and _____ would require two answers.

- Never assume that the length of the blank has anything to do with the length of the answer.

- Remember that your initial response is usually correct.

- Pay close attention to the word immediately preceding the blank; if the word is *an,* give a response that begins with a vowel (a, e, i, o, u).

- Look for keywords in the sentence that may trigger a response.

Sample Test 4

DIRECTIONS: Fill in the blanks with the correct response. Write clearly.

LISTENING SKILLS

1. Listening is a _____ act. We choose to do it.
2. The three elements of listening are listening objectively, _____, and _____.
3. _____ is the same as listening with an open mind.
4. Prejudging is an _____ to listening.
5. Leaning forward, giving eye contact, being patient, and leaving your emotions at home are characteristics of _____ listeners.

STRATEGIES FOR ESSAY QUESTIONS.   Most students look at essay questions with dismay because they take more time. Yet essay tests can be one of the easiest tests to take because they give you a chance to show what you really know. An essay question requires you to supply the information. If you have studied, you will find that once you begin to answer an essay question, your answer will flow more easily. Some tips for answering essay questions are the following:

■ More is not always better; sometimes more is just more. Try to be as concise and informative as possible. An instructor would rather see one page of excellent material than five pages of fluff.

■ Pay close attention to the action word used in the question and respond with the appropriate type of answer. Keywords used in questions include the following:

discuss	illustrate	enumerate	describe
compare	define	relate	list
contrast	summarize	analyze	explain
trace	evaluate	critique	interpret
diagram	argue	justify	prove

■ Write a thesis statement for each answer.

■ Outline your thoughts before you begin to write.

■ Watch your spelling, grammar, and punctuation.

■ Use details, such as times, dates, places, and proper names, where appropriate.

■ Be sure to answer all parts of the question; some discussion questions have more than one part.

■ Summarize your main ideas toward the end of your answer.

■ Write neatly.

■ Proofread your answer.

Sample Test 5

DIRECTIONS: Answer each question completely. Use a separate paper if you wish.

STUDY SKILLS

1. Identify and discuss two examples of mnemonics.
2. Justify why it is important to use the SQ3R method when reading.
3. Compare an effective study environment with an ineffective study environment.

Do you find it easier or harder to take tests online?

iStockPhoto

Learning how to take a test and learning how to reduce your anxiety are two of the most important gifts you can give yourself as a student. Although tips and hints may help you, don't forget that there is no substitute for studying and knowing the material.

STRATEGIES FOR TAKING ONLINE EXAMS.   Many of the techniques used for taking online exams are the same as those that you will use to take a traditional exam. As with traditional exams, the same is true for online exams: There is *no* substitute for studying.

Depending on your learning management system and instructor, the rules for an online exam may vary. You may have a time requirement; some instructors may set the exam so that after a limited time period, the question is gone and you cannot come back to it. You will need to find out their rules before the exam.

Some instructors allow you to use your text and notes for an online exam, but the questions are usually more complex and higher on Bloom's Taxonomy scale. You will have to understand the material in much more depth than an in-class exam.

The following tips will assist you in taking an online exam:

- If at all possible, find out what the exam will cover. Is it comprehensive or on a specific chapter?

- Read the directions and questions carefully.

- Ask about the time limit for each question and whether you will be able to come back to skipped questions. Manage your time well for an online exam.

- Find out if you have to answer the questions in sequence.

- Find out if you can change an answer once you have clicked on or entered your response.

- Make sure that you have a strong network connection so that you are not disconnected in the middle of the exam.

- Understand the method of submission, whether through the learning management system (LMS), e-mail, or some other means.

- If at all possible, practice using the testing feature in the LMS before you actually have to take an exam.

- Once you begin your exam, do not close the window for any reason.

- If allowed, write down all formulas, dates, definitions, and rules that you may need for the exam. Have all materials with you before you log onto the computer to begin the exam.

- If possible, save a copy of your exam before you send it.

REFLECTIONS ON **NOTE TAKING AND TESTING**

Just as reading is a learned skill, so is memory development, studying, and learning how to take tests. You can improve your memory, but it will take practice, patience, and persistence. You can improve your study skills, but it will take time and work. And you can increase your ability to do well on tests, but it will take a commitment on your part to study smarter and put in the time and dedication required. By making the decision that you can do this, you've won the battle; for when you make that decision, your studying and learning become easier.

Your challenge is to focus on developing excellent memory techniques, study patterns, and test-taking abilities while earning the best grades you can. When you have done this, you can look in the mirror and be proud of the person you see without having to be ashamed of your character, worrying about being caught cheating, or wondering

if you really did your best. When studying for your next class or taking your next text, consider the following:

- Study your hardest material first.
- Review your classroom and textbook notes frequently.
- Use mnemonics to help you remember lists.
- Learn the material from many different directions.
- Ask questions of the instructor before the test.
- Glance at the entire test before beginning.
- Write your name on every test page.
- Ignore the pace of your classmates.
- Watch time limits.

As you study and learn to enter your chosen profession, remember this: You are building your character for the long haul—not just a few short years.

"Change occurs, progress is made, and difficulties resolved if people merely do the right thing—and rarely do people not know what the right thing is."

—*Father Hessburg*

REDUCING TEST ANXIETY

Utilizes levels 1 and 6 of the taxonomy

Each chapter-end assessment is based on Bloom's Taxonomy of Learning. See pages xxvi–xxviii in the front of this book for a quick review.

Explanation: Now that you have read and studied this chapter and no doubt taken a few tests this semester, you have a better understanding of what happens to you physically and mentally during an exam.

On the next page, you will find listed six of the common physical or mental symptoms of anxiety reported by students while testing.

Process: Beside each symptom, create a list of at least three concrete, doable, realistic strategies to overcome this physical or emotional anxiety symptom before or during a testing situation.

SYMPTOM	HOW TO REDUCE IT
Fatigue	1. _____ 2. _____ 3. _____ 4. _____ 5. _____
Frustration	1. _____ 2. _____ 3. _____ 4. _____ 5. _____
Fear	1. _____ 2. _____ 3. _____ 4. _____ 5. _____
Anger	1. _____ 2. _____ 3. _____ 4. _____ 5. _____
Nervousness/Nausea	1. _____ 2. _____ 3. _____
Uncertainty/Doubt	1. _____ 2. _____ 3. _____ 4. _____ 5. _____

SQ3R MASTERY STUDY SHEET

EXAMPLE QUESTION *(from page 257)*
Why are mnemonics important?

ANSWER:

EXAMPLE QUESTION *(from page 259)*
Discuss three strategies for studying math.

ANSWER:

AUTHOR QUESTION *(from page 247)*
What is the difference between short-term and long-term memory?

ANSWER:

AUTHOR QUESTION *(from page 248)*
Discuss the five steps in VCR3.

ANSWER:

AUTHOR QUESTION *(from page 260)*
What is H2 FLIB, and how can it help you?

ANSWER:

AUTHOR QUESTION *(from page 261)*
Discuss five ways to reduce text anxiety.

ANSWER:

AUTHOR QUESTION *(from page 264)*
Discuss one strategy for each type of testing situation.

ANSWER:

YOUR QUESTION *(from page _____)*

ANSWER:

YOUR QUESTION *(from page _____)*

ANSWER:

YOUR QUESTION *(from page _____)*

ANSWER:

YOUR QUESTION *(from page _____)*

ANSWER:

YOUR QUESTION *(from page _____)*

ANSWER:

Finally, after answering these questions, recite in your mind the major points covered here. Consider the following general questions to help you master this material.

- What was it about?
- What does it mean?
- What was the most important thing you learned? Why?
- What were the key points to remember?

chapter eleven

THINK

BUILDING CRITICAL-THINKING, EMOTIONAL INTELLIGENCE, AND PROBLEM-SOLVING SKILLS

"Many people think they are thinking when they are merely rearranging their prejudices." —William James

THINK

Why read this chapter?

Because you'll learn:

- To define critical and creative thinking
- The steps in the critical-thinking process
- To identify false arguments

Because you'll be able to:

- Tolerate uncertainty
- Identify, narrow, and solve problems
- Tell the difference between fact and opinion

Scan and QUESTION

Take a few moments, **scan this chapter,** and on page 303, write **five of your own questions** that you think will be important to your mastery of this material. You will also find five questions listed from your authors.

Example:

☑ **Why is emotional intelligence important to critical thinking?** (from page 279)

☑ **What are fallacious arguments?** (from page 293)

MyStudentSuccessLab

MyStudentSuccessLab (www.mystudentsuccesslab.com) is an online solution designed to help you "Start strong, Finish stronger" by building skills for ongoing personal and professional development.

How
COLLEGE CHANGED MY LIFE

Name: Jennifer Rosa
Institution: Graduate! InterCoast College
Age: 24
Major: Alcohol and Drug Counseling
Career: Alcohol and Drug Counselor

Often, when we decide to do something, it is because we have had experiences that influenced and shaped those decisions. This was the case with me when I began my studies at InterCoast College. I had a problem with alcohol and drugs until I became pregnant with my son. At that moment, I realized that I would have to change my life. My past problems helped me make the decision to become a drug and alcohol counselor. I knew that because of my past experiences, I would be able to help those who wanted to stop using. I knew that because of my addiction, I would be able to relate and give them my perspective on things. I hoped that I would be able to help them see another path and show them other options because I had been down the same road. It was a great decision for me.

I began at InterCoast College because of their alcohol and drug counseling program and stayed there because of the wonderful help I received from my instructors. They were so willing to work with all of us. They shared their life experiences, which made the classroom come alive. We learned a great deal from the books and readings, but we also learned from what they had to offer from real-world trials, failures, and successes.

There were several challenges in going back to school, but the biggest challenge I faced in returning was the fact that I was a single mom. Because my son is an only child, he is "mommy-oriented" and needed me. Shortly after I began my studies at InterCoast, he became quite ill and was hospitalized. Soon after this illness, he got pneumonia. My instructors were more than happy to work with me and help me catch up and adjust to life in college. Another challenge I faced was getting back into the groove of studying and reading. Thankfully, I had always been a good test taker and this helped me greatly. Another challenge was public speaking. I had never been good at communicating in public, but I quickly realized that to be an effective counselor, I needed to be able to listen to others and express myself clearly. My classes and practical experiences at InterCoast helped me overcome my fears.

One of the best experiences I had was my internship. I got on-the-job training in a nonthreatening environment. I learned the processes of intake, paperwork, and questioning clients. I learned what we could ask and what was off limits. I got to work in an actual treatment facility. This was such a great experience for me that they hired me full time after graduation. So, my advice would be to work hard and have an open mind in your internship, because you may be working for your future employer.

The biggest lesson that I learned from going back to school was that anything is possible if you want it badly enough. Sure, there are going to be hard times, trying times, and times when you want to just give up, but if you stick with it, success will come to you. I quickly learned because of the diversity of students in school that it is never too late to start and never too late to finish.

Think about it

1. Jennifer praised her internship experience. What experience do you hope to get from your internship or part-time employment in your field of study?

2. Jennifer mentions that she had an early setback because of her son's health. What steps should you take to notify and work with your instructors if something major happens in your life?

THINKING ABOUT THINKING

Do You Know *Why* You Think *What* You Think?

Same-sex couples should be able to marry and adopt children. Think about that statement for a moment. You may be saying to yourself, "I don't have to think about it—I know what my opinions on same-sex marriage and adoption are." However, do you know *why* you have these opinions? Can you trace your decisions back to certain events or moments in your life? Do you think that your emotions cloud your thoughts on the issue? Is there a right or wrong side to this debate? Does your religion or culture come into play when thinking about this issue? Did someone else influence your thoughts or are they your very own, developed through research and conversations regarding this issue?

What are you thinking right now? More importantly, why are you thinking the way you are right now? What is causing you to believe, feel, or think one way or the other regarding this issue? What are the facts and/or opinions that have led you to your conclusion? At this moment, what are the origins on which you are basing your thoughts about this issue—emotions or facts, fallacies or truths, data or opinions, interviews or hearsay, reason or misjudgment, fear or empathy?

We purposefully chose a "hot topic" issue because understanding why and how we formulate thoughts and ideas is the main objective of this chapter and critical thinking in general. This chapter is about believing and disbelieving, seeking, uncovering, debunking myths, uncovering bias, identifying and solving problems, using information correctly, and proving the impossible possible. It is about proof, logic, evidence, and developing ideas and opinions based on hard-core facts and credible research. It is about seeking truth and expanding your mind to unimaginable limits, about the fundamental hallmarks of becoming an educated citizen, and about human thought and reasoning.

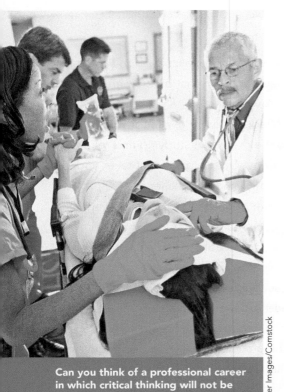

Can you think of a professional career in which critical thinking will not be required?

Jupiter Images/Comstock

THE IMPORTANCE OF CRITICAL THINKING

When Will I Ever Use It?

Have you ever made a decision that turned out to be a mistake? Have you ever said to yourself, "If only I could go back and . . ." Have you ever regretted an action you took toward a person or situation? Have you ever planned a paper or speech that was flawless? Have you ever had to make a hard, painful decision that turned out to be the best decision of your life? If the answer to any of these questions is yes, you might be able to trace the consequences back to your ***thought process*** at the time of the decision. Let's face it, sometimes good and bad things just happen out of luck or circumstance. More often than not, however, many events in our lives are driven by the thought processes involved when we made the initial decision and chose to act on it.

Critical thinking can serve us in many areas as students and citizens in a free society. As a student, ***critical thinking can help you:***

- Focus on relevant issues/problems and avoid wasting time on trivia

- Gather relevant, accurate information regarding finances, goals, decision making, relationships, civic responsibility, environmental issues, and many other areas

- Understand and remember facts and organize thoughts logically

- Look more deeply at problems, analyze their causes, and solve them more accurately

- Develop appropriate and meaningful study plans and manage your priorities

- Assist in your problem-solving skills

- Help you control your emotions so that you can make rational judgments and become more open-minded

- Produce new knowledge through research and analysis

- Help you determine the accuracy of printed and spoken words

- Assist you in detecting bias and determining the relevance of arguments and persuasion

AN EIGHT-POINT PLAN FOR CRITICAL THINKING

Can You Really Make Critical Thinking Work for You in Everyday Life?

Does critical thinking really matter? Seriously? Can it do anything to improve the quality of your life? The answer is yes. Critical thinking has daily, practical uses, from making sound financial decisions to improving personal relationships to helping you become a better student to helping you make a good deal on purchasing a car. You can improve your critical-thinking skills by watching your emotional reactions, using solid research and facts to build your examples and thoughts, and practicing open-mindedness.

Conversely, can the lack of critical-thinking skills cause real problems? The answer, once again, is yes. Poor critical-thinking skills can impair your judgment, lead you to make rash decisions, and even cause you to let your emotions rule (and sometimes ruin) your life. Critical thinking can be hampered by a number of factors, including closed-mindedness, unflappable opinions based on rumor instead of facts, cultural and/or religious bias, lack of accurate information, faulty arguments, and negativity.

As you begin to build and expand your critical-thinking skills, consider the eight steps in Figure 11.1.

 ## Step 1: Understanding and Using Emotional Intelligence

Emotions play a vital role in our lives. They help us feel compassion, help us support others, help us reach out in times of need, and help us relate to others. Emotions, on the other hand, can cause some problems in your critical-thinking process. You do not—and should not—have to eliminate emotions from your thoughts, but it is crucial that you know when your emotions are clouding an issue and causing you to act and speak before thinking.

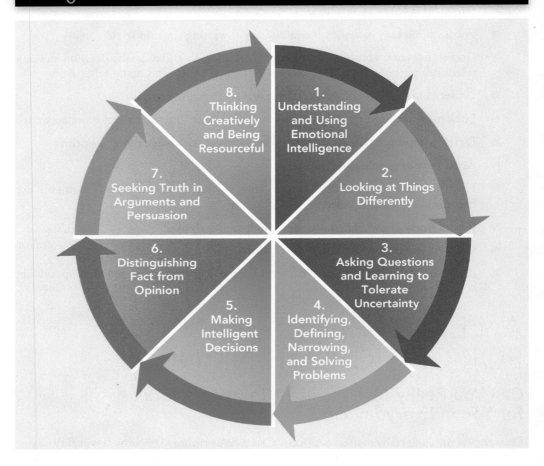

Figure 11.1 **The Eight Steps in Critical Thinking**

Consider the following topics:

- Should drugs and prostitution be totally legalized in the United States?
- Can the theories of evolution and creationism coexist?
- Is affirmative action reverse discrimination?
- Should illegal aliens be given amnesty and made U.S. citizens?
- Should the legal drinking age be lowered to 18?
- Should terminally ill patients have the right to assisted suicide?
- Should prayer be allowed in public schools?

"Simply stated, people who are emotionally intelligent harness emotions and work with them to improve problem solving and boost creativity."
—Snyder and Lopez

As you read these topics, did you immediately form opinions? Did old arguments surface? Did you feel your emotions coming into play as you thought about the questions? If you had an immediate answer, it is likely that you allowed some past judgments, opinions, and emotions to enter the decision-making process, unless you have just done a comprehensive, unbiased study of one of these issues. If you had to discuss one of these issues in class or with your friends and had to defend your position, how would you react? Do you think you would get angry? Would you find yourself groping for words? Would you find it hard to explain why you held the opinion that you voiced? If so, these are warning signs that you are allowing your emotions to drive your decisions. If you allow your emotions to run rampant and fail to use research, logic, and evidence, you may not be able to examine the issues critically or have a logical discussion regarding the statements.

SHARPENING YOUR EMOTIONAL INTELLIGENCE (EI) SKILLS

How Does EI Affect Critical Thinking and Problem Solving?

If you have ever heard the old saying "Think before you act," you were actually being told to use *emotional intelligence.* Everyone knows that *IQ* (intelligence quotient) is important to success in college, work, and life, but many experts also believe that *EI* (emotional intelligence) is just as important to being successful. Emotional intelligence helps people cope with the social and emotional demands in daily life. "Emotional intelligence is the single most influencing variable in personal achievement, career success, leadership, and life satisfaction" (Nelson and Low, 2003). "The data that exist suggest it can be as powerful, and at times more powerful, than IQ" (Goleman, 2006).

Exactly what is EI? EI includes all the skills and knowledge necessary for building strong, effective relationships through managing and understanding emotions. *It is knowing how you and others feel and managing feelings and emotions in a rational manner that is good for both parties.* Consider Figure 11.2 (adapted from Snyder and Lopez, 2007).

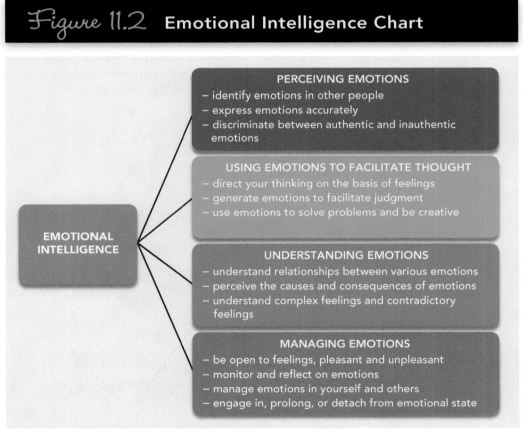

Figure 11.2   Emotional Intelligence Chart

EMOTIONAL INTELLIGENCE

PERCEIVING EMOTIONS
– identify emotions in other people
– express emotions accurately
– discriminate between authentic and inauthentic emotions

USING EMOTIONS TO FACILITATE THOUGHT
– direct your thinking on the basis of feelings
– generate emotions to facilitate judgment
– use emotions to solve problems and be creative

UNDERSTANDING EMOTIONS
– understand relationships between various emotions
– perceive the causes and consequences of emotions
– understand complex feelings and contradictory feelings

MANAGING EMOTIONS
– be open to feelings, pleasant and unpleasant
– monitor and reflect on emotions
– manage emotions in yourself and others
– engage in, prolong, or detach from emotional state

Source: Adapted from Snyder and Lopez, 2007.

Our emotions originate in the brain. If you have emotional intelligence skills, your ***thinking mind*** and ***emotional mind*** should function together, making it more likely that you will craft sound, rational decisions. In other words, you will ***think*** before you ***act.*** When these two minds do not operate in harmony, you might make highly emotional decisions that can be viewed as irrational.

The amygdala, discussed in Figure 11.3, remembers frustrations, fears, hurt feelings, and anger from our past. The tension from these past experiences causes the amygdala to go into default behavior—we ***feel*** before we ***think***—and this can create a potentially explosive situation. If you had a bad experience several years ago and are placed in a similar situation, the amygdala will remember and trigger emotions that cause the body to respond. These feelings often cause people to bypass critical thinking (the logical brain) and to respond with angry words or actions (the emotional brain). For example:

- They get angry; you get angry.

- They curse you; you curse them.

- They use physical violence; you use physical violence.

Figure 11.3   The Amygdala

Don't let this word or concept frighten you. If you have never heard of the amygdala (pronounced ah-MIG-da-la), you're not alone. Most people have not. But this term and concept are important for you to be able to understand the overall aspects of EI. The amygdala is simply a part of the brain's emotional system and can cause us to go into default behavior based on what we remember from a similar experience. Do I use ***fight or flight?*** Basically, the amygdala is there to protect us when we become afraid or emotionally upset. When influenced by the amygdala, everything becomes ***about us***. We become more judgmental. We don't stop to think about differences or the other person's feelings or the relationship. The amygdala can trigger an emotional response ***before*** the brain has had time to understand what is happening, and this situation causes us to have problems with others.

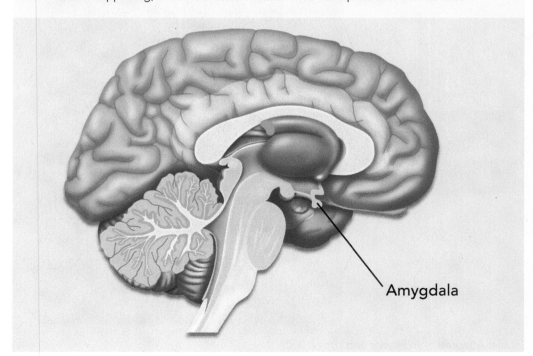

Amygdala

However, if you remain calm and level-headed, you will begin to see that the other person usually begins to calm down, too. He or she follows your emotional lead, positively or negatively, and if you're calm and rational, anger and violence become out of place for most people.

To become a successful, happy person, interpersonal relationships are important, and so learning to manage the entire spectrum of your personal emotions will be vitally important. This spectrum ranges from the darker side of your emotions (extreme negative pole) to the optimistic side (extreme positive pole). Study the spectrum of emotions illustrated in Figure 11.4. Think about which of these emotions you experience frequently and where you are located most of the time on this emotional continuum.

As you can see, the restraint and management of your personal emotional spectrum can greatly affect you and your thinking skills at home, school, and work. Today, this relatively new concept is being given a great deal of attention on college campuses and in the workplace. Not only will you find it helpful and necessary to manage your emotions at school, you will also need to be able to apply emotional management techniques with family, friends, and work associates.

Think about one experience you've had in the past where your negative emotions took over. Perhaps it was anger, fear, sorrow, hatred, or rage. What was the situation, and where were you when it happened? Be specific.

_____

_____

_____

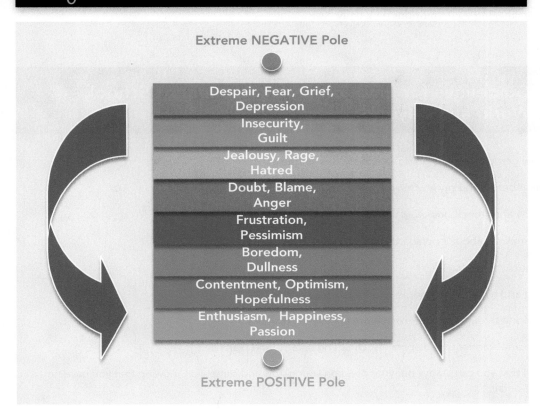

Figure 11.4   Emotional Spectrum

Extreme NEGATIVE Pole

Despair, Fear, Grief, Depression

Insecurity, Guilt

Jealousy, Rage, Hatred

Doubt, Blame, Anger

Frustration, Pessimism

Boredom, Dullness

Contentment, Optimism, Hopefulness

Enthusiasm, Happiness, Passion

Extreme POSITIVE Pole

What triggered these emotions?

_____

_____

_____

_____

What were the negative consequences to you (or someone else) because of your emotions?

_____

_____

_____

_____

How did these emotions affect your ability to think clearly and critically?

_____

_____

_____

_____

Because emotional intelligence skills and knowledge are so important to your success in all areas of your life, you are encouraged to read extensively about this subject and to design your own personal plan for dealing with emotional concerns. Consider the tips in Figure 11.5 for managing your emotions on a daily basis.

Figure 11.5 Guidelines for Emotional Management at School, Work, and Beyond

Face each day with an "I feel great, nothing is going to ruin my day" attitude.

Hear all sides of an argument before you say anything, make a decision, or take an action.

Practice a win–win philosophy at all times, and work tirelessly to make it happen.

Avoid letting your personal feelings about a person dictate your decisions.

Never, never, never lose control!

Avoid negative stereotyping and typecasting people into negative categories.

Never look at or judge someone through someone else's eyes or experiences.

Learn to keep a tight rein on any emotional "hotspots," such as anger, rage, and jealousy.

Strive to treat people so well that you can always put your head on your pillow and sleep well knowing that you have not been underhanded, rude, or unfair.

Step 2: Looking at Things Differently

Critical thinking involves examining something you may have seen many times from many different angles and perspectives. It involves going beyond the obvious or "easy" to seek new understanding and rare solutions. It encourages you to dig deeper than you have before; to get below the surface; to struggle, experiment, and expand. It asks you to look at something from an entirely different view so that you might develop new insights and understand more about the problem, situation, question, or solution. Critical thinking involves looking at **common issues** with uncommon eyes; **known problems** with new skepticism; **everyday conflicts** with probing curiosity; and **daily challenges** with greater attention to detail.

Review the brain teasers in Figures 11.6, 11.7, and 11.8. Take the time to solve them, even though you may not "get" them quickly. You may need to break down a few barriers in your thought process and look at them from a new angle. Remember, these exercises do not measure intelligence. They are included to prod your thought process along and help you look at things differently.

Figure 11.6 Brain Teaser 1, Looking at Common Terms Backward

Consider the following clues. Two examples are given to help you get started. Answer the following 10 teasers based on the clues.

Example	4 W on a C	Four Wheels on a Car
	13 O C	Thirteen Original Colonies

1. SW and the 7D _____
2. I H a D by MLK _____
3. 2 Ps in a P _____
4. HDD (TMRUTC) _____
5. 3 S to a T _____
6. 100 P in a D _____
7. T no PLH _____
8. 4 Q in a G _____
9. I a SWAA _____
10. 50 S in t U _____

Figure 11.7 Brain Teaser 2, Seeing What Is Not Given

Look at the design below. You will find nine dots. Your mission is to connect all nine dots with four straight lines without removing your pencil or pen from the paper. Do not retrace your lines.

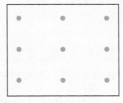

Figure 11.8 **Brain Teaser 3, The Penny**

Pretend that all life on Earth has ended and all traces of civilization are gone. There are no buildings, no people, no animals, no plants—nothing is left but dirt and one penny. Someone from another planet who knows our language comes to Earth and finds the penny. List all of the things that could be inferred about our civilization based on this one small penny. You should find at least 10.

1. _____
2. _____
3. _____
4. _____
5. _____
6. _____
7. _____
8. _____
9. _____
10. _____

How did you do? Was it hard to look at the situation backward or look for clues within a series of letters and numbers? Most of us are not used to that. But part of critical thinking is trying to find ***clues or patterns.*** Perhaps the easiest teaser in Figure 11.6 is number two. Most people know MLK as Martin Luther King Jr. When you figure that part out, the name of his most popular speech, "I Have a Dream," becomes easier. Often, when trying to solve problems or dealing with unknowns, things become easier when you can find a clue or a pattern and build from what you already know.

Examine the brain teaser in Figure 11.7. This teaser is included to help you look at an issue beyond what is actually given to you and considering what is not given.

Once again, you are given a basic clue, but you must go beyond what is given. You must look at the nine dots, but you must not let them confine you. You can't let the nine dots control your thoughts—you must move beyond what is given; beyond what you actually see. When you do this, the answer will come to you.

As you continue to look at common things differently and think beyond the obvious, examine the penny in Figure 11.8.

Drawing inferences often takes the ability to examine something very common like you have never examined it before. Just as you looked at the penny, you learned new things about it by studying it with different eyes. Think about how you might solve a common problem that you face every day simply by looking at that problem with different eyes, too.

While these activities may seem somewhat trivial, they are provided to help you begin to think about and consider information from different angles. This is a major step in becoming a critical thinker: looking beyond the obvious, thinking outside the box, examining details, and exploring possibilities—basically, looking *beyond* what is given to you.

 ## Step 3: Asking Questions and Learning to Tolerate Uncertainty

You've asked questions all your life. As a child, you asked your parents "What's that?" a million times. You probably asked them "Why do I have to do this?" In later years, you've asked questions of your friends, teachers, strangers, store clerks, and significant others.

Questioning is not new to you, but it may be a new technique to you for exploring, developing, and honing your critical-thinking skills. Curiosity may have killed the cat, but it was a smart cat when it died! Your curiosity is one of the most important traits you possess. It helps you grow and learn, and sometimes it may cause you to be uncomfortable. That's OK. This section will teach you how to ask questions to promote knowledge, solve problems, foster strong relationships, and critically analyze difficult situations. It will also help you to understand the value of knowing how to tolerate uncertainty and avoid jumping to faulty conclusions because uncertainty got the better of you. It is important to know that sometimes, *the question is more important than the answer*—especially a faulty answer.

> "It is not possible to become a good thinker and be a poor questioner. Thinking is not driven by answers, but, rather, by questions."
> —Paul and Elder

Types of Questions

There are three basic types of questions, according to Paul and Elder (2006):

- **Questions of Fact.** Require answers based in facts and evidence and have a correct or incorrect answer.
  - **Example:** What is the freezing point of water?

- **Questions of Preference.** Require answers that state a subjective preference and do not necessarily have a correct or incorrect responses.
  - **Example:** What is your favorite color?

- **Questions of Judgment.** Require answers based on your judgment drawn from logic and evidence. These questions can have more than one defensible answer.
  - **Example:** Should *Roe v. Wade* be overturned?

Asking questions helps us gain insight where we may have limited knowledge. Answering properly posed questions can also help us expand our knowledge base. For example, if you were assigned to write a paper or give a speech on the topic of *creationism versus evolution*, what five questions would you definitely want that paper or speech to answer when you were finished? Take some time to think about the issue. Write down at least five questions that you consider essential to the topic of creationism versus evolution.

1. _____
2. _____
3. _____
4. _____
5. _____

Learning to ask probing questions can help you in everyday situations by challenging you to look beyond the obvious and critically examine those situations. Examine the car advertisement in Figure 11.9. The car dealership has provided some information, but it is not enough to make a smart, rational decision. What other questions would you ask the dealer to make sure that you are getting a good deal?

1. _____
2. _____
3. _____
4. _____
5. _____

Figure 11.9   Auto AD

I AM 100 PERCENT SURE THAT I AM NOT SURE

Can You Tolerate Uncertainty?

Asking questions that can be answered is vitally important to critical thinking, but so is learning to tolerate uncertainty and ask questions that may not have immediate answers. Uncertainty causes you to keep going—to not get lazy or give up. If we thought we knew the answers to everything, we would still be beating rocks together to make fire and we would still be walking everywhere instead of driving or flying. Uncertainty causes humanity to move forward and create new knowledge, to try new things, to consider the impossible. Uncertainty also breeds creative thinking.

Think about all of the uncertainty that can arise your daily life:

"Can I be certain my spouse/partner will not leave me?" No.
"Can I be certain that I will remain healthy?" No.
"Can I be certain my children will turn out as good, caring, loving adults?" No.
"Can I be certain what happens to me after I die?" No.
"Can I be certain the plane won't crash or someone won't crash into my car?" No.
"Can I be certain that this will not embarrass me or someone else?" No.
"Can I be certain that my investments will grow and I can retire comfortably?" No.

The inability to tolerate uncertainty can cause stress and anxiety. Sometimes, we just have to let go and accept that we do not know the answers. We can work hard to try to find the answers and/or direct our actions so that the answers will be favorable to us, but ultimately, many things in this universe require our tolerance of uncertainty. Sometimes, the best we can hope for is to keep asking questions and seeking truth.

Think of the good things that initially unanswered questions and uncertainty brought to humanity in many fields of study:

"Can we send people to the moon and have them return safely?"
"Can we transplant a human heart and have that person live and prosper afterwards?"
"Can we establish a new country with a new constitution and have it work?"
"Can we design and build a skyscraper that is over 140 stories high and have it remain safe?"
"Can we create an automobile that will get over 50 miles per gallon of fuel?"
"Can we help reduce global warming and its effects on the polar ice caps?"

All of these uncertainties have contributed to the development of new knowledge, new skills, new jobs, new outlooks, and new ways of living. Therefore, it is important to remember in your quest for answers, sometimes uncertainty can be the most important thing you discover.

Step 4: Identifying, Defining, Narrowing, and Solving Problems

What would your life be like if you had no problems? Most people do not like to face or deal with problems, but the critical thinker knows that problems exist every day and that they must be faced and hopefully solved. Some of our problems are larger and more difficult than others, but we all face problems from time to time. You may have transportation problems. You may have financial problems. You may have child care problems. You may have academic problems or interpersonal problems. Many people don't know how to solve problems at school, home, or work. They simply let the problem go unaddressed until it is too late to reach an amicable solution. There are many ways to address and solve problems. In this section, we will discuss how to *identify and narrow* the problem, *research and develop* alternatives, *evaluate* the alternatives, and *solve* the problem.

Not every problem may have a solution. That can be a hard pill for many people to swallow, but it is a raw truth and a part of the uncertainty we just discussed. Many problems have solutions, but the solution may not be what you wanted. It is imperative to remember the words of Mary Hatwood Futrell, president of the NEA. She states that "finding the right answer is important, of course. But more important is developing the ability to see that many problems have multiple solutions, that getting from X to Y demands basic skills and mental agility, imagination, persistence, patience." Consider the problem-solving model in Figure 11.10.

DID YOU *Know?*

CESAR CHAVEZ was born in 1927 near Yuma, Arizona. He was raised during the Great Depression in unspeakable poverty. His parents owned a small store but lost everything during the Depression. The entire family became migrant workers just to survive. He spent his youth working in the fields of Arizona and California. From the first through eighth grade (when he left school), he attended over 30 schools. Often his family did not have even the basic necessities of water and toilets. They faced not only poverty, but extreme prejudice and injustice.

Later, Chavez joined the Navy. Upon his return, seeing the many problems faced by migrant families, he vowed to try to find a way to make life better for his family and the families living in such poverty. He founded the United Farm Workers, which was responsible for increasing public awareness of the plight of the migrant workers in the United States. He is considered to be one of the greatest civil rights activists in U.S. history.

PHOTO: Najlah Feanny/Corbis

"When I'm getting ready to reason with a man, I spend one-third of my time thinking about myself and what I am going to say—and two-thirds thinking about him and what he is going to say."
—Abraham Lincoln

IDENTIFY THE SYMPTOMS. *Symptoms* and *problems* are not the same thing. Symptoms are *part* of the problem, but may not be the problem itself. Think of a problem like you think of your health. For example, you may have aches in your joints, chills, and a severe headache. Those seem like problems, but in actuality, they are really symptoms of something larger—perhaps the flu or an infection. You can treat the headache with medicine, and soothe your joint pain with ointment, but until you get at the root of the problem, these symptoms will come

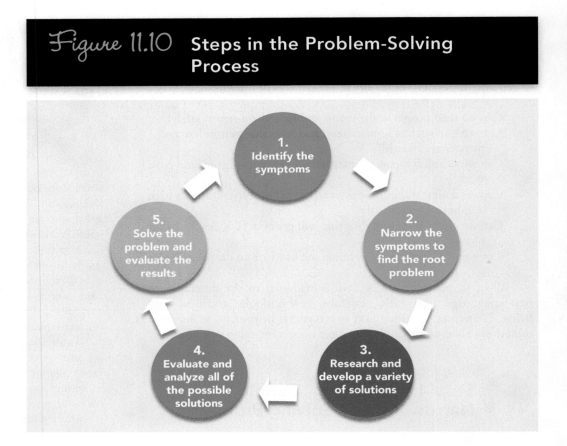

Figure 11.10   Steps in the Problem-Solving Process

back. Problems are much the same way. If you don't move beyond symptoms, the problem may seem to be solved, but shortly, it will reappear, usually worse than before. Therefore, it is imperative that you identify the symptoms of the greater problem before you begin solving anything.

NARROW THE SYMPTOMS TO FIND THE ROOT PROBLEM.   Often, problems keep coming up because we dealt with a symptom instead of the ***real problem.*** Getting to the heart of a problem is hard work that requires a great deal of thought, research, and patience. Begin by putting your symptoms in writing, perhaps on note cards, so that you can lay them out and see them all at once. When doing this, be sure to jot down all of the major and minor symptoms, such as:

■ What are the daily challenges that keep coming up?

■ Who is involved?

■ How are the symptoms hindering your overall goals?

■ Who or what is responsible for creating these symptoms?

■ Are the symptoms internal (self-inflicted) or external (other-inflicted)?

■ What obstacles are these symptoms creating?

■ Are the symptoms part of one major problem or several problems?

RESEARCH AND DEVELOP A VARIETY OF SOLUTIONS.   It is a mistake to try to solve a problem when you don't have enough information to do so. It may be that you need to conduct

Successful Decisions
AN ACTIVITY FOR CRITICAL REFLECTION

arson's class was assigned an activity asking them to determine whom they would like to meet if they could meet anyone and what questions they would like to ask the individual. Some of the class members thought it was a stupid assignment—and Carson was not so sure that she wanted to spend any time on this "weird" activity either. That evening, she began to think about the question seriously. "Who has been important to the world?" she thought. "Who has done something powerful and extraordinary?" "Who has been awful and caused needless pain?"

She decided that if she could ask anyone anything, she would choose Hitler. She decided that she would ask him these questions: 1) If you had to do it all over again, would you? 2) From where did your hatred come? 3) Why did you have everyone killed who could have revealed your own past? 4) You did not look like the master race you chose to promote; why did you chose to promote it?

5) Why did you become such a coward in the end and kill yourself?

This interesting project let Carson use WWII, Hitler, and the German occupation as the basis for her presentation in speech class. She did not just brush off what seemed to be a "crazy" assignment.

In your own words, what three suggestions would you give to a classmate who thinks an assignment is crazy or useless? Be specific.

1. _____
   _____
2. _____
   _____
3. _____
   _____

interviews, research what others have done who have faced similar issues, read current data and reports, or even explore historical documents. Paul and Elder (2006) suggest that the type of information you need is determined by the type of problem you have and the question(s) you are trying to answer. "If you have a historical question, you need historical information. If you have a biological question, you need biological information. If you have an ethical question, you must identify at least one relevant ethical principle." Therefore, part of the problem solving process is to gather your facts—the correct facts—before you try to reach a resolution.

EVALUATE AND ANALYZE ALL OF THE POSSIBLE SOLUTIONS.   After you have gathered your research (through formal methods and/or brainstorming), you must now evaluate your solutions to determine which would work best and why. After careful study and deliberation, without emotional interference, analyze the solutions you came up with and determine if they are appropriate or inappropriate. To analyze, create Columns A and B. Write each possible solution in Column A and an evaluative comment in Column B.

EXAMPLE PROBLEM: I don't have enough time to study due to my job.

A (Possible Solutions)	B (Comments)
Quit the job.	Very hard to do. I need the money for tuition and car.
Cut my hours at work.	Will ask my boss.
Find a new job.	Hard to do because of the job market—but will look into it.
Get a student loan.	Visit financial aid office tomorrow.
Quit school.	No—it is my only chance for a promotion.

With your comments in Column B, you can now begin to eliminate some of the alternatives that are inappropriate at this time.

SOLVE THE PROBLEM AND EVALUATE THE RESULTS.   Now that you have a few strong possible solutions, you have some work to do. You will need to talk to your boss, go to the financial aid office, and possibly begin to search for a new job with flexible hours. Basically, you are creating a plan to bring this solution to life. After you have researched each possible solution further, you will be able to figure out which solution is the best option for you and make a decision based on solid information and facts.

Your Turn

Using the diagram in Figure 11.11, work through the following situation and determine the steps that could be taken to solve this problem.

Pretend that your best friend, Nathan, has just come to you with a problem. He tells you that his parents are really coming down hard on him for going to college. It is a strange problem. They believe that Nathan should be working full time and that he is just wasting his time and money, since he did not do well in high school. They have threatened to take away his car and kick him out of the house if he does not find a full-time job. Nathan is doing well and does not want to leave college. He has a goal of becoming an architect and knows that he has talent in this area. He is making A's and B's in all of his classes. This does not matter to his parents. They do not value education and see it as a luxury.

 ## Step 5: Making Intelligent Decisions

You make decisions every day. These decisions may be small, such as "What am I going to have for lunch?" or large decisions like "Should I change jobs in this economy?" There are many factors that influence our decisions such as our past experiences, our tolerance for risk, our comfort level, our desire to change, and our relationships with others. To further complicate the issue of decision making, we are faced with immediacy. In today's information-centered world, we seldom have time to sit back and digest all of the facts and angles before we're required to make life-altering decisions. Because of the pace at which decision making is required in today's business world, we sometimes add two and two together and get five (MindTools, 2011).

Decision making is such an important tool when it comes to being effective in the workplace and enhancing your leadership skills. When faced with a difficult decision, we've all asked the age-old question "How do I know if I'm making the right decision?" With so many factors tugging at us, including people in our lives, past experiences, and our amygdala (the emotional brain), it is difficult to know if the decision we're making is a wise one. The amygdala, once again, tries to play tricks on us. It wants us to make decisions based on our emotions and not our intellect. Then, you have your brain telling you to make the decision based on logic, reasoning, and facts and leave your heart out of it. It's enough to drive you crazy, or worse yet, enough to drive you to make a poor decision or no decision at all.

In his book *How We Decide* (2010), Jonah Leher speaks of "The Sin of Certainty." This is a situation when our strong desire to believe we're right flies in the face of the evidence that clearly states otherwise. It is a neurological condition where we convince ourselves that our actions are just, fair, and based in fact when in actuality, we have simply told ourselves the lie so many times that we believe the incorrect assumptions. We have given our brain so many facts and figures that it begins to "cherry pick" only what is needed to make the decision *we want* to make, not the decision *we need* to make based on evidence and logical reasoning. Leher states that our brains are very complex and sometimes the best decisions are going to come from our head and sometimes the best decisions are going to come from our heart. We have to know when to use both—either separately or together.

One of the most effective ways to make a decision is to use a numerical scale to actually assign a "grade" to each choice before you. This works by doing several things:

■ **Create an "Element" column.** This column lists the aspects of the decision that are important to you, such as pay, potential for growth, joy of work, and so on.

Figure 11.11 Effective Problem Solving

Summarize the situation in your own words.

_____
_____
_____
_____
_____
_____

Symptom 1 that the problem is real

_____
_____

Symptom 2 that the problem is real

_____
_____

Symptom 3 that the problem is real

_____
_____

Identify the ROOT problem.

_____
_____
_____
_____
_____
_____
_____

Possible solution 1

_____
_____

**Research possible solutions.
What did you find?**

Possible solution 2

_____
_____

Possible solution 3

_____
_____

Evaluate the solutions.

Solution 1
Comments

_____
_____
_____
_____

Solution 2
Comments

_____
_____
_____
_____

**Create a PLAN to solve the problem.
I plan to. . .**

_____
_____
_____
_____
_____
_____
_____

Solution 3
Comments

_____
_____
_____
_____

- **Create a "Rating of Importance" column.** This column gives each element a rating that you assign. Using a scale of 1 to 10, you will decide if pay is very important (an 8, 9, or 10) or not very important (a 1, 2, or 3).

- **Create a "Choice 1" column.** This column will list the numerical calculations for your first choice. You will decide on its importance and then multiply that number by your importance rating.

- **Create a "Choice 2" column.** This column will list the numerical calculations for your second choice. You will decide on its importance and then multiply that number by your importance rating.

Once you have created your columns (see Figure 11.12), you will work through your decisions using your head and your heart.

A numerical score may not be the ultimate in decision making, but at least you have taken the time to think about what is important to you, what is offered within the choices, and how it ranks in importance to you. By using this system, you are calling on your head and your heart to make decisions that could affect your life for a very long time.

 ## Step 6: Distinguishing Fact from Opinion

An important aspect of critical thinking is the ability to distinguish fact from opinion. ***In most mediums—TV, radio, newspapers, magazines, and the Internet—opinions surface more often than facts.*** Reread the previous sentence. This is an example of an opinion cloaked as a fact. There is no research supporting this opinion. It sounds as if it could be true, but without evidence and proof, it is just an opinion.

> "Everyone is entitled to their own opinion, but not their own facts."
>
> —Senator Daniel Patrick Moynihan

A fact is something that can be **proven**, something that can be **objectively verified**. An opinion is a statement that is held to be true, but one that has no objective proof. *Statements that cannot be proven should always be treated as opinion.* Statements that offer valid proof and verification from credible, reliable sources can be treated as factual.

Learning to distinguish fact from opinion can be a paramount step in building your critical-thinking skills at work, with family, and especially when analyzing media.

Figure 11.12 Decision-Making Chart

The following example shows a decision-making chart for considering two job offers for Samantha. The "Element" column lists the items that are most important to Samantha in selecting a new job.

ELEMENTS IMPORTANT TO ME	MY RATING OF IMPORTANCE 1–10	CHOICE 1 JOB AT MERCY HOSPITAL		CHOICE 2 JOB AT GRACE HOSPITAL	
Distance to work from home	8	My rating = 5	8 × 5 = 40	My rating = 2	2 × 8 = 16
Pay	10	My rating = 9	10 × 9 = 90	My rating = 7	10 × 7 = 70
Benefits	9	My rating = 2	9 × 2 = 18	My rating = 7	9 × 7 = 63
Potential for growth	5	My rating = 5	5 × 5 = 25	My rating = 5	5 × 5 = 25
Upgraded facility	7	My rating = 6	7 × 6 = 42	My rating = 4	7 × 4 = 28
			TOTAL SCORE = 215		TOTAL SCORE = 202

BRING the Change

TIPS FOR PERSONAL SUCCESS

Consider the following tips when distinguishing fact from opinion:

- Take nothing for granted.
- Understand who is making the assertion.
- Listen for what is not stated.

Now, it is your turn. List two more tips that you would offer a fellow classmate to assist him or her with distinguishing a fact from an opinion.

1. _____

_____

2. _____

_____

Step 7: Seeking Truth in Arguments and Persuasion

Whether or not you realize it, arguments and persuasive efforts are around you daily—hourly, for that matter. They are in newspaper and TV ads, editorials, news commentaries, talk shows, TV magazine shows, political statements, and religious services. It seems at times that almost everyone is trying to persuade us through arguments or advice. This section will assist you in recognizing faulty arguments and implausible or deceptive persuasion.

First, let's start with a list of terms used to describe faulty arguments and deceptive persuasion. As you read through the list, try to identify situations in which you have heard arguments that fit these descriptions.

Terminology for Fallacious Arguments	
Ad baculum	Ad baculum is an argument that tries to persuade based on force. Threats of alienation, disapproval, or even violence may accompany this type of argument.
Ad hominem	Ad hominem is when someone initiates a personal attack on a person rather than listening to and rationally debating his or her ideas. This is also referred to as "slander."
Ad populum	An ad populum argument is based on the opinions of the majority of people. It assumes that because the majority says X is right, then Y is not. It uses little logic.
Ad verecundiam	This argument uses quotes and phrases from people in authority or popular people to support one's own views.
Bandwagon	The bandwagon approach tries to convince you to do something just because everyone else is doing it. It is also referred to as "peer pressure."
Scare tactic	A scare tactic is used as a desperate measure to put fear in your life. If you don't do X, then Y is going to happen to you.

Straw man argument	The straw man argument attacks the opponent's argument to make one's own argument stronger. It does not necessarily make argument A stronger; it simply discounts argument B.
Appeal to tradition	This argument looks only at the past and suggests that we have always done it "this way" and we should continue to do it "this way."
Plain folks	This type of persuasion is used to make you feel that the people making the argument are just like you. Usually, they are not; they are only using this appeal to connect with your values and lifestyle.
Patriotism	This form of persuasion asks you to ignore reason and logic and support what is right for state A or city B or nation C.
Glittering generalities	This type of persuasion or argumentation is an appeal to generalities (Bosak, 1976). It suggests that a person or candidate or professional is for all the "right" things: justice, low taxes, no inflation, rebates, full employment, low crime, free tuition, progress, privacy, and truth.

Identifying Fallacious Arguments

Below, you will find statements intended to persuade you or argue for a cause. Beside each statement, identify which type of faulty persuasion is used.

AB	Ad baculum	SA	Straw man argument	AH	Ad hominem
AT	Appeal to tradition	AP	Ad populum	PF	Plain folks
AV	Ad verecundiam	PM	Patriotism	BW	Bandwagon
ST	Scare tactic	GG	Glittering generalities		

_____ 1. This country has never faltered in the face of adversity. Our strong, united military has seen us through many troubled times, and it will see us through our current situation. This is your country; support your military.

_____ 2. If I am elected to office, I will personally lobby for lower taxes, a new comprehensive crime bill, a $2,500 tax cut on every new home, and better education, and I will personally work to lower the unemployment rate.

_____ 3. This is the best college in the region. All of your friends will be attending this fall. You don't want to be left out; you should join us, too.

_____ 4. If you really listen to Governor Wise's proposal on health care, you will see that there is no way that we can have a national system. You will not be able to select your doctor, you will not be able to go to the hospital of your choice, and you will not be able to get immediate attention. His proposal is not as comprehensive as our proposal.

_____ 5. My father went to Honors College, I went to Honors College, and you will go to Honors College. It is the way things have been for the people in this family. There is no need to break with tradition now.

_____ 6. The witness's testimony is useless. He is an alcoholic; he is dishonest and corrupt. To make matters worse, he was a member of the Extremist Party.

_____ 7. The gentleman on the witness stand is your neighbor; he is your friend; he is just like you. Sure, he may have more money and drive a Mercedes, but his heart never left the Elm Community.

_____ 8. John F. Kennedy once said, "Ask not what your country can do for you; ask what you can do for your country." This is the time to act, my fellow citizens. You can give $200 to our cause, and you will be fulfilling the wish of President Kennedy.

_____ 9. Out of the 7,000 people polled, 72 percent believed that there is life beyond our planet. Therefore, there must be life beyond Earth.

_____ 10. Without this new medication, you will die.

_____ 11. I don't care what anyone says. If you don't come around to our way of thinking, you'd better start watching your back.

As you develop your critical-thinking skills, you will begin to recognize the illogical nature of many thoughts, the falsehoods of many statements, the deception in some advertisements, and the irrational fears used to persuade. You will also begin to understand the depths to which you should delve to achieve objectivity, the thought and care that should be given to your own decisions and statements, and the methods by which you can build logical, truthful arguments.

> "There is nothing so powerful as truth, and often, nothing so strange."
> —Daniel Webster

Step 8: Thinking Creatively and Being Resourceful

Creative thinking is a major and important aspect of critical thinking in that you are producing something that is uniquely yours—introducing something to the world that is new, innovative, and useful. Creative thinking does not mean that you have to be an artist, a musician, or a writer. Creative thinking means that you have examined a situation and developed a new way of explaining information, delivering a product, or using an item. It can be as simple as discovering that you can use a small rolling suitcase to carry your books around campus instead of the traditional backpack. Creative thinking means that you have opened your mind to possibilities!

Creative thinking is really about being resourceful—and in today's times, resourcefulness is a powerful tool. Resourcefulness is an **internal** quality, not an **external** gift. If you have ever seen the TV series *Survivor Man* or *Man versus Wild,* you know that it takes a strong person to eat a slug just carved out of a tree trunk. It takes internal will to drink water with so many bacteria that flies die when they drink it. Yes, both shows are somewhat staged, but they show the basics of creativity, intelligence, imagination and resourcefulness.

To truly understand resourcefulness, you need look no further than a child playing in the backyard. "What can a worthless old stick become?" Because of a child's inability to see limitations, the stick becomes a medieval sword, Luke Skywalker's laser beam, an old man's cane, a crutch, a magic wand, a bat, a witch's stirring stick, or a marshmallow roaster. An old stick now has limitless possibilities because the child refused to see it only as a stick. The child's refusal to be boxed into the confines of our adult reality created possibilities. Sometimes, we have to become that child and use every stick we have just to survive.

Think of internal resourcefulness as **renewable energy**. When you have to draw on your wits, creativity, and determination, these qualities multiply. The more you are required by circumstance to use them, the stronger and more plentiful they become. Conversely, if you've always been able to buy anything you want or all that you need is provided to you by an external force, your internal resourcefulness begins to wither and die like uneaten fruit on the winter vine. You are not forced to use the whole of yourself. Your energy fades. Your harvest dies.

Your inner resourcefulness and creativity also make you more secure and offer more protection from outside forces. When you know how to make ends meet, you can always do it. When you know how to pay the rent on limited income, you can always do it. When you know how to cut firewood to heat your home, you can always do it. When you know how to navigate the public transportation system in your town, you can always do it—even when the time comes when you don't have to do it anymore, you could if you had to. The more you know and the more inner strength and resourcefulness you have, the safer you are against the unknown. The more confidence you possess, the greater the likelihood that you can survive anything at any time. The more resourceful you

Getty Images RF

If you had to use your creativity to survive in the wild, could you do it?

from ORDINARY to *Extraordinary*

Dr. Wayne A. Jones
Assistant Professor and Thurgood Marshall Pathways Fellow
Department of Political Science and Public Administration,
Virginia State University, Petersburg, Virginia

I COME FROM a fine family. My mother is a retired social worker, college professor, and community activist and my father a retired Presbyterian minister and college professor. They provided a safe, structured environment and always have encouraged me to do well. Clearly, I had the foundation to do well in school. However, I have not always followed my parents' advice to look out for my best interests. This was especially true for my senior year in high school. The outcome was that I did not graduate. So at 18, I started working and got my own apartment. Things were OK. At least, so I thought.

I had always been interested in anything that had wheels on it. If it had wheels, I wanted to drive! I drove a school bus for a few years, and then I drove an ambulance. Additionally, I had a part-time job driving a taxi. One day, however, I saw our local bookmobile and I wanted to drive it, as it was different from anything that I had previously operated. I applied to do so, but found out that I had to have a high school diploma to be able to drive the bookmobile. At 19, this became my reason for going back to get a GED. Now, I could master driving yet another "thing" with wheels. It was not, however, as exciting as I thought it would be.

With my GED in hand, my parents encouraged me to begin my college studies. Subsequently, I enrolled at Virginia Commonwealth University. After only one year, I decided that college was not for me. I did not return for a third semester. In 1975, I began working for the police department in Chesterfield, Virginia. I was only the second African American police officer on the force. I held this position for four years.

My desire for wheels was still with me. I left the police department and began working for the Virginia Overland Transportation Company as a safety supervisor and bus driver. A short time later, I was promoted to operations manager. With this experience under my belt, I went to work for a larger bus company in Richmond, Virginia, driving a city transit bus.

I left the second bus company after a year to drive for a local construction company. This work, however, turned out to be seasonal and I found myself frequently without income. This company also operated trash trucks, so I asked to be allowed to drive one of their trash trucks so that I could have a steady income and overtime, too. So, there I was in my early 30s, without a college degree, driving either a dump or trash truck. There was not a lot to look forward to.

My grandmother called me one day and asked me why I didn't go back to college. "You are far from dumb," I remember her telling me. I tried to explain to her that I was making decent money and I really liked the company I was working

are, the more you understand that this one quality will help you rebuild all that may have been lost. When the world *has* been handed to you on a silver platter, you cannot be ready for what the world *can* hand you.

To begin the creative process, consider the items in Figure 11.13. These are some of the characteristics creative thinkers have in common. Using your imaginative and innovative juices, think about how you would *creatively* solve this problem. Write down at least five possibilities. Come on, make it count!

for and would not quit my job. I told her that if I went back to college part time, it would take me at least eight years to get a bachelor's degree. "I'll be too old by then," I told her.

She posed a question to me, the answer to which was a turning point in my life. "Son," she asked, "how old will you be in eight years if you do not go back to college?" That was my wake-up call. I enrolled at John Tyler Community College with no idea of what I wanted to become. The start of my second semester would bring a devastating event, as my grandmother died unexpectedly of cardiac arrest. Her final gift to me was her wonderful words of wisdom.

So, there I was, working full time, attending classes several nights a week, and studying the nights when I did not have classes. One night, I received another phone call that changed my life again. My parents told me that they wanted to talk with me about my education.

In just a few short years, I went from driving a trash truck to being a university professor.

To my surprise, they asked me to quit work and concentrate on my studies. "Grandma had a vision," my mother told me. "She knew that you were going to do great things." They told me that if I quit, they would help with my bills until I finished college. I agreed to take their help.

I transferred from John Tyler Community College and enrolled again at Virginia Commonwealth University, where I completed my bachelor's degree. However, my GPA was not great and I scored very badly on the Graduate Record Exam (GRE). I was turned down for the graduate program in public administration. I was now 35. I met with the chair of the department and said to him, "Just give me a chance. I know I can do this." After some conversation, he agreed to give me that opportunity. I completed my master's of public administration in only 18 months. Then, I applied to the doctoral program in public administration at VCU. The chairman of the doctoral program reviewed my GRE scores and basically told me that based on them, I should not have been able to

obtain a master's degree. I then applied to the doctoral program in higher education administration at George Washington University. They accepted me provisionally. However, I again rose to the occasion and only five years later, I graduated with a 3.85. My dissertation won the Outstanding Dissertation of the Year Award in 2000 from the George Washington University chapter of Phi Delta Kappa.

While working on my master's degree I obtained a position as adult day coordinator for a local nonprofit agency. Eventually, I would become the agency's executive director. It was during this time the thought of becoming a college professor came to mind. I saw an ad in the local newspaper for an adjunct teaching position at Richard Bland College, instructing a class of Advanced Placement high school students in U.S. government. It was through this part-time position that I found the love of my life—teaching. I later applied to become a full-time faculty member at Virginia State University, and today, I teach freshman studies and public administration classes.

It may seem like a lifetime to an outsider, but in a few years, I managed to go from driving a trash truck to being a university professor. With hard work, dedication, and help from those around you, you too can change your life and find your dream job. I wish you much luck in your search.

EXTRAORDINARY REFLECTION

Read the following statement and respond in your online journal or class notebook.

Dr. Jones was brave enough to take an enormous risk, quit his full-time job, accept help, and reach his goals. Who do you have in your life that you can depend on for support (maybe not monetary support, but crucial support of your goals, dreams, and educational plans)? Why?

The Problem

Jennifer is a first-year student who does not have enough money to pay her tuition, buy her books, and purchase a few new outfits and shoes to wear to class and her work-study job on campus.

What should she do? Should she pay her tuition and purchase her books, or pay her tuition and buy new clothes and shoes to wear to class and work? What creative, resourceful ideas (solutions) can you give Jennifer?

BLOOM LEVEL 6

Figure 11.13   Characteristics of Creative Thinking

Compassion	Creative thinkers have a zest for life and genuinely care for the spirit of others.	*Example:* More than 40 years ago, community members who wanted to feed the elderly created Meals on Wheels, now a national organization feeding the elderly.
Courage	Creative thinkers are unafraid to try new things, to implement new thoughts and actions.	*Example:* An NBC executive moved the *Today Show* out of a closed studio onto the streets of New York, creating the number-one morning news show in America.
Truth	Creative thinkers search for the true meanings of things.	*Example:* The astronomer and scientist Copernicus sought to prove that Earth was *not* the center of the universe—an unpopular view at the time.
Dreams	Creative thinkers allow themselves time to dream and ponder the unknown. They can see what is possible, not just what is real.	*Example:* John F. Kennedy dreamed that space exploration was possible. His dream became reality.
Risk Taking	Creative thinkers take positive risks every day. They are not afraid to go against popular opinion.	*Example:* Barack Obama took a risk and ran for President of the United States. He became one of only a few African Americans to ever run for the office and the only African American to be nominated by his party. In November of 2008, he became the first African American President of the United States.
Innovation	Creative thinkers find new ways to do old things.	*Example:* Instead of continuing to fill the earth with waste such as aluminum, plastic, metal, and old cars, means were developed to recycle these materials for future productive use.
Competition	Creative thinkers strive to be better, to think bolder thoughts, to do what is good, and to be the best at any task.	*Example:* A textbook writer updates the publication every three years to include new and revised information so the product remains competitive.
Individuality	Creative thinkers are not carbon copies of other people. They strive to be true to themselves.	*Example:* A young man decides to take tap dancing instead of playing baseball. He excels and wins a fine arts dancing scholarship to college.
Curiosity	Creative thinkers are interested in all things; they want to know much about many things.	*Example:* A 65-year-old retired college professor goes back to college to learn more about music appreciation and computer programming to expand her possibilities.
Perseverance	Creative thinkers do not give up. They stick to a project to its logical and reasonable end.	*Example:* Dr. Martin Luther King Jr. did not give up on his dream in the face of adversity, danger, and death threats.

My creative solutions:

1. _____

2. _____

3. _____

4. _____

5. _____

REFLECTIONS ON **CRITICAL AND CREATIVE THINKING**

Critical thinking, emotional intelligence, and information literacy require a great deal of commitment on your part. They may not be easy for everyone at first, but with practice, dedication, and an understanding of the immense need of all three, everyone can think more critically and logically, evaluate information sources, and use emotional intelligence to his or her best advantage.

Critical thinking and emotional intelligence can affect the way you live your life, from relationships to purchasing a new car, from solving family problems to investing money, from taking the appropriate classes for graduation to getting a promotion at work. Both are vitally important to your growth and education.

As you continue on in the semester and work toward personal and professional motivation and change, consider the following ideas:

■ Use only credible and reliable sources.
■ Learn to distinguish fact from opinion.
■ Be flexible in your thinking and avoid generalizations.
■ Use emotional intelligence and restraint.
■ Avoid stereotyping and prejudging and strive for objectivity in your thinking.
■ Reserve judgment until you have looked at every side.
■ Do not assume—do the research and ask questions.
■ Work hard to distinguish symptoms from problems.

Critical thinking is truly the hallmark of an educated person. It is a hallmark of character and integrity, and a hallmark of successful students. Let it be yours.

"The significant problems we face cannot be solved at the same level of thinking we were at when we created them."

—Albert Einstein

ANSWERS TO TEASERS

Brain Teaser 1, Looking at Common Terms Backwards

1. Snow White and the Seven Dwarfs
2. "I Have a Dream" by Martin Luther King Jr.
3. Two peas in a pod
4. Hickory dickory dock, the mouse ran up the clock
5. Three sides to a triangle
6. 100 pennies in a dollar
7. There's no place like home
8. Four quarts in a gallon
9. "It's A Small World After All"
10. 50 states in the Union

Brain Teaser 2, Thinking Beyond What Is Given To You

(Hint: You have to think "outside the box." Look beyond what is given to you.)

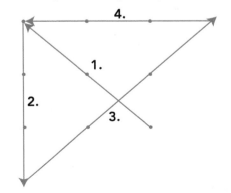

Brain Teaser 3, The Penny

Your answers might include things such as:

■ We had more than one language.
■ We knew geometry.
■ We had a calendar system.
■ We honored people.
■ We knew metallurgy.
■ We had a numeric system.
■ We knew architecture.
■ We were united.
■ We valued liberty.

Knowledge
in Bloom

DEVELOPING A RATIONAL, LOGICAL ARGUMENT

Utilizes level 3 of the taxonomy

Each chapter-end assessment is based on Bloom's Taxonomy of Learning. See pages xxvi–xxviii in the front of this book for a quick review.

Explanation: Thousands of articles are written every day for magazines, newspapers, online journals, and other print media. Depending on the article and where it is published, it can have a slant. You may have heard this called *bias* (as in liberal or conservative bias). One of journalism's objectives should be to present the facts of an incident or the facts of what is being discussed. Bias should not enter the argument unless it is an editorial.

Process: For this activity, you are to find an article (not an editorial) in a mainstream newspaper or magazine (*USA Today, Newsweek, Time, New York Times, The Washington Post, The National Review,* etc.), read the article, and determine

if the article has bias, unsubstantiated opinions, or research that is weak.

To assist you in this project, you will find a list of questions below to help you evaluate and assess your article.

Name of the article: _____

Writer of the article: _____

His/her affiliation: _____

Publication in which the article was found: _____

Date of publication: _____

Before you read this article, based on the title and subject matter, what five questions do you want to be able to answer once you have read the article?

1. _____

2. _____

3. _____

4. _____

5. _____

After reading the article, what is the author's main reason for writing it?

_____

_____

_____

What is the most important fact(s) or information in the article?

_____

_____

_____

By writing this article, what is the author implying?

_____

_____

_____

By writing this article, what is the author proving?

_____

_____

_____

In writing this article, what assumptions were made?

_____

_____

_____

What sources does the write cite to prove his or her point?

_____

_____

_____

Is the article fairly presented? In other words, does the author examine both sides of the issue or just one side? Justify your answer.

_____

_____

_____

Do you believe and trust the article? Why or why not? Justify your answer.

_____

_____

_____

If this article is accurate (or inaccurate, depending on your judgment), what are the implications for society?

_____

_____

_____

Answer the five questions you wrote earlier in this exercise.

1. _____

2. _____

3. _____

4. _____

5. _____

List one way that you can use the information in this article to enhance your creativity and/or resourcefulness.

_____

_____

_____

(This project is based on the work of Richard Paul and Linda Elder.)

SQ3R MASTERY STUDY SHEET

EXAMPLE QUESTION *(from page 279)* Why is emotional intelligence important to critical thinking?	**ANSWER:**
EXAMPLE QUESTION *(from page 293)* What are fallacious arguments?	**ANSWER:**
AUTHOR QUESTION *(from page 284)* Why is asking questions so important in critical thinking?	**ANSWER:**
AUTHOR QUESTION *(from page 284)* Why is uncertainty essential to educational growth?	**ANSWER:**
AUTHOR QUESTION *(from page 287)* When solving problems, why is it essential to find the root of the problem?	**ANSWER:**
AUTHOR QUESTION *(from page 292)* Define fact and opinion, and give an example of each.	**ANSWER:**
AUTHOR QUESTION *(from page 293)* Define ad hominem, and find an example of this in a recent newspaper or magazine.	**ANSWER:**
YOUR QUESTION *(from page _____)*	**ANSWER:**
YOUR QUESTION *(from page _____)*	**ANSWER:**
YOUR QUESTION *(from page _____)*	**ANSWER:**
YOUR QUESTION *(from page _____)*	**ANSWER:**
YOUR QUESTION *(from page _____)*	**ANSWER:**

Finally, after answering these questions, recite in your mind the major points covered here. Consider the following general questions to help you master this material.

- What was it about?
- What does it mean?
- What was the most important thing you learned? Why?
- What were the key points to remember?

chapter twelve

COMMUNICATE

COMMUNICATING, APPRECIATING DIVERSITY, AND MANAGING CONFLICT

"Words can destroy relationships. What we call each other ultimately becomes what we think about each other, and what we think about each other matters."—Jeanne J. Kirkpatrick

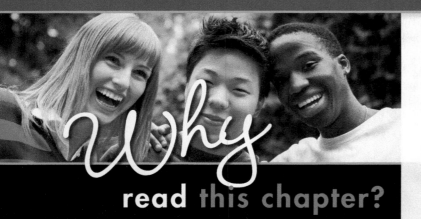

Why read this chapter?

Because you'll learn:

- About the Sapir–Whorf Hypothesis and its role in interpersonal communication
- How computer mediated communication relates to interpersonal communication
- How to deal with difficult people

Because you'll be able to:

- Choose an appropriate communication path to deliver your messages
- Understand the dimensions of diversity and how they affect relationships
- Navigate and learn how to manage conflict more effectively

Scan and QUESTION

Take a few moments, **scan this chapter,** and on page 329, write **five of your own questions** that you think will be important to your mastery of this material. You will also find five questions listed from your authors.

Example:

☑ **What are the six elements of the communication process?** (from page 308)

☑ **What is self-disclosure, and why is it important for healthy relationships?**
(from page 315)

MyStudentSuccessLab

MyStudentSuccessLab (www.mystudentsuccesslab.com) is an online solution designed to help you "Start strong, Finish stronger" by building skills for ongoing personal and professional development.

How
COLLEGE CHANGED MY LIFE

Name:	Lawrence A. Cain Jr.
Institution:	Graduate! Lincoln College of Technology
Age:	22
Major:	Business Management
Career:	U.S. Bank Customer Representative—Teller Services

I was not the first in my family to attend college, but I am the first to be able to say "I have a degree!" I can also say and write on my resumé that I made the President's List and Dean's List, received the Perfect Attendance Award, and graduated with a 3.6 GPA. Because of my degree from Lincoln College of Technology, I can also write that I have knowledge and experience in business law, accounting, payroll, accounts receivable, customer service, QuickBooks, and Microsoft Office. I'm not bragging—I just worked hard and I'm proud.

I began my studies at LCT because of their degree in business management and because they were adult friendly, had day and evening classes, and allowed me to graduate early. I also began my degree because I looked around and saw that people with degrees were getting and keeping jobs in this economy. There are many people who have knowledge, skills, and experience, but employers want you to have a degree as well.

The biggest challenge that I faced in going to college was getting back into the "school zone." I had been out of high school for several years, and learning to balance homework, classes, and a job was a huge task. I had to quickly learn how to manage my time and set priorities. I also had to learn to be patient and listen to my instructors.

The thing I liked most about LTC was that it afforded me the opportunity to experience a positive, encouraging atmosphere of learning. I got to associate, interact, and learn from people from all walks of life. I also loved learning and focusing on many different things. You don't often get that chance at work, but you can get it from college.

The most important lesson I learned was that I control my own destiny. As long as I know and live this, I have no excuses. I have to create my own future through goal setting and hard work. By getting my degree, doors began to open for me. I gained the resources to help me in the world of work. I learned how to network and meet people. These skills have served me well in my current position, and I know that they will serve me well into the future.

My advice to anyone just starting college would be to be patient with yourself, your instructors, and your program of study. Sure, there will be classes that you do not want to take and classes where you do not see their benefit, but believe me, they all begin to fit in the greater puzzle—the bigger picture. Going to college, getting my degree, and entering the professional world made me a better person who is more confident, optimistic, and hopeful. It makes me want to help others achieve their dreams, too.

THINK about *it*

1. Lawrence states that he is proud of the work he has done and skills he has acquired. What are you studying now that you are proud to master?

2. Do you think you control your own destiny? Why or why not? What proof do you have to justify your response?

THE COMMUNICATION PROCESS

How Does Communication Work?

Look around any store, at any red light, in any restaurant, and often, in any classroom, and you will see someone on a cell phone. Increasingly, people are not talking, but texting. Technology is one of the dominant forms of communication in today's world. Does texting count as communication? You bet it does. Does talking on a phone or writing an e-mail count as communication? Yes, it does, too. We are living in a world where communication through technology is a way of life that is here to stay. This chapter will help you understand the process of face-to-face or technological communication, how to communicate more effectively, how to appreciate the diverse nature of your institution and work environments, and how to manage the inevitable conflicts that arise from time to time.

Communication is not something we do **to people**, but something that is done **between people.** Communication can take on a variety of forms, such as oral speech, the written word, body movements, electronic messages, and even yawns. All of these actions communicate something to another person. As you begin thinking about communication, it is paramount that you know this: If you are in the presence of another person, communication cannot be stopped.

Basically, the communication process involves **six elements:** the source, the message, the channel, the receiver, barriers, and feedback. Consider Figure 12.1.

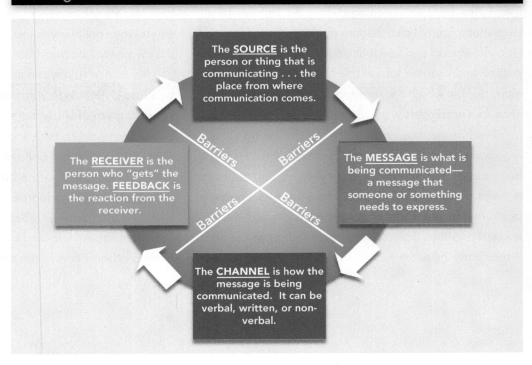

Figure 12.1 **Six Elements of Communication**

The **SOURCE** is the person or thing that is communicating . . . the place from where communication comes.

The **MESSAGE** is what is being communicated— a message that someone or something needs to express.

The **CHANNEL** is how the message is being communicated. It can be verbal, written, or non-verbal.

The **RECEIVER** is the person who "gets" the message. **FEEDBACK** is the reaction from the receiver.

Barriers

Barriers (represented by the lines in Figure 12.1) are things that can interfere with the source, the message, the channel, or the receiver. Barriers can occur anywhere within the communication process and can include things like external noise (others talking, cell phones, and traffic), internal noise (self-talk, doubt, and questioning), interference, and poor communication habits. Your emotions, past experiences, social norms, communication expectations, and prejudices can also be barriers to effective communication. Think about a time when your feelings for someone interfered with your ability to listen to him or her objectively. This would be a perfect example of a barrier. **Feedback** is the verbal and nonverbal response given to you by the receiver.

> "I see communication as a huge umbrella that covers and affects all that goes on between human beings."
>
> —Joseph Adler

What Is the Role of Interpersonal Communication in Everyday Life?

Interpersonal communication is a part of the greater communication spectrum. It is "a dynamic form of communication between two (or more) people in which the messages exchanged significantly influence their thoughts, emotions, behaviors, and relationships" (McCornack, 2007). The messages in interpersonal communication are not necessarily static, like the words in a book, a written letter, or a text message; they are fluid and constantly changing, potentially causing your relationships to change along with them. Texting and e-mails are components of interpersonal communication, as well as computer mediated interpersonal communication, which we will discuss later in this chapter.

In his book *Reflect and Relate* (2007), Steven McCornack suggests that there are three interpersonal communication goals, as shown in Figure 12.2. They are **self-presentation,** **instrumental,** and **relationship goals.**

Take a moment and identify one way that you could use each of the interpersonal communication goals to help you succeed in college and establish strong relationships.

BLOOM LEVEL 3

Self-Presentation Goal	I can use this to _____ _____
Instrumental Goal	I can use this to _____ _____
Relationship Goal	I can use this to _____ _____

Figure 12.2 Interpersonal Communication Goals

TYPE OF GOAL	EXPLANATION	EXAMPLE
Self-Presentation Goals	Goals that help us present ourselves to others in a particular fashion and help others see us as we wish to be seen	If you want a new acquaintance or love interest to see you as a caring, compassionate person, you will use words and actions that reveal yourself as caring, trustworthy, honest, and compassionate.
Instrumental Goals	Goals that help us present information in a way so that we get what we want or need from another person; to possibly win approval	If you wanted to borrow your best friend's laptop, you would remind him or her that you are always careful and respect others' property.
Relationship Goals	Goals that help us build meaningful, lasting, and effective relationships with other people	If your friend loaned you his or her computer, you might write a thank you note or buy a small gift to show your gratitude.

Later, we will discuss how to use interpersonal communication to your best advantage in understanding and learning from others, building lasting relationships, and dealing with inevitable conflicts both in person and through technology.

THE STORY OF ONE WILD BOY

Why Is Interpersonal Communication Important?

You do not have a choice: If you are in the presence of another human being, you are communicating. Period! Smiling is communication. Reading a newspaper is communication. Turning your back to the wall and hiding your face from everyone is communication. Silence is communication. It is just the law of nature—if you are around one or more people, you are communicating with them. With that said, understanding the impact of your communication is paramount.

Consider this: Nothing in your life is more important than effective communication. Nothing! Your family is not. Your friends are not. Your career is not. Your religion is not. Your money is not. "Why?" you may ask. "That's a harsh, drastic statement." We make this assertion because without effective communication, you would not have a relationship with your family and friends. You would not have a career or money or even religious beliefs. Communication is that important. In fact, it is so important that communication gives us our identity. That's right. Without communication and interaction, *we would not even know that we were human beings.*

Take into account the true story of the Wild Boy of Aveyron. It may sound like this story was taken from *The National Enquirer,* but it was not. This story has been documented in many science, psychology, sociology, and communication texts over the years. In January of 1800, a gardener in Aveyron, France, went out one morning to collect vegetables for the day. To his surprise, he heard an unusual moaning and groaning sound. Upon further inspection, he found a "wild boy" squatting in the garden eating vegetables as an animal might do. This boy showed no signs or behaviors associated with human beings. He appeared to be between 12 and 14 years old, but stood just a little more than four feet tall. He had scars and burns on his body, and his face showed traces of smallpox. His teeth were brown and yellow, and his gums were receding. It can only be assumed that when he was an infant, he was abandoned in the woods and left to die. It has also been suggested that someone may have tried to kill him as an infant because of the long scar across his trachea (Lane, 1976).

When he was found in 1800, he could not speak and barely stood erect. "He had no sense of being a human in the world. He had no sense of himself as a person related to other persons" (Shattuck, 1980). Because of his lack of communication and contact with other humans, he had no identity, no language, no self-concept, and no idea that he was even a human being in a world of human beings. Of course, he had no religious beliefs or relationships with other human beings. That is how **powerful** communication is in our world today—it gives us our identity. It lets us know we are human! It helps establish our place and purpose in the world.

The Sapir–Whorf Hypothesis

Much work has been done on the topic of identity, communication, and personal actions, but perhaps the most widely cited research comes from the *Sapir–Whorf Hypothesis* (1956). Edward Sapir and Benjamin Whorf researched the relationships among language, culture, and thought. Basically, their theory suggests the language we know, hear, and speak *determines the way we interpret and understand the world.* Just like the Wild Boy of Aveyron had never heard human language, his actions suggested that he did not know he was human. The theory also suggests that as humans, we are *unconscious* of this language/action situation and live our lives accordingly without choice. At its core, the Sapir–Whorf Hypothesis suggests that because of the language we hear, our "realities" and interpretations of the world around us vary from culture to culture and person to person.

Consider this example: In the Native American culture, there are no words for "to own the earth." The concept of land ownership does not exist. Native Americans do not believe that the earth can be owned by human beings. Think about that for a moment. If you have no concept of what it means to own the earth, then your actions and beliefs about the earth differ greatly from those who think they can and do own the earth. Language, in this and many cases, would determine our thoughts and actions.

Another example comes from the civil rights movement of the 1960s. We've all seen the photos of fire hoses being used to "control" African Americans who were marching for equal rights. According to the Sapir–Whorf Hypothesis, if you were raised where segregation was normal and natural and African Americans were considered second-class citizens, this footage may not have affected you at all. In fact, you may have even thought the police who used the hoses were justified. You may have seen it and thought, "They deserve it." If the only language to which you have ever been exposed consists of bigotry and prejudice, then you might naturally believe that supremacy is OK and your thoughts and actions will mirror this.

However, if you were reared in an atmosphere where you were taught that everyone is equal and racial prejudice is shameful and disgraceful, you would see these fire hose photos as barbaric and horrific. The language we hear and live with on a daily basis determines how we think and how we act. *That* is the important lesson of the power of language and communication. It gives us our identity. It defines us. It determines our actions. And, perhaps most importantly, language can help us grow, change, and overcome negative influences, people, and events that might have shaped our backgrounds and held us back. Just because we were raised with language that may well be harmful, language can still be the driving force that teaches us to live in a more positive, optimistic space.

THE ROLE OF NONVERBAL BEHAVIOR IN INTERPERSONAL COMMUNICATION

Can We Communicate Without Words?

Nonverbal communication is any and all communication other than words—and it is constant. We cannot escape our body language or the body language of others. Why is it important to study nonverbal communication? Because there can be so many interpretations of a single nonverbal clue, we must understand that not every action is equal or carries the same message. We must consider everything from cultural traditions to unconscious acts to fully grasp what may be intended by a look, a smile, a touch, or how close we stand to someone. We must consider that many of our nonverbal clues are accidental. Think about how many interpretations there can be from a pat on the shoulder. It could mean "congratulations," or "welcome back," or "way to go," or "I'm sorry," or "Hey, friend" (Lane, 2008).

Nonverbal clues mean different things to different people and cultures and can be interpreted in vastly different ways. Our facial expressions are perhaps one of the if not *the* most telling of our nonverbal clues. "One research team found that some facial expressions such as those conveying happiness, sadness, anger, disgust, and surprise were the same in 68 to 92 percent of all cultures examined" (Beebe, Beebe, and Redmond, 2008).

Proximity is also a strong nonverbal clue. Maybe you are not overly fond of a person who has approached you and you decide to keep your distance from him or her. Conversely, if a friend or confidant approaches you, you may move closer to him or her.

How do your physical actions influence your message?

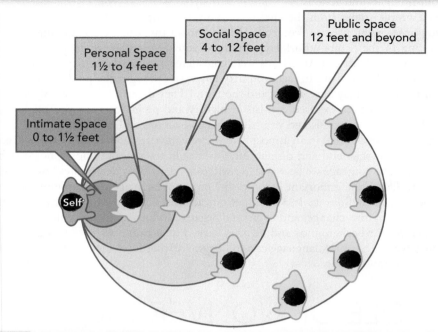

Figure 12.3   The Classification of Spatial Zones

Zone	Distance from Individaul	Example
1	0 feet–1½ feet	Communicatinig with our most intimate acquaintances
2	1½ feet–4 feet	Conversing with good friends and family members
3	4 feet–12 feet	Working in small groups and professional situations
4	12 feet and beyond	Public speaking situations

The rules vary from culture to culture, but consider the classification of spatial zones diagram in Figure 12.3, as described by interpersonal expert Edward T. Hall (1966).

Also consider the chart in Figure 12.4 describing more common nonverbal clues. As you study each action and example, try to determine what it would mean to you, based on your thoughts and cultural traditions.

Understanding forms of nonverbal communication and the cultural clues that can accompany them can greatly enhance your ability to establish effective interpersonal relationships and avoid conflicts caused by misunderstanding. As you grow in your ability to communicate effectively, work hard to hear the verbal message and learn to decode the nonverbal clues in conjunction with each other. This will help you establish a rich, rewarding communication environment.

COMPUTER MEDIATED COMMUNICATION

R U OTT (Are You Over the Top)?

Believe it or not, there was a time not too long ago when there was no such term as *computer mediated communication* (CMC). There were no e-mails, Blackberries, iPhones, tablets, text messages, blogs, tweets, Facebook pages, or instant messages. OMG, YKM! No, we're not kidding you. As a matter of fact, it was not until a few years ago that the study of interpersonal communication even mentioned CMC. It was not considered to be a part of interpersonal communication at all. It was believed that interpersonal communication had to take place *in person*.

Figure 12.4   Nonverbal Communication

NONVERBAL ACTION	EXAMPLES	WHAT THEY COULD MEAN
Eye contact	Looking directly at someone Avoiding eye contact Fixed gaze	
Posture	Slumping Standing very erect Leaning forward when seated	
Facial expressions	Smiling/Frowning Squinted eyes Blank stare	
Clothing/Emblems	Well dressed and pressed Wrinkled and sloppy "Smelly"	
Artifacts	Jewelry Tattoos Body/Facial piercings	
Gestures	Waving arms Fingers pointed toward person Crossed arms	
Touch	Patting someone on the back Firm handshake Weak handshake	

Today, it is widely considered that CMC is a vital subcategory of interpersonal communication studies. "There is some evidence that those wishing to communicate a message to someone, such as a message ending a relationship, may select a less-rich communication message—they may be more likely to send a letter or an e-mail rather than share the bad news face-to-face" (Beebe, 2008). Technology has become an integral part of our communication strategies.

Some may ask, can CMC really be considered "interpersonal" when you are not meeting face-to-face with another person? The answer is "yes." Why? Because in today's rich CMC environment, we can *infer or imply emotions* as we send and receive electronic communication. For example, we use symbols such as 😊 to indicate happiness or funny and 😞 to indicate sad or upset. We use abbreviations such as LOL (for laugh out loud). We even SCREAM AT OTHERS or SPEAK WITH EMPHASIS when we use all capital letters in our communication. Additionally, many people have cameras connected to their computers, and the sender and receiver can see each other's facial expressions on the screen. Therefore, emotions can be conveyed through CMC, although there are not as many nonverbal clues to view and interpret as in face-to-face communication (Lane, 2008). Because we cannot see all the nonverbal clues associated with face-to-face communications, we are more likely to misunderstand the message when using CMC.

> "The information superhighway is clearly not just a road for moving data from one place to another, but a roadside where people can pass each other, occasionally meet, and decide to travel together."
>
> —Beebe, Beebe, and Redmond

BRING the *Change*

TIPS FOR PERSONAL SUCCESS

Consider the following tips for using CMC (e-mails, text and instant messaging, etc.):

■ Never send an electronic message that you would not want the public to see. They are not private and quite difficult, if not impossible, to destroy. If you put things in writing that attack or libel other people, you could be sued.

■ When using CMC, choose your words carefully. You cannot change them once the "send" button has been pressed.

■ Never send CMC when you are angry, frustrated, or stressed. Even if you write a message when you're angry, wait at least 24 to 48 hours before you consider sending it.

Now, it is your turn. Create a list of at least three more tips that you would offer a fellow classmate to assist him or her with using CMC more effectively.

1. _____

_____

2. _____

_____

3. _____

_____

The fact that we are not face-to-face does not seem to negatively affect our communication efforts via technology. Several studies suggest that CMC relationships differ very little from those who meet face-to-face. Further research also suggests that CMC relationships may even be stronger than face-to-face relationships because people using CMC ask more pointed and direct questions, reveal more about themselves, and communicate more frequently (Tidwell and Walther, 2002; Walther and Burgoon, 1992). Think about the last time you revealed something online that you may have never revealed to that person face-to-face.

There can be a downside and some challenges to CMC, however. For years, communication experts have worried about the effects of electronic communication on the entire communication process, especially traditional interpersonal communication. In today's technologically advanced world, we do not have to speak to anyone if we don't want to. We purchase gasoline at the pump, pay for groceries at self-checkout, use automated tellers to get money, go to Amazon or iTunes to purchase our music and books, search e-Bay for sale items, and text others rather than pick up the phone or visit someone. Social isolation is a major concern, and you have to work hard to guard against becoming *emotionally detached* and *technologically reclusive.*

When deciding which communication channel to use, consider Figure 12.5 for the timeline of delivery, richness of your message, and control over the outcome. Do you want to say "I love you" via Facebook or in person? Would you rather hear "I'm sorry" over the phone or in an e-mail? Would you approach your instructor about an extension for a project in person or with a text message? These are decisions faced by today's communicators.

You will have to discover how you want to deliver your message and understand there is no "one best way" for any communication effort. What works well and is effective for you and John in situation Y may not work well or be effective for you and Jane in situation X. What works well with someone from your own culture, sex, or religion may not work well with

Figure 12.5 Choosing Your Communication Path

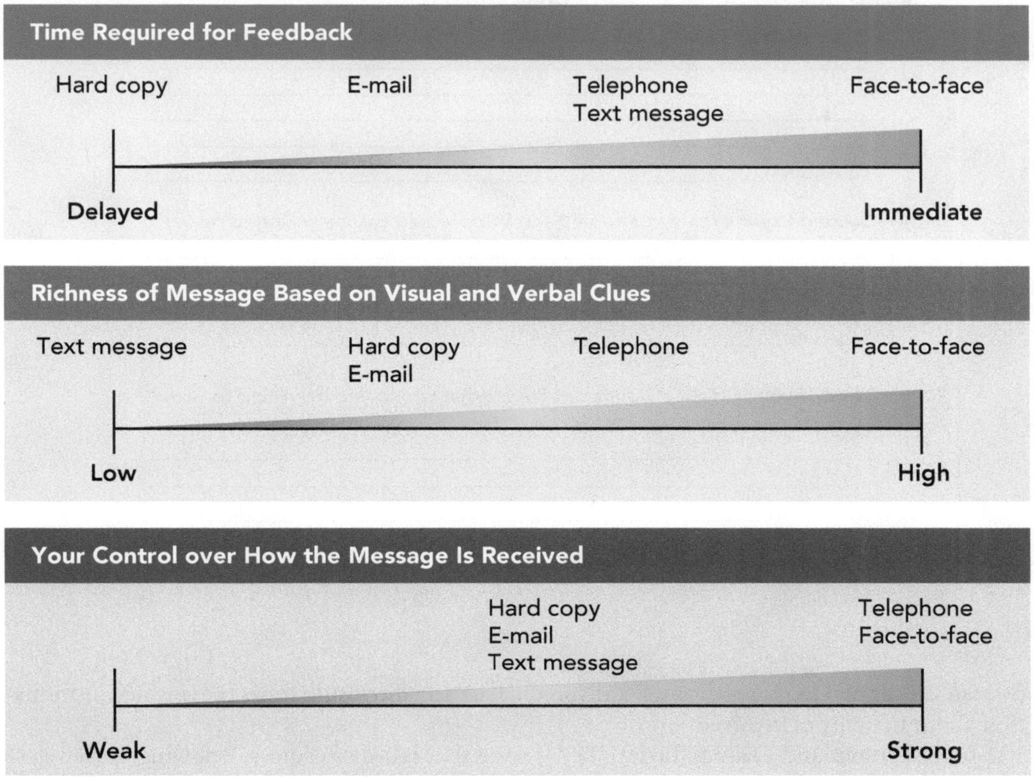

Time Required for Feedback

| Hard copy | E-mail | Telephone Text message | Face-to-face |

Delayed ——————————————————————————— Immediate

Richness of Message Based on Visual and Verbal Clues

| Text message | Hard copy E-mail | Telephone | Face-to-face |

Low ——————————————————————————— High

Your Control over How the Message Is Received

| | Hard copy E-mail Text message | | Telephone Face-to-face |

Weak ——————————————————————————— Strong

Source: Based on Adler, Rosenfeld, and Proctor (2010).

someone from another culture, sex, or religion. A communication path that works well for you in one situation may turn out horribly in another. In today's technologically advanced communication environment, you will have to make these decisions based on your experiences, knowledge of the media, and message to be conveyed.

SELF-DISCLOSURE AND INTERPERSONAL COMMUNICATION

Are You Willing to Let Others into Your Life?

Self-disclosure is how much you are willing to share with others about your life, your goals, your dreams, your fears, and your set-backs. Often, self-disclosure determines the quality of your interpersonal relationships. The level of self-disclosure is up to you, and it can vary from *insignificant* facts (I had dinner at O'Toole's last night or I'm a Leo) to *informational* facts (I'm majoring in history or I have two children) to *highly significant* facts (I'm fighting

"Good communicators don't use the same approach in every situation. They know that sometimes it's best to be blunt and sometimes tactful, that there is a time to speak up and a time to be quiet."
—Ronald Adler

"Confiding a secret to an unworthy person is like carrying grain in a bag with a hole in it."
—Ethiopian Proverb

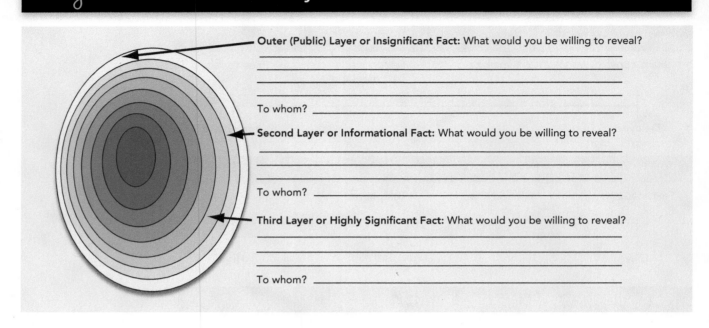

Figure 12.6 **The Third Layer**

Outer (Public) Layer or Insignificant Fact: What would you be willing to reveal?

_____
_____
_____
_____

To whom? _____

Second Layer or Informational Fact: What would you be willing to reveal?

_____
_____

To whom? _____

Third Layer or Highly Significant Fact: What would you be willing to reveal?

_____
_____

To whom? _____

BLOOM LEVEL 1

ovarian cancer or I'm going through a divorce). True self-disclosure must present new information about the parties involved.

Irwin Altman and Dalmas Taylor (1973) state that self-disclosure is "showing ourselves to others on a conscious and unconscious level." They use the analogy of an onion and suggest that you think of your life with multiple layers. As you know, an onion has layer after layer, each hidden beneath the other. The outer layer is different from the inner layers and is only the covering of what lies inside—much like our clothes are a covering for what is inside us. The skin of an onion is easily peeled away. The further you peel into the onion, the smaller it becomes and the more protected those inner layers are. We too have many layers and we can choose to "peel" them away or keep them all intact.

Consider Figure 12.6. What would you be willing to reveal (peel away) about yourself, and to whom would you feel comfortable revealing this information?

Everyone has more than three layers, but this figure gives you a good example of how you can peel away layers to let others know you more intimately. By self-disclosing and getting past your outer layers, you can enrich the quality of your relationships with others and also strengthen your own self-concept. You must, however, self-disclose (tell the truth) to yourself before you can ever self-disclose to others. Without personal and interpersonal self-disclosure, you cannot have mature, intimate, well-developed, sincere interpersonal relationships because your inner life remains hidden.

THE TIES THAT BIND

How Can You Strengthen Your Relationships with Friends?

Think about your best friend. How did you meet? In class? Through another person? By chance? What was the force that brought you together? More importantly, what is the "glue" that holds you together? If you compare your relationships with your closest friends, you will probably recognize that honest communication, self-disclosure, and trust are paramount in these relationships. You can't choose your family, but you can, and do, choose your friends.

So, why are friendships important? Friendships can bring a plethora of joys, including comfort, understanding, a loyal confidant, and a listening ear. They give you someone to talk with about happiness and sorrow and someone to laugh with when things are funny. You can share your hopes and dreams and fears with good friends. Take a moment and list the qualities that you like in your close friends. Consider the emotional, intellectual, spiritual, and physical aspects of friendship.

> "The worst solitude is to be destitute of sincere friendship."
> —Francis Bacon

_____

_____

_____

_____

_____

_____

When making new friends, consider adding people to your life who:

- Treat you kindly, fairly, and equally
- Bring new and different ideas and experiences to your life
- May be very different from friends you have had in the past
- Have ambition and courage and are outgoing and adventurous
- Have healthy work habits, strong ethics, and take pride in their character
- Enjoy learning new things
- Have found their goals and mission in life

APPRECIATING DIVERSITY

How Can You Strengthen Your Relationship with People of Diverse Backgrounds?

A few pages back, you read about the rule of communication suggesting that if you are in the presence of another person, ***you are communicating.*** It is inescapable. It is also inescapable that we all live in a diverse world with people from different socioeconomic, cultural, religious, and ideological backgrounds. The U.S. culture is one of the most diverse of any on earth! We are a nation of immigrants that still welcomes people from all over the world to its shores.

This fact is one of our greatest strengths, because ideas from all over the world come together in an environment that allows anyone to pursue his or her dreams and ambitions. On the other hand, all this diversity is accompanied by the problems of throwing so many people from diverse cultures together and expecting them to function together as one society. In a society such as ours, it is almost inevitable that prejudice will arise. However, by understanding what it means to live in a diverse society, we can learn how to communicate more effectively and hopefully learn more about the cultures and traditions of others.

What Are Ethnocentrism and Xenocentrism?

Many people truly believe that they are not prejudiced against any group and that they have no stereotypes in their thought processes about certain groups of people. If we dig deep enough,

> *"We don't see things as they are, we see things as we are."*
>
> —Anaïs Nin

however, we would find that most of us have some kind of prejudices and that we all discriminate in some ways. Because many of us have lived in rather homogeneous neighborhoods and primarily hang out with people "like us," we tend to be ***ethnocentric,*** believing that our particular ethnic background is superior and tending to stay with "our kind."

Ethnocentrism suggests that we tend to fear people from other ethnic backgrounds or we lump them together and view them ***as a group*** rather than ***as individuals.*** We don't think that their culture, religion, or race could possibly be as important or worthwhile as our own. Think about the ramifications to your own life if you were judged by "your group" of people instead of as an individual—if everyone judged you *as a woman* and not as Suzanne; if everyone judged you *as a Northerner* and not as Joe; if everyone judged you *as a Pentecostal* and not as Raymond; if everyone judged you *as a lesbian* and not as Sandra.

Think about the negative terms many people use to describe just a few practices from other cultures:

"People in England drive on the **wrong** side of the road."

"The Islamic language is written and read **backward.**"

"Europeans use the **wrong kind** of money."

"Africans dress **funny.**"

"Asians eat **weird** things."

"Arabs listen to **strange** music."

Ask yourself this: "Is it really wrong?" "Is it really backward?" "Is it really weird?" Or are these customs simply ***different*** from your own? You know the true answer.

Xenocentrism is the opposite of ethnocentrism in that one believes that other cultures are superior to one's own culture and that one's own culture has very little value or nothing to offer. Some people use xenocentrism as an "overcorrection" for their ethnocentrism. This can be just as dangerous as ethnocentrism because once again, we cut ourselves off from learning from everyone and everything we encounter. All people, places, cultures, religions, races, genders, and orientations have something to offer. It does not mean that we have to accept and embrace every idea or characteristic from every person or every culture, but being an educated citizen does mean learning to listen, evaluate, analyze, and then make our decisions.

What Are the Dimensions of Diversity?

Among the kinds of diversity you might encounter are race, religion, gender, age, ethnic groups, nationality, cultural, sexual orientation, social class, geographic region, and physical challenges. It is important for you to become open to individuals in all dimensions of diversity. The most significant thing you can do is to think of people who have different backgrounds than you as individuals, not as a group. Some of you will need to make bigger changes in your overall belief system than others; it all depends on what kind of background you came from and what experiences you have had. Figure 12.7 shows some of the dimensions of diversity.

Have you ever made a snap judgment about something unfamiliar to you?

iStockPhoto

Figure 12.7   The Dimensions of Diversity

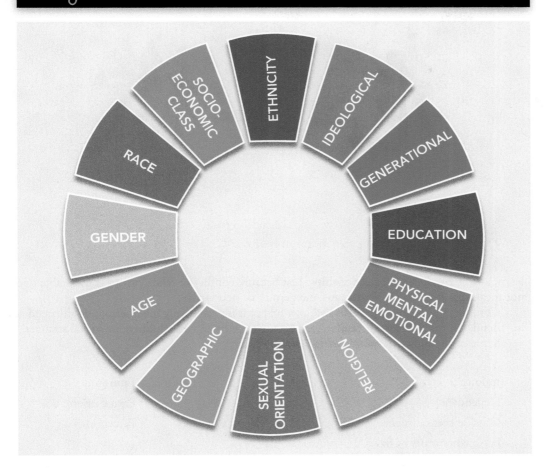

CONFLICT IN RELATIONSHIPS IS INEVITABLE

Why Is It Important to Learn How You Deal with Conflict?

Many people intensely dislike conflict and will go to extreme measures to avoid it. On the other hand, some people seem to thrive on conflict and enjoy creating situations that put people at odds with each other. While in college, you certainly will not be sheltered from conflicts. In fact, on a college campus, where a very diverse population lives and learns together, conflict is likely to arise on a regular basis. The simple truth is, conflict is pervasive throughout our culture, and you simply cannot avoid having some confrontations with other people. Therefore, you should not try to avoid conflict; rather, you can use it to create better relationships by exploring workable solutions—hopefully win–win solutions.

Consider the Chinese symbol for *conflict* in Figure 12.8. You will see that it is made up of two different symbols: **danger** and **hidden opportunity.** Why? Because when you are engaged in a conflict, you have the potential to enter into *dangerous* territory. Violence, alienation, and irreparable damage could be caused. However, you also have the ***hidden opportunity*** to grow,

Figure 12.8 **Chinese Symbol for Conflict**

Danger

Hidden Opportunity

learn, and strengthen your relationships. Just because conflict in relationships is inevitable does not mean that it has to be permanent, dangerous, or destructive.

Conflict can occur in any relationship, whether it is with family members, your girlfriend or boyfriend, your best friend, a roommate, a spouse or partner, your children, or a total stranger. Some of the causes of ***relationship tensions*** include:

Jealousy	Honesty	Emotions
Dependency	Culture	Sexual orientation
Outside commitments	Opinions, values, or beliefs	Perceptions
Personality traits or flaws	Affiliations	

Dealing with Conflict

Conflict does not happen in just one form. Conflict can be personal or situational. There are several ways that people deal with issues. They include the following:

- **Blowing your lid.** This involves screaming, uncontrolled anger, hurling insults, and being unwilling to listen.

- **Shunning.** This involves shutting the other person out and being unwilling to engage in any type of communication or resolution.

- **Sarcasm.** This involves using stinging remarks to make the other person feel small, unimportant, insignificant, or stupid.

- **Mocking.** This involves using past experiences or words to mock or ridicule the other person, laughing or poking fun at him or her or the situation.

- **Civility.** This involves sitting down and logically, rationally discussing the issues or problems and trying to come to a win–win solution (adapted from Baxter, 1993).

from ORDINARY to *Extraordinary*

Vivian Wong
Founder, Global Trading Consortium, Greenville, South Carolina

I WAS A very young woman and a new wife when my husband began talking about coming to the United States in the early 1960s. We dreamed of living in our own house with a yard rather than a flat as we did in China. We were working as front desk clerks in a Hong Kong hotel when fate intervened in the person of Robert Wilson, who was in China marketing his Barbeque King grills. We told him about our dream, and he decided to help us. Many people would have never followed through, but Mr. Wilson gave us $100 and told us to get photos made and to acquire passports. He promised to work on a visa for us. It took a year for us to finally be granted a trainee visa, and we headed to Greenville, South Carolina, to work for Mr. Wilson, leaving our little girl behind with her grandparents.

In South Carolina we trained and learned to sell Barbeque King grills in China. After about 10 months, we were very homesick for China, so we went home. We realized after we got to Hong Kong that our hearts were really in the United States because now we were homesick for Greenville. Without even realizing it, the United States had become our home. Mr. Wilson brought us back and this time, we brought our little girl.

In 1967 we were blessed with twin girls, and in 1968 we were given a permanent visa and U.S. citizenship. I often say, "We spent the first 20 years in America simply trying to earn a meager living and put food on the table." We didn't want to work for other people the rest of our lives, so we began to look around to try to figure out what kind of edge we had that we could use to start our own business in Greenville. In 1970, with Mr. Wilson as a partner, we opened our first business, a Chinese restaurant, but before we opened, my husband spent two years in Washington, D.C., training for restaurant ownership. We opened other restaurants in 1975, 1976, and 1988. By now, I could put food on the table, and I wanted to do something other than sell egg rolls.

> *We spent the first 20 years in America simply trying to earn a meager living and put food on the table.*

I became very interested in commercial real estate and began to learn everything I could. Today I own several hotels in the United States, and I am starting a chain in China with my brother. This chain will be called Hotel Carolina and is aimed at business travelers. We found a niche that had not been tapped—a clean, reasonable, three-star hotel for business travelers who couldn't afford five-star accommodations. We also own and operate a large business park and foreign trade zone in Greenville, South Carolina. We are partners and franchisees of the Medicine Shoppe, China's first American pharmacy.

I am also a partner in three banks located in Greenville, Atlanta, and Myrtle Beach. People ask me how I know how to own and manage such a disparate collection of businesses. My answer is simple: "I know how to connect the dots; this is what I do best." I also believe strongly in networking and communicating with partners and people who know how to get things done. I have partners all over the world in a great variety of businesses. I have developed the vision, action plans, and good teams to make things happen. I take nothing for granted!

We have been very blessed to live in the United States and now to open businesses in our native land. In this wonderful country, we have succeeded beyond our wildest dreams! So can you!

EXTRAORDINARY REFLECTION

Read the following statement and respond in your online journal or class notebook.

Mrs. Wong mentions how important it is to establish relationships, communicate, and network with other people. How can communication, networking, and strong relationships help you in your chosen field?

Successful Decisions
AN ACTIVITY FOR CRITICAL REFLECTION

In a meeting for the American Institute of Architecture Students, John made a suggestion that the council sponsor a fundraiser to send the officers to a design workshop. His suggestion included having all members of the council participate in raising the funds even though only the officers would get to attend. This suggestion set Barry off and he began to talk very animatedly with a loud, intimidating voice about how this would be unfair to everyone who worked and didn't get to attend the workshop. He stood up and towered over John and continued to use abusive language.

Rather than fuel Barry's argument, John remained calm, and in a very quiet, controlled, but firm voice, said, "Barry, I understand your feelings, but what you need to realize is that next year you will be an officer, and all of us will be working to send you and your team. Why don't we move to another agenda item and come back to this one after we have all had time to collect our thoughts."

In your own words, what two suggestions would you give John to further help control the situation at hand?

1. _____
   _____
   _____
   _____

2. _____
   _____
   _____
   _____

THE FACES OF CONFLICT

Uggggh! How Do I Deal with Negative, Nasty, Difficult People?

We've all encountered them from time-to-time—difficult people who are negative, angry, unhappy, destructive, argumentative, sad, depressed, and judgmental. They are people who seem to walk around with a black cloud above their heads and seem to enjoy causing interpersonal conflict, like the negative people discussed in Chapter 3. They are likely to pop up everywhere—at work, in class, in traffic, in restaurants, and even in places of worship. They cannot be avoided. Figure 12.9 profiles the most common type of negative, difficult people. Perhaps you recognize some of them. Read the descriptions, and try to develop at least two to three strategies to effectively deal with each type of difficult person. In developing your strategies, you may have to rely on others in your class for assistance, pull from your past experiences (what worked and what did not), and do some research on your own.

Learning to manage conflict and interact with difficult people are very important steps in developing sound communication practices and healthy relationships. If you can learn to stay calm, put yourself in the other person's shoes, and try to find mutually beneficial solutions, you will gain admiration and respect from your friends, family, peers, and colleagues. As you consider conflicts in your life and relationships, take a moment and complete the Conflict Management Assessment (Figure 12.10) to determine your awareness of issues related to conflict and managing conflict.

Figure 12.9 **Types of Difficult Behaviors and People**		
TYPES OF DIFFICULT BEHAVIORS BY DIFFICULT PEOPLE	**DESCRIPTION**	**WHAT CAN YOU DO TO EFFECTIVELY DEAL WITH THEM?**
Gossiping	They don't do a lot of work, but would rather spread rumors and untruths about others to make themselves feel better.	_____ _____ _____ _____
Manipulating	The person who constantly tries to negotiate every aspect of life: "I'll do this for you if you do this for me."	_____ _____ _____ _____
Showing Off	They usually talk more than they work. They know everything about every subject and are not willing to listen to anything or anybody new.	_____ _____ _____ _____
Goofing Off	They usually do very little, and what they do is incorrect. They pretend to be involved, but spend time looking busy more than actually being busy.	_____ _____ _____ _____
Standing By	They do not get involved in anything or any cause, but then complain because something did not go their way.	_____ _____ _____ _____
Complaining	They may produce work and be involved, but complain about everything and everybody and seem to exist under a rain cloud. Nothing is ever good enough.	_____ _____ _____ _____
Dooming and Glooming	They are so negative they make death look like a joy ride. They are constantly thinking about the worst-case scenario and don't mind voicing it.	_____ _____ _____ _____

Figure 12.10 Conflict Management Assessment

Read the following questions carefully and respond according to the key below. Take your time and be honest with yourself.

1 = NEVER typical of the way I address conflict

2 = SOMETIMES typical of the way I address conflict

3 = OFTEN typical of the way I address conflict

4 = ALMOST ALWAYS typical of the way I address conflict

1. When someone verbally attacks me, I can let it go and move on.	1	2	3	4
2. I would rather resolve an issue than have to "be right" about it.	1	2	3	4
3. I try to avoid arguments and verbal confrontations at all costs.	1	2	3	4
4. Once I've had a conflict with someone, I can forget it and get along with that person just fine.	1	2	3	4
5. I look at conflicts in my relationships as positive growth opportunities.	1	2	3	4
6. When I'm in a conflict, I will try many ways to resolve it.	1	2	3	4
7. When I'm in a conflict, I try not to verbally attack or abuse the other person.	1	2	3	4
8. When I'm in a conflict, I try never to blame the other person; rather, I look at every side.	1	2	3	4
9. When I'm in a conflict, I try not to avoid the other person.	1	2	3	4
10. When I'm in a conflict, I try to talk through the issue with the other person.	1	2	3	4
11. When I'm in a conflict, I often feel empathy for the other person.	1	2	3	4
12. When I'm in a conflict, I do not try to manipulate the other person.	1	2	3	4
13. When I'm in a conflict, I try never to withhold my love or affection for that person.	1	2	3	4
14. When I'm in a conflict, I try never to attack the person; I concentrate on his or her actions.	1	2	3	4
15. When I'm in a conflict, I try to never insult the other person.	1	2	3	4
16. I believe in give and take when trying to resolve a conflict.	1	2	3	4
17. I understand and use the concept that kindness can solve more conflicts than cruelty.	1	2	3	4
18. I am able to control my defensive attitude when I'm in a conflict.	1	2	3	4
19. I keep my temper in check and do not yell and scream during conflicts.	1	2	3	4
20. I am able to accept "defeat" at the end of a conflict.	1	2	3	4

Number of 1s _____ Number of 2s _____ Number of 3s _____ Number of 4s _____

If you have mostly 1s, you do not handle conflict very well and have few tools for conflict management. You have a tendency to anger quickly and lose your temper during the conflict.

If you have mostly 2s, you have a tendency to want to work through conflict, but you lack the skills to carry this tendency through. You can hold your temper for a while, but eventually it gets the best of you.

If you have mostly 3s, you have some useful skills in handling conflict. You tend to work very hard for a peaceful and mutually beneficial outcome for all parties.

If you have mostly 4s, you are very adept at handling conflict and do well with mediation, negotiation, and anger management. You are approachable; people turn to you for advice about conflicts and resolutions.

© Robert M. Sherfield

STANDARDS FOR DEALING WITH DIFFICULT PEOPLE AND MANAGING CONFLICT

- Check your own behavior before anything else. Don't become the same type of difficult person as the ones with whom you are dealing. Fighting fire with fire will only make the flame hotter. Learn to be the "cool" one.

- Don't take the other person's attitude or words personally. Most of the time, the person doesn't know you or your life.

- Avoid physical contact with others at every expense.

- If you must give criticism, do so with a positive tone and attitude.

- Remember that everyone is sensitive about themselves and their situations. Avoid language that will set someone off.

- Do not verbally attack the other person; simply state your case and your ideas.

- Allow the other person to save face. Give the person a way to escape embarrassment. People may forgive you for stepping on their toes, but they will never forgive you for stepping on their feelings.

- If you have a problem with someone or someone's actions, be specific and let him or her know before it gets out of hand. People can't read your mind.

- If someone shows signs of becoming physically aggressive toward you, get help early, stay calm, talk slowly and calmly to the other person, and if necessary, walk away to safety.

- Allow the other person to vent fully before you begin any negotiation or resolution.

- Try to create "win–win" situations, where everyone can walk away having gained something.

- Determine if the conflict is a "person" conflict or a "situation" conflict.

- Ask the other person what he or she needs. Try to understand the situation.

- Realize that you may very well be "in the wrong."

- When dealing with conflict and other people, ask yourself, "If this were my last action on earth, would I be proud of how I acted?"

DID YOU Know?

DITH PRAN was born in 1942 in Cambodia. He learned English and French and worked for the U.S. government as a translator, then for a British film crew, and then as a hotel receptionist. In 1975, after meeting a *New York Times* reporter, he taught himself how to take pictures.

After U.S. forces left Cambodia, he stayed behind to cover the fall of Phnom Penh to the communist Khmer Rouge. Having stayed behind, he was forced to remain in Cambodia while foreign reporters were allowed to leave. From this point, Dith witnessed many atrocities and had to hide the fact that he was educated or knew any Americans. He pretended to be a taxicab driver.

Cambodians were forced to work in labor camps and Dith was not immune. He endured four years of starvation and torture before Vietnam overthrew the Khmer Rouge and he escaped the camp. He coined the term "The Killing Fields" because of the number of dead bodies he encountered during his escape. He later learned that his three brothers and 50 members of his family were killed during the genocide.

Dith escaped to Thailand in 1979, fearing for his life because of his association with Americans and his knowledge of what had happened. He moved to America in 1980. In 1984, the movie *The Killing Fields* was released, detailing the horrors and triumphs of his life. He died of pancreatic cancer in 2008.

PHOTO: Richard B. Levine/Newscom

REFLECTIONS ON INTERPERSONAL COMMUNICATION AND CONFLICT MANAGEMENT

In today's fast-paced, ever-changing, cell phone–addicted, text message–crazy, pay-at-the-pump, "don't have to talk to anyone unless I want to," action-packed world, it is easy to forget that communication is paramount in so many areas of your life. From building healthy and meaningful relationships with your fellow students to talking to your instructors to managing conflict, few tools will ever give you the power to affect change more than effective interpersonal communication skills.

By working to improve your interpersonal communication skills, your appreciation of diversity, and your conflict management skills, you will see the relationships in your life begin to change and improve. Properly nourished and cultivated relationships will grow from superficial, insignificant encounters to powerful, meaningful bonds where trust, honesty, and maturity are commonplace. As you continue on in your studies and work toward personal and professional growth, consider the following ideas related to interpersonal communication and conflict management:

- Work every day to strengthen your interpersonal communication skills.
- Use computer mediated communication in conjunction with face-to-face communication.
- Strive to let people into your life by "turning off" technology from time to time.
- Work hard to understand all aspects of your own life and develop a positive sense of self.
- Peel away "layers" and let people into your life through self-disclosure.
- Develop and welcome relationships with people from a variety of backgrounds.
- Maintain close friendships through honesty and loyalty.
- Learn to manage conflict instead of ignoring or running from it.

"Everything we shut our eyes to, everything we run away from, everything we deny, denigrate or despise, serves to defeat us in the end. What seems nasty, painful, and evil can become a source of beauty, joy, and strength, if faced with an open mind."

—Henry Miller

Knowledge
in Bloom

MANAGING CONFLICT IN INTERPERSONAL RELATIONSHIPS

Utilizes levels 1–6 of the taxonomy

Each chapter-end assessment is based on Bloom's Taxonomy of Learning. See pages xxvi–xxviii in the front of this book for a quick review.

Explanation: Read the following brief case study. After you have familiarized yourself with the situation, work through each level of Bloom's Taxonomy to discuss, analyze, and solve the conflict.

Case: My (*choose one:* boyfriend, girlfriend, husband, wife, partner, best friend) is a nice person. Most of the time, he/she is very affectionate and passionate toward me. He/she is supportive of my career, and most of the time, we get along well. However, it seems that when something goes wrong or he/she gets angry or stressed, I am the person who receives the brunt of his/her aggression, regardless of the cause. He/she can become very verbally abusive, sometimes yelling, screaming, cursing, and hurling insults. Sometimes, I just get the "silent treatment." On certain occasions, he/she has used personal and private information that I shared with him/her to hurt me or insult me. He/she has never physically abused me, but I sometimes worry that the verbal aggression may turn into physical aggression. I'm not sure what to do or what to make of this situation.

Procedure: Answer the following questions related to the case from each level of Bloom's Taxonomy. Be specific and use the information from this chapter, your own experiences, and outside research to aid in your responses.

Bloom Level	Question	Response
Level 1 Remember	In your own words, define the conflict(s) and the cause(s).	_____ _____ _____ _____ _____ _____ _____
Level 2 Understand	Identify at least three major problems with this interpersonal relationship.	1. _____ _____ 2. _____ _____ 3. _____ _____

Bloom Level	Question	Response
Level 3 Apply	What solutions would you offer to both parties?	_____ _____ _____ _____ _____ _____ _____ _____ _____
Level 4 Analyze	Compare and contrast this interpersonal relationship with a healthier, more mature, productive relationship.	_____ _____ _____ _____ _____ _____ _____ _____
Level 5 Evaluate	Develop a brief argument as to why you think this relationship is more the norm than exception.	_____ _____ _____ _____ _____ _____ _____ _____
Level 6 Create	Develop/design a plan that you would make this situation better. List at least five positive steps to bring about change.	1. _____ _____ _____ 2. _____ _____ _____ 3. _____ _____ _____ 4. _____ _____ _____ 5. _____ _____ _____

SQ3R MASTERY STUDY SHEET

EXAMPLE QUESTION (*from page 308*) What are the six elements of the communication process?	**ANSWER:**
EXAMPLE QUESTION (*from page 315*) What is self-disclosure and why is it important for healthy relationships?	**ANSWER:**
AUTHOR QUESTION (*from page 309*) Why is interpersonal communication important to your professional growth?	**ANSWER:**
AUTHOR QUESTION (*from page 312*) What is computer mediated communication (CMC)?	**ANSWER:**
AUTHOR QUESTION (*from page 314*) In your own words, define "technological recluse."	**ANSWER:**
AUTHOR QUESTION (*from page 317*) Define ethnocentrism and give one example.	**ANSWER:**
AUTHOR QUESTION (*from page 319*) Discuss at least two strategies for managing conflict.	**ANSWER:**
YOUR QUESTION (*from page ___*)	**ANSWER:**
YOUR QUESTION (*from page ___*)	**ANSWER:**
YOUR QUESTION (*from page ___*)	**ANSWER:**
YOUR QUESTION (*from page ___*)	**ANSWER:**
YOUR QUESTION (*from page ___*)	**ANSWER:**

Finally, after answering these questions, recite in your mind the major points covered here. Consider the following general questions to help you master this material.

- What was it about?
- What does it mean?
- What was the most important thing you learned? Why?
- What were the key points to remember?

chapter thirteen

PLAN

CREATING A DYNAMIC EMPLOYMENT PACKAGE AND JOB SEARCH PLAN

"No one can tell you what your life's work is, but it is important that you find it. There is a part of you that already knows; affirm that part."
—Willis W. Harman

PLAN

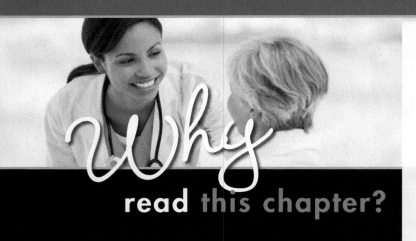

Why read this chapter?

Because you'll learn:

- How to make yourself a desirable employee
- About cover letters and resumés
- Important tips for having a dynamic interview

Because you'll be able to:

- Use the D.O.C.T.O.R. system to write a powerful cover letter and resumé
- Use the R.E.W.A.R.D.S. system to prepare for an interview
- Write a compelling thank you note

Scan and QUESTION

Take a few moments, **scan this chapter**, and on page 367, write **five questions** that you think will be important to your mastery of this material. You will also find five questions listed from your authors.

Example:

☑ **Why is it important to write an excellent resumé?** (from page 338)

☑ **What does D.O.C.T.O.R. stand for?** (from page 338)

MyStudentSuccessLab

MyStudentSuccessLab (www.mystudentsuccesslab.com) is an online solution designed to help you "Start strong, Finish stronger" by building skills for ongoing personal and professional development.

Name: Zack Karper

Institution: Honor Graduate! The Art Institute of Philadelphia

Major: Digital Film and Video Production

Age: 21

Career: Head of Video Production, Dream Camp Foundation (www.buggleproductions.com)

My childhood was filled with trouble. It is hard to think of it, much less speak of it. I had little direction and no future. I did not respect authority, began missing school, and fell into the "wrong" crowd. My life was headed in a direction where the ending was not going to be good. I was then asked, and decided to attend, the Patane Foundation's first "Dream Camp" for challenged youth, and my life changed forever. At the camp, I found support, advice, guidance, love, and a sense of my own future. I also learned how to produce movies and eventually found that not only was I good at it, but that I loved it!

After camp, I decided to enroll at The Art Institute of Philadelphia to major in digital film and video production, never realizing that soon I would return to the camp that changed my life to be a part of the change in others' lives. Today, I am head of the newly named Dream Camp Foundation's video production arm, Buggle Productions. We film almost all of the foundation's nonprofit activities.

The biggest challenge in attending college was adapting to a new life and being on my own. I had to learn how to manage my day and leave enough time for rest and sleep. I learned how to create lists and plan out my days. I posted the lists so that I could see them daily. This helped me develop a schedule that worked for me.

During my time at The Art Institute of Philadelphia, I learned how to push myself and get out of my comfort zone. I learned how to actually do things and not just talk about doing things. I did not waste my time on partying and mindless activities. I began to explore new avenues and seek new skills that would carry me into the future. By learning how to step outside my comfort zone, I learned how to become who and what I wanted to be. I was no longer the person others wanted me to be. By focusing on my career and my future, my life began to change. I never dreamed that I could be an award-winning filmmaker. But with hard work and perseverance, I won awards at school, nationally, and internationally. Some of my films have received recognition and won awards at film festivals in Colorado, New Jersey, California, and even the International Youth Film Festival in England!

The biggest lesson that I learned in college was to treat every project, whether a paper, a speech, or a film, as if it was your baby. Nurture it. Care for it. Feed it. Make it great and never raise it halfway. Give your baby your all. Today, as Head of Video Production at Buggle Productions, I live my dream of working in film and I get to help troubled kids who were in the same shoes I was in. I get to make a difference.

1. Zack mentioned that he had some things in his past to overcome. What areas of your past will you have to overcome to be successful in your chosen field?

2. Zack has won many awards for his work in documentary film. What are your hopes and dreams for your future? What do you hope to accomplish with your education and degree?

PLANNING FOR THE FUTURE

What Am I Going to Do for the Rest of My Life?

"What am I going to do for the rest of my life?" is an overwhelming question for anyone, especially in a dramatically changing, global, technologically driven environment. What was true last year—and sometimes even last week—is no longer true. While many things that worked for your parents and grandparents are still important and relevant today—like ethics, integrity, hard work, education, honesty, teamwork—many practices that were true in their times are no longer valid. Your grandfather may have gone to work for a company and stayed there all his life. Employers were loyal to employees, and employees were loyal to their employers. Work stayed pretty much the same one year to the next. All that has changed. You will have many different jobs during your lifetime—you will most likely have three or four different careers, and what constitutes your work will be constantly changing.

> "The four great questions: Why are you here? Where have you been? Where are you going? What difference will you make?"
>
> —Hal Simon

WORKIN' 9 TO 5—OR TRYING TO

Is It Really Possible to Sell Yourself Through a Cover Letter and Resumé?

You've got it all together—education, experience, and a strong sense of self. A positive attitude. What do you do now? How do you pull all of this together? How do you find the job of your dreams? The job for which you have prepared?

Know this! Getting a job—the **right job**—is hard work! Regardless of your status in school, now is the time to begin your job search. If you are in the last months of your program, your job search should be a top priority. If you are just beginning your educational plan, it is never too early to begin assembling a dynamic employment package.

Selling Yourself

Remember the old saying "You are what you eat"? When searching for a professional position, you could change that to read "You are what you write." Most likely, the people conducting the job search have never met you and know nothing about you except what you provide to them. A carefully crafted resumé communicates your past history (skills and experience) that makes you the ideal candidate for their position. Your resumé is the first marketing piece and in many cases must stand alone when a recruiter is determining whether to interview you. Just as a well-designed and written resumé can be a wonderful first step, a poorly designed and written resumé can doom you before you ever leave

What changes do you foresee coming in your chosen career field in the next five years?

Getty RF

your house. A good thing to remember is this: A resumé gets you the interview; the interview gets you the job. Although there is no single way to develop your career resumé and formats may vary from discipline to discipline, this chapter will outline the key components of resumés and discuss how to develop a resumé that will represent your best efforts.

Your second "advertising tool" is your cover letter. A cover letter is basically an expansion of your resumé. A cover letter gives you the chance to link your resumé, skills, and experience together with your interest in a specific company's position. You will need to write many cover letters to make this link work properly; in other words, you most likely need to write a cover letter designed for each job for which you apply. Your cover letter will often be the stepping stone to get an employer to even look at your resumé. Consider it a "teaser," if you will, to all of your talents and experience. Just as you would never send someone a greeting card and not sign it, you would never send a resumé and not tell the person or committee *why* you sent it. Your cover letter tells why.

WRITE A POWERFUL AND CONCISE COVER LETTER

How Do You Get Your Foot in the Door?

Careful preparation must be done **prior to starting** the interview process. Two key elements of this preparation are your cover letter and resumé. Both are key components in your career search. A carefully crafted letter and resumé communicate your past history (education, skills, and experience) that makes you the ideal candidate for the position you are seeking. They are the first marketing pieces, and in many cases must stand alone when a recruiter is determining whether or not to interview you.

Whenever you send your resumé to a company, whether it is in response to a posted advertisement or it was requested, you must send a cover letter with it. Cover letters are extremely important; in fact, most recruiters say that they read four times as many cover letters as they do resumés, because if the cover letter does not "strike a chord," then they never look past it to the resumé.

Career development expert, author, and speaker Carolyn Robbins (2006) states, "During my 25 plus years that I've been involved in career development, I have found that of all the paperwork associated with job searching, cover letters give job searchers the most difficulty." The information presented below will help you overcome any anxiety associated with writing your cover letter or resumé. As you begin your cover letter and resumé process, consider the general tips in Figure 13.1.

Simply put, the cover letter's purpose is to get the interviewer to read your resumé. It sets the tone for who you are, what you have to offer, and what you want. "It screams—ever so politely—that you have the intelligence, experience, and soft skills to be the answer to an employer's staffing problem" (Britton-Whitcomb, 2003). The cover letter should say to the reader, "You have an opening and a detailed description of what you need and I can fill your opening and be the person who gets the job done—and done well."

Consider the following **four steps to success** when writing your cover letter:

1. **A effective cover letter will be *personally addressed and job specific.*** If at all possible (and yes, it is possible with just a little research), address your letter to a specific person. Avoid at all cost the dreaded "Dear Sir or Madam" or "To Whom It May Concern." In most cases, a phone call to the company will provide the name of the person, as well as his or her title and address. Always verify spelling, even with common names. This single step can set you apart from lazy job-seekers. Also, make sure you spell the company's name correctly.

2. **Once your letter is correctly addressed, your first paragraph should be an "attention grabber" and it should answer the question "Why am I writing?"** Susan Britton-Whitcomb, author of *Resumé Magic* (2003), calls this "the carrot." This simply means that your first paragraph has an interesting fact, an appeal, or maybe even a quote—something that makes the reader (hopefully, your future employer) read further. Your first paragraph should also have a

Figure 13.1   Successful Cover Letters and Resumés

- Both your resumé and cover letter *must be typed*. There are no exceptions to this rule. Ever! Seriously, EVER!

- Your cover letter and resumé must be printed on the same type and color of *fine-quality paper*. Cheap paper sends the message that you don't care. This is not the place or time to pinch pennies; buy excellent quality, 100 percent cotton stock, resumé-quality paper.

- Check your printer and be sure that the print quality is impeccable. Never send a cover letter or resumé with smudges, ink smears, or poor print quality.

- When you print your cover letter and resumé, be certain that the watermark on the paper is turned in the correct direction. Hold it up to the light and you will see the watermark embedded in the paper. This may sound silly and picky, but people notice attention to detail.

- Do not fold your cover letter or resumé. Purchase a packet of 9" × 13" envelopes in which to send your materials.

- Do not handwrite the address on the envelope. Use a label or type the address directly on the envelope. Remember, first impressions are important.

- Never send a generic photocopy of a cover letter or resumé, even on the finest paper.

- Layout, design, font, spacing, and color must be considered in the building of your cover letter and resumé.

- Unless you are specifically asked to do so, never discuss money or salary history in either your cover letter or resumé. This could work against you. When asked for a salary history, use ranges.

- Your resumé and cover letter must be free of errors. That's right, not one single error is acceptable, including grammar, spelling, punctuation, layout/spacing, dates, or content.

- Each cover letter must be signed in black or blue ink.

transition statement that makes the reader want to read on. For example, your last statement might read, "With a degree in medical assisting and four years experience at Desert Medical Center, I know that I can make a valued contribution to Grace Care Center."

3. **Your second (and maybe third) paragraph(s) should clearly state why you are qualified for the position you are seeking.** Use your cover letter to highlight those areas of your experience that specifically qualify you for the job. Your cover letter is not the time to list all of your qualifications, but to indicate the two or three components that most qualify you for the position and closely match the position announcement. You may also include specific attributes that may not be on your resumé. The keyword to consider here is your *value*. Relate your education, experience, and talents to the company's need. Mention facts and statistics of how you've been successful in the past. Remember, "Employers are not interested in you for your sake, but rather because of what you can bring to the organization. This might sound harsh, but businesspeople have an obligation to improve the success of their organization. If you consistently show how you can help them do this . . . they will be much more motivated to talk to you" (Farr and Kursmark, 2005).

4. **Your final paragraph should address the question of "Where do we go from here?"** Do not be ambiguous by saying something trite like "I hope to hear from you in the near future," or "If you have any questions please do not hesitate to call me." Remember, your job search is none of their business, nor is it their responsibility. Be proactive by stating that you will be following up with a phone call to discuss your resumé and experience(s) in more detail. Make sure that once you have told them that you are going to call that you actually do call.

Your final paragraph should also continue to express what you can do for the company. You should end your letter with a statement about your qualities and the company's needs such as, "Mr. Thompson, I will call you on Monday, January 24th at 11:30 a.m. to discuss how my past experiences can help streamline operations and continue superior patient care at Grace Care Center."

Don't forget to **sign your letter.** Figure 13.2 provides a sample cover letter and indicates the correct format and spacing to the left of the letter's content.

Figure 13.2 Sample Cover Letter with Formatting Information

Your name and address —→	**BENJAMIN SHAW**
Your name should be larger and/or in a different font to draw attention (then double space)	1234 Lake Shadow Drive (123) 555-1234 Maple City, PA 12345 Scott@bl.com
The date (then double space) —→	January 3, 2011
The specific person, title, and address to whom you are writing (then double space) —→	Mr. James Pixler, RN, CAN Director of Placement and Advancement Grace Care Center 123 Sizemore Street, Suite 444 Philadelphia, PA 12345
The formal salutation followed by a colon (then double space) —→	Dear Mr. Pixler:
Paragraph 1 (then double space) —→	Seven years ago, my mother was under the treatment of two incredible nurses at Grace Care Center in Philadelphia. My family and I agree that the care she was given was extraordinary. When I saw your ad in today's *Philadelphia Carrier*, I was extremely pleased to know that I now have the qualifications to be a part of the Grace Care Team as a Medical Assistant.
Paragraph 2 (then double space) —→	Next month, I will graduate with an Occupational Associate's Degree from Victory College of Health and Technology as a certified Medical Assistant. As my resumé indicates, I was fortunate to do my internship at Mercy Family Care Practice in Harrisburg. During this time, I was directly involved in patient care, records documentation, and family outreach.
Paragraph 3 (then double space) —→	As a part of my degree from Victory, I received a 4.0 in the following classes: • Management Communications • Microsoft Office (Word, Excel, Outlook, PowerPoint) • Business Communications I, II, III • Anatomy and Physiology I, II, III • Medical Coding I, II • Principles of Pharmacology • Immunology I, II, III, IV • Urinalysis and Body Fluids • Clinical Practicum I, II, III This, along with my past certificate in Medical Transcription and my immense respect for Grace Care Center, makes me the perfect candidate for your position.
Final paragraph or closing (then double space) —→	I have detailed all of my experience on the enclosed resumé. I will call you on Monday, January 24, at 11:30 a.m. to discuss how my education and experiences can help streamline operations and continue superior patient care at Grace. In the meantime, please feel free to contact me at the number above.
The complimentary close (then four spaces) —→	Sincerely,
Your handwritten signature in black or blue ink within the four spaces —→	*Benjamin Shaw*
Your typed name —→	Benjamin Shaw
Enclosure contents —→	Enclosure: Resumé

UNDERSTAND THE DO'S AND DON'TS OF MEMORABLE RESUMÉS

How Do You Sell Yourself?

Eight seconds. That is all you have to gain the attention of your potential employer, according to Susan Ireland, author and consultant (2003): "In eight seconds, an employer scans your resumé and decides whether she will invest more time to consider you as a job candidate. The secret to passing the eight-second test is to make your resumé look inviting and quick to read" (p. 14).

A resumé is the blueprint that details what you have accomplished with regards to education, experience, skills acquisition, workplace successes, and progressive responsibility and/or leadership. It is a painting (that you are able to "paint") of how your professional life looks. It is the ultimate advertisement of you! Your resumé must create interest and hopefully a *desire* to find out more about you!

As you begin to develop your resumé, make sure to allow plenty of time. Plan to enlist several qualified proofreaders to check your work. We cannot stress strongly enough the need for your resumé to be perfect. A simple typo or misuse of grammar can disqualify you from the job of your dreams. Don't allow a lack of attention to detail to stand between you and your future career.

Further, your resumé must be 100 percent completely accurate and truthful. Do not fabricate information or fudge dates to make yourself look better. It will only come back to haunt you in the long run. Dennis Reina, organizational psychologist and author of *Trust and Betrayal in the Workplace*, states, "I think that what you put in a resumé absolutely has to be rock-solid, concrete, and verifiable. If there are any questions, it will immediately throw both your application and your credibility into question" (Dresang, 2007). People have been fired from positions after they were hired because they misrepresented themselves on their resumé, cover letter, or application.

As you begin to build your resumé, remember to "call in the **D.O.C.T.O.R**."

D: Design

Visual **design** and format are imperative to a successful resumé. You need to think about the font that you plan to use; whether color is appropriate (usually, it is not); the use of bullets, lines, or shading; and where you are going to put information. You also need to pay attention to the text balance on the page (centered left/right, top/bottom). The visual aspect of your resumé will be the first impression. "Make it pretty" (Britton-Whitcomb, 2003).

O: Objective

Writing a clear and specific **objective** can help get your foot in the door. The reader, usually your potential employer, needs to be able to scan your resumé and gather as much detail as possible as quickly as possible. A job-specific objective can help. Consider the following two objectives:

- **Vague objective:** To get a job as an elementary school teacher in the Dallas Area School District
- **Specific objective:** To secure an elementary teaching position that will enable me to use my 14 years of creative teaching experience, curriculum development abilities, supervisory skills, and commitment to superior instruction in a team environment.

C: Clarity

Clarity is of paramount importance, especially when including your past responsibilities, education, and job responsibilities. Be certain that you let the reader know exactly what you have done, what specific education you have gained, and what progress you have made. Being vague and unclear can cost you an interview.

T: Truth

When writing your resumé, you may be tempted to fudge a little bit here and there to make yourself look better. Perhaps you were out of work for a few months and you think it looks bad to have this gap in your chronological history. Avoid the urge to fudge. Telling the absolute **truth** on a resumé is essential. A lie, even a small one, can (and usually will) come back to haunt you.

O: Organization

Before you begin your resumé, think about the **organization** of your data. We will provide a model resumé; however, there are several other formats you might select. It is most important that you present your information in an attractive, easy-to-read, comprehensive format.

R: Review

Reviewing your resumé and cover letter is important, but having someone else review them for clarity, accuracy, spelling, grammar, formatting, and overall content can be one of the best things you can do for your job search.

The basic tips in Figure 13.3 will help you as you begin building a dynamic resumé. Some other tips to help you begin building a dynamic resumé include the following:

- Do not date stamp or record the preparation date of your resumé in any place.
- Limit your resumé (and cover letter) to one page each (a two-page resumé is appropriate if you have more than 10 years' experience).
- Use a standard resumé paper color, such as white, cream, gray, or beige.
- Use bullets (such as these) to help profile lists unless you are preparing an electronic resumé.
- Avoid fancy or hard-to-read fonts.
- Use a standard font size between 10 and 14 points.
- Do not staple anything to your resumé (or cover letter).
- Try to avoid the use of *I, me,* or *my* in your resumé. (If you must use them, do so sparingly.)
- Avoid contractions such as *don't*, and do not use abbreviations.
- Use action verbs such as *designed, managed, created, recruited, simplified*, and/or *built*.
- Avoid the use of full sentences; fragments are fine on a resumé, but not in a cover letter.
- Use the correct verb tense. You will use past tense (such as *recruited*), except when referring to your current job.
- Do not include irrelevant information that does not pertain to this particular job search.
- Choose a format that puts your "best foot" or greatest assets forward.

$\mathcal{F}igure$ 13.3 **General Inclusion Tips**

Contact information (name, complete mailing address, phone and cell numbers, fax number, e-mail address, webpage URL)	MUST include
Education, degrees, certificates, advanced training (to include dates and names of degrees)	MUST include
Current and past work history, experience, and responsibilities	MUST include
Past accomplishments (this is *not* the same as work history or responsibilities)	MUST include
Specific licensures	MUST include
Specific career objective (different for each position for which you apply)	SHOULD include
Summary or list of qualifications, strengths, specializations	SHOULD include
Special skills (including special technical skills or multiple language skills)	SHOULD include
Volunteer work, public service, and/or community involvement	SHOULD include
Internships, externships, and/or extracurricular activities	SHOULD include
Awards, honors, certificates of achievement, special recognitions (at work or in the community)	SHOULD include
Military experience	CONSIDER including
Professional/Preprofessional memberships, affiliations, and/or associations	CONSIDER including
Publications and presentations	CONSIDER including
Current business phone number and/or address (where you are working at the moment)	DO NOT include
Availability (date/time to begin work)	DO NOT include
Geographic limitations	DO NOT include
Personal hobbies or interests	DO NOT include
Personal information such as age, sex, health status, marital status, parental status, ethnicity, or religious affiliations	DO NOT include
Photos	DO NOT include
Salary requirements or money issues	DO NOT include (unless specifically asked to provide a salary history)
References	DO NOT include, but have the information ready on a separate sheet of paper that matches your resumé

Remember that the job market is highly competitive. Your job is to write a resumé that is solid, appealing, comprehensive, and brief. The idea is to get someone to read it and make him or her want to know more about you.

BUILDING YOUR RESUMÉ

What Are the Major Differences?

There are different types of resumés, but primarily, they can be classified as chronological resumés, functional resumés, accomplishment resumés, or a combination of these. Your job package may also contain a portfolio. You might also consider submitting a video resumé or a resumé that can be easily scanned and sent electronically. Each is described below.

- A **chronological resumé** (Figure 13.4) organizes education and work experience in a reverse chronological order. (Your last or present job is listed first.)

- A **functional resumé** (Figure 13.5) organizes your work and experience around specific skills and duties.

- An **accomplishment resumé** (Figure 13.6) resumé allows you to place your past accomplishments into categories that are not necessarily associated with an employer, but shows your track record of "getting the job done."

- A **video resumé** is a resumé that showcases your experiences and talent through a brief (three- to five-minute) video recording. A video resumé is often used to supplement a traditional resumé and shows your creative and technological skills. Some employers will not accept video resumés because they can lead to claims of bias.

- A **scannable resumé** (Figure 13.7) is a resumé with very little formatting and a clear font, such as Arial. It may appear to be less visually appealing, but it is easier to read once scanned and read by a computer.

- A **portfolio** is a binder, website, CD-ROM, flash drive, or cloud that showcases your very best work. It details your projects, awards, certificates, certifications, degrees, transcripts, military experience, and major accomplishments. Your portfolio should always be specific to the position for which you are applying.

CHOOSE APPROPRIATE REFERENCES

Who Can Speak Positively about My Talents and Skills?

If an employer is interested in you, he or she will most likely ask that you provide three to five references; people who can attest to your professional skills, work ethic, and workplace knowledge. There are five steps for successfully soliciting letters of reference.

STEP 1: SELECT THREE TO FIVE PEOPLE WITH WHOM YOU HAVE HAD PROFESSIONAL CONTACT.   As you are determine the best ones to select, choose people who are very familiar with your work ability. Current and former employers with whom you have experienced a good working relationship are excellent sources of references. Your instructors are also excellent sources. If you do not have anyone who falls into these two categories, consider asking friends of your family who are respected members of the community. As you consider possible

from ORDINARY to *Extraordinary*

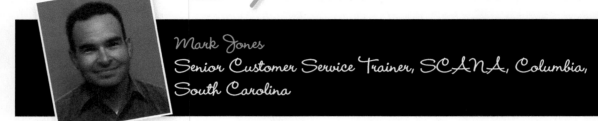

Mark Jones
Senior Customer Service Trainer, SCANA, Columbia,
South Carolina

MY PROUDEST moment? Finally coming to the realization that I am a functional member of a highly dysfunctional family. I know, I know; many people say they have a dysfunctional family—but in my case, it is the raw, inescapable truth. My realization may not sound like much to an outsider, but when you finally realize that you do not have to be a victim of your family or your past, it is a proud moment! I can confidently say, "I am not like them."

I don't have any memories of a time when my family was "normal." My mother, who has been clinically depressed my entire life, attempted suicide when I was four years old. I have never known a day when she was not heavily medicated. My father had the first of four heart attacks when I was six. My parents divorced when I was 11 and I remained with my father. My mother remarried when I was 13. When I was 15, my father died, leaving us very little. Even the mobile home in which we lived was repossessed.

My new stepfather was legally blind and had never driven a car. My mother did not drive either. They never wanted me to get my permit or drive and fought my attempts to do so for years. They thought walking everywhere was perfectly normal. My stepfather did not have any children of his own and did not have any parenting skills. I was treated more as a tenant than a son or stepson. As a matter of fact, I had to pay rent to live with him and my own mother. Due to my father's death, I drew a small Social Security check until I graduated from high school. Every month, much of that money had to be turned over to my stepfather. I even had to buy my own bed to sleep in. Of course, we had our share of good times, too. But I knew this situation was far from "normal"—whatever that was.

When I was in my early 20s, I begged a dear friend, Stella, to let me use her car so I could try for my driver's license. I had practically no driving experience, but somehow, I passed the test. I paid $200 for my first car in two installments of $100 each. It was a 1973 Buick LaSabre that was wrecked down one entire side and had been used in demolition donut field races. But, it was much better than walking everywhere. This

reference sources, be sure to choose individuals who are responsible and timely in their reply to your request. Typically, you should not use your minister, rabbi, or other religious figures as references.

References are a reflection of you, and if the reference sources do not respond in the appropriate manner, they will cast a shadow on your credibility. Your references should have excellent written communication skills. A poorly written recommendation letter reflects badly on you.

STEP 2: REQUEST PERMISSION FROM YOUR REFERENCE SOURCES. Always ask someone before you list him or her as a reference on an application or resumé. During your conversation with the individual, discuss your career goals and aspirations. Give him or her a copy of your resumé and cover letter. Ask him or her to critique them for you and make any necessary changes. You should also ask the person to put your letter on his or her company letterhead and send your potential employer an original copy, not a photocopy.

was a turning point in my life. I was in my early 20s and working in a local grocery store. I enrolled in the university right after high school, but I had to drop out because I could not get a grant and did not make enough money to pay tuition. I later enrolled in the local community college, but after one semester, I realized I could not afford this either.

Basically, I had to make a hard, life-altering decision. I did not want to live my life in debt, as my father had done, so I made up my mind that I would have to take a few steps back to eventually go forward. I began to look for a job that offered educational benefits. I scanned the phone book for hospitals, utility companies, banks, and government agencies that offered this benefit. Every Monday night, their job lines would be updated and I would call, fill out an application, and wait. Nothing!

Finally, I learned how to properly fill out an application. I would call the job line many times and write down every word in its advertisement. Then, I would craft my application and letter based on those needs, not my experiences. I had to learn to apply for a job as if I already had it. After two years and many attempts to secure a suitable position, a utility company hired me—*and* they had educational benefits. Finally, I could go back to school and get another car! I began working toward my degree and after six long, hard years, I graduated with a bachelor of science in business management. It was not easy, as I am sure you know. I had

> *I paid $200 for my first car . . . a 1973 Buick LaSabre that was wrecked down one entire side and had been used in demolition donut field races.*

to take some courses online, and I was in class every Friday night for years and years.

During my time in college, I worked my way up in the company and today, 17 years later, I am a senior trainer for SCANA, an eleven-billion-dollar, Fortune 500 utility holding company founded in 1846. I design training programs and development materials for new hires, system enhancements, and employee upgrades.

I look back on my childhood and early adulthood, and I am proud of the fact that I did not let my past or my family dictate my future. I survived. I refused to succumb to their life. I knew that I had to have my own life with my own fate. You can have this, too. Never let your past or your family tell you what you're capable of doing. Take chances. Take risks. And, if you have to take a step backward to go forward, never be ashamed to do that, too.

EXTRAORDINARY REFLECTION

Read the following statement and respond in your online journal or class notebook.

Mr. Jones came from a family that did not support him financially, emotionally, or educationally. What advice would you give to someone who might be experiencing the same type of environment? Does your family have to play a role in your life for you to be successful?

STEP 3: OBTAIN ALL NECESSARY CONTACT INFORMATION FROM REFERENCES. You should know your reference's professional name, job title, business address, e-mail address, phone number, and fax number so that your potential employer can contact him or her with ease.

STEP 4: SEND THANK YOU LETTERS TO THOSE WHO AGREE TO SERVE AS REFERENCES FOR YOU. Stay in contact with them throughout your job search. Give them updates and a periodic thank you in the form of a card, an e-mail, or a phone call. At the end of your job search, a small token of your appreciation may be appropriate, but a thank you note is essential.

STEP 5: DEVELOP A TYPED LIST OF ALL REFERENCES—INCLUDING CONTACT INFORMATION—AND TAKE IT WITH YOU TO ALL INTERVIEWS. It is now customary that you do not include the names of references on your resume. You simply state "References available upon request" or do not mention references at all. Employers will ask if they need them.

Figure 13.4 **Chronological Resumé**

BENJAMIN SHAW

1234 Lake Shadow Drive, Maple City, PA 12345   (123) 555-1234   Scott@bl.com

OBJECTIVE: To work as a medical assistant in an atmosphere that uses my organizational skills, compassion for people, desire to make a difference, and impeccable work ethic.

PROFESSIONAL EXPERIENCE:

January 2007–Present

Medical Assistant Intern
Mercy Family Care Practice, Harrisburg, PA
▶ Responsible for completing patient charts
▶ Take patients' vitals
▶ Assist with medical coding

February 2003–December 2006

Medical Transcriptionist
The Office of Brenda Wilson, MD, Lancaster, PA
▶ Interpreted and typed medical reports
▶ Worked with insurance documentation
▶ Assisted with medical coding
▶ Served as Office Manager (1/05–12/06)

March 1998–February 2003

Ward Orderly
Wallace Hospital, Lancaster, PA
▶ Assisted nurses with patient care
▶ Cleaned patient rooms
▶ Served patient meals

August 1995–March 1998

Administrative Assistant
Ellen Abbot Nursing Care Facility
▶ Typed office reports
▶ Organized patient files

EDUCATION:

Occupational Associate's Degree—Medical Assistant
Victory Health Institute, Harrisburg, PA
May 2008 (with honors)

Certificate of Completion—Medical Transcription
Philadelphia Technical Institute
December 2002

Vocational High School Diploma—Health Sciences
Philadelphia Vocational High School
August 1995

Figure 13.5 **Functional Resumé**

BENJAMIN SHAW

1234 Lake Shadow Drive, Maple City, PA 12345   (123) 555-1234   Scott@bl.com

OBJECTIVE: To work as a medical assistant in an atmosphere that uses my organization abilities, people skills, compassion for patients, desire to make a difference, and impeccable work ethic.

SKILLS:

Bilingual (English/Spanish)	Data Protection
Claims Reimbursement	Client Relations
Highly Organized	Problem-Solving Skills
Motivated, Self-starter	Team Player
Priority Management Skills	Delegating Ability
Strategic Planning	Budget Management

PROFESSIONAL PREPARATION:

Occupational Associate's Degree—Medical Assistant
Victory Health Institute, Harrisburg, PA
May 2008 (with honors)

Certificate of Completion—Medical Transcription
Philadelphia Technical Institute
December 2002

Vocational High School Diploma—Health Sciences
Philadelphia Vocational High School
August 1995

PROFESSIONAL EXPERIENCE:

January 2007–Present	Medical Assistant Intern Mercy Family Care Practice, Harrisburg, PA
February 2003–December 2006	Medical Transcriptionist The Office of Brenda Wilson, MD, Lancaster, PA
March 1998–February 2003	Ward Orderly Wallace Hospital, Lancaster, PA
August 1995–March 1998	Administrative Assistant Ellen Abbot Nursing Care Facility

References: Provided upon request

Figure 13.6 **Accomplishment Resumé**

BENJAMIN SHAW

1234 Lake Shadow Drive
Maple City, PA 12345
(123) 555-1234

ben@online.com
www.bjs@netconnect.com

Career Target:

MEDICAL ASSISTANT

A highly qualified medical professional with eight years' experience in patient care, client relations, and medical coding seeking a challenging career that uses my strong problem-solving skills, deep compassion for the people, and medical training.

PROFESSIONAL ACCOMPLISHMENTS
Mercy Family Care Practice
✓ Revised and updated medical coding procedures
✓ Increased insurance payments by 11%
✓ Revised and streamlined new patient intake process
✓ Assisted Lead MA with ethics plan revision
✓ Revamped treatment procedure guidelines

Office of Brenda Wilson, MD
✓ Developed new medication administration checklist
✓ Implemented new guidelines for lab specimen collection
✓ Assisted with compliance of OSHA regulations

SKILLS/STRENGTHS
✓ Highly organized
✓ Team player
✓ Impeccable work ethic
✓ Bilingual (English and Spanish)
✓ Budget minded
✓ Motivated, self-starter
✓ Excellent client relations
✓ Superior time management skills

PROFESSIONAL PREPARATION
Occupational Associate's Degree—Medical Assistant
Victory Health Institute, Harrisburg, PA
May 2008 (with high honors)

Certificate of Completion—Medical Transcription
Philadelphia Technical Institute
December 2002 (with honors)

Vocational High School Diploma—Health Sciences
Philadelphia Vocational High School
August 1995

PROFESSIONAL EXPERIENCE

January 2007–Present	**Medical Assistant Intern** Mercy Family Care Practice
February 2003–December 2006	**Medical Transcriptionist** The Office of Brenda Wilson, MD
March 1998–February 2003	**Ward Orderly** Wallace Hospital
August 1995–March 1998	**Administrative Assistant** Ellen Abbot Nursing Care Facility

Figure **13.7   Scannable Resumé**

BENJAMIN SHAW
1234 Lake Shadow Drive, Maple City, PA 12345
(H) 123-456-7890 (C) 123-456-1232

OBJECTIVE
To work as a medical assistant in an atmosphere that uses
my organizational skills, compassion for people, a desire to
make a difference, and impeccable work ethic.

PROFESSIONAL EXPERIENCE
January 2006–Present
Medical Assistant Intern
Mercy Family Care Practice, Harrisburg, PA
Responsible for completing patient charts
Take patients' vitals
Assist with medical coding

February 2003–December 2006
Medical Transcriptionist
The Office of Brenda Wilson, MD, Lancaster, PA
Interpreted and typed medical reports
Worked with insurance documentation
Served as Office Manager (1/05–12/06)

March 1998–February 2003
Ward Orderly
Wallace Hospital, Lancaster, PA
Assisted nurses with patient care
Cleaned patient rooms
Served patient meals

EDUCATION
Occupational Associate's Degree—Medical Assistant
Victory Health Institute, Harrisburg, PA
May 2008 (With Honors)

Certificate of Completion—Medical Transcription
Philadelphia Technical Institute
December 2002

Vocational High School Diploma—Health Sciences
Philadelphia Vocational High School
August 1995

Successful Decisions

AN ACTIVITY FOR CRITICAL REFLECTION

Richard had never held a professional job. He had only held a series of odd jobs for friends and family members. When it came time for Richard to begin applying for a full-time position, he was unsure who to ask to serve as his references.

He began to think about his past part-time job and decided that his old boss at the gas station, James Cartman, might help him. His boss was a friend of his father's, and he only worked for him for two months during class break, but he knew that he had done a good job for Mr. Cartman.

Richard stopped by the gas station to ask if he could use Mr. Cartman's name on his applications. Mr. Cartman told Richard that he would be happy to speak about his work ethic and reliability. Now, Richard only needed two more people.

How could Richard locate two more people to serve as his references?

_____

_____

Should Richard contact these people by phone, e-mail, or Facebook? Justify your answer.

_____

_____

_____

Figure 13.8   Selecting References

In the space provided in Figure 13.8, list three people you could ask to serve as references for you (or write you a reference letter). Once you have identified these three people, list the skills that each person could speak to on your behalf. Think about this carefully, as it is important to choose references who can speak to your many qualifications, not just one or two. Choose people who know you in different areas of success.

PERSON	QUALIFICATIONS HE/SHE CAN WRITE ABOUT
JoAnna Thompson	My oral communication skills My attention to detail My ability to get along with others
Beau DeTiberious	My ability to form a team My ability to motivate team members My ability to meet deadlines
Person 1 _____	Qualifications he/she can write about _____ _____
Person 2 _____	Qualifications he/she can write about _____ _____
Person 3 _____	Qualifications he/she can write about _____ _____

BLOOM LEVEL 1

DESIGN AND DISTRIBUTE ATTRACTIVE PERSONAL BUSINESS CARDS

Does a Small Card Really Help?

Setting yourself apart from other job seekers is important, and designing and distributing attractive personal business cards can help with this endeavor. Business cards give you a professional edge, provide your potential employer another contact source, and help contacts stay in touch with you.

Business cards should be the standard size of 2" × 3.5" and should, if possible, be professionally designed and printed. If this is not possible, there are many computer programs and graphic packages to assist you. You can also purchase sheets of blank business cards for your home printer. You simply design, print, and separate them.

While including a simple graphic is fine (and can be very helpful), avoid flashy, unprofessional colors or "cutesy" graphics. Be certain to include your vital information such as:

Full name
Full address with zip code
Phone numbers (residence, business, cellular, and fax)
E-mail address
Website

Study the examples of appropriate and inappropriate personal business cards in Figure 13.9.

NETWORKING

How Do I Form a Circle of Peers in the World of Work?

It will be important for you to develop a network among the people you know who may work for a company in which you have an interest. People on the inside have an advantage in helping you get your foot in the door. What about your dad's coworker? Your wife's friend? What about a friend who knows your work style and works for a company in which you have an interest? Use every method you have to get the interview. Some important networking opportunities include:

- Attending events and conferences on and off campus
- Joining professional organizations in your field of study
- Shadowing professionals in your field
- Volunteering within your community
- Working in externships or internships in your field
- Contacting family and friends about opportunities
- Logging onto websites and job search social networking sites such as:
  - www.monster.com
  - www.career.com
  - www.careerbuilder.com
  - www.indeed.com
  - www.craigslist.com
- Talking to your instructors
- Working with headhunters or recruiters

Figure 13.9   Sample Business Cards

Benjamin Shaw

BIKER • SKIER • ALL AROUND COOL DUDE

Babes, call me at
(702) 555-1212

or email me at
realDude@shaw.net

Inappropriate personal card for business use

Benjamin Shaw

1234 Lake Shadow Drive, Maple City, PA 12345
702-555-1212 • ben.shaw@online.com

Student
Victory Health Institute
Medical Assistant Program

More appropriate personal card for business use

- Contacting a temp agency in the city in which you hope to work
- Working with your school's counselors and career officers
- Interviewing and connecting with guest speakers who came to your class

THE BIG DAY IS HERE

How Do You Make the Impression of a Lifetime?

Remember the ***eight-second rule*** for making an impression. Consider this: During the interview process, you have even less. A judgment is made immediately about you: your dress, your grooming, your stance, your handshake, and your overall visual impression. Right or wrong, the interviewer will form an immediate first opinion of you—just as you will form an immediate first impression of your interviewer.

There are several ways your potential employer might choose to conduct the interview. In today's globally connected world, the standard face-to-face interview may not be the first choice

B R I N G the *Change*

TIPS FOR PERSONAL SUCCESS

Consider the following tips for preparing to be successful in your future career:

- Read about a variety of careers that interest you.
- Study several websites that provide information about career planning.
- Identify jobs and careers that appear to be "rising" and not "setting."

Now, it is your turn. Create a list of three action steps to help you create a successful job search plan.

1. _____

2. _____

3. _____

of an employer—especially if he or she has to pay to have you visit the office. Your interview may be conducted in one of the following ways:

- **In person.** This type of interview takes place one on one with one person or with a group of people. The interview usually happens at the place of business.

- **Electronic.** With so many electronic ways to communicate, some employers are using the Internet to interview potential employees through Skype, GoToMeeting, WebEx, or other networking sites.

- **Social.** You may have an interview where you are asked to join the members of the interview team at a restaurant or outside the business location.

- **Phone.** Because of the high cost of bringing in someone to an interview, many employers will conduct the first interview over the phone. If you do well and they are impressed, they will then bring you in for an in-person interview

As you begin to prepare for your interview, consider the following mnemonic. If you confidently carry *R.E.W.A.R.D.S.* with you to an interview, you will most likely *get* rewards after the interview, such as a job offer, benefits, and a career in which you can grow and prosper.

R: RAPPORT.   Rapport is basically your "relationship" (intended or unintended) with another person—the emotional alliance you establish with someone. Consider how you come across to others. Rapport involves your verbal and nonverbal communication efforts. You should strive to establish a positive relationship with potential employers and future colleagues.

E: EDUCATION AND TRAINING.   Be confident about what you know and eloquently promote your abilities, skills, and talents to the interviewer. Remember, if you don't promote yourself, it is unlikely that anyone else will.

Brand X/Jupiter RF

In the past, what preparations have served you best in getting ready for an interview?

W: WILLINGNESS.   Project a sense of willingness to learn new things, to become a team member, to assist the company with growth and new projects, and to keep up with advancements and changes in the modern world of work. Potential employers enjoy seeing an attitude of willingness and engagement.

A: APPEARANCE.   Dress for success. Pay close attention to your grooming, your hygiene, your hair, your clothing, and yes, even your shoes and socks (or hosiery). It all matters—and it is all noticed. Never make the mistake of thinking that appearance is not important. You will also want to consider dressing for a specific type of job. Careers in health studies may require a different type of interview dress than careers in aviation maintenance, engineering, and business.

R: RESPONSE.   Project positivity and optimism in your responses to the questions asked in the interview. Even if you have to talk about your weaknesses or past experiences of conflict and turmoil, put a positive spin on them. Let the interviewer know that you have learned from adversity.

D: DEMEANOR.   Cast a quality of confidence (not cockiness), intelligence, professionalism, and positivity. Carrying yourself with confidence during the interview will not go unnoticed. Pay attention to your handshake, eye contact, posture, mannerisms, and facial expressions.

S: SINCERITY.   No one likes phony people, especially a potential employer. Be yourself and strive to be sincere in your answers, your emotions, and your passion.

Getting Prepared

Just as you prepared for exams, you will need to prepare for interviews. Please do not make the common mistake of thinking that your degree or past work experience will get you the job. It may, but more often than you would believe, it is the interview and the relationship that you establish that day that gets you the offer. Your experience and credentials are important, but nothing is more important than how well you are prepared for this day and how well you represent yourself. As you prepare for your interview, consider the following sound advice:

DAYS BEFORE THE INTERVIEW

- Prepare extra copies of your resumé to take to the interview. Though one person typically conducts interviews, some employers designate several people to sit in on the interview process.

- Place your extra resumés, references, and other job search information in a professional portfolio (leather binder) or nice folder. Avoid carrying loose papers, and never carry a backpack to an interview.

- Prepare a typed reference sheet, and take several copies to the interview.

- If achievement portfolios are required, update your portfolio with any last-minute, applicable information.

- Using the research that you have done on the company, make a list of questions that you want to ask the interviewer. Never attend an interview without asking questions yourself. You are interviewing them just as they are interviewing you. Interviewers are much more impressed if they think you have researched the company and if you have questions to ask.

- Have a friend or colleague sit with you and ask you questions that you might anticipate. Have them throw a few "surprise questions" your way, too.

- Ask someone whose opinion you trust to look at your interview outfit and give you advice and suggestions for improvement.

- Make sure you know how to get to the interview site. Make a dry run if you have to. Being late for your interview will be the "kiss of death" for that job.

- Check the night before to make certain that you have transportation and that all of your personal needs are met, such as child care.

- Be sure you have enough gas to reach your destination if you are driving yourself. What is the availability for parking? Will you need to allow time for finding a parking place?

THE DAY OF THE INTERVIEW

- Get up early and spend some time alone reviewing the job announcement, your resumé, your portfolio, the company's profile, and other important information.

- Bring a pen, paper, and calendar with you to the interview. These can be kept in your portfolio, too.

- Know where your items are located so that you do not have to search for them during an interview. Fumbling around makes you look disorganized and unprepared.

- Prepare for the unknown: Take an umbrella, even if it is sunny; leave your home early, even though the interview site is only a few miles away; and so on.

- Be certain that your clothes are clean and pressed.

- Be certain that your shoes are spotless and shined.

- Be certain that you are groomed and that your breath is fresh. Breath mints or sprays go a long way.

- Arrive at the interview at least 15 minutes early.

- If you are a smoker, *do not* smoke in the car on the way to the interview, and try to avoid smoking in your interview clothes. Often, the smell of cigarette smoke lingers for hours and clings to your clothing. For many, this is an immediate turn-off. Some employers will find a way not to hire a smoker because of increased insurance premiums paid for smokers.

- Do not carry any type of food or drink into the interview with you.

- Do not chew gum during the interview.

- Before you enter the building, turn off your cell phone, pager, Blackberry, iPod, tablet, or any other electronic device except your hearing aid, pacemaker, or other life-assisting device. *Turn them off.* Period! There is *no* excuse for your cell phone to ring during an interview. No one, including you, is that important.

- Do not take anyone with you to the interview unless the person remains in the car. Under no circumstances should you take anyone with you into the building!

DURING THE INTERVIEW

- Establish eye contact.

- Work to develop an immediate rapport.

- Offer a firm handshake to everyone in the room.

- Pay close attention to your posture (straight shoulders, positive stride, etc.).

- Speak with clarity and enunciate your words.

- Ask where to sit if you are not told on entering the room.

- Enter with a positive and upbeat attitude.

- Jot down the names of all the people in the room as they are introduced to you. You may even draw an impromptu "seating chart" to remind you of who's who in the room.

- Refer to people by their names if you address them during the interview.

- Take notes during the interview.

- Answer every question asked, as long as the question is legal.

- You don't have to be deadly serious or stodgy, but it is advisable to avoid jokes or off-color humor during the interview process.

- Consider your grammar, and strive to use correct speech.

- If you need clarification on a question, ask for it before you begin your answer.

- Never degrade or talk badly about a past job or employer. This will only come back to haunt you.

- If at all possible, do not discuss any aspect of your personal life, such as children, marriage, or family.

- During the interview, jot down any questions that may arise that you did not already consider.

- If you are offered anything to eat or drink, accept only water, just in case your mouth becomes dry during the interview.

- Never ask about money or company benefits during an interview, especially during the first interview, unless the interviewer approaches the topic. Let him or her lead this discussion. If you are asked about salary requirements, respond with this question: "What is the range for this job?" In negotiations of any kind, you want the other person to offer information first. If you think you are highly qualified, respond with a salary amount close to the top of the range by saying, "Based on my qualifications and experience, I would consider a salary of \$_____."

- Strive to never appear desperate or "begging" for the job. There is a difference between excitement and desperation.

AFTER THE INTERVIEW

- Shake hands with all the people in the room, and thank them for the opportunity to meet with them. Let them know that you were honored to have the opportunity. Humility goes a long way.

- Politely let them know that you enjoyed the interview and that you are very interested in the position.

- Ask each person in the room for a business card. This provides you with his or her correct name spelling, address, and e-mail address for use in future correspondence.

- Don't linger around the site unless you are told to wait. This makes you look desperate.

- Always follow up with a personalized thank you note to each person.

GENERAL TIPS

- Remember the cardinal rule of interviewing: Interviewers are not interested in what the company can do for you; they are interested in what you can do for the company. Therefore, you must present your case on why you want to work for the company and the contributions you are prepared to make.

- Be truthful in every aspect of the job search: the application, your resumé, your cover letter, your portfolio, your references, your question responses, your salary history, and yes, your interest in the position.

- Be nice and gracious to everyone you meet. That may be the person with whom you interview in a few moments.

ANTICIPATING THE INTERVIEWER'S QUESTIONS

Can You Answer Hard Questions with a Positive Attitude?

Richard Nelson Bolles, author of *What Color is Your Parachute?* (2011), the most widely published job-hunting book in history with over 10 million copies in print, makes an astounding assertion. He states, "You don't have to spend hours memorizing a lot of 'good answers' to potential questions from the employer; There are only five questions that matter." Wow. Five questions!

With this statement, do not think that you will only be asked five questions. Rather, Mr. Bolles is suggesting that with every question asked of you, the interviewer is trying to get to the heart of the matter—the five basic questions are:

1. Why are you here?

2. What can you do for us?

3. What kind of person are you?

4. What distinguishes you from the 19 other people who can do the same tasks that you can?

5. Can I afford you?

So, how do interviewers get to "the heart of the matter?" How do they pull the answers to these five questions from you? Ironically, they do it by asking many, many other questions. This section will offer you insight into some common and not-so-common questions asked by today's employers.

It is usually customary that the interviewer will make "small talk" for a few minutes to give you time to relax and get comfortable. You should avoid answering questions with a simple "yes" or "no." Briefly elaborate on your answers without talking too much. For example, if the interviewer says, "I hope you had no trouble finding our building," you should not just answer "No." You might say something like, "Not at all. I live near here so I was familiar with the location. Actually, I had a part-time job when I was a sophomore, and I brought materials to one of your managers from my department chair."

Interviewers will often say to you, "Tell me about yourself." They are not looking for your life history as much as they are gathering background information on you and observing how well you can present information. Provide highlights of your education, experience, and accomplishments. If you are just yourself and enjoy the process, this will show.

The interviewer might then ask you, "What do you know about our company?" This is a good opportunity for you to show how prepared you are. You could open your portfolio and tell the interviewer, "When I was researching the company, I found some interesting facts on your website. I know that you are an international company based in New York and that you have over 4,000 employees. I learned that you have several divisions, including food processing and distribution, restaurants, and contract food sales. In fact, this information is the reason I applied for a

What do you have to offer an employer that is unique to you?

Image 100 RF

job with you through our Career Center. My minor in college is restaurant management, and I think this company will be a great place to put my knowledge and the skills to great use."

You will, of course, have to adapt your answer to your own situation. There is no way to be completely prepared for the questions an interviewer may ask. The key is to have anticipated the interviewer's questions and to be so comfortable with the message you want to convey about yourself that you sound confident and decisive. As you talk, remember to look at the interviewer and to lean forward slightly, which indicates that you are listening intently.

After a brief "let's-get-to-know-each-other" session, you can anticipate more direct and important questions. Some of the more common questions that you might expect include:

- Why should we hire you?
- Why are you interested in this company and in the position?
- When did you decide on a career in _____?
- Tell me about your extracurricular activities.
- What are your strengths?
- What are your weaknesses?
- Why did you leave your last job?
- Do you have a geographic preference? Why?
- Are you willing to relocate?
- Are you willing to travel?
- Do you have job experience in _____?
- What can you do for the company?
- What other companies are you interviewing with?
- Tell me about a difficult problem you have had and how you solved it.
- Tell me about a time when you worked under stress.
- What kind of accomplishment gives you the greatest satisfaction?
- What are your long- and short-range goals?
- Where do you see yourself in five years?
- What one word best describes you?
- How do you deal with difficult people?
- Describe one goal you have set over the past six months and how you went about accomplishing it.
- What is the biggest mistake you ever made? What did you learn from it?
- What subject in school gave you the most challenges? Why?
- What past experiences or courses have prepared you for this position?
- Would you prefer to work alone or with a group of people? Why?

Some more in-depth and less common questions might be:

- What type of manager would bring out the best in you? Why?
- What is the most important thing to you in a job? Why?
- Who has been the most influential person in your life? Why?

- If I called your past supervisor, how would he or she describe you?

- In what area do you lack the most confidence?

- In what area of this position do you lack the most experience? How do you plan to accommodate for this?

- If you could design your own job evaluation form with only five qualities to be evaluated, what five qualities would you list? Why?

- Tell us about a time when you put your best forward and the end result was still unfavorable. Why do you think this happened? What did you do about it? What did you learn from the situation?

- What is the biggest change to which you have ever had to adapt? What strategies did you employ to adjust to this change?

- How do you effectively deal with interpersonal conflicts?

- How do you effectively deal with miscommunication?

- How do you effectively deal with gossip?

- Of what are you most proud in your professional life? Why?

- If you could not be involved in this job or profession any longer, what would you do for a vocation? Why? Why are you not doing that now?

Regardless of the question asked, your primary responsibility in the interview is to be straightforward, honest, and answer the question to the very best of your ability.

Look over the position advertisement, the company's website, and your own application materials and think about questions that may be asked of you. Write down five questions that you might anticipate that are not listed above.

1. _____

2. _____

3. _____

4. _____

5. _____

ASK INFORMED QUESTIONS

Am I Allowed to Interview the Interviewer?

You should feel free to ask the interviewer questions during the interview, but the interviewer should lead the majority of the first part of the interview. At the close of the interview, you may be asked if you have any questions. If this opportunity is not offered, you should say, "I have a few questions, if you don't mind." Asking questions of the interviewer is impressive and indicates that you are interviewing him or her, as well. Some typical questions follow:

- How would you describe a typical day in this position?

- What kind of training can I anticipate?

- What is the probationary period of employment?

- What are the opportunities for personal growth and professional development?

- To whom would I report?

- Will I have an opportunity to meet some of my coworkers?
- Would you describe the training program?
- When will my first job performance evaluation take place?
- Why do you enjoy working for this company?
- How would you describe the most successful person working at this company? Why?
- What objectives do you expect to be met by your new employee in the first six months?
- Can you tell me about an assignment I might be asked to do?
- What happened to the person who most recently held this position?
- What do you see as the major challenges facing this organization? Why?
- How would you describe the culture of the workplace in this organization?
- What does this company value?

ROUGH, TOUGH, HARD QUESTIONS

How Do You Effectively Manage Inappropriate or Illegal Questions?

Sadly, you may encounter questions that are inappropriate or even illegal. Remember, federal and state laws may prohibit many questions that deal with your personal life, but, "No single federal, state, or local agency or court defines for all cases which interview questions are legal or illegal. Instead, a plethora of court rulings, legislative decisions, agency regulations, and constitutional laws combine to produce the often confusing and frequently changing list of what you can and can't ask a job applicant" (Bell and Smith, 2004). Federal laws such as the Civil Rights Act of 1964 and the Americans with Disabilities Act of 1990 do regulate certain questions that can be asked during an interview.

If illegal or inappropriate questions are asked in person or on an application, it can be challenging to manage them and still retain your composure and decorum. It is up to you how much you want to tell a potential employer about your personal life or lifestyle, and he or she cannot demand an answer unless it relates directly to the line of work for which you are applying, such as tending bar or flying an airplane.

First, review the list of questions that many experts consider illegal, or at best inappropriate and/or taboo, and later in this section, we will discuss how to respond if you are asked an illegal or unethical question.

With some exceptions, employers should not ask you about:

- **Your age.** You should generally not be asked this question. However, some professions are age-restricted (such as airline pilots and bartending) and this question is perfectly legal.

- **Your marital status, your parental status, or your living situation (who lives with you or why).** If you are asked this question, the interviewer is really trying to find out if you will be at work on a regular basis or if you can travel. It is legal to ask, "Does your personal schedule permit extensive travel?" but it is not legal to ask, "Would you get into trouble with your wife or children if you were asked to travel a lot?" It is illegal to ask if you are planning a family, if you are pregnant, or if you have ever had an abortion.

- **Your race or national origin.** You should not be asked about either of these categories, nor should you ever be asked to provide a photo of yourself. However, every employer can, on employment, ask that you provide legal documentation that you are eligible and clear to work in the United States. At this point, he or she can also ask for a photograph for security and identification purposes.

- **Your sexual orientation.** This is tricky, but generally, an employer may ask about your sexual orientation. However, many states and cities ban discrimination based on sexual orientation. "Don't be lulled into complacent mistakes because of the rapid acceleration during the past decade of sexual orientation as a protected class by both company declarations and government (state and local) laws. Discrimination is alive and well" (Kennedy, 2011).

- **Your religious affiliation.** This question is illegal and should never be asked. However, if you are asked this question, the interviewer is probably trying to determine if your religion might **prevent you from working on** weekends, Sundays, or certain holidays. It is legal to ask, "Would you be willing to work on Sunday?" or "Would you be willing to work on Christmas?"

- **Your political affiliation.** It is legal to ask this question; however, "Some states ban discrimination on this basis and political affiliation may not be used for discriminatory purposes in federal-government employment" (Smith, 2007).

- **Your physical, mental, or emotional limitations.** You cannot be asked a question such as "Have you ever been treated for depression or any mental illness?" but you can be asked a question such as "This position requires that you deal with many stressful situations and many situations in which you will encounter conflict. Do you feel that you have any limitations that might prevent you from managing these situations effectively?" It is never legal to ask about your HIV status, your disabilities, or any prescription drugs that you may take.

- **Your physical attributes.** You cannot be asked questions about your height or weight unless this is directly tied to job performance due to specific, predetermined limitations.

- **Your financial status.** An employer cannot ask you if you have a checking or savings account, how much money you save each month, or any question about your credit rating. However, many states do allow potential employers to run credit checks on applicants.

- **Your personal habits.** Generally, employers can ask if you smoke at home, but this question has lead to some lawsuits. "Currently, 31 states ban policies prohibiting off-duty smoking" (Smith, 2007).

- **Your arrest status.** Your arrest status is different from your conviction status. It *is* legal to ask if you have ever been convicted of a crime. A few states do allow an employer to ask if you have been arrested if it is job related.

- **Your affiliations.** It is not legal to ask you to which organizations you belong, except for certain professional organizations (such as The National Association of Architects if you are applying for a position in the architectural field). An employer, cannot, however, ask if you belong to the Shriners, Freemasons, or any union.

- **Your military status.** You may not be asked what type of discharge you had from the military. You should not be asked if you ever belonged to the military unless it is job related.

- **Your school and/or college records.** School and college records may be sought only with your consent. Usually, you have to order the official transcript and have it sent directly to your employer.

Basically it comes down to money. It is very expensive to hire, train, and retain an employee in today's workforce. An employer wants to know as much about you as possible—basically, he

How would you handle an illegal question during an interview?

or she wants to know if you are qualified, if you will get along with others, and if you will be at work when you say you will be there.

So, how do you handle questions that may be illegal or inappropriate? This can be tricky at best and "the kiss of death" at worst. Consider this: Can an employer ask you if you are married? No, he or she cannot. However, if this type of question arises, you have to decide if you will answer, but you can always view these types of questions as a positive moment, too. You might respond: "Yes, I am married, and my spouse and I fully support each other's careers and advancement possibilities."

Can an employer ask, "Are you gay?" Generally, yes, but again, you have to decide how you would answer this question (whether the answer is "yes" or "no"). If you are uncomfortable with this question, you may respond, "Before I answer that question, can you discuss how this is related to this particular position?" or "I choose not to answer that question based on my personal beliefs."

Sometimes, you will have to do an evaluation of the employer. You may need to ask yourself, "Do I really want to work for a company that would ask an illegal or inappropriate question?" Ultimately, the choice is yours.

As an exercise, choose one area above and pretend that you were asked a question that was illegal, inappropriate, or taboo. State the question below then give your response to this question.

BLOOM LEVEL 3

Question:

_____

_____

_____

My response:

WIN, LOSE, OR DRAW, ALWAYS SAY THANK YOU IN WRITING

Do I Have to Say Thank You Even If I Don't Get the Job?

Indeed, it is safe to say that sending a thank you note is "the most overlooked step in the entire job search process" (Bolles, 2011). Yes, this is a mandatory step for every interview, and you must send one to every person who interviewed you. Period. In today's world of high-tech and run, run, run, this one act will set you apart from the thousands who interview on a daily basis. And yes, you must send a thank you letter even if you do not get the job. "When do I send the thank you note?" you might ask. *Immediately after the interview.*

Sending a simple thank you note does many things. It lets the employer know that you have good manners, that you respect other people's time and efforts, that you are considerate, that you really do care about the position, and that you have positive people and communication skills. Yes, all of that from a card and stamp that can cost less than $2.00.

Figures 13.10 and 13.11 show examples of two thank you notes. Review them and consider using them as templates to build your own notes.

DID YOU *Know?*

MAYA ANGELOU was born in St. Louis, Missouri, in 1928. By the time she was in her 20s, she had been a cook, streetcar conductor, cocktail waitress, dancer, madam, high school dropout, and unwed mother. As a young girl, she was raped by her mother's boyfriend and did not speak again for four years.

Today, Dr. Angelou is a world-renowned poet, civil rights activist, historian, screenwriter, and director. She is only the second poet in history to write and deliver an original poem at a presidential inauguration (for President Clinton).

She won three Grammy awards in the spoken word category and has been nominated twice for Broadway's prestigious Tony award.

PHOTO: Judy Eddy/Wenn Photos/Newscom

Figure 13.10 **Thank You Note: After the Interview**

BENJAMIN SHAW
1234 Lake Shadow Drive
Maple City, PA 12345
Scott@bl.com

January 20, 2011

Mr. James Pixler, RN, CAN
Director of Placement and Advancement
Grace Care Center
123 Sizemore Street, Suite 444
Philadelphia, PA 12345

Dear Mr. Pixler,

Thank you for the wonderful opportunity to meet with you and the team at Grace Care Center on Monday. Your facilities are amazing, and the new wing is going to be a remarkable addition to your center.

I enjoyed learning more about the new position in Medical Assisting, and I think that my qualifications and experiences have prepared me for this challenging opportunity. I would consider it an honor to answer any further questions that you might have or to meet with you again if you consider it necessary.

I look forward to hearing from you at your convenience. If you need any additional information, you can reach me at 123-555-1234.

Thank you,

Benjamin Shaw

Benjamin Shaw

Figure 13.11 **Thank You Note: After a Position Rejection**

BENJAMIN SHAW
1234 Lake Shadow Drive
Maple City, PA 12345
Scott@bl.com

January 20, 2011

Mr. James Pixler, RN, CAN
Director of Placement and Advancement
Grace Care Center
123 Sizemore Street, Suite 444
Philadelphia, PA 12345

Dear Mr. Pixler,

Thank you for the opportunity to meet with you and the team at Grace Care Center on Monday. I enjoyed learning more about your center and the planned addition.

While I was not offered the position, I did want to let you know that I appreciate your time and I would like for you to contact me if you have any future openings where you feel my qualifications and experiences would match your needs. Grace is an incredible facility, and I would consider it an honor to hold a position there.

If you need to contact me in the future, you can reach me at 123-555-1234.

Thank you for your time and assistance, and good luck to you and your colleagues.

Sincerely,

Benjamin Shaw

Benjamin Shaw

CHANGING IDEAS *to Reality*

REFLECTIONS ON CAREER AND LIFE DEVELOPMENT

This is your one lifetime! You need to prepare to do something you love. No matter how much money you make, you won't be happy unless you are doing something that matters to you, something that allows you to keep learning and becoming, something that provides you opportunities to give back—perhaps the best gift of all.

As you reflect on this chapter, keep the following pointers in mind:

- Learn how to make yourself a desirable employee.
- Set yourself apart with a dynamic cover letter and resumé.
- Select references who can speak to your many talents and skills.
- Learn to promote and sell yourself in an interview.
- Send thank you notes after your interview.
- Present yourself in a professional, educated manner.

*"If you follow your bliss, doors will open for you
that wouldn't have opened for anyone else."*

—*Joseph Campbell*

Knowledge
in Bloom

PREPARING YOUR RESUMÉ

Utilizes levels 1–6 of the taxonomy

Each chapter-end assessment is based on Bloom's Taxonomy of Learning. See pages xxvi–xxviii in the front of this book for a quick review.

Now, it is your turn. After reviewing the information for resumé writing and the examples of several resumés, begin compiling information to build your own chronological resumé using this template.

Your Resumé Worksheet

Personal Information

Name

_____

Address

_____

_____

Phone number(s)

_____

E-mail address

_____

Website

_____

Work Experience (Employment History)

1. (most recent)

Company name

_____

Your position

_____

Your duties

_____

_____

_____

2. (next most recent)

Company name

_____

Your position

_____

Your duties

_____

_____

_____

3. (next most recent)

Company name

_____

Your position

_____

Your duties

_____

_____

_____

Education and Training

1. (latest degree)

Name of institution

_____

Name and date of degree

_____

Honors/Recognition

_____

_____

2. (degree)

Name of institution

_____

Name and date of degree

_____

Honors/Recognition

_____

_____

Additional Training

Name of institution

_____

Name and date of certificate or training program

_____

_____

Name of institution

_____

Name and date of certificate or training program

_____

Special Skills and Qualifications

List any skills and qualifications you possess that may be of interest to an employer.

_____

_____

_____

_____

College or Community Service (optional)

List any relevant service you have performed that the potential employer might need to know.

_____

_____

_____

References

List the names, addresses, and phone numbers of at least three people whom you could call on to serve as references for you if needed.

1. _____

2. _____

3. _____

Locate a position for which you would like to apply. Practice writing a job-specific objective.

_____

_____

_____

_____

_____

SQ3R MASTERY STUDY SHEET

EXAMPLE QUESTION (from page 338) Why is it important to write an excellent resumé?	**ANSWER:**
EXAMPLE QUESTION (from page 338) What does D.O.C.T.O.R. stand for?	**ANSWER:**
AUTHOR QUESTION (from page 339) Why is it important to be truthful with your job search package?	**ANSWER:**
AUTHOR QUESTION (from page 341) How do you select a reference?	**ANSWER:**
AUTHOR QUESTION (from page 341) What are the three major types of resumés?	**ANSWER:**
AUTHOR QUESTION (from page 341) What is a portfolio? What should it include?	**ANSWER:**
AUTHOR QUESTION (from page 361) Why do you need to write a thank you note even if you do not get the position?	**ANSWER:**
YOUR QUESTION (from page ___)	**ANSWER:**
YOUR QUESTION (from page ___)	**ANSWER:**
YOUR QUESTION (from page ___)	**ANSWER:**
YOUR QUESTION (from page ___)	**ANSWER:**
YOUR QUESTION (from page ___)	**ANSWER:**

Finally, after answering these questions, recite in your mind the major points covered here. Consider the following general questions to help you master this material.

- What was it about?
- What does it mean?
- What was the most important thing you learned? Why?
- What were the key points to remember?

REFERENCES

Adler, R., Rosenfeld, L., & Proctor, R. (2010). *Interplay: The Process of Interpersonal Communication* (11th ed.). New York: Oxford University Press.

Altman, I., & Taylor, D. (1973). *Social Penetration: The Development of Interpersonal Relationships.* New York: Holt.

American Library Association. (1989). *Presidential Committee on Information Literacy. Final Report.* Chicago: American Library Association.

American Psychological Association. (2008). *For a Better Understanding of Sexual Orientation and Homosexuality.* Retrieved August 12, 2008, from www.apa.org/topics/orientation.html.

Anderson, L., & Bolt, S. (2008). *Professionalism: Real Skills for Workplace Success.* Upper Saddle River, NJ: Pearson/Prentice Hall.

Bach, D. (2003). *The Finish Rich Notebook.* New York: Broadway Books.

Barrett, D. (2008). *Average Student Loans Top $19,000.* Retrieved on September 2, 2008, from http://encarta.msn.com/encnet/departments/financialaid/?article=averagestudentloans.

Baxter, L. A. (1993). Conflict Management: An Episodic Approach. *Small Group Behavior, 13*(1), 23–42.

Beebe, S., Beebe, S., & Redmond, M. (2008). *Interpersonal Communication: Relating to Others* (5th ed.). Boston: Allyn and Bacon.

Begley, S. (March 7, 2011). I Can't Think. *Newsweek,* pp. 28–33.

Bell, A., & Smith, D. (2004). *Interviewing for Success.* Upper Saddle River, NJ: Prentice Hall.

Block, S. (February 22, 2006). Students Suffocate under Tens of Thousands in Loans. *USA Today.*

Bolles, R. N. (2010). *What Color Is Your Parachute? A Practical Manual for Job-Hunters and Career-Changers, 2010 Edition.* Berkeley, CA: Ten Speed Press.

Bosack, J. (1978). *Fallacies.* Dubuque, IA: Educulture.

Britton-Whitcomb, S. (2003). *Resumé Magic: Trade Secrets of a Professional Resumé Writer.* Indianapolis, IN: JIST Works.

Broderick, C. (2003). *Why Care about Your Credit Score?* Orlando, FL: InCharge Education Foundation.

Chronicle of Higher Education. (August 28, 2011). *Almanac Edition, 2011-2012. 57*(1), 20.

Cojonet (City of Jacksonville, FL). (2006). *Consumer Affairs Gets New Tough Law on Car Title Businesses.* Retrieved from www.coj.net/Departments/Regulatory+and+Environmental+Services/Consumer+Affairs/TITLE?LOANS.htm.

College Board. (2008). *College Prices Increase in Step with Inflation: Financial Aid Grows But Fewer Private Loans Even Before Credit Crisis.* Retrieved from www.collegeboard.com/press/releases/201194.html.

College Learning for the New Global Century. (2008). National Leadership Council for Liberal Education and America's Promise. Washington, DC: Association of American Colleges and Universities.

Consumer Reports. Money Advisor. (September 2008). Protecting Your Identity.

Consumer Reports. (September 2008). Protect Yourself Online: The Biggest Threats and the Best Solutions.

Consumer Response Center. (2003). *Identity Theft and Fraud.*

Cooper, M. (2002). Alcohol Use and Risky Sexual Behavior among College Students and Youth. *Journal of Studies on Alcohol, 63*(2), S101.

Cooper-Arnold, A. L. (2006). *Credit Card Debt: A Survival Guide for Students.* Retrieved from www.youngmoney.com/credit_debt/credit_basics/050804-02.

Daly, J., & Engleberg, I. (2006). *Presentations in Everyday Life: Strategies for Effective Speaking.* Upper Saddle River, NJ: Allyn and Bacon.

DeVito, J. A. (2007). *Interpersonal Messages: Communication and Relationship Skills.* Boston: Pearson.

The Digerati Life. (2008). *Lost Money: How Money Drains Add Up to $175,000 in 10 Years.* Retrieved September 5, 2008, from www.thedigeratilife.com/blog/index.php/2008/07/31/lost-money-how-money-drains.

Donatelle, R., & Davis, L. (2002). *Health: The Basics.* Upper Saddle River, NJ: Prentice Hall.

Dresang, J. (April 23, 2007). Liar! Liar! Won't get hired. In age of easy information, resume fibs can sabotage hunts for work. *Las Vegas Review Journal,* reprinted from *Milwaukee Journal Sentinel.*

Dunn, R., and Griggs, S. (2000). *Practical Approaches to Using Learning Styles in Higher Education.* New York: Bergin & Garvey.

ERIC Digest. (2010). Retrieved April 3, 2010, from www.ericdigests.org/1992-3/college.htm.

Farr, M., & Kursmark, L. (2005) *15 Minute Cover Letter: Write an Effective Cover Letter Right Now.* Indianapolis, IN: JIST Works.

Feagin, J. R., & Feagin, C. B. (2008). *Racial and Ethnic Relations.* Upper Saddle River, NJ: Pearson/Prentice Hall.

Forbes. (March 11, 2009). *The World's Billionaires.* Retrieved from www.forbes.com/lists/2009/10/billionaires-2009-richest-people_Warren-Buffett_C0R3.html.

Gardner, H. (1983). *Frames of Mind: The Theory of Multiple Intelligences.* New York: Basic Books.

Get More Done. (2009). Retrieved January 3, 2009, from www.getmoredone.com.

Girdano, D., Dusek, D., & Everly, G. (2009). *Controlling Stress and Tension* (8th ed.). Boston: Benjamin Cummings.

Glenn, J. M. L. (October, 2007). Generations at Work: The New Diversity. *Business Education Forum, 62*(1), 47–49.

The Goddess Path. (2009). *Mnemosyne, the Goddess of Memory.* Retrieved from www.goddessgift.com.

Goleman, D. (2006). *Emotional Intelligence: Why It Can Matter More than IQ* (10th Anniv. Ed.). New York: Bantam.

Gordon, E. E. (2005). *The 2010 Meltdown: Solving the Impending Jobs Crisis.* Westport, CT: Praeger.

Hall, E. (1966). *The Hidden Dimension.* Garden City, NY: Doubleday.

Heath, C., & Heath, D. (2010). *Switch: How to Change Things When Change Is Hard.* New York: Broadway Books.

Housden, R. (2007). Taking a Chance on Joy. *O's Guide To Life: The Best of the Oprah Magazine.* Birmingham, AL: Oxmoor House.

Ireland, S. (2003). *The Complete Idiot's Guide to the Perfect Resumé.* Indianapolis, IN: Alpha.

Jung, C. (1921). Psychology Types. In *Collected Works of C. G. Jung* (Volume 6; R. Hull, Translator). Princeton, NJ: Princeton University Press. (Reprinted 1976)

Kabani, S. H. (2010). *The Zen of Social Media.* Dallas, TX: BenBella Books.

Kallock, A. (April 16, 2009). Sunstein: Lack of Ideological Diversity Leads to Extremism. *The Harvard Law Review.*

Kennedy, J. (2011). *Responding to Job Interview Questions about Sexual Orientation.* Retrieved September 14, 2011, from http://www.dummies.com/how-to/content/responding-to-job-interview-questions-about-sexua0.html.

Kennon, J. (n.d.). Warren Buffett Biography. *About.com.* Retrieved from http://beginnersinvest.about.com/cs/warrenbuffet/a/awarrenbio.htm.

Kiewra, K., & Fletcher, H. (1984). The Relationship Between Note Taking Variables and Achievement Measure. *Human Learning, 3,* 273–280.

Kirszner, L., & Mandell, S. (1995). *The Holt Handbook.* Orlando, FL: Harcourt Brace College.

Konowalow, S. (2003). *Planning Your Future: Keys to Financial Freedom.* Columbus, OH: Prentice Hall.

Lane, H. (1976). *The Wild Boy of Aveyron.* Cambridge, MA: Harvard University Press.

Lane, S. (2008). *Interpersonal Communication: Competence and Contexts.* Boston: Pearson/Allyn and Bacon.

Leher, J. (2010). *How We Decide.* New York: Mariner Books.

Leinwood, D. (September 23, 2002). Ecstasy-Viagra Mix Alarms Doctors. *USA Today,* p. D4.

Light, R. (2001). *Making the Most of College: Students Speak Their Minds.* Cambridge, MA: Harvard University Press.

Maslow, A. (1943). A Theory of Human Motivation. *Psychological Review, 50,* 370–396.

McCornack, S. (2007). *Reflect and Relate: An Introduction to Interpersonal Communication.* Boston: Bedford/St. Martin's Press.

MindTools. *The Ladder of Influence: Avoiding Jumping to Conclusions.* Retrieved May 2, 2011, from at www.mindtool.com.

Nellie Mae. (2005). *Credit Cards 101.* Wilkes-Barre, PA: Author.

Nelson, D., & Low, G. (2010). *Emotional Intelligence: Achieving Academic and Career Excellence.* Upper Saddle River, NJ: Prentice Hall.

Nobel Foundation. (1993). *Nelson Mandela—Biography.* Retrieved from http://nobelprize.org/nobel_prizes/peace/laureates.

NPR Staff. (August 30, 2011). *College Student Debt Grows. Is It Worth It?* Retrieved from http://www.npr.org/2011/05/16/136214779/college-student-debt-grows-is-it-worth-it.

Ormondroyd, J., Engle, M., & Cosgrave, T. (2001). *How to Critically Analyze Information Sources.* Cornell University Libraries. Retrieved from www.library.cornell.edu.

Pauk, W. (2007). *How to Study in College* (8th ed.). New York: Houghton Mifflin.

Paul, R., & Elder, L. (2006). *A Miniature Guide to Critical Thinking: Concepts and Tools.* Dillon Beach, CA: Foundation for Critical Thinking.

Payday Loan: Consumer Information. (2008). Retrieved February 12, 2009, from www.paydayloaninfo.org.

Personality Type Portraits. (n.d.) Retrieved December 2, 2008, from www.personalitypage.com.

Potter, J. (2005). *Becoming a Strategic Thinker: Developing Skills for Success.* Upper Saddle River, NJ: Pearson/Prentice Hall.

Ritchie, J. (2010). *Strategies for Success.* Upper Saddle River, NJ: Pearson Education.

Robbins, C. (2006). *The Job Searcher's Handbook* (3rd ed.). Upper Saddle River, NJ: Prentice Hall.

Rosato, D. (July 2008). Life Without Plastic. *Money,* pp. 91–95.

Russell, N. S. (2004). *Words, Words, Words.* Retrieved October 7, 2008, from www.careerknowhow.com/improvement/words.htm.

Schmalleger, R. (2006). *Criminal Justice: A Brief Introduction* (6th ed.). Upper Saddle River, NJ: Prentice Hall.

Seyler, D. (2003). *Steps to College Reading* (2nd ed.). Boston: Allyn and Bacon.

Shattuck, R. (1980). *The Forbidden Experiment: The Story of the Wild Boy of Aveyron.* New York: Farrar, Straus & Giroux.

Sherfield, R. (2004). *The Everything Self-Esteem Book.* Avon, MA: Adams Media.

Sherfield, R., & Moody, P. (2009). *Solving the Professional Development Puzzle: 101 Solutions for Career and Life Planning.* Upper Saddle River, NJ: Pearson.

Sieben, L. (January 27, 2011). College Freshman Report Record-Low Levels of Emotional Health. *The Chronicle of Higher Education,* p. 21.

Slavin, R. E. (2009). *Educational Psychology: Theory and Practice* (10th ed.). Upper Saddle River, NJ: Pearson Education.

Smilkstein, R. (2003). *We're Born To Learn: Using The Brain's Natural Learning Process to Create Today's Curriculum.* Thousand Oaks, CA: Corwin Press.

Smith, B. (2007). *Breaking Through: College Reading* (8th ed.). Upper Saddle River, NJ: Pearson Education.

Snyder, C. R. (2000). Hope Theory: Rainbows of the Mind. *Psychology Inquiry, 13,* 249–275.

Snyder, C. R., & Lopez, S. (2007). *Positive Psychology: The Scientific and Practical Explorations of Human Strength.* Thousand Oaks, CA: Sage.

The State (Newspaper). (August 31, 2008). Protecting Your Identity, p. B12.

Steinke, R. (2007). Women on the rocks. *O's Guide to Life: The Best of the Oprah Magazine.* Birmingham, AL: Oxmoor House.

Sycle, B., & Tietje, B. (2010). *Anybody's Business.* Upper Saddle River, NJ: Pearson.

Tarkovsky, S. (2006). *Mind, Body, and Soul: The Key to Overall Wellness and Health.* Ezine articles.com. Retrieved September 11, 2006, from http://ezinearticles.com/?Mind,-Body,-and-Soul---The-Key-To-Overall-Wellness-and-Health.

Texas A&M University. (n.d.). *Improve Your Memory.* Retrieved January 5, 2009, from www.scs.tamu.edu/selfhelp/elibrary/memory.asp.

Tidwell, L., & Walther, J. Computer-Mediated Communication Effects on Disclosure, Impressions, and Interpersonal Evaluations: Getting to Know One Another a Bit at a Time. *Human Communication Research, 28,* 317–348.

Tieger, P., & Barron-Tieger, B. (2007). *Do What You Are: Discover the Perfect Career for You Through the Secrets of Personality Type* (3rd ed.). Boston: Little, Brown.

TimMcGraw.com (n.d.). About Tim. Retrieved from www.timmcgraw.com/#about-tim.html.

Trudeau, K. (2007). *Debt Cures They Do Not Want You To Know About.* Pueblo, CO: Equity Press.

Turnitin.com. (n.d.). Retrieved September 30, 2008, from www.turnitin.com/static/home.html.

21 Facts About the Internet. Retrieved January 24, 2009, from www.bizwaremagic.com/quick_internet_history.htm.

UC Berkeley—Teaching Library Internet Workshop. (2005). *Evaluating Web Pages: Techniques to Apply and Questions to Ask.* Retrieved from www.lib.berkeley.edu/TeachingLib/Guides/Internet/Evaluate.htm.

U.S. Bureau of Labor Statistics. (2006). *How Americans Spend Time.* Washington, DC: Department of Census. Retrieved February 9, 2009, from www.bls.gov.

U.S. Bureau of Labor Statistics. (2010). *Education and Training Pay.* Washington, DC: U.S. Government Printing Office.

U.S. Department of Education. (2008). *Newsblade.* Retrieved from http://newsblaze.com/story/2007091202000800001.mwir/topstory.html.

U.S. Department of Education/National Center for Education Statistics. (June, 1998). *First-Generation Students: Undergraduates Whose Parents Never Enrolled in Postsecondary Education,* NCES 98-082. Washington, DC: Author.

Waitley, D. (1997). *Psychology of Success: Developing Your Self-Esteem.* Boston: Irwin Career Education Division.

Wallechinsky, D., & Wallace, A. (2005). *The New Book of Lists: The Original Compendium of Curious Information.* Edinburgh, Scotland: Conongate Books.

Walther, J., & Burgoon, J. (1992). Relational Communication in Computer-Mediated Interaction. *Human Communication Research, 19,* 50–88.

Warner, J. (November 5, 2002). Celebratory Drinking Culture on Campus: Dangerous Drinking Style Popular among College Students. *Parenting and Pregnancy,* p. 37.

Webster's College Dictionary. (1995). New York: Random House.

Wechsler, H., and Wuethrich, B. (2002). *Dying to Drink: Confronting Binge Drinking on College Campuses.* New York: Rodale Press.

Wetmore, D. (2008). *Time Management Facts and Figures.* Retrieved December 1, 2008, from www.balancetime.com.

White House. (n.d.). *Abraham Lincoln.* Retrieved from www.whitehouse.gov/about/presidents.

Whorf, B. (1956). *Language, Thought, and Reality.* Cambridge, MA: MIT Press.

Wikipedia. (n.d.). *Tim McGraw.* Retrieved from www.wikipedia.org/wiki/Tim_McGraw.

Wikipedia. (n.d.). *Warren Buffett.* Retrieved from www.wikipedia.org/wiki/Warren_Buffett.

Williams, E. (June 26, 2008). Students Need Help Combating Credit Card Debt. Testimony before the House Financial Services Subcommittee on Financial Institutions and Consumer Credit. Retrieved September 2, 2008, from www.americanprogress.org/issues/2008/06/williams_testimony.html.

Woolfolk, A. (2006). *Educational Psychology* (10th ed.). Boston: Allyn and Bacon.

Yip, P. (August 31, 2008). College Campuses Are Ripe for the Picking. *The State* (newspaper), p. B22.

Zarefsky, D. (2001). *Public Speaking: Strategies for Success* (3rd ed.). Boston: Pearson/Allyn and Bacon.

Zen Habits. (2008). *Simple Living Manifesto: 72 Ways to Simplify Your Life.* Retrieved from http://zenhabits.net.

INDEX

R.E.W.A.R.D.S., interviewing strategy, 351–352

Review, as step in SQ3R, 154. *See also* SQ3R

Rhymes/jingles, as mnemonic devices, 252

Richardson, John, Jr., 5

Riopelle, Maureen, 174

Robinson, Francis P., 146

Roosevelt, Eleanor, 15

Rosa, Jennifer, 275–276

Rousseau, Jean-Jacques, 197

Sapir-Whorf Hypothesis, 310–311

Satir, Virginia, 243

Saving/investing, of money, 33

Scan, as step in SQ3R, 146–147. *See also* SQ3R

Schedules/scheduling, 168–169, 176–180. *See also* Time management

Schleigh, Catherine, 225

Scholarships, for college students, 34, 36. *See also* Financial aid

Schuller, Robert, 69

Science, studying/testing strategies for, 258–259

Second-language speakers, listening by, 227–228

Second term, planning for, 99–101

Sections/paragraphs, reading of, 144–145, 150

Self-actualization, and motivation, 63, 64

Self-defeating behaviors, 66–68

Self-discipline, and time management, 163–164

Self-disclosure, and interpersonal communication, 315–316

Self-esteem
  characteristics of, 77
  definitions of, 76–77
  development of, 75–78
  and goals, 71
  guidelines for, 78
  and motivation, 75–76
  and values, 71

Self-talk
  and anxiety, 187
  guidelines for, 70–71
  and math/science, 63, 258
  and reading, 138, 142
  and self-discipline, 164
  and self-esteem, 78
  and tests/testing, 261

Sensing/intuition, and personality type, 209–210

Sensory memory, 247. *See also* Memory

Sentences
  as mnemonic devices, 252–253
  and topics of paragraphs, 144–145, 150

Services/resources, of career colleges, 93, 94, 101, 103–104

Sherfield, Robert M., 1, 3–4

Short-answer tests, strategies for, 266–267

Short-term memory, 247. *See also* Memory

Simon, Hal, 334

Simplification, guidelines for, 168, 169

Skype, 110, 119, 261, 351

Smith, Fred, 99

Smith-Ransome, Odette, 210–211

Social media
  and education, 115–119
  effective use of, 7, 115–119
  purpose of, 112
  tools for, 112, 115–118

Social skills, value of, 7

Socrates, 197

Sophocles, 92

Spatial zones, 312

Stoll, Clifford, 131

Spending habits, 33, 43–44, 46–47, 48, 51. *See also* Money management

Split-page system, for note taking. *See* Cornell system, for note taking

SQ3R, as reading/study method
  effectiveness of, 146, 154
  steps in, 151–156

Standard of living, vs. quality of life, 32–33

State loans/grants, 34. *See also* Financial aid

Stone, Clement, 90

Story lines, as mnemonic devices, 253

Strategies for Lifetime Success, 66–78

Stress
  assessment of, 181, 182
  causes of, 184–185
  definition of, 180
  physical signs/symptoms of, 181, 183. *See also* Anxiety; Depression
  reduction of, 184–185, 188–190
  research about, 183
  and time management, 180–181, 182
  types of, 180–181, 184–185

Student loans, sources/types of, 34, 36, 38. *See also* Financial aid

Study groups, 261

Studying
  cramming as, 146, 257–260
  and distraction by children/family, 255–257
  for math, 258–259
  and multiple intelligences, 202–203
  and personality type, 211, 212–213
  reading for, 146
  for science, 258–259
  strategies for, 260, 261
  for tests, 261–262, 264. *See also* Tests/testing
  and time management, 17

Success
  change needed for, 11–12
  elements of, 14, 17, 86
  formula for, 8–10
  guidelines for, 66–78

Support
  from college resources/services, 93, 94
  from personal sources, 16, 63, 65

Tactile learning style, 203, 206. *See also* Learning style(s)

Talking, as obstacle to listening, 224–226

Technology
  changes in, 110, 111
  and college education, 110, 111, 112–113, 119, 120
  for communication, 110, 112, 118–119, 121–122, 312–315, 326

effective use of, 110–111, 119–120

fear of, 87

and globalization, 110

and interpersonal relationships, 314

language of, 111, 113–114

privacy/security issues with, 119–121

skills for, 111, 112, 122. *See also* Information literacy

and time management, 111

tools of, 110, 111, 112–113. *See also* *specific tools*

Tests/testing
  anxiety about, 259, 261–262, 268, 269–270
  attitude about, 261
  in math, 259
  for placement, 87, 95, 96
  responses types for, 262–264
  in science, 259
  strategies for, 259, 262–28
  studying for, 261–262, 264
  types of, 264–268. *See also specific types*

Texting/text messaging, 122. *See also* E-communication

Thank-you notes
  following job interviews, 354, 361, 362
  for references, 343

Thinking, nature of, 276. *See also* Critical thinking

Thinking/feeling, and personality type, 210

Tick marks, for segmenting text, 152

Time management
  assessment of, 175, 176
  daily approach to, 179–180
  and distractions/interruptions, 176, 179
  and free time, 165
  and habits, 162–163, 170, 175, 176
  and personality, 165, 166, 170, 171
  and procrastination, 164, 169–170, 171
  and productivity, 162–163
  and saying "no," 165–167
  and schedules/scheduling, 168–169, 176–180
  and self-discipline, 163–164
  and simplification, 168, 169
  and stress, 180–181, 182. *See also* Stress
  and studying, 17, 146, 257–260
  tools for, 175, 177–178, 180, 181
  and values, 163, 168
  and willpower, 163–164

Time-oriented listeners, 223

Toffler, Alvin, 250

Topics/topic sentences, of paragraphs, 144–145, 150

Tracy, Brian, 169

Transitional words/phrases, listening for, 227

True-false tests, strategies for, 264–265

T-system, for note taking. *See* Cornell system

Tullins, M., 125

Turner, Tina, 180

Tutor, John, 111

Twain, Mark, 135, 152

Twitter, 110, 111, 112, 114, 118, 119. *See also* Social media